OCCUPATIONAL ENGLISH

OCCUPATIONAL ENGLISH

Fourth Edition

Ann A. Laster / Nell Ann Pickett
Hinds Junior College District
Raymond Campus

1817

HARPER & ROW, PUBLISHERS, New York
Cambridge, Philadelphia, San Francisco,
London, Mexico City, São Paulo, Singapore, Sydney

For
Wrenna McGehee Poirrier

Sponsoring Editor: Phillip Leininger
Project Editor: Ronni Strell
Text Design: Robert Sugar
Cover Design: Betty L. Sokol
Cover Photo: © Freis, Image Bank
Text Art: Fineline Illustrations, Inc.
Production: Delia Tedoff
Compositor: Progressive Typographers
Printer and Binder: The Murray Printing Company

Occupational English
4th edition

Library of Congress Cataloging in Publication Data

Laster, Ann A.
    Occupational English.

    Includes bibliographies and index.
    1. English language—Rhetoric.   2. English language—
Business English.   3. English language—Technical English.
I. Pickett, Nell Ann.   II. Title.
PE1408.L32   1985   808'.0666   84-25350
ISBN 0-06-043858-4

85 86 87 88 89 9 8 7 6 5 4 3 2 1

CONTENTS

Inside front cover: General Format Directions for Writing

Preface   vii

CHAPTER 1
Instructions and Process: Explaining a Procedure   14

CHAPTER 2
Description of a Mechanism: Explaining How Something Works   55

CHAPTER 3
Definition: Explaining What Something Is   84

CHAPTER 4
Analysis Through Classification and Partition: Putting Things in Order   107

CHAPTER 5
Analysis Through Effect-Cause and Comparison-Contrast: Looking at Details   151

CHAPTER 6
The Summary: Getting to the Heart of the Matter   184

CHAPTER 7
Memorandums and Letters: Sending Messages   212

CHAPTER 8
Reports: Conveying Needed Information   303

CHAPTER 9
The Research Report: Becoming Acquainted with Resource Materials   368

CHAPTER 10
Oral Communication: Saying It Clearly   436

CHAPTER 11
Visuals: Seeing Is Convincing   460

HANDBOOK

CHAPTER 1
Grammatical Usage   487

CHAPTER 2
Mechanics 521

Index 557

Inside back cover: Checklist for Common Problems in Revising a Report

PREFACE

Occupational English is a practical writing guide designed for students in occupational education curricula. Students are entering these programs in ever-increasing numbers, preparing themselves for jobs in a wide variety of areas. Regardless of their orientation, however, students need the ability to communicate orally and in writing.

What's New in the Fourth Edition

The fourth edition includes:

- a new, introductory section on readability
- stronger emphasis on layout and design
- more coverage on memorandums, inclusion of current practices in letter writing, additional specific types of letters
- expanded discussion of microforms and library research tools
- inclusion of documentation style from *MLA Handbook* (1984)
- additional attention to practices in business communication

Rationale

The basic writing text is designed to fill the needs of those students who, out of necessity or interest, require instruction in writing with utilitarian emphasis. It was written with two underlying principles in mind. These have been formulated from our formal training in English and in technical education, our teaching experiences, and our visits to industries, businesses, and service facilities.

    1. First, emphasis in an English course for career-oriented students should be on *practical* application rather than on theory, rules, or rhetoric.

    2. Second, the preparation and selection of class materials for such an English course require more discrimination than do those for the regular academic English course because the occupational student frequently has only two years to prepare to become a productive member of society.

Organization

With these ideas in mind, the text deals with the principles and forms of writing that any student needs to know, but with emphasis on occupational writing demands. In a logical and selective fashion, the basic rhetorical devices are covered; then there are chapters on business letters, report writing, and the library paper. Each chapter leads students to end-of-chapter writing assignments through a logical sequence: **chapter-opening objectives** stating what students should be able to do upon completion of a chapter, clearly explained **principles** and **examples** of specific kinds of presentations, **step-by-step procedures** for organizing presentations, and **plan sheets** to guide the selection and organization of material.

We offer special thanks to the following groups of the Hinds Junior College District for their help in preparing the text: our students, the English department, and the McLendon Library staff.

Ann A. Laster
Nell Ann Pickett

Achieving Readability: Some Basic Guidelines

Communication is an active process with at least three parts: a message to be sent, a way to send the message, and a receiver to comprehend, analyze, and respond or react to the message.

As a future communicator on the job you must be very aware of this process, for you may be the person with a message to send, the person who must find the most effective way to send a message, or the person to receive a message. Making a sale, convincing management of needed change, giving employees instructions on operating new equipment, preparing a report on work in progress, proposing the purchase of new materials or equipment — a worker daily conveys and receives many different types of messages to and from many different audiences.

This introductory section deals with the communicator on the job in the role of the person who has a written message to send and who must decide on the most effective way to send it. You want to get the message across to the intended audience so that you get the desired response.

One major consideration in planning the message is readability. What can you, the writer, do to make the message easier to read and comprehend? Of course, readability to a great extent depends on the content of the message and on what the reader brings to the reading of the message, that is, the reader's mental state, reason for reading, and special skills. The writer can, however, make use of various techniques to improve readability. This introductory section will explain and illustrate some techniques that can make a message more readable. As you prepare the assignments throughout the text, you can select and adapt these techniques to enhance the readability of a particular message.

Audience analysis, organization, and content are dealt with at length in the various chapters of the text.

LAYOUT

One of the simplest ways for a writer to make a message more readable is layout — that is, placement of words and sentences, paragraphs, lists, tables, graphs, and the like on the page. Layout makes an important visual impression on the reader.

For many years writers followed the nineteenth-century essay form, paragraph after paragraph after paragraph with only an occasional indentation to mark the beginning of a new paragraph. Sometimes no indentation appeared on an entire page; the page was literally filled with words with space only at the outer edges of the page. Look at Figure 1, Example A.

Today's occupational writer uses layout to enhance writing and reading. Look at Example B in Figure 1. This example puts into practice some of the usual techniques for making a page "come alive."

Various basic layout techniques can be grouped into two general categories:

- White space providers
- Emphasis markers

White Space Providers White space providers yield an uncluttered, easily readable, inviting page. Indenting for paragraphs, double spacing, and allowing ample margins (1½ inches minimum on all four perimeters) are the most usual ways of allowing for plenty of white space. Additional white space providers include headings (with triple spacing before a major heading and double spacing after the heading), vertical listing (placing the items up and down rather than across the page), and columns (setting up the page with several columns of short lines, as in a periodical, rather than a page of long lines).

Emphasis Markers A number of techniques can be used in drawing attention, lending variety, or giving emphasis to material. Different sizes and styles of typefaces can be used, such as Roman, italic, and boldface. Underlining gives emphasis, as do uppercase (capital) letters. Boxes can be used to set off material, such as a caution in a set of instructions, or to enclose an entire page (as used throughout this book to set off sample pieces of writing). Insets — small boxes that set off material — may provide a legend or an explanation of symbols for such visuals as maps, charts, and drawings; insets are often used to set off key thoughts, a summary, or supplementary material. Bars (heavy straight lines) typically separate a table or other visual from the text. Also, writers can employ multiple colors (for contrast) and shading (for depth) and a border (particularly in a paper requiring a title page).

Symbols are additional emphasis markers. Frequently used are the bullet (O), the square (□), other geometric shapes, such as a triangle or diamond (△ ◇), the dash (—), the asterisk (°), and arrows (→↓). The various geometric shapes can be solid (● ■ ▲) or open (○ □ △). Especially easy to make is the bullet: use the letter "o" or the period on a typewriter, or hand insert the bullet with a pen.

All of these emphasis markers are fairly easy to produce. Readily available commercially prepared aids such as templates, transfer lettering sheets, transfer shading sheets, and charting tape can help to provide a professional look to a report.

DESIGN

Design concerns not only the individual pages but also the report as a whole. In designing the report, the writer makes careful, conscious decisions concerning matters that affect the appearance and the impact of the total document.

Design involves the elements of composition: contrast, balance, propor-

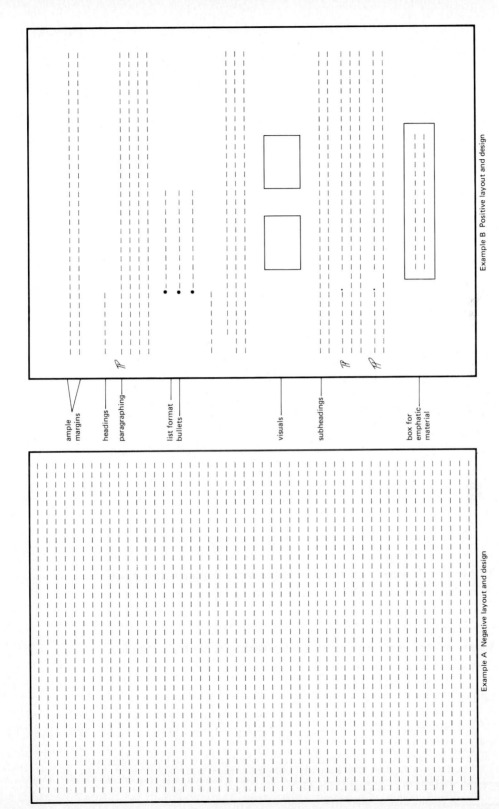

ample
margins

headings

paragraphing

list format
bullets

visuals

subheadings

box for
emphatic
material

Example B Positive layout and design

Example A Negative layout and design

3

tion, dominance, harmony, opposition, unity. These elements are used to direct the reader's attention and to establish hierarchies of emphasis.

Among the tools used in design are color, format, column width, visuals (including kind, size, and placement), spacing, texture, geometric shapes, and sizes and styles of typefaces (for text, headings, and special materials). Through the use of these tools, the designer consciously makes choices to achieve the desired intellectual and psychological impact on the reader.

HEADINGS

A heading identifies the subject or topic written about in a block of information. Each heading should be meaningful, that is, clearly tell the reader what the block of information is about. The heading helps the writer to stay on the subject; the heading plus the white space marking the block of information helps the reader by making the pages of writing more inviting. Even a glance at a page of print without headings and one with headings (such as this page) will attest to the importance of headings. Headings give the reader a visual impression of major and minor topics and their relation to one another; headings reflect the organization of the material. Headings remind the reader of movement from one point to another. Headings help the reader interested only in particular sections, not the whole report, to locate these sections. And headings give life and interest to what otherwise would be a solid page of unbroken print.

For headings to show organization of material, the form and placement of each heading must indicate its rank or level. Use of capital letters and underlining and position of the headings on the page help to differentiate rank or level. Headings that identify higher levels of material should *look* more important than those that identify lower levels.

The writer should work out a system of headings to reflect the major points of the report and their supporting points. (Should a report contain an outline or table of contents, the headings in them should correspond exactly to the headings in the body of the report.)

Following are suggested systems of headings for reports.

2 Levels of Headings (The underlining may be omitted)

MAJOR HEADING (This heading may be centered)
Division of Major Heading

3 Levels of Headings (The underlining may be omitted)

MAJOR HEADING (This heading may be centered)
Division of Major Heading
   Subdivision of division of major heading. The paragraph
begins here.

4 Levels of Headings

MAJOR HEADING (This heading may be centered)
Division of Major Heading
Subdivision of Division of Major Heading

<u>Sub-subdivision of division of major heading</u>. The paragraph begins here.

5 Levels of Headings

<u>MAJOR HEADING</u>

<u>DIVISION OF MAJOR HEADING</u>
<u>Subdivision of Division of Major Heading</u>
<u>Sub-Subdivision of Division of Major Heading</u>
  <u>Sub-sub-subdivision of division of major heading</u>. The paragraph begins here.

Headings must be visibly obvious if they are to be effective. Leave plenty of white space. As a general rule, triple space above a heading and double space below a heading (unless the heading is indented as a part of the paragraph).

TITLES

The title of a report is the first thing a reader sees. It should, therefore, specifically identify the topic, suggest the writer's approach and coverage, and interest the reader. A title should indicate to the reader what to expect in the content of the report.

A title such as "The Brentsville Police Department" is vague and broad, giving a reader no idea of the writer's approach to the topic or the coverage. A title such as "Brentsville Police Department: Organization and Responsibilities" clearly suggests the approach and coverage.

Be honest with your reader. A report entitled "Customizing a Van at Home" suggests the report covers everything an individual would need to know to customize a van. If the report discusses only special tools needed to customize a van at home, then the writer has misled the reader. An accurate title would be "Special Tools Needed for At-Home Van Customizing."

A title is usually a phrase rather than just one word or a complete sentence.

WORD CHOICE

The technical communicator must be very aware of words selected to convey a message. The English language is filled with a rich, diverse vocabulary. Thus, you have a wide choice of words to use to express an idea. To select the words that best convey intended meaning to an intended audience, you must use denotative and connotative words as needed, choose between specific and general words, avoid inappropriate jargon, practice conciseness where desirable, and select the appropriate word for the specific communication need.

Denotation and Connotation

Language could be used more easily and communication would be much simpler if words meant the same things to all people at all times. Unfortunately they do not. Meanings of words shift with the user, the situation, the section of the country, and the context (all the other words surrounding a particular word). Every word has at least two areas of meaning: denotation and connotation.

The denotative meaning is the physical referent the word identifies, that is, the thing or the concept: it is the dictionary definition. Words like *flower, book, shoe, tractor, desk,* and *car* have physical referents; *hope, love, faith, courage, bravery,* and *fear* refer to qualities or concepts.

The connotative meaning of a word is what an individual feels about that word because of past experiences in using, hearing, or seeing the word. Each person develops attitudes toward words because certain associations cause the words to suggest qualities either good or bad. For some people, such words as *communist, Red, liberal, leftist, democrat, republican,* or *right-wing* are favorable; for others, they are not. The effects of words depend on the emotional reactions and attitudes that the words evoke.

Consider the words *fat, large, portly, obese, plump, corpulent, stout, chubby,* and *fleshy.* Each of these could be used to describe a person's size, some with stronger connotation than others. Some people might not object too much to being described as *plump,* but they might object strongly to being described as *fat.* On the other hand, they probably would not object to receiving a *fat* paycheck. So, some words may evoke an unfavorable attitude in one context, "*fat* person," but a favorable attitude in another, "*fat* paycheck."

Some words always seem to have pleasant connotations; for example, *truth, success, bravery, happiness, honor, intelligence,* and *beauty.* Other words, such as *lust, hate, spite, insanity, disease, rats, poverty,* and *evil,* usually have unpleasant connotations.

You should choose words that have the right denotation and the desired connotation to clarify your meaning and evoke the response you want from your reader. Compare the following sentences. The first illustrates a kind of writing in which words point to things (denotation) rather than attitudes; the words themselves call for no emotional response, favorable or unfavorable.

> Born in the Fourth Ward with its prevailing environment, John was separated from his working mother when he was one year of age.

The second sentence, through the use of words with strong connotative meaning, calls for an emotional response — an unfavorable one.

> Born in the squalor of a Fourth Ward ghetto, John was abandoned by his barroom-entertainer mother while he was still in diapers.

Specific and General Words

A specific word identifies a particular person, object, place, quality, or occurrence; a general word identifies a group or a class. For example, *lieutenant* indicates a person of a particular rank; *officers* indicates a group. For any general word there are numerous specific words; the group identified by *officers* includes such specific terms as *lieutenant, general, colonel,* and *admiral.*

There are any number of levels of words that can take you from the general to the specific:

GENERAL transportation automobile
SPECIFIC Buick Electra

GENERAL athletes team football team professional football team
SPECIFIC Green Bay Packers

The more specific the word choice, the easier it is for the reader to know exactly the intended meaning.

GENERAL   The gift was expensive.
SPECIFIC   The alligator billfold cost $49.50.

GENERAL   The bird was in a tree.
SPECIFIC   The robin was perched on the topmost branch of the cherry tree.

GENERAL   The place was damaged.
SPECIFIC   The tornado blew out all the windows in the administration building at Midwestern College.

Using general words is much easier, of course, than using specific words; the English language is filled with "umbrella" terms with broad meanings. These words come readily to mind, whereas the specific words that express exact meaning require thought. To write effectively, you must search until you find the right words to convey your intended meaning.

Jargon

Jargon is the specialized or technical language of a trade, profession, class, or group. This specialized language used in particular fields of activity is often not understandable by persons outside those fields.

Jargon is appropriate (1) if it is used in a specialized occupational context and (2) if the intended audience understands the terminology. For example, a computer programmer communicating with persons knowledgeable about computer terminology and discussing a computer subject may use such terms as *input, interface, menu driven,* or *48K.* The computer programmer is using jargon appropriately.

If, however, these specialized words are applied to actions or ideas not associated with computers, jargon is used inappropriately. Or if such specialized words are used extensively — even in the specialized occupational context — with an audience who does not understand the terminology, jargon is used inappropriately.

The problem with inappropriate use of jargon is that the speaker or writer is not communicating clearly and effectively with the audience. Study these examples of inappropriate jargon:

The computer revolution has impacted on business.
The bottom line is a 10 percent salary increase.
Nurse to patient: "A myocardial infarction is contraindicated." (No heart attack)
TV repairperson to customer: "A shorted bypass capacitor removed the forward bias from the base-emitter junction of the audio transistor." (A capacitor shorted out and killed the sound)

Gobbledygook   Jargon enmeshed in abstract pseudo-technical or pseudo-scientific words is called *gobbledygook* (from *gobble,* to sound like a turkey). Examine these sentences:

The optimum operational capabilities and multiple interrelationships of the facilities are contiguous on the parameters of the support systems.
Integrated output interface is the basis of the quantification.

Is the message of either sentence clear? No. The sentences are made up of jargon and pseudo-technical and pseudo-scientific words—words that *seem* to be technical or scientific but in fact are not. Further, the words are all abstract; that is, they are general words that refer to ideas, qualities, or conditions. They are in contrast with concrete words that refer to specific persons, places, or things which one can see, feel, hear, or otherwise perceive through the senses. Examine again the two gobbledygook sentences above. Not one word in either sentence is a concrete word; not one word in either sentence creates an image in the mind of the reader.

Conciseness

In communication, clarity is of primary importance. One way to achieve clarity is to be concise, whenever possible. Conciseness — saying much in a few words — omits nonessential words, uses simple words and direct word patterns, and combines sentence elements.

It is important to remember that you can be concise without being brief and that what is short is not necessarily concise. The essential quality in conciseness is making every word count.

It is indeed misleading to suggest that all ideas can be expressed in simple, brief sentences. Some ideas by the very nature of their difficulty require more complex sentences. And frequently a longer sentence is necessary to show relationships between ideas.

Omitting Nonessential Words   Nonessential words weaken emphasis in a sentence by thoughtlessly repeating an idea or throwing in "deadwood" to fill up space. Note the improved effectiveness in the following sentences when unnecessary words are omitted.

WORDY   The train arrives at 2:30 P.M. in the afternoon.
REVISED   The train arrives at 2:30 P.M.

WORDY   He was inspired by the beautiful character of his surroundings.
REVISED   He was inspired by his surroundings.

WORDY   In the event that a rain comes up, close the windows.
REVISED   If it rains, close the windows.

Eliminating unnecessary words makes writing more exact, more easily understood, and more economical. Often, care in revision will weed out the clutter of deadwood and needless repetition.

Simple Words and Direct Word Patterns   An often-told story illustrates quite well the value of simple, unpretentious words stated directly to convey a message. A plumber who had found that hydrochloric acid was good for cleaning out pipes wrote a government agency about his discovery. The plumber received this reply: "The efficiency of hydrochloric acid is indisputable, but the corrosive residue is incompatible with metallic permanence." The plumber responded that he was glad his discovery was helpful. After several more garbled and misunderstood communications from the agency, the plumber finally received this clearly stated response: "Don't use hydrochloric acid. It eats the hell out of pipes.'' Much effort and time could have been saved if this had been the wording of the agency's *first* response.

Generally, use simple words instead of polysyllabic words and avoid giving too many details in needless modifiers. When necessary, show causal relationships or tie closely related ideas together by writing longer sentences.

WORDY AND OBSCURE	Feathered bipeds of similar plumage will live gregariously.
SIMPLE AND DIRECT	Birds of a feather flock together.
WORDY AND OBSCURE	Verbal contact with Mr. Jones regarding the attached notification of promotion has elicited the attached representations intimating that he prefers to decline the assignment.
SIMPLE AND DIRECT	Mr. Jones does not want the job.
WORDY AND OBSCURE	Believing that the newer model air conditioning unit would be more effective in cooling the study area, I am of the opinion that it would be advisable for the community library to purchase a newer model air conditioning unit.
SIMPLE AND DIRECT	The community library should buy a new air conditioning unit.
IMPLIED RELATIONSHIP	The area was without rain for ten weeks. The corn stalks turned yellow and died.
STATED RELATIONSHIP	Because the area was without rain for ten weeks, the corn stalks turned yellow and died.

Combining Sentence Elements Many sentences are complete and unified yet ineffective because they lack conciseness. Parts of sentences, or even entire sentences, often may be reduced or combined.

Study the following examples.

REDUCING SEVERAL WORDS TO ONE WORD	the registrar *of the college* the *college* registrar
REDUCING A CLAUSE TO A PHRASE OR TO A COMPOUND WORD	a house *that is shaped like a cube* a house *shaped like a cube* a *cube-shaped* house
REDUCING A COMPOUND SENTENCE	Mendel planted peas for experimental purposes, and from the peas he began to work out the universal laws of heredity.
TO A COMPLEX SENTENCE	As Mendel experimented with peas, he began to work out the laws of heredity.
OR TO A SIMPLE SENTENCE	Mendel, experimenting with peas, began to work out the laws of heredity.
COMBINING TWO SHORT SENTENCES	Many headaches are caused by emotional tension. Stress also causes a number of headaches.
INTO ONE SENTENCE	Many headaches are caused by emotional tension and stress.

ACTIVE AND PASSIVE VOICE VERBS

Generally use active voice verbs. Active voice verbs are effective because the reader knows immediately the subject of the discussion; the writer mentions first who or what is doing something.

The machinist *values* highly the rule depth gauge.
Roentgen *won* the Nobel Prize for his discovery of X rays.

Passive voice verbs are used when the who or what is not as significant as the action or the result and when the who or what is unknown, preferably unnamed, or relatively insignificant.

The lathe *has been broken* again. (More emphatic than "Someone has broken the lathe again.")
The blood sugar test *was made* yesterday.
The transplant operation *was performed* by an outstanding heart surgeon.
Light *is provided* for technical drawing classrooms by windows in the north wall.

A good rule is choose the voice of the verb that permits the desired emphasis.

ACTIVE VOICE   The ballistics experts *examined* the results of the tests. (Emphasis on *ballistics experts*)
PASSIVE VOICE   The results of the tests *were examined* by the ballistics experts. (Emphasis on *results of the tests*)
ACTIVE VOICE   Juan *gave* the report. (Emphasis on *Juan*)
PASSIVE VOICE   The report *was given* by Juan. (Emphasis on *report*)

WORD ORDER

Word order plays a major role in readability. Writing sentences so that a reader is able to make sense out of word clusters improves readability. (Arranging groups of sentences or paragraphs developing one aspect of a topic into a block of information also improves readability.)

One desirable arrangement of words in sentences is placing the subject and the verb close together.

Also try to keep sentences within a maximum of four or five units of information. Look at the following two examples.

                    Unit 1   Unit 2
The dimensions on a blueprint are called scale dimensions.
           Unit 1   Unit 2   Unit 3
Because the corners of the nut may be rounded or damaged and because the wrench
       Unit 4   Unit 5   Unit 6   Unit 7
   may slip off the nut and cause an accident, choose a wrench with size and type
       Unit 7
   suited to the nut.

Notice that the second example becomes difficult to read and comprehend because of the many units of information.

COORDINATION AND SUBORDINATION

Coordination and subordination are techniques used by the writer to combine ideas and to show the relationship between ideas.

The ideas in sentences may be combined to make meaning clearer by adding a word, usually a subordinate conjunction or a coordinate conjunction, to show the relationship between the ideas.

From the two sentences

1. The company did not hire him.
2. He was not qualified.

a single sentence

1. The company did not hire him *because* he was not qualified.

makes the relationship of ideas clearer with the addition of the subordinate conjunction, "because." The second sentence is changed to an adverb clause, "because he was not qualified," telling why the company did not hire the him.

The two sentences

1. John applied for the job.
2. He did not get the job.

might be stated more clearly in

1. John applied for the job, but he did not get it.

The addition of the coordinate conjunction, "but," indicates that the idea following is in contrast to the idea preceding it.

Study the following examples.

1. Magnetic lines of force can pass through any material.
2. They pass more readily through magnetic materials.
3. Some magnetic materials are iron, cobalt, and nickel.

The ideas in these three sentences might be combined into a single sentence.

1. Magnetic lines of force can pass through any material, but they pass more readily through magnetic materials such as iron, cobalt, and nickel.

The addition of the coordinate conjunction, "but," indicates the contrasting relationship between the two main ideas; sentence 3 has been reduced to "such as iron, cobalt, and nickel." The three sentences might also be combined as follows:

1. Although magnetic lines of force can pass through any material, they pass more readily through magnetic materials: iron, cobalt, and nickel.

Using coordination and subordination, a writer can eliminate short, choppy sentences. The following five sentences

1. The mission's most important decision came.
2. It was early on December 24.
3. Apollo was approaching the moon.
4. Should the spacecraft simply circle the moon and head back toward earth?
5. Should it fire the Service Propulsion System engine and place the craft in orbit?

might be combined:

1. As Apollo was approaching the moon early on December 24, the mission's most important decision came.
2. Should the spacecraft simply circle the moon and head back toward earth or should it fire the Service Propulsion System engine and place the craft in orbit?

Combining sentences gives a flow of thought as well as makes relationships between ideas clearer.

Coordination and subordination are used to emphasize details; important details appear in independent clauses and less important details appear in dependent clauses and phrases. Almost any group of ideas can be combined in several ways. The writer chooses the arrangement of ideas that best "fits in with" preceding and following sentences. More importantly the writer arranges ideas to make important ideas stand out.

Consider the following group of sentences:

1. Carmen Diaz is the employee of the year.
2. She has been with the company only one year.
3. She has had no special training for the job she performs.
4. She is highly regarded by her colleagues.

The four sentences might be combined in several ways.

1. Although Carmen Diaz, the employee of the year, has been with the company only one year and has had no special training for the job she performs, *she is highly regarded by her colleagues.*
2. *Carmen Diaz is the employee of the year* although she has been with the company only one year and has had no special training for the job she performs; *she is highly regarded by her colleagues.*
3. Although Carmen Diaz, highly regarded by her colleagues, is the employee of the year, *she has been with the company only one year and has had no special training for the job she performs.*

Each sentence contains the same information; through coordination and subordination, however, different information is emphasized.

The way you arrange information, as well as what you say, affects meaning.

POSITIVE STATEMENTS

Generally, statements worded positively are easier to read and comprehend. To understand negative wording, the reader reads the negative statement, mentally changes it to positive, and then changes it to negative, therefore taking a longer time to comprehend the statement.

Look at the following example.

NEGATIVE   If enrollment does not increase, the trustees will not vote to build new dormitories.

POSITIVE   The trustees will vote to build new dormitories only if enrollment increases.

The positively worded statement can be read and understood much more quickly.

The purpose of this introductory section has been to give you some basic guidelines for achieving readability as you prepare assignments suggested throughout the text. Further, you may want to consider the following general principles in occupational writing which pervade the entire book.

GENERAL PRINCIPLES IN OCCUPATIONAL WRITING

- *Occupational writing is functional.* Occupational writing serves a need. Typically, that need is to communicate factual, objective information to someone who requests or requires that information.
- *Occupational writing is concerned with an intended audience.* The occupational writer asks: Who will be reading this material? Why? What kind of details will the reader need? What approach to the material and which order in presenting the material are most appropriate for the reader's purpose?
- *Occupational writing involves choices in format.* Purpose and intended audience largely determine whether the writer uses a memorandum, an informal report, a computer printout, a letter, a conference telephone call, a formal report, a printed form, or some other format for communicating the needed information.
- *In occupational writing, the organization is readily apparent.* The introductory section includes a statement of purpose or a statement indicating the major aspects of the topic to be covered. Headings and subheadings throughout the paper signal movement from one aspect to another.
- *In occupational writing, accurate, precise terminology is essential.* Occupational writing uses exact, specific, concrete words.
- *In occupational writing, conventional standards of grammar, usage, spelling, punctuation, and so on, are observed.* Since the emphasis in occupational writing is on conveying factual information—for a specific purpose, to a specific audience, in an appropriate format—anything that detracts from that emphasis is to be avoided.
- *In occupational writing, layout and design are an integral part of the communication.* Layout is concerned with such matters as spacing (paragraphing, ample white space), use of headings, and the placement of material on the page for optimum readability. Design includes such overall considerations as format, sizes and kinds of typefaces, color, and such composition components as balance, unity, and emphasis.
- *In occupational writing, visuals are important.* Drawings, charts, graphs, tables, photographs, and the like are often as important as the written material. Visuals clarify verbal explanation, focus attention, and add interest.
- *Occupational writing requires the ability to think critically, objectively, thoroughly, and creatively.* Effective occupational writing is based on logical thinking applied to problem solving. The writer must solve such problems as audience analysis and adaptation, choice of format, decisions as to organization and layout and design, creation of appropriate visuals, and formulating a communication so clear that the recipient knows exactly what the writer means.

CHAPTER 1

Instructions and Process: Explaining a Procedure

OBJECTIVES   15
INTRODUCTION   15
CLASSIFYING INSTRUCTIONS   15
    Locational Instructions   16
    Operational Instructions   17
INTENDED AUDIENCE   20
ORAL PRESENTATION   22
VISUALS   23
LAYOUT AND DESIGN   23
GENERAL PRINCIPLES IN GIVING INSTRUCTIONS   25
PROCEDURE FOR GIVING INSTRUCTIONS   26
    Form   26
    Content   26
    Length of Presentation   27
PLANNING AND GIVING INSTRUCTIONS   27
APPLICATIONS   32
DESCRIPTION OF A PROCESS   37
INTENDED AUDIENCE   37
    Process Description for a General Audience   38
    Process Description for a Specialized Audience   43
ORAL PRESENTATION AND VISUALS   48
GENERAL PRINCIPLES IN DESCRIBING A PROCESS   48
PROCEDURE FOR DESCRIBING A PROCESS   49
    Form   49
    Content   49
    Length of Presentation   50
APPLICATIONS   50

OBJECTIVES

Upon completing this chapter, the student should be able to:

- Define instructions
- Classify instructions
- Plan a presentation giving instructions to several audiences
- Use visuals in giving instructions
- Plan the layout and design of instructions
- Explain the relationship between planning and giving instructions
- Give instructions in writing and orally
- Define process description
- Explain the difference between giving instructions and describing a process
- Give a process description directed to a general audience
- Give a process description directed to a specialized audience
- Use visuals in describing a process
- Give process descriptions in writing and orally

INTRODUCTION

You have been a giver and receiver of instructions practically from the beginning of your life. As a child, you were told how to drink from a cup, how to tie your shoes, how to tell time, and so on. As you matured, you became involved with more complex instructions: how to parallel park an automobile, how to throw a block in football, how to tune an electric guitar, how to stock grocery shelves. Since entering college, you have been confronted with even more complex and confusing instructions: how to register as an incoming freshman, how to write an effective report, how to get along with a roommate, how to spend money wisely, how to study.

Since all aspects of life are affected by instructions, every person needs to be able to give and to follow instructions satisfactorily. Frequently, clear, accurate, complete instructions save the reader or listener time, help do a job faster and more satisfactorily, or help get better service from a product. Being able to give and to follow instructions is essential for any employee. Certainly, in order for workers to advance to supervisory positions, they must be able to give intelligent, authoritative, specific, accurate instructions; and they must be able to follow the instructions of their superiors.

CLASSIFYING INSTRUCTIONS

Giving instructions seems much simpler than following them. Telling someone how to study for a test, for instance, appears to be much easier than studying for it. But giving instructions—telling someone how to get somewhere or how to perform a particular operation—is deceptively simple.

You may find it helpful to look at two categories of instructions: locational and operational. As a student and a future employee you will have to give and receive both locational and operational instructions.

Locational Instructions

Locational instructions, as the term suggests, help you locate a person, place, or thing. These instructions should clearly identify the starting point and the destination, the distance between the two, and the general direction. As with all instructions, giving them can be deceptively simple. Which of us at one time or another has not experienced the confusion of the delivery boy in the following dialogue.

DELIVERY BOY Could you tell me where Mr. Sam Smith lives so I can deliver this load of fertilizer?

LOCAL INHABITANT Go down the road a piece and turn left at the mailbox — the one just on this side of Mr. Jenkins's house. After you leave the main road and pass that bad curve, you should see the house you're looking for, not too far off up the road to the right.

The delivery boy receiving these instructions may have difficulty in reaching his destination. Obviously, "down the road a piece" and "not too far" are, at best, indefinite; the inquirer has no idea where Mr. Jenkins lives; and what might be a "bad curve" to one person might not be to someone else. These instructions might have been more accurately and more clearly stated as follows:

LOCAL INHABITANT Continue down this highway for about two miles. When you come to the second gravel road, turn left onto it. At this intersection, there is a large mailbox on a white wooden frame. When you take the gravel road, you will be about a half mile from where Mr. Smith lives. His is the second house on the right, the one that has a white paling fence around it.

In contrast to the lack of clarity and accuracy in the first instructions given to the delivery boy, consider these instructions given to the driver of a moving van in an unfamiliar city:

DRIVER After I took Exit 53 off the Interstate, I got balled up somehow, and I can't seem to find Porter Drive, much less 4437 Porter Drive. It's supposed to be around here somewhere.

SERVICE STATION ATTENDANT You took the right exit OK. As a matter of fact, you're only about three or four miles due south from where you want to be. If you knew where you were going and how to get there, it would take you ten minutes or less. Got a piece of paper to jot this down on? Now this street you are on, Charles Avenue, comes within three blocks of Porter Drive. Stay on Charles for about two-and-one-half or three miles until you get to Richard Street. You will turn left onto Richard. And Richard Street comes up just after you pass a fire station on the left. Got that? After you turn left on Richard from Charles, go three blocks. You run right into Porter Drive, which intersects with Richard Street. The address you are looking for is a few blocks on your left.

DRIVER I think maybe I can find it now. Does this map I've sketched look right?

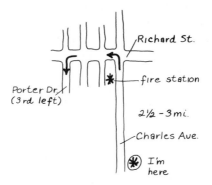

SERVICE STATION ATTENDANT   That looks perfect. Remember—just stay on this street till after you pass a fire station on your left, a couple of miles from here. Turn left onto Richard. Go three blocks. Take a left onto Porter.

Those directions are clear and easy to follow.

Or perhaps you have been in a situation similar to the following:

LOCKSMITH   I'm Jack Jones from National Lock and Key Company. I'm supposed to change a lock on Ms. Grady's desk.

RECEPTIONIST   Yes, I've been expecting you. Ms. Grady's office is on the third floor, Office 301. You'll notice identifying numbers over the door. After you enter the office, go to the desk on the left. As you face the desk, the drawer on the right is the one that needs to have the lock replaced.

Those directions are also clear and easy to follow.

Operational Instructions

Operational instructions tell how to carry out a procedure or an operation, for example, how to put a child's outdoor gym set together, how to run a lathe, how to prepare a blood smear, how to fill out an accident report, how to rescue a person from the tenth floor of a burning building, or any number of other "how to's."

The following student-written operational instructions explain how to make cheese at home.

HOW TO MAKE CHEESE AT HOME

Everyone knows how expensive things have become in the past few years. Some individuals are now making many items in their own homes, to save money, and have found enjoyment and satisfaction at the same time.

Foods are no exception. Many in our generation are so used to the convenience of buying certain foods in the grocery, we are willing to overlook the expense. We are completely unaware of how simple some of our "staples" are to make and of how inexpensive the materials are.

Soft cheese is one example. You probably already have everything you need to make cheese today in your kitchen.

Necessary Materials

- Nonaluminum saucepan
- Double boiler (or two pots, as shown in Figure1)

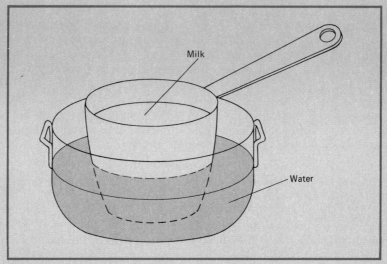

Figure 1. Makeshift double boiler.

- Cheesecloth square (or a cotton cloth napkin or cotton fabric) approximately 16″ x 16″
- Strainer or colander
- Small, perforated container (such as a small basket or perforated milk carton)
- Starter (used to speed up the coagulation process)—any <u>one</u> of the following:

    Rennet tablets (extract made from the stomach lining of a calf; can be purchased in health food stores)
    Lemon juice
    Vinegar
    Buttermilk

- One quart of any <u>one</u> of the following:

    Fresh or sour raw milk
    Light or heavy cream
    Yogurt
    Buttermilk
    Skimmed milk

Make sure that all the equipment is scrupulously clean and sterilized, to avoid contamination.

Use only <u>nonaluminum</u> pots or pans. The taste of the cheese can be affected by cooking with aluminum pans.

After you have assembled all of the necessary materials, you are ready to begin making the cheese.

Step 1

Place a quart of milk in a saucepan. Add rennet tablets, or a tablespoon of one of the other starters listed. The starter contains active bacteria cultures, which, when added to the milk, will multiply rapidly and speed up coagulation. Set the mixture aside for a day.

Step 2

Heat the soured milk gently, in a double boiler. This is to promote the separation of the curd (a thick, white, cheesy substance) and the whey (the thin, bluish, watery part of milk). See Figure 2. The separation of curds and whey should occur within three to five minutes.

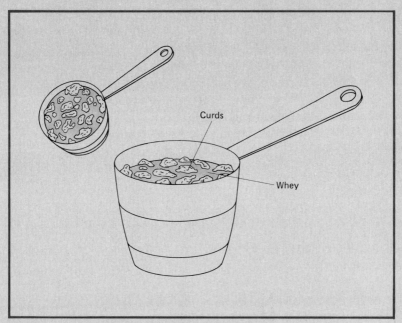

Figure 2. Heating to promote curds and whey.

Step 3

Turn the curds into the cheesecloth square (or other cotton fabric), lining the colander. Then gather the four corners of the cloth together, tie them, and hang the bundle of curds over a bowl or over the sink to drain off any remaining whey. See Figure 3.

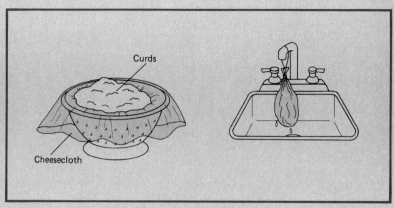

Figure 3. Draining the curds from the whey.

Step 4

When the curds have reached the desired consistency, they are ready to eat — as cheese. The curds (cheese) should be eaten on this day, unless salt is added. The addition of salt will allow the cheese to keep in the refrigerator for two to three days.

Step 5

For those who desire a richer cheese, add butter or cream. For a party spread, or simply a more flavorful cheese, add your favorite spices (as in the recipe for herbed cheese).

There is a good feeling of accomplishment when you have successfully made something yourself. You can savor the flavor of your food a little more when it is completely homemade; and you have saved some money in the process.

Herbed Cheese Recipe

Add to your soft cheese:
  2 tbsp half and half
  1 clove of garlic
  2 tbsp each chopped chives
    and parsley
  1 tbsp chopped tarragon or
    fresh basil
  salt and pepper to taste

INTENDED AUDIENCE

Giving instructions that can be followed requires thought and careful planning. One of the first things to be considered is the intended audience, that is, who will be hearing or reading and thus trying to follow the instructions. An explanation of how to operate the latest model X-ray machine would differ for an experienced X-ray technologist and for a student just being introduced to X-ray equipment. Instructions on how to freeze corn would differ for a food specialist at General Mills, for a homemaker who has frozen other vegetables but not corn, and for a seventh-grade student in a beginning home economics course.

Writing or speaking on a level that the intended audience will understand determines the kind and extent of details presented and the manner in which they are presented. Therefore, you must know who will be reading or hearing the explanation and why. You must be fully aware whether a particular background, specialized knowledge, or certain skills are needed in order to understand the explanation.

Consider, for example, the following instructions included with an **FM/AM** portable radio, Juliette Model FPR-1281B.

INSTRUCTIONS FOR USE OF JULIETTE FM/AM PORTABLE RADIO MODEL FPR-1281B

Helpful Operating Guide

Carefully unpack your new Juliette receiver and place it face down on a flat surface. Remove the back cover, exposing the battery compartment and AC line cord. Install 4 "C" size (UM-2) batteries, observing polarity as shown inside the battery compartment.

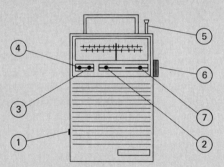

Batteries not included. Use 4 pcs. UM-2 or "C."

Control Locations

1. Output Jack
2. Volume Control
3. FM/AM Band Switch
4. Power Switch

5. Telescopic Antenna
6. Tuning Control
7. Tone Control

WARNING: To prevent fire or shock hazard, do not expose this appliance to rain or moisture.

To Operate Radio

- Slide the POWER SWITCH (4) to the ON position.
- Slide the FM/AM BAND SWITCH (3) to the band of your choice. When listening to

FM, you must extend the TELESCOPIC ANTENNA (5) and adjust the height for best reception.
- Select the station of your choice by rotating the TUNING CONTROL (6).
- Using the precision engineered slide controls, adjust the VOLUME and TONE controls (2 & 7) to your listening pleasure.
- To shut radio off, slide the POWER SWITCH to the OFF position.

Dual Power

Your Juliette radio will operate from the self-contained batteries or regular 105–120V. AC household power.

This radio is completely automatic; no adjustments of controls are needed to switch from battery to household power operation. Simply remove the AC power cord stored under the back cover and insert the plug into any standard electrical outlet.

Whenever possible, operate your unit from household power to conserve batteries.

Output Jack (1)

We have provided, for your convenience, an audio output jack that may be used for private listening with the use of an earphone (NOT INCLUDED), or you may use this jack to tape-record directly from your radio.

An Ounce of Prevention

Keep your Juliette radio from being exposed to extreme high temperatures or humidity, as damage could result. When storing or operating your radio on household power for prolonged periods of time, remove the batteries, as they may leak and damage your receiver.

Performance of your radio can be severely impaired, both in volume and sensitivity, by weak batteries. Should your radio fail to operate properly, check to see that your batteries are fully operational.

For what readers were the instructions for using the radio written? In what specific ways has the intended audience determined the kind and extent of details presented and the manner in which they are presented? Obviously the audience could be anyone able to purchase the radio; the person might or might not be familiar with the operation of a radio. Therefore, the instructions are kept simple.

ORAL PRESENTATION

The content of oral instructions is very similar to that of written instructions. But the delivery, of course, is different. In speaking, you don't have to be concerned with such things as spelling and punctuation, and you have the advantage of a visible audience with whom you can interact.

Your delivery of oral instructions will be successful if you follow these suggestions, whether addressing only one or two persons or a large group:

1. *Look at your audience.* Use eye-to-eye contact with your audience, but without special attention to particular individuals. Avoid continuously looking at your notes, the floor, the ceiling, or a particular individual.
2. *Speak, don't read, to the audience.* Avoid memorizing or reading your presentation. Rather, have it carefully outlined on a note card.
3. *Repeat particularly significant points.* Remember that the audience is *listening*. Repeat main points and summarize frequently. The hearer cannot reread material as the reader can; therefore repetition is essential.
4. *Speak clearly, distinctly, and understandably.* Follow the natural pitches and stresses of the spoken language, and use acceptable pronunciation and grammar. Speak on a language level appropriate for the audience and the subject matter.
5. *Use bodily movements and gestures naturally.* Put some zest in your expression; be alive; show enthusiasm for your subject. Stand in an easy, natural position, with your weight distributed evenly on both feet. Let your movements be natural and well-timed.
6. *Involve the audience, if practical.* Invite questions or ask someone to carry out the procedure or some part of it.
7. *Use visuals where needed.* Whenever visuals will make the explanation clearer, use them. The visuals should be large enough for everyone in the audience to see clearly.

For a detailed discussion of oral presentations, see Chapter 10, Oral Communication.

VISUALS

Often in giving locational and operational instructions, it is helpful to the reader or listener if the instructions include such visuals as maps, drawings, photographs, diagrams, real objects, models, demonstrations, slides, and overhead-projected transparencies. Consider, for instance, the freehand map included with the locational instructions on page 17. Even this crudely drawn map with key points identified is extremely helpful to the individual in reaching the destination more quickly and easily. Such a map usually depicts pertinent streets, intersections, turns, landmarks, and distances.

Or consider the drawings included with the instructions on how to make cheese on pages 17–20, the drawing included with the instructions for using a portable radio on pages 21–22, and the drawings with the instructions for sharpening a ruling pen on pages 31–32. The drawings help to make the instructions clearer.

For a detailed discussion of visuals, see Chapter 11, Visuals.

LAYOUT AND DESIGN

Especially in instructions, layout and design are of prime importance. The placement of material on the page should provide maximum ease in reading and

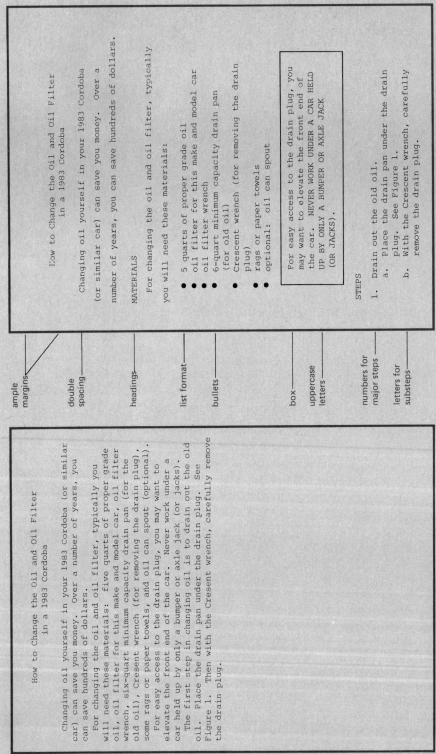

Example A Negative layout and design

Example B Positive layout and design

Figure 1. **Examples of negative (poor) and positive (good) layout and design.**

24

comprehension. The overall design of the set of instructions must provide ready access to needed information, in a convenient format.

Consider, for example, the opening page of two sets of instructions for changing the oil and oil filter in a 1983 Cordoba (Figure 1).

Example A in Figure 1 gives the same information that Example B does. But which example is easier to read and comprehend? Example B, of course. Example B has plenty of *white space;* the material is uncluttered and so placed on the page that the eye easily and quickly sees the relationship of one part of the material to another. The *headings* provide key words for each section. Emphasis is achieved in several ways: through *uppercase letters* for the headings and for the precaution; the *box* to set off material about elevating the car; the *bullets* for a list in which sequence is not important; the *numbers* for the major steps (where sequence is very important); and the *letters of the alphabet* (for substeps in a sequence).

For a detailed discussion, see Layout and Design, pages 1 – 4.

GENERAL PRINCIPLES IN GIVING INSTRUCTIONS

1. *Knowledge of the subject matter is essential.* To give instructions that can be followed, you must be knowledgeable about the subject. If need be, consult sources — knowledgeable people, your textbooks, reference works in the library — to gain further understanding and information about the subject.
2. *The intended audience influences what information is to be presented and how it is to be presented.* Consider the audience's degree of knowledge and understanding of the subject and consider how the information will be used. Avoid talking down to the audience as well as overestimating the audience's knowledge or skills.
3. *Effective instructions are accurate and complete.* The information must be correct. Instructions should adequately cover the subject, with no step or essential information omitted.
4. *Visuals help to clarify instructions.* Whenever instructions can be made clearer by the use of such visuals as maps, diagrams, graphs, pictures, drawings, slides, demonstrations, and real objects, use them.
5. *Instructions require careful layout and design.* An integral part of effective instructions is consideration of how material is placed on the page and of how the document as a whole is presented.
6. *Conciseness and directness contribute to effective communication.* An explanation that is stated in the simplest language with the fewest words is usually the clearest. If the instructions call for terms unfamiliar to the audience or for familiar terms with specialized meanings, explain them.
7. *Instructions that can be followed have no unexplained gaps in the procedure or vagueness about what to do next.* Well-stated instructions do not require the audience to make inferences, to make decisions, or to ask, "What does this mean?"

PROCEDURE FOR GIVING INSTRUCTIONS

Form

The steps in a set of instructions are usually presented as a list, with numbers indicating the major steps. For nonsequential lists (such as a list of needed materials or equipment) and for indicating emphasis, symbols such as these are used: the open or closed bullet ○ ● (see page 2), the open or closed square or box □ ■, the dash —, and the asterisk *.

In giving instructions, use the second person pronoun *you* (usually understood) and imperative or action verbs.

EXAMPLE

First, *(you* understood) *unplug* (imperative verb) the appliance. Then with a Phillips screwdriver *(you* understood) carefully *remove* (imperative verb) the back plate.

Content

In giving instructions, be sure to tell your audience not only *what* to do but also *how* to do each activity, if there is any doubt that the audience might not know how.

EXAMPLE

Remove the plug (tells *what*). Use the fingers to turn it counterclockwise until it can be removed (tells *how*).

Also use good judgment in selecting details. For example, if you are explaining how to pump gasoline, it is not necessary to say you must have a car and a gasoline pump.

The following suggestions may also be helpful. Generally include *a*, *an*, and *the*. Avoid shifting from the active to the passive voice. (For further discussion, see pages 9–10, 498–499.) In writing locational instructions, avoid run-on sentences. (For further discussion, see page 502.)

When organizing material for giving instructions, whether in writing or orally, divide the presentation into two or three parts, as shown below.

I. The identification of the subject is usually brief, depending on the complexity of the operation.
   A. State the operation to be explained.
   B. If applicable, give the purpose and significance of the instructions and indicate who uses them, when, where, and why.
   C. State any needed preparations, skills, equipment, or materials.
II. The development of the steps is the main part of the presentation and thus will be the lengthiest section.
   A. Take up each step in turn, developing it fully with sufficient detail.
   B. In a more complex operation, it may be necessary to subdivide each major step.
   C. Explain in clear detail exactly what is to be done to complete the operation.

      D. Sometimes it is helpful to emphasize particularly important points and to caution the reader where mistakes are most likely to be made.

      E. Plan the layout and design of the instructions, using headings and visuals wherever needed.

  III. The closing may be:

      A. The completion of the discussion of the last step.

      B. A summary of the main steps, especially in complex or lengthy instructions.

      C. A comment on the significance of the operation.

      D. Mention of other methods by which the operation is performed.

Length of Presentation

The length of the presentation is determined by the complexity of the operation, the degree of knowledge of the reader, and the purpose of the presentation. In explaining how to do a simple operation, such as taking a temperature or changing a typewriter ribbon, the entire presentation may be very brief.

PLANNING AND GIVING INSTRUCTIONS

Planning instructions requires several steps. As with any planning, you need first to answer two questions:

1. Why am I giving the presentation? (Purpose)
2. For whom is the presentation intended? (Audience)

Although these two items do not necessarily appear in the actual presentation, purpose and audience directly affect the way you select and present details in a set of instructions, as illustrated by the three examples of instructions on pages 17–20, 21–22, and 29–32.

    Review the General Principles in Giving Instructions on page 25. These principles summarize the major points of the chapter. Now review the Procedure for Giving Instructions on pages 26–27 on the form and the content for instructions. In the content outline, note that the suggestions under Roman numeral I help you to know what kinds of information you may include in the introductory material; suggestions under II identify content for the body; and the suggestions under III give choices for the closing material. Then decide if including visuals will make the instructions clearer to the intended audience. Remember, if you use a visual, refer to the visual within the content of the instructions (see page 463).

    The Plan Sheet (see the illustration on pages 29–30) includes parts of the content outline that are of major importance in planning the instructions. It serves as a guide to help you plan what you will write or tell; it helps you to clarify your thinking on a topic and helps you to select and organize details.

    You may or may not use every bit of information on the Plan Sheet. Nevertheless, fill it in completely and fully so that once you begin to prepare a preliminary draft you will have thought through all major details needed in the presentation.

As you work, refer frequently to the Procedure for Giving Instructions and the Plan Sheet. These two guides should help you plan and develop an acceptable presentation.

Following is a sample presentation of instructions. The filled-in Plan Sheet is included, and marginal notes are added to outline the development of the instructions.

PLAN SHEET
FOR GIVING INSTRUCTIONS

Analysis of Situation Requiring Instructions

What is the procedure to be explained?
how to sharpen a ruling pen

For whom are the instructions intended?
a classmate in drafting

How will the instructions be used?
to sharpen a ruling pen

In what format will the instructions be given?
a written explanation

Importance or Usefulness of the Instructions

Used regularly, a pen becomes dull. Anyone using one needs to know how to sharpen it. A sharp pen is required for neat, clean lines.

Organizing Content

Equipment and materials necessary:
sharpening stone; silicone carbide cloth, if desired

Terms to be defined or explained:
ruling pen, nibs

Major steps (list as command verbs), with identifying information:
1. Close the nibs.
2. Hold the sharpening stone correctly in left hand.
3. Hold the ruling pen correctly in right hand.
4. Round the nibs.
5. Sharpen the nibs.

Precautions to emphasize (crucial steps, possible difficulties, or places where errors are likely to occur):
Hold ruling pen and stone correctly to avoid an injured hand and a ruined pen.

Types and Subject Matter of Visuals to Be Included

Drawings to show:
1. Hand holding pen for sharpening
2. Nibs to show correct shape

Sources of Information

class lecture in drafting, textbook in drafting, personal experience

HOW TO SHARPEN A RULING PEN

A major instrument in making a mechanical drawing is the ruling pen, which is used to ink in straight lines and noncircular curves. To assure neat, clean lines, the ruling pen must be kept sharp and in good condition. It must be sharpened from time to time after extensive use because the nibs (blades resembling tweezers) wear down.

Identification of ruling pen

Reason for sharpening pen

Definition of *nib*

To sharpen the dull ruling pen, you need a 3- or 4-inch sharpening stone, preferably a hard Arkansas knife piece that has been soaked in oil, and possibly a silicone carbide cloth. Following these five simple sharpening procedures will ensure a longer life for the ruling pen and neater, more accurate drawings: close the nibs, hold the sharpening stone in the left hand, hold the ruling pen in the right hand, round the nibs, and sharpen the nibs.

Materials needed

Listing of steps

1. Close the nibs. They should be screwed together until they touch.
2. Hold the sharpening stone in the left hand in a usable position. With the stone lying across the palm of the left hand, grasp it with the thumb and fingers to give the best control of the stone.
3. Hold the ruling pen in the right hand. Pick up the ruling pen with the thumb and index finger of the right hand as if it were a drawing crayon. The other three fingers should rest lightly on the pen handle (see Figure 1). CAUTION! Failure to hold the sharpening stone and ruling pen correctly may result in an injured hand and a ruined ruling pen.

Each step numbered and explained in detail

Comparison with a familiar action

Figure 1. Holding the pen for sharpening.

4. Round the nibs. To round (actually to make elliptical) the nibs, stroke the pen back and forth on the stone, starting with the pen at a 30-degree angle to the stone and following through to past a 90-degree angle as the line across the stone moves forward. Be sure that both nibs are the same length and shape. When the nibs are satisfactorily rounded, they will be left dull (see Figure 2).

Particular emphasis

Figure 2. Correct shape of pen nibs.

5. Sharpen the nibs. Open the blades slightly, and only on the outside sharpen each blade, one at a time. To sharpen, hold the stone and the ruling pen in the hands as in rounding the nibs; the pen should be at a small angle with the stone. Rub the pen back and forth with a rocking, pendulum motion to restore the original shape.

    If desired, the nibs may be polished with a silicone carbide   Optional step
cloth. It is a good idea to test the ruling pen after sharpening it.   Added suggestion
If the job has been done well, the pen is capable of making clean, sharp lines.

APPLICATION 1   GIVING INSTRUCTIONS

Make a list of five persons to interview about their jobs. After interviewing each of the five, make a list of examples showing how they use instructions on the job. From this experience, what can you speculate about the importance of instructions in your own future work?

APPLICATION 2   GIVING INSTRUCTIONS

Explain to a new student how to get from the classroom to another campus building or location (the library, another classroom, the student center, etc.).

APPLICATION 3   GIVING INSTRUCTIONS

Explain to a late-entering freshman in a lab how to find needed supplies and equipment.

APPLICATION 4   GIVING INSTRUCTIONS

Explain to a visitor from out of town how to get from the airport, bus station, or train station to your home. Include a freehand map you have drawn.

APPLICATION 5   GIVING INSTRUCTIONS

Find and attach to your paper a set of instructions that a manufacturer included with a product.

>   a. Evaluate in a paragraph the layout and design of the instructions (see pages 1 – 4, and 23 – 25).
>   b. Evaluate in a paragraph the clarity and completeness of the instructions by applying the General Principles in Giving Instructions, page 25.

APPLICATION 6   GIVING INSTRUCTIONS

Assume that you are a foreman or a supervisor with a new employee on the job. Explain to the employee in writing how to carry out some simple operation.

>   a. Make a Plan Sheet like the one on pages 35 – 36, and fill it in.
>   b. Write a preliminary draft.
>   c. Revise.
>   d. Write the final draft.

APPLICATION 7   GIVING INSTRUCTIONS

Give orally the instructions called for in Application 6 above. Remember to use visuals whenever they will be helpful. Ask your classmates to evaluate your speech by making an Evaluation of Oral Presentations sheet like the one on page 459 and filling it in.

APPLICATION 8   GIVING INSTRUCTIONS

Choose a topic for an assignment on giving instructions from the following list, or choose a topic from your own experience. Consult whatever sources necessary for information.

>   a. Make a Plan Sheet like the one on pages 35 – 36, and fill it in.
>   b. Write a preliminary draft.
>   c. Revise.
>   d. Write the final draft.

How to:

>   1. Copy a disk on a personal computer
>   2. Take a patient's blood pressure
>   3. Water ski
>   4. Install a room air conditioner
>   5. Sharpen a drill bit
> * 6. Read the resistor color code
>   7. Clean a chimney
>   8. Produce a business letter — individualized to several people — on a word processor
>   9. Cure an animal hide
>   10. Plant a garden
>   11. Operate a piece of heavy-duty equipment

12. Rescreen a window
13. Open a checking account
14. Change a tire on a hill
15. Plant a garden
16. Change oil in a car
17. Read a micrometer or a dial caliper
18. Hang wallpaper
19. Set out a shrub
20. Replace a capacitor in a television set
21. Sterilize an instrument
22. Use a microfiche reader
23. Make a tack weld
24. Operate an office machine
25. Prepare a laboratory specimen for shipment
26. Input data into a computer
27. Fingerprint a suspect
28. Tune up a motor
29. Repair (or rebind) a book
30. Develop black and white film
31. Use a compass, architect's scale, divider, or French curve
32. Administer an intramuscular injection
33. Start an airplane engine
34. Set up a partnership
35. Topic of your choosing

APPLICATION 9   GIVING INSTRUCTIONS

Give orally the instructions for one of the topics in Application 8 above. Remember to use visuals whenever they will be helpful. Ask your classmates to evaluate your speech by making an Evaluation of Oral Presentations sheet like the one on page 459 and filling it in.

PLAN SHEET
FOR GIVING INSTRUCTIONS

Analysis of Situation Requiring Instructions

What is the procedure to be explained?

For whom are the instructions intended?

How will the instructions be used?

In what format will the instructions be given?

Importance or Usefulness of the Instructions

Organizing Content

Equipment and materials necessary:

Terms to be defined or explained:

Major steps (list as command verbs), with identifying information:

Precautions to emphasize (crucial steps, possible difficulties, or places where errors are likely to occur):

Types and Subject Matter of Visuals to Be Included

Sources of Information

DESCRIPTION OF A PROCESS

Describing a process — explaining how something is done — is similar to giving instructions. There are, however, two basic differences: a difference in the purpose and a difference in the procedure of presentation. The purpose in giving instructions is to enable an individual to perform a particular operation. The giver of the instructions expects the reader or hearer to *act*. In describing a process, however, the purpose is to describe a method or operation so that the intended audience will understand what is done. The presenter expects the reader or hearer to *understand* what happens.

Processes may be carried out by people, by machines, or by nature. Descriptions of processes carried out by people might be: how steel is made from iron, how glass is made, how diamonds are mined. Machine processes include how a clock works, how a Xerox copier works, or how a gasoline engine operates. Natural processes include how sound waves are transmitted, how rust is formed, how food is digested, and how mastitis is spread.

With instructions, you use commands (for example, *unplug, remove, insert*) so that the audience can act. You present and explain each step the reader or listener must carry out to perform the operation. In the description of a process, you emphasize the sequence of actions that is the procedure for an operation. The audience is unlikely to perform the operation. Notice below a comparison of possible procedures for giving instructions and for describing a process.

Giving Instructions	*Describing a Process*
"(you) Fasten the left strand . . ."	"The left strand is fastened . . ."
1. Imperative mood (orders or commands	1. Indicative mood (statements of fact)
2. Active voice (subject does the action)	2. Passive (subject is acted upon)
3. Second person (person spoken to is subject). Subject is understood *you*.	3. Third person (thing spoken about is subject)

Through reading or hearing a description of a process, the audience develops an *understanding* of the operation. It would, in fact, be impossible to perform some processes, for example those carried out by nature. It is possible, however, to understand what happens as these natural processes occur; for instance, you can understand how sound is transmitted or how a tornado develops. Further, you can understand how bricks are made, but you would probably never make a brick.

INTENDED AUDIENCE

Just as in giving instructions, in giving a description of a process you must aim your presentation at a particular audience. You then write your explanation so that the intended audience will clearly understand. The intended audience influences your choice of the kind and extent of details you include in the description and the manner in which you present them. Audiences may be grouped into two broad categories: general audiences and specialized audiences.

Process Description for a General Audience

The general adult audience requires a fairly inclusive description. The writer should assume that this audience has little, if any, of the particular background, knowledge, or skill necessary to understand a description of a technical process. Therefore, you need to describe that process as clearly and simply as possible, defining any terms that might have special meaning.

The following description of how the heart works is directed to a general audience. Note the use of drawings as well as simplified language in describing the process.

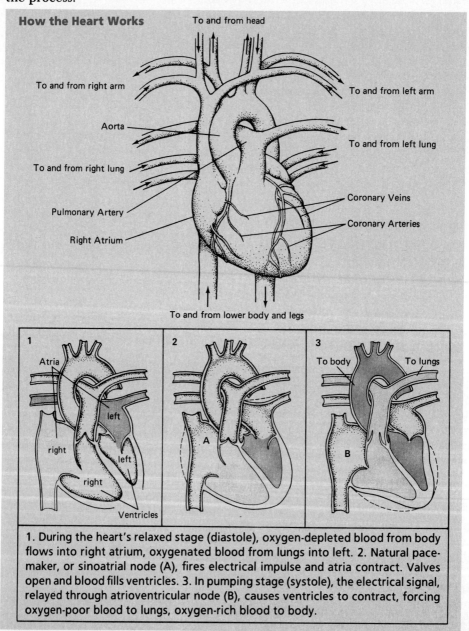

How the Heart Works

1. During the heart's relaxed stage (diastole), oxygen-depleted blood from body flows into right atrium, oxygenated blood from lungs into left. 2. Natural pacemaker, or sinoatrial node (A), fires electrical impulse and atria contract. Valves open and blood fills ventricles. 3. In pumping stage (systole), the electrical signal, relayed through atrioventricular node (B), causes ventricles to contract, forcing oxygen-poor blood to lungs, oxygen-rich blood to body.

The following description of how plywood is made illustrates an oral presentation for a general audience. A filled-in Plan Sheet and the description with directions for oral presentation are included.

PLAN SHEET
FOR DESCRIBING A PROCESS

Analysis of Situation Requiring Description of a Process

What is the process to be described?
how plywood is made

For whom is the description intended?
a general adult audience

How will the description be used?
for general understanding

In what format will the description be given?
an oral presentation

Importance or Significance of the Process

*Plywood is stronger and lighter than a piece of lumber the same size.
Durable.*

Major Steps and Description of Each Step

(List the major steps as -*ing* verb forms or in third person, present tense, active or passive voice.)

1. *Peeling the layers of wood from the log:*
    A lathe turns the log against a blade.
    Thin layers of wood are peeled off.
    The layers are sorted.
    The layers are dried.
2. *Gluing the layers of wood together:*
    Layers are placed on one another at right angles.
    Plywood can be made in various thicknesses.
3. *Pressing the sheets in large hydraulic presses:*
    The glue is set with heat and pressure.
    The sheets of plywood are sanded and trimmed.

Important Points to Receive Special Emphasis

Plywood is popular construction material in making houses, boats, furniture, etc.

Types and Subject Matter of Visuals to Be Included

A flow chart to outline major stages and show what each stage includes

Put on chalkboard as each step is mentioned:

Peeling
{ *the log*
thin layers
sorting
drying }

Gluing
{ *angle placement*
various thicknesses }

Pressing
{ *heat and pressure*
sanding and trimming }

Sources of Information

Pamphlet from Georgia-Pacific, World Book Encyclopedia

HOW PLYWOOD IS MADE

Have you ever wondered why plywood is so strong, lightweight, and durable? Plywood is a building material composed of thin sheets of wood glued together. The process of making plywood involves three major stages: peeling the thin layers of wood from the log, gluing the layers together, and pressing the sheets in large hydraulic presses.

As each major step is listed, write on the chalkboard:

Peeling
   ↓
Gluing
   ↓
Pressing

Peeling the thin layers of wood from the log is done by a huge lathe. Logs, with the bark removed, are placed in the lathe, which turns them against a long, razor-sharp knife. As the thin, continuous layers of wood are peeled from the log, they slide onto conveyor tables. At this point the layers of wood are inspected for defects, sorted into needed lengths and widths, and graded. Then, to reduce the amount of moisture in the layers, they are put through automatic driers.

As each aspect of peeling is stated, jot it down on the chalkboard:

Peeling $\begin{cases} \textit{the log} \\ \textit{thin layers} \\ \textit{sorting} \\ \textit{drying} \end{cases}$

The next major stage in making plywood is gluing together the dried layers of wood. Each layer, as it is placed on another, is turned so that the grain is at right angles with the layer below it. Then the layers are glued together. Each layer, or ply, may be as thin as $1/100$ of an inch or as thick as $1/2$ inch. Any number of plies may be glued together.

As each aspect of gluing is stated, jot it down on the chalkboard:

Gluing $\begin{cases} \textit{angle placement} \\ \textit{various thicknesses} \end{cases}$

The final stage is pressing the plywood to set the glue. The plywood is put in large hydraulic presses, where heat and pressure are applied. As the plywood comes from the presses, it is sanded and trimmed to specified lengths and widths, depending on the use it will be put to. The finished plywood sheets are now ready to be shipped to the dealer or consumer.

As each aspect of pressing is stated, jot it down on the chalkboard:

Pressing $\begin{cases} \textit{heat and pressure} \\ \textit{sanding and trimming} \end{cases}$

When this last stage is completed, the complete process will be outlined in a flow chart:

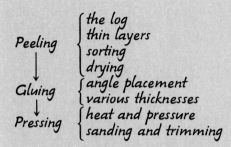

Plywood has become an enormously popular construction material for airplanes, houses, furniture, boats, and hundreds of other items. Because of the cross-laying of the plies, plywood is very strong, and it is relatively lightweight. The waterproof glue used in some plywood is so strong that the plywood will stand up under repeated changes of boiling and drying and continuous exposure to salt water. Plywood is the best choice for a strong, lightweight, and durable building material.

In the description of how plywood is made, the speaker's purpose is to give the average adult listener a general view of the process. The speaker, being knowledgeable about the subject and understanding the process of manufacturing plywood sufficiently to give a general description of it, is successful in accomplishing that purpose. The speaker remembers the audience throughout the presentation by using a vocabulary and level of speaking that the average adult can easily understand.

The speaker is accurate and complete in the description, and the information is correct. All the necessary steps in manufacturing plywood are given, and at no time is the wood unaccounted for, from the log to the finished product. Certainly, there is much more information about plywood that the speaker *could* have included, such as the kinds of trees from which plywood is made or differences in making interior and exterior plywood. Or the speaker could have elaborated further about each step in the manufacturing process. The important thing, however, is that the speaker included all *essential* information.

Process Description for a Specialized Audience

A specialized audience, as the term implies, has at least an interest in a particular subject and probably has the background, either from reading or from actual experience, to understand a description of a process related to that subject. For example, a person whose hobby is working on cars and reading about them would understand a relatively technical description of the operation of the Wankel engine. The specialized reader may even have a high degree of knowledge and skill. For example, sanitation engineers, fire chiefs, inhalation therapists, research analysts, programmers, or machinists would understand technical descriptions related to their fields of specialization. If, however, you have any doubt about the audience's level of knowledge, clarify any part of the description that you feel the reader might have difficulty understanding. (See also Accurate Terminology, page 58.)

The following description of how a fire company officer sizes up a fire is directed to a person interested in fire science. The Plan Sheet used in preparing the description is included.

PLAN SHEET
FOR DESCRIBING A PROCESS

Analysis of Situation Requiring Description of a Process

What is the process to be described?
how fires are sized up

For whom is the description intended?
a fire science trainee

How will the description be used?
to learn the duties of a company officer

In what format will the description be given?
a written explanation

Importance or Significance of the Process

Accurate sizing up of a fire determines fire fighting techniques to be employed and the effectiveness of those techniques.

Major Steps and Description of Each Step

(List the major steps as -*ing* verb forms or in third person, present tense, active or passive voice.)

1. *Determining the location of the fire:*
   Noticing the alarm code (alarm box report)
   Checking with caller (call-in report)
2. *Assessing the danger to life and materials:*
   Noticing time of day
   Noticing season of the year
3. *Judging what the fire can do:*
   Consulting water resources map
   Checking building and its surroundings
4. *Reviewing available resources:*
   Noting kinds of companies responding, including types and amounts of equipment, numbers of men, and the availability of additional help
   Estimating the amount of water needed
   Evaluating the adequacy of the water supply

5. *Checking progress of the fire:*
   Watching for drastic changes
   Considering any new information about building, occupants, contents

Important Points to Receive Special Emphasis

omit

Types and Subject Matter of Visuals to Be Included

omit

Sources of Information

Lecture by company officer, observation of company officers at fires, training manual

THE PROCESS OF SIZING UP A FIRE

A key person in a fire company is the fire company officer. When an alarm sounds, the officer must note several factors immediately and others at the site of the fire in order to direct other fire fighters in putting out the fire. Sizing up a fire involves these five factors: determining the location of the fire, assessing the danger to life and materials, judging what the fire can do, reviewing available resources, and checking the progress of the fire. The entire process of fighting a fire is largely determined by the decisions of the company officer.

Determining the Location of the Fire

Upon the sound of the alarm, the officer notices the alarm code to determine the location of the fire. If the alarm box is tied directly into the fire department's alarm system, the exact location of the fire may be determined. If not, only the area of the fire can be determined. If someone calls in to report a fire, the caller may or may not identify the exact location. Generally, the fire company responding must find the fire once the officer's unit reaches the general area.

Assessing the Danger to Life and Materials

Next the officer looks at the clock to determine whether danger to life is high, moderate, or low. For example, an early morning fire in a hotel or a hospital or any other place where people are sleeping is a high danger to life. The time also helps the officer to anticipate traffic problems and to decide whether police are needed to clear the streets or if the drivers of mobile fire fighting units should take an alternate route to reach the scene of the fire more quickly. Another time factor considered is the season of the year. If it is Christmas season and the fire is in a large department store, there will be more people in the store and extra large stocks of merchandise.

Judging What the Fire Can Do

As the fire unit moves toward the fire, the officer consults the company water resources map to focus clearly in mind the location of hydrants or other water resources in the area. Radio communication may reveal the exact building on fire; more than likely, however, the exact building will not be identified until the unit reaches the scene of the fire.

Upon reaching the site of the fire, the officer notices the building and its surroundings: facts about smoke — the amount, its color, its location; visible flame, if any; facts about people involved, if any — at the windows, on the roof and the fire escapes, or in the streets. To assess hazards, the officer determines where within the building the fire is burning; notices the type of construction, the age, and the structural features of the building; and identifies any special hazards, such as explosive materials. An old building with open stairways and with wood used for much of its structure will burn rapidly.

Reviewing Available Resources

Next the officer reviews the resources available to handle the fire, noticing at least three factors. The first factor is the kinds of companies responding to the alarm (pump company, ladder company, and so on), the types and amount of equipment, the number of men, and the availability of additional help, if the severity of the fire indicates a need for such help. The second factor is the estimated amount of water needed to extinguish the fire. The third factor is the adequacy of the water supply.

Checking the Progress of the Fire

Identifying resources available enables the officer to plan and direct tactics to fight the fire. During the course of the fire, the officer watches for any drastic changes. Any new facts about the building, its occupants, or its contents, whether observed by the officer or reported by another person, may mean new tactics and operations.

Conclusion

The ability of a fire company officer to size up a fire determines fire fighting effectiveness. Therefore, a high degree of skill in sizing up a situation would surely be a desirable trait for a company officer. Decisions may mean great economic loss or small economic loss, a building burned to the ground or a building partially burned but restorable, or, more significantly, life or death.

ORAL PRESENTATION AND VISUALS

For detailed discussions of oral presentation and visuals, see Chapter 10, Oral Communication, and Chapter 11, Visuals.

GENERAL PRINCIPLES IN DESCRIBING A PROCESS

1. *The purpose of a description of a process is for audience understanding, not audience action.*
2. *The intended audience influences the kind and extent of details included and the manner in which they are presented.* Take into consideration the audience's degree of knowledge and understanding of the subject, and use a language level that will make the process description clear.
3. *Audiences may be grouped into two broad categories: general audiences and specialized audiences.*
4. *Accuracy and completeness are essential.* The process description should be correct in its information, and it should adequately cover all necessary aspects of the process.
5. *Visuals can enhance a process description.* Whenever a process description can be made clearer by such visuals as flow charts, diagrams, drawings, real objects, demonstrations, and the like, include them.

PROCEDURE FOR DESCRIBING A PROCESS

Form

In a description of a process you may arrange the steps or stages of the process in a numbered list, in information blocks, or in paragraphs. Remember the purpose of the description is to make the reader understand *what happens* during a process. The usual way to describe what happens is to use the third person, present tense, active or passive voice.

> **EXAMPLES**
>
> An *officer* (third person) *fingerprints* (present tense, active voice) a suspect by . . .
> *Glass* (third person) *is made* (present tense, passive voice) by . . .

Or, the description might use *-ing* verb forms.

> **EXAMPLES**
>
> *Peeling* (*-ing* verb form) the thin layers . . .
> The final stage is *removing* (*-ing* verb form) the seeds . . .

Remember to be consistent with person, tense, and voice in a single presentation. For example, if you select third person, present tense, active voice, use the third person, present tense, active voice throughout the presentation. Do not shift to some other person, tense, or voice. (See pages 498, 499, 503, 505.)

Content

When organizing a description of a process, divide the description into two or three parts, as shown below.

    I. The identification of the subject may be brief, perhaps only one or two sentences, depending on the complexity of the process.
        A. State the process to be explained.
        B. Identify or define the process.
        C. If applicable, give the purpose and significance of the process.
        D. Briefly list the main steps or stages of the process, preferably in one sentence.
   II. The development of the steps is the main part of the presentation and thus will be the lengthiest section.
        A. The guiding statement is a list of the main steps given in the introduction.
        B. Take up each step in turn, developing it fully with sufficient detail.
        C. Subdivide major steps, as needed.
        D. Insert headings for at least the main steps or stages.
        E. Use visuals whenever they will be helpful.
  III. The closing is determined largely by the purpose of the presentation.
        A. If the purpose is simply to inform the audience of the specific procedure, the closing may be:
            1. The completion of the discussion of the last step.
            2. A summary of the main steps.

    3. A comment on the significance of the process.

    4. Mention of other methods by which the process is performed.

B. If the presentation serves a specific purpose, such as evaluation of economy or practicality, the closing may be a recommendation.

Length of Presentation

The length of a presentation describing a process is determined by the complexity of the process, the degree of knowledge of the audience, and the purpose of the presentation. In a simple process, such as how a cat laps milk or how a stapler works, the steps may be adequately developed in a single paragraph, with perhaps a minimum of two or three sentences for each step. In a more complex process, the steps may be listed and numbered, and the description of each step may require a paragraph or more. The closing is usually brief.

APPLICATION 1   DESCRIBING A PROCESS

Choose one of the following topics or another, similar topic of interest to you for describing a process for a general audience. Consult any sources needed.

    a. Make a Plan Sheet like the one on pages 53–54, and fill it in.

    b. Write a preliminary draft.

    c. Revise.

    d. Write the final draft.

Processes Carried Out by People. How:

    1. A synthetic heart is transplanted

    2. A diamond is cut and polished

    3. Ceramic tile, bricks, tires, sugar (or any other material) is (are) made

    4. A person becomes a "star"

    5. Community colleges and technical institutes are helping to alleviate the skilled labor shortage

    6. A site is chosen for a business or industry

    7. Flood prevention helps to eliminate soil erosion

    8. Gold, silver, or coal is mined

    9. An industrial plant works with community leaders

   10. Penicillin (or any other "miracle" drug) was developed

   11. An alcoholic beverage is produced

   12. A buyer selects merchandise for a retail outlet

   13. A television repairperson troubleshoots a television set

   14. A college cafeteria dietician plans meals

   15. A topic of your choosing

APPLICATION 2   DESCRIBING A PROCESS

Give an oral process description of one of the topics in Application 1 above. Ask your classmates to evaluate your speech by making an Evaluation of Oral Presentations sheet like the one on page 459 and filling it in.

APPLICATION 3   DESCRIBING A PROCESS

Choose one of the following topics or another, similar topic for writing a process description for a specialized audience. Consult any sources needed.

   a. Make a Plan Sheet like the one on pages 53–54, and fill it in.
   b. Write a preliminary draft.
   c. Revise.
   d. Write the final draft.

Processes Carried Out by Machines. How:

   1. A telephone answering service works
   2. A space satellite works
   3. A tape recorder works
   4. A Xerox (or similar machine) reproduces copies
   5. A computer copies a disk
   6. An automatic icemaker works
   7. A jet (diesel or gas turbine) engine works
   8. Air brakes work
   9. A mechanical cotton picker (or any other piece of mechanical farm or industrial machinery) operates
   10. A lathe (or any other motorized piece of equipment in a shop) works
   11. An autoclave works
   12. A printing press prints material
   13. An electronic calculator displays numbers
   14. A dental unit works
   15. A topic of your choosing

APPLICATION 4   DESCRIBING A PROCESS

Give an oral process description of one of the topics in Application 3 above. Ask your classmates to evaluate your speech by making an Evaluation of Oral Presentations sheet like the one on page 459 and filling it in.

APPLICATION 5   DESCRIBING A PROCESS

Choose one of the following topics or another, similar topic for writing a process description. Consult any sources needed.

   a. Make a Plan Sheet like the one on pages 53–54, and fill it in.
   b. Write a preliminary draft.
   c. Revise.
   d. Write the final draft.

Processes Carried Out by Nature. How:

   1. The human eye works
   2. Oxidation occurs
   3. Tornadoes are formed
   4. Foods spoil
   5. Aging affects the body
   6. Gold, silver, granite, oil, peat (or any other substance) is formed

7. An acorn becomes an oak tree
8. Infants change during the first year
9. Microorganisms produce disease
10. Wood becomes petrified
11. A tadpole becomes a frog
12. Freshwater fish spawn
13. Sound is transmitted
14. An amoeba reproduces
15. A topic of your choosing

APPLICATION 6   DESCRIBING A PROCESS

Give an oral process description of one of the topics in Application 5 above. Ask your classmates to evaluate your speech by making an Evaluation of Oral Presentations sheet like the one on page 459 and filling it in.

PLAN SHEET
FOR DESCRIBING A PROCESS

Analysis of Situation Requiring Description of a Process

What is the process to be described?

For whom is the description intended?

How will the description be used?

In what format will the description be given?

Importance or Significance of the Process

Major Steps and Description of Each Step

(List the major steps as -*ing* verb forms or in third person, present tense, active or passive voice.)

Important Points to Receive Special Emphasis

Types and Subject Matter of Visuals to Be Included

Sources of Information

CHAPTER 2

Description of a Mechanism: Explaining How Something Works

OBJECTIVES   56
INTRODUCTION   56
GENERAL DESCRIPTION   56
   Frames of Reference in General Description   57
    Function   57
    Physical Characteristics   57
    Parts   57
ACCURATE TERMINOLOGY   58
PURPOSE AND AUDIENCE IN DESCRIPTION   58
SAMPLE GENERAL DESCRIPTIONS   58
SPECIFIC DESCRIPTION   64
   Uses of Specific Description   64
COMPARING GENERAL AND SPECIFIC DESCRIPTIONS   70
MECHANISM AT REST AND IN OPERATION   73
ORAL DESCRIPTION   73
VISUALS   74
GENERAL PRINCIPLES IN DESCRIBING A MECHANISM   75
PROCEDURE FOR A GENERAL DESCRIPTION OF A MECHANISM   75
PROCEDURE FOR A SPECIFIC DESCRIPTION OF A MECHANISM   76
APPLICATIONS   76

OBJECTIVES

Upon completing this chapter, the student should be able to:

- Define mechanism
- Explain the difference between a general description and a specific description
- List and explain the three frames of reference (points of view) from which a mechanism can be described
- Use accurate and precise terminology in describing a mechanism
- Use visuals in a description of a mechanism
- Give a general description of a mechanism
- Give a specific description of a mechanism
- Describe orally or in writing a mechanism at rest and a mechanism in operation

INTRODUCTION

A mechanism is defined broadly as any object or system that has a functional part or parts. Thus, a mechanism is any item that performs a particular function. Items regarded as mechanisms are as diverse as a fingernail file, a diesel engine, a computer, a ballpoint pen, or a lawn mower. Another example of a mechanism is a heart, which receives and distributes blood through dilation and contraction. The human body could also be defined as a mechanism. And systems like the universe or a city, which are composed of parts that work together, could also be described as mechanisms. Most often perhaps, the term *mechanism* suggests tools, instruments, and machines.

A technician constantly works with mechanisms and always needs to understand them: what they do, what they look like, what parts they have, and how these parts work together. At times an employee — when writing bid specifications, a memorandum for a repairperson, or purchase requests; when demonstrating a new piece of equipment; when learning how to perform heart catheterization or kidney dialysis; or when planning changes in a city department's activities — may need to describe a mechanism or a part of it, using a written or an oral presentation.

Such a description may be brief or it may be lengthy, depending upon audience and purpose. It may be a general description or a specific description.

GENERAL DESCRIPTION

General description focuses on describing a group or class of mechanisms, or on describing one mechanism as representative of the group or class. Examples are a word processor, a camera, a book, a cat, a pogo stick, or a rose.

The general description identifies and explains aspects *usually* associated with the mechanism. These aspects may include what the mechanism can do or can be used for, what it looks like, what its parts (components) are, what each part looks like, what each part does, and how these parts interact.

Frames of Reference in General Description

Logically there are three frames of reference, or points of view, from which a mechanism can be described generally: its function, its physical characteristics, and its parts.

Function A mechanism is created to perform a particular function or task. The typewriter, for example, produces characters resembling printed ones, as a substitute for handwriting. The wedging board eliminates bubbles of air in clay. The fire hydrant provides a source of water for fire fighting. The hypodermic needle and syringe are used to inject medications under the skin. The microscope makes a very small object, such as a microorganism, appear larger so that it is clearly visible to the human eye. An automobile serves as a means of transportation. The kidney separates water and the waste products of metabolism from the blood. An elevator transports people, equipment, and goods vertically between floors.

Thus, the key element in a general description of a mechanism is an explanation of its function, that is, the answer to: What is it used for? This question automatically raises other questions: When is this mechanism used? By whom? How? These questions need answers if the general description is to be adequate.

Physical Characteristics A general description points out the physical characteristics of the mechanism. The purpose is to help the audience "see," or visualize, the object, to give an overall impression of the appearance of the mechanism. Physical characteristics to consider include size, shape, weight, material, color, and texture.

Often, comparison with a familiar object is helpful too. The dividers, described on pages 61–62, are compared to a printed capital letter "A." Magnetic tape, described on pages 62–64, is compared to tape for a tape recorder and to movie film on a reel.

Sometimes a drawing of the parts of the mechanism is even more helpful. Notice the use of drawings with the descriptions, pages 61, 63, 64, 65, 66, 71, and 74; notice the use of cutaway diagrams on pages 63, 71, and 74.

Parts A third frame of reference in describing a mechanism is its parts, or construction. The mechanism is divided into its parts, the purpose of each part is given, and the way that the parts fit together is explained. A typewriter, for example, would be described as having four major parts: frame, keyboard, ribbon, and carriage. When a key is struck against the ribbon, a character is printed on the paper in the carriage. In the part-by-part description, the frame, keyboard, ribbon, and carriage would each be described in turn. In essence, each of these parts becomes a new mechanism and is subsequently described according to its function, physical characteristics, and parts.

Identifying the parts is similar to partitioning (see pages 134–147), and explaining how they work together is similar to explaining a process (see pages 37–50).

ACCURATE TERMINOLOGY

In describing a mechanism, use accurate and precise terminology. It is easier, of course, to use terms like *thing, good, large, narrow, tall,* and so forth. But your writing will be more effective if you use precise, specific words (see pages 5–9). Take time to think of or look up and use precise words.

Rather than "Magnetic tape is narrow" (not precise), use "Magnetic tape is ½-inch wide." Use "The chart shows manufactured goods representing 44 percent of the goods produced in Manitoba," not "The chart shows manufactured goods representing a large [not precise] percentage of goods produced in Manitoba." Or "Breaker points in use more than 10,000 miles need cleaning or replacing," not "Breaker points in use more than a few thousand miles [not precise] need cleaning or replacing."

Be careful to show variances. For example, rather than "Dividers may vary in size," use "Dividers may vary in size from 2 to 12 inches." Also be careful to refer to sizes by the standard method of measurement. The size of a bicycle, for instance, is referred to by the diameter of the wheels (such as 24-inch or 26-inch), not by the length of the frame or the minimum height of the saddle to the ground.

If you are not certain about precise words, many sources are available. Such sources include general dictionaries; general encyclopedias; textbooks; specialized dictionaries, handbooks, and encyclopedias; knowledgeable people; advertisements; mail order catalogs; and instruction manuals.

PURPOSE AND AUDIENCE IN DESCRIPTION

As always in planning a written or an oral presentation, you must identify the purpose of the presentation and the needs of the audience. For instance, descriptions of a hi-fi speaker would differ in emphasis and in detail, depending on whether the descriptions were given so a hi-fi buff could construct a similar speaker, or so a prospective buyer could compare the speaker to a similar one, or so the general public could simply understand what a hi-fi speaker is.

SAMPLE GENERAL DESCRIPTIONS

General descriptions are illustrated in the following two student-written descriptions. The first description includes the Plan Sheet that the student filled in before writing. Marginal notes have been included to help you analyze the description.

Analysis of Situation Requiring a General Description of a Mechanism

What is the general mechanism to be described?
dividers

For whom is the description intended?
an apprentice draftsperson

How will the description be used?
to understand dividers as a mechanism used by draftspersons

In what format will the description be given?
a written description

Analysis of the Mechanism

Definition, identification, and/or special features:
a tool commonly used by draftspersons, machinists, welders, and navigators to transfer measurements, to scribe circles, and to compare distances

Function, use, or purpose:
included in definition above

Who uses:
included in definition

When:
omit

Where:
omit

Physical characteristics:
   Size:
   2 to 12 inches
   3 to 18 inches
   (point range)

   Shape:
   printed capital letter "A" with a circle on top

   Weight:
   1 to 10 ounces

   Material:
   hardened steel

Other:
two adjustable legs or points joined at the top by a hinge and a circular spring

Major parts and a description of each:

Parts	Function	Physical Characteristics
legs	*mark the points of measurement*	*thin rectangles of hardened steel; one end of each leg is sharpened to a point*
hinge	*allows the legs to pivot*	*small steel spool*
spring	*holds ends of legs together*	*flat piece of steel shaped into a circle*
adjustable screw	*makes it possible to change distance between the two legs*	*threaded rod with a nut, a round, knuckled piece of metal with a center hole to fit onto the rod. The nut is threaded to match the rod. A small knob on the end of the rod stops the nut.*
handle	*for holding the divider*	*metal rod with knurled finger grip*

Operation Showing Parts Working Together

The handle is grasped between the thumb and first finger of one hand. Next, one point is placed on a scale. The other point is adjusted to the desired measurement by turning the adjustment screw.

Variations or Special Features

included under physical characteristics

Types and Subject Matter of Visuals to Be Included

figure showing hand holding dividers

Sources of Information

textbook, demonstration by instructor

A GENERAL DESCRIPTION OF DIVIDERS

Dividers are a tool commonly used by draftspersons, machinists, welders, and navigators to transfer measurements, to scribe circles, and to compare distances. Dividers can be described by physical characteristics, parts, and use.

Dividers defined; definition includes function

Control sentence naming topics to be covered

Physical Characteristics

The appearance of dividers is like a printed capital letter "A" with a small circle on top. Made of hardened steel, dividers have two adjustable legs or points joined at the top by a hinge and a circular spring. (See Figure 1.)

Physical characteristics: shape

material made from

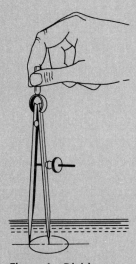

Figure 1. Dividers.

Dividers may vary in size from 2 to 12 inches. They are classified, however, according to the maximum opening between the points, which ranges from 3 to 18 inches. Depending on the size, the weight may be 1 to 10 ounces. Although the dividers vary in size and weight, they have the same parts and are used in the same way.

size

weight

Control sentence renaming topics to be covered

Parts

The five parts of dividers are the legs, the hinge, the circular spring, the adjustment screw, and the handle.

Parts listed

<u>Legs</u>. The two legs, thin rectangles of hardened steel, are used to mark the points of measurement; the lower end of each leg is tapered to a point. At the ends opposite the points, the two legs are joined by a hinge and a spring.

Parts described by physical characteristics and function of each

<u>Hinge</u>. The hinge is a small steel spool that allows the legs to pivot.

<u>Spring</u>. The spring is a flat piece of steel shaped into a circle to hold the ends of the legs together.

<u>Adjustment Screw</u>. The adjustment screw, which fits below the hinge, makes it possible to change the distance between the two legs. It is a threaded rod with one end anchored to one leg of the dividers. On the opposite end of the rod is a nut, a round, knurled piece of metal with a center hole threaded to match the rod.

A small knob on the end of the rod stops the nut at the maximum opening of the dividers. Turning the nut moves the other leg back and forth along the threads from 0 to the maximum opening. The movable leg can be anchored at any point between 0 and the maximum opening by the nut.

<u>Handle</u>. Centered on top of the spring is a handle, a metal rod with a knurled finger grip for holding the dividers.

Using Dividers

Dividers are used in the following way. First, the handle is grasped between the thumb and first finger of one hand. Next, one point is placed on a scale. The other point is adjusted to the desired measurement by turning the adjustment screw. The measurement can then be transferred to another drawing, a circle can be drawn, or distances can be compared.

Description of dividers "in use." A miniprocess explanation

A General Description of Magnetic Tape

Definition

Magnetic tape is a data representation medium that looks very much like tape recorder tape. It is used in a computer system for both input and output information. Magnetic tape can be described by its physical characteristics, parts, and use.

Magnetic tape defined
Use
Control sentence naming topics to be covered

Physical Characteristics

Most often, magnetic tape is ½-inch wide, although it may be ¾-inch or 1-inch wide. The tape is wound on a reel, very similarly to the way movie film is wound on a reel. See Figure 1.

Physical characteristics: width

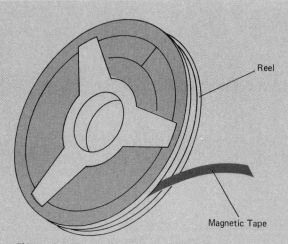

Figure 1. Magnetic tape on a reel.

The length of a reel of tape may range from 50 to 3600 feet, depending on the purpose of the tape. The most common length is 2400 feet and requires a 10½-inch-diameter reel.

length

At the beginning and at the end of each reel of tape is a small strip of reflecting material that "marks" for the computer where usable information begins and when the end of the tape is near (to keep the tape from running off the reel). The strip at the beginning is appropriately called the load-point marker; the strip at the end, the end-of-reel marker.

end markers

Parts

Magnetic tape has two basic parts: the base and the magnetic coating. See Figure 2.

Two parts listed

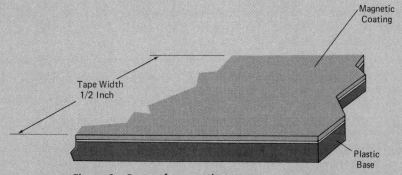

Figure 2. Parts of magnetic tape.

The base comprises the major portion of the tape. Made of a type of flexible plastic, it provides a place on which the magnetic coating can be applied.

First part described by material made from and use

Composed of ferric oxide, the magnetic coating is the most important part of the tape. On its surface in magnetized areas coded data representing numbers, letters, and special characters can be recorded.   *Second part described by material made from and use*

Magnetic tape may have a seven-track or a nine-track coding area. A track is simply a horizontal row on the tape. The code is the computer language; short vertical lines are the coded language on the magnetized areas.

The magnetized areas containing data are called blocks. Blocks can carry tremendous amounts of information in a very small area. For example, more than 1000 letters and numbers can be recorded on 1 inch of tape.

Each block is separated by a space called an interblock gap (IBG). The interblock gaps allow starting and stopping and speeding and slowing as the tape is used. See Figure 3.

Figure 3. Tape showing data blocks and IBGs.

Using Magnetic Tape

To use magnetic tape requires a tape drive, a machine that reads and records in the magnetized areas. Also the tape drive makes possible rewinding, backspacing, and skipping ahead.   *Use of magnetic tape*

SPECIFIC DESCRIPTION

In contrast with the general description, the specific description of a mechanism emphasizes particular characteristics, aspects, qualities, or features. It focuses on particular characteristics of an identified model, style, or brand of mechanism. It tries to show what sets this mechanism apart from all similar mechanisms.

For example, a specific description of Acco (brand) 20/30 (model) staplers might include facts about color, cost, guarantee, and unique construction features. See the sample description, page 69.

Uses of Specific Description

Specific description is used in bid specifications, in advertisements for products, or in any description for an audience that wants to know particular features of a mechanism.

One example of specific description is bid specifications. Bid specifications name a product and describe the unique characteristics, qualities, or features the product must have to meet a need. A company or business that sells the product looks at the specifications, determines if the company can offer the product as it is described, and then offers to sell it at a stated price.

While there is no standard form for recording or presenting bid specifications, they always identify a model and the desired qualities clearly and precisely.

The following is an example of bid specifications for a lawn mower to be used in cutting a golf course. (See also page 73.)

Bid No. 519
Opening Date: April 23, 1985
Name: 7 Gang Blitzer Mower

Item No.	Quantity	Description
1	1	7 unit Gang Blitzer for cutting golf course roughs, 30" or wider cut per unit
		Reel to be a five-blade, 10" diameter unit with pneumatic or semipneumatic tires. Wheel shaft to rotate on tapered roller bearings. Internal gears to rotate on ball or roller bearings (rotation of gear drive train on brass/bronze bushing not acceptable). Reels to be 10" diameter and with hardened steel blades
		Separate drive train required for wheel of the unit
		Quick disabling of reel drive for transportation required
		Reversible bed knife preferred but not mandatory. (Bed knife must be hardened steel)
		Frames readily attachable or detachable to expand or reduce number of reel units in use
		Heavy duty frames equal to or better than Jacobsen Blitzer Frames or Toro "Aero-Frames"

Another use of specific description is in magazines and journals in sections advertising products and in catalogs. The following description appeared in a section on new products in an issue of *The Office.*

Marvel Metal Products Co., 3843 West 43rd St., Chicago, Ill. 60632, introduces its Model 11-3030 utility stand for copiers, duplicators, audiovisual, and other office equipment. Stand is 30" wide, 20" deep, 30" high, with top and shelf of skid-resistant textured steel. Stud-welded 1" sq. steel legs and welded shelf corners provide rigid nonsway strength. Hooded ball casters, two with locks, allow mobile or stationary use. Stand can support up to 300 lbs.

Specific descriptions of mechanisms also appear in all types of merchandise catalogs. The description of hedge trimmers appeared in a merchandise catalog.

CRAFTSMAN® Cord-type Electric Bushwacker® Hedge Trimmers

- Double-edged blades cut in both directions for fast, clean trimming
- Helper handle on top lets you grip with both hands for better control and stability while trimming

(6 thru 8) Craftsman® Bushwacker® Hedge Trimmers
HOUSING: Thermoset polyester housing is impact-resistant. Rear hand grip and top helper handle made of durable plastic. Rear grip contoured to fit hand. Plastic blade barrier helps protect hand from blade.
BLADE: Double-edged steel blade cuts in both directions. Deep gaps between blade teeth makes grabbing branches easier.
ELECTRICAL INFORMATION: 110–120-volts, 60-Hertz. AC. UL listed. Double-insulated. Stub-length, 2-wire cord.
ORDER INFO: Order from chart at right. See warranty (C) for (6) and (7) and warranty (A) for (8), page 1052. Order extension cord on page 1049.

Hedge Trimmer	(6)	(7)	(8)
HP	.22	.20	.19
Bearings	Permanently lubricated ball and sleeve bearings	Permanently lubricated sleeve bearings	
Switch	Trigger switch for quick start-up and stop		Thumb switch
Blade size	22 inches	18 inches	16 inches
Teeth	58	48	40
Cutting strokes per minute	3000		2600
Catalog Number	9 H 8159C	9 H 8157C	9 H 8156C
Shipping weight	8 lbs. 15 oz	8 lbs. 11 oz.	7 lbs.
Price	$63.99	$48.99	$26.88

Following is a specific description of a mechanism prepared by a student. The description includes the Plan Sheet the speaker filled in; marginal notes have been added to outline the development of the description.

The description of Acco 20/30 staplers, to be given as an oral presentation, emphasizes the features that make the staplers desirable to own and use. These features include an unconditional one-year guarantee, a metal base that provides extra weight for improved performance and durability, a no-skid cushion, and jam-proof design. The function, physical characteristics, and parts of these specific staplers are very similar to those in any other stapler; therefore, treatment of the *usual* aspects is kept to a minimum, and the *unusual* aspects are emphasized.

Try reading the description aloud to approximate an oral presentation.

PLAN SHEET
FOR A SPECIFIC DESCRIPTION OF A MECHANISM

Analysis of Situation Requiring a Specific Description of a Mechanism

What is the specific mechanism to be described?
Acco 20/30 staplers

For whom is the description intended?
a general adult audience

How will the description be used?
to promote sales of Acco 20/30 staplers

In what format will the description be given?
an oral presentation

Analysis of the Mechanism

Who uses:
secretaries, teachers, businesspeople, anyone

When:
omit

Where:
home, office

Physical characteristics:
    Size:
    omit

    Shape:
    omit

    Weight:
    heavier than ordinary

    Material:
    zinc/magnesium alloy
    chrome

    Other:
    omit

Special features to be emphasized:
no-skid cushion
one-year unconditional guarantee
front loading
jam-proof
heavyweight metal base

Variations available:
two models: Acco #20 and #30

Types and Subject Matter of Visuals to Be Included

Sample stapler to show features mentioned and to demonstrate the loading and jam-proof device

A poster listing features mentioned (to be pointed out as each feature is discussed)

A poster illustrating each color of stapler and suggested price for each (to be pointed out as each is mentioned)

Sources of Information

brochure from Acco Company

ACCO 20/30 STAPLERS

For office and home use, Acco International, Inc., suggests the new Acco Staplers.

Hold up sample staplers.

These staplers, which look and perform like precision hand tools, are available in two models: the Acco #20 and #30.

The Acco #20 stapler is available in beige with choice of wood grain, blue, orange, brown, or green top, or charcoal with wood grain, gray, or black top. All #20 models feature a chrome cap. The suggested retail price for the stapler is $9.50 except for the one with the wood grain finish, which has a suggested retail price of $10.50.

Show poster illustrating each color stapler, pointing to each as it is mentioned, and stating suggested prices, pointing to each as it is mentioned.

The Acco #30 stapler is available in beige with a brown top or charcoal with a black or gray top. The suggested retail price is $8.50.

The main difference in the two models is appearance. The more expensive model is a bit handsomer and has a chrome cap. But both models function with equal efficiency.

Several features make Acco 20/30 staplers unique. Each is unconditionally guaranteed for one year. Each has a no-skid cushion that covers the entire bottom of the stapler, protecting surfaces and preventing sliding. Two features are of revolutionary design. One is the front loading channel, which pops out at the touch of the finger to receive a full strip of standard staples. Another is the jam-proof "floating" inner rail, which opens automatically to clear any misaligned staples.

Perhaps most important, however, is the zinc/magnesium alloy, used in place of aluminum. This new heavyweight metal base provides the extra weight needed for improved performance and rugged durability.

Show poster listing each feature briefly. As each feature is mentioned, point to it on the poster. Then, point out these features on the sample stapler. Demonstrate the loading and jam-proof devices.

Also, Acco International will imprint an individual's name, company logo, or message in color at no charge for quantities of 72 staplers or more. There is a small charge for lesser quantities.

Show sample imprint on a stapler.

For an attractive, easy-to-use stapler, choose an Acco stapler!

Marginal annotations:

- Identification of mechanism
- Topic sentence for following three paragraphs; key word: *models*
- First model colors and costs
- Second model colors and costs
- Comparison of two models
- Key words in main idea sentence: *features* and *unique*
- Paragraph gives four features: guarantee, no-skid cushion, front loading channel, jam-proof rail
- Paragraph gives material made from and advantages
- Paragraph explains imprint availability
- Closing

COMPARING GENERAL AND SPECIFIC DESCRIPTIONS

The general description of a mechanism emphasizes what the mechanism does or can be used for and what it looks like. It includes a description of the parts, what each part looks like, and what each does. Then the general description describes the parts as they relate to one another, that is, the mechanism in operation. This section of the description describes a process (see pages 37–50).

The general description explains a type of mechanism or a mechanism representing a class. It describes what all types of a stated mechanism or all mechanisms in a class have in common, even though variations may exist for different brands and different models.

A general description of a mechanism is the kind of description given in an encyclopedia. The following description of a microscope appears in *The World Book Encyclopedia.*°

> **MICROSCOPE,** *MY kruh skohp,* is an instrument that magnifies extremely small objects so they can be seen easily. It produces an image much larger than the original object. Scientists use the term *specimen* for any object studied with a microscope.
>
> The microscope ranks as one of the most important tools of science. With it, researchers first saw the tiny germs that cause disease. The microscope reveals an entire world of organisms too small to be seen by the unaided eye. Physicians and other scientists use microscopes to examine such specimens as bacteria and blood cells. Biology students use microscopes to learn about algae, protozoa, and other one-celled plants and animals. The details of nonliving things, such as crystals in metals, can also be seen with a microscope.
>
> There are three basic kinds of microscopes: (1) *optical,* or *light;* (2) *electron;* and (3) *ion.* This article discusses optical microscopes. For information on the other types, see the WORLD BOOK articles on ELECTRON MICROSCOPE AND ION MICROSCOPE.
>
> **How a Microscope Works.** An optical microscope has one or more lenses that bend the light rays shining through the specimen (see LENS). The bent light rays join and form an enlarged image of the specimen.
>
> The simplest optical microscope is a magnifying glass (see MAGNIFYING GLASS). The best magnifying glasses can magnify an object by 10 to 20 times. A magnifying glass cannot be used to magnify an object any further because the image becomes fuzzy. Scientists use a number and the abbreviation *X* to indicate (1) the image of an object magnified by a certain number of times or (2) a lens that magnifies by that number of times. For example, a 10X lens magnifies an object by 10 times. The magnification of a microscope may also be expressed in units called *diameters.* A 10X magnification enlarges the image by 10 times the diameter of the object.
>
> Greater magnification can be achieved by using a *compound* microscope. Such an instrument has two lenses, an *objective lens* and an *ocular,* or *eyepiece, lens.* The objective lens, often called simply the *objective,* produces a magnified image of the specimen, just as an ordinary magnifying glass does. The ocular lens, also called the *ocular,* then magnifies this image, producing an even larger image. Many micro-scopes have three standard objective lenses that magnify by 4X, 10X, and 40X. When these objective lenses are used with a 10X ocular lens, the compound microscope magnifies a specimen by 40X, 100X, or 400X. Some microscopes have *zoom* objective lenses that can smoothly increase the magnification of the specimen from 100X to 500X.

° Excerpted from *The World Book Encyclopedia.* © 1983 World Book, Inc.

In addition to magnifying a specimen, a microscope must produce a clear image of the closely spaced parts of the object. The ability to provide such an image is called the *resolving power* of a microscope. The best optical microscopes cannot resolve parts of objects that are closer together than about 0.000008 of an inch (0.0002 of a millimeter). Anything smaller in the specimen—such as atoms, molecules, and viruses—cannot be seen with an optical microscope.

Parts of a Microscope. The microscopes used in most schools and colleges for teaching have three parts: (1) the *foot,* (2) the *tube,* and (3) the *body.* The foot is the base on which the instrument stands. The tube contains the lenses, and the body is the upright support that holds the tube.

The body, which is hinged to the foot so that it may be tilted, has a mirror at the lower end. The object lies on the *stage,* a platform attached above the mirror. The mirror reflects light through an opening in the stage to illuminate the object. The upper part of the body is a slide that holds the tube and permits the operator to move it up and down with a *coarse-adjustment* knob. This movement focuses the microscope. Most microscopes also have a *fine-adjustment* knob, which moves the tube a small distance for final focusing of a high-power lens.

The lower part of the tube contains the objective lens. In most microscopes, this lens is mounted on a revolving *nosepiece* that the operator can rotate to bring the desired lens into place. The upper end of the tube holds the ocular lens.

Using a Microscope. A microscope is an expensive instrument and can be damaged easily. When moving one, be sure to hold it with both hands and set it down gently on a firm surface.

Parts of a Microscope

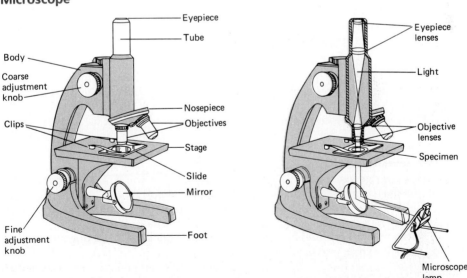

The diagram at the left shows the external parts of a microscope. A person adjusts these parts to view a specimen. The cutaway diagram at the right shows the path that light follows when passing through the specimen and then through the lenses and tubes of the microscope.

To prepare a microscope for use, turn the nosepiece so that the objective with the lowest power is in viewing position. Lower the tube and lens by turning the coarse-adjustment knob until the lens is just above the opening in the stage. Next, look through the eyepiece and adjust the mirror so a bright circle of light appears in the eyepiece. The microscope is now ready for viewing a specimen. Most people keep both eyes open when looking into the eyepiece. They concentrate on what they see through the microscope and ignore anything seen with the other eye.

Most specimens viewed through a microscope are transparent, or have been made transparent, so that light can shine through them. Objects to be viewed are mounted on glass slides that measure 3 inches long and 1 inch wide (76 by 25 millimeters). The technique of preparing specimens for microscopic viewing is called *microtomy* (see MICROTOMY). See also the *Science Project* with this article.

To view a slide, place it on the stage with the specimen directly over the opening. Hold the slide in place with the clips on the stage. Look through the eyepiece and turn the coarse-adjustment knob to raise the lens up from the slide until the specimen comes into focus. Never lower the lens when a slide is on the stage. The lens could press against the slide, breaking both the slide and the lens.

After the specimen has been brought into focus, turn the nosepiece to an objective lens with higher power. This lens will reveal more details of the specimen. If necessary, focus the stronger objective with the fine-adjustment knob. A zoom microscope is changed to a higher power by turning a part of the zoom lens. Different parts of the specimen can be brought into view by moving the slide on the stage.

The specific description of a mechanism, on the other hand, describes the outstanding or unique features or characteristics of a stated brand or model. It emphasizes the aspects of the stated brand or model that set it apart from other brands or models of the same mechanism. The specific description below appears in a merchandise catalog from Arthur H. Thomas Company (note the omission of noncontent words to save space).

6545-H10   MICROSCOPES, Teaching
6545-H30   American Optical Series Sixty

Designed to withstand classroom handling. Advanced features include unique, spring-loaded focusing mechanism which protects slide and objective, avoids conventional rack and pinion. Equipped with in-base illuminator.

Revolving ball-bearing nosepiece is raised or lowered to effect focus, by means of coaxial coarse and fine adjustments, low-positioned for convenience. Adjustable stop (Autofocus) limits objective travel, permitting rapid focus while safeguarding objective and slide.

Stage, with clips, is 125×135 mm. Integral in-stage condenser with adjustable diaphragm has reference ring for centering specimen.

Inclined body is reversible for viewing from front or back of stage. Huygenian eyepiece, $10\times$, with pointer and measuring scale, is locked in.

Optics on both models have Americote magnesium fluoride coating on air-glass surfaces to reduce internal reflection and improve image contrast.

6545-H10 Microscope has 5-aperture disc diaphragm, double revolving nosepiece, $10\times$ and $43\times$ achromatic objectives, providing $100\times$ and $430\times$ magnification.

6545-H30 Microscope has iris diaphragm; triple revolving nosepiece; $4\times$, $10\times$, and $43\times$ achromatic objectives, providing $40\times$, $100\times$, and $430\times$ magnification.

With switch, cord, and plug, for 120 volts. For replacement bulb, see 6625-D30.

Still another type of specific description is illustrated in the following bid specifications for a microscope.

Bid No. 215
Opening Date: May 10, 1985
Name: Microscope, AO Series 10

Item No.	Quan-tity	Description	Unit Price	Total Price
	1	MICROSCOPE, AO Series 10 Microscope to permit simultaneous viewing of the same image by two persons in side-by-side position. To have dual viewing adapter binocular body, 10X, wide-field eyepieces. To have illuminated green arrow, to be powered by microscope transformer, to be controlled by lever at base of adapter, and positioned anywhere in the field of view. To be equipped with ungraduated mechanical stage, Aspheric, N.A. 1.25, condenser with auxiliary swing-in lens, 2 pair 10X widefield eyepieces. SPECIFICATIONS: Viewing position—side by side Planachromatic 4X, 40X, 100X		

MECHANISM AT REST AND IN OPERATION

In either a general or a specific description of a mechanism, the mechanism may be described at rest or in operation or both, depending on the purpose of the description.

A description of a mechanism at rest would perhaps mention the function and the physical appearance, but it would emphasize the parts of the mechanism, particularly their location in relation to one another. A description of a mechanism in operation would perhaps mention the function and the parts, but it would emphasize these parts working together to perform the function.

Occasionally you might want to emphasize only the operation of a mechanism. The illustration on page 74 describes the four-cycle engine in operation.

ORAL DESCRIPTION

As an employee in such areas as sales, supervision, or training you may find occasions when you must describe a mechanism orally. This description might be given to a large group of potential buyers, to several newly hired workers, to students in a training program, or to a single individual. As a student, you may also be asked to give oral descriptions of mechanisms.

The content of an oral description might be organized following the procedures outlined within this chapter. Presenting the material, however, might require other considerations. For a detailed discussion on oral presentations, see Chapter 10, Oral Communication.

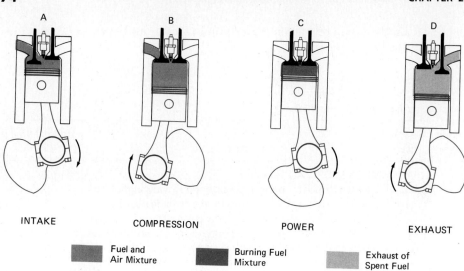

INTAKE   COMPRESSION   POWER   EXHAUST

Fuel and
Air Mixture

Burning Fuel
Mixture

Exhaust of
Spent Fuel

Four-cycle Engine. Provides one power impulse for four strokes of piston; each two revolutions of crankshaft. A—On Intake Stroke, inlet valve opens; piston draws fuel and air mixture into cylinder. B—On Compression Stroke, both valves are closed. Rising piston compresses mixture. C—At upper limit of piston movement; both valves closed, mixture is ignited. Explosion forces piston downward on Power Stroke. D—On Exhaust Stroke, exhaust valve opens, rising piston pushes spent gas from cylinder. (Redrawn by permission from William K. Toboldt and Larry Johnson, eds., *Goodheart-Wilcox's Automotive Encyclopedia* [South Holland, Ill.: Goodheart-Wilcox Co., Inc., 1977].)

VISUALS

Visuals are especially valuable in describing a mechanism. Generally in describing a mechanism, the goal is to enable the audience to see what the mechanism looks like and what its parts are and to understand how these parts work together to allow the mechanism to function.

Pictorial illustrations, such as photographs, drawings, and diagrams, that are included with a verbal description accomplish the goal more readily. The illustration above describes the four-cycle engine in operation; the illustration plus the verbal explanation provides a clear description, easily understood, of a fairly complex operation.

Photographs, drawings, and diagrams are useful in describing mechanisms. Photographs can provide a clear external or internal view; they can show the size of a mechanism; they can show color and texture. Drawings, ranging from simple, free-hand sketches done with pencil, pen, crayon, or brush to engineers' or architects' minutely detailed drawings done with drafting instruments, machines, and computers, can do the same. Diagrams can outline an object or system, showing such things as its parts, its operation, its assembly. These outlines may be picture, schematic, or block diagrams. Drawings and diagrams can show the entire exterior or interior of a mechanism or only a part; they can show the shapes of parts, the relationships between parts, and the functions of parts as they work together; they can show cross sections. Or they can be exploded views that show the parts disassembled but arranged in sequence of assembly. Obviously, visuals such as these are of great value in describing mechanisms.

For a detailed discussion, see Chapter 11, Visuals.

GENERAL PRINCIPLES IN DESCRIBING A MECHANISM

1. *The description of a mechanism may be a general description.* In a general description, emphasis is on giving an overall view of what the mechanism can do or can be used for.
2. *The three frames of reference in a general description are function, physical characteristics, and parts.* Although these three frames of reference are closely related, ordinarily they should be kept separate and in logical order.
3. *Accurate and precise terminology should be used.* Sources for such terminology are dictionaries, encyclopedias, textbooks, knowledgeable people, instruction manuals, and merchandise catalogs.
4. *The purpose of the description and the intended audience must be clear.* These two basic considerations determine the extent and the kind of details given and the manner in which they are given.
5. *The description may be a specific description of a particular mechanism.* In a specific description, emphasis is on particular characteristics or aspects of a mechanism identifiable by brand name, model number, and the like.
6. *The description may be of a mechanism at rest or in operation.* In an at-rest description, emphasis is on parts of the mechanism and their location in relationship one to another. In an in-operation description, emphasis is on the parts and the way these parts work together to perform the intended function.

PROCEDURE FOR A GENERAL DESCRIPTION OF A MECHANISM

I. The identification of the mechanism is usually simple and requires only a few sentences.
   A. Define or identify the mechanism.
   B. Indicate why this description is important, if appropriate.
   C. In a sentence, list the points (frames of reference) about the mechanism to be described.

II. The explanation of the function, physical characteristics, and parts is the lengthiest section of the presentation.
   A. Give the function, use, or purpose of the mechanism.
      1. If the mechanism is part of a larger whole, show the relationship between the part and the whole.
      2. If applicable, state who uses the mechanism, when, where, and why.
   B. Give the physical characteristics of the mechanism.
      1. Try to make the reader "see" the mechanism.
      2. Describe, as applicable, such physical characteristics as size, shape, weight, material, color, texture, and so on.
   C. Give the parts of the mechanism.
      1. List the major parts of the mechanism in the order in which they will be described.

2. Identify each part.
3. State what each part is used for — its function.
4. Tell what each part looks like — its physical characteristics.
5. Give the relationship of each part to the other parts.
6. If necessary, divide the part into its parts and give their functions, physical characteristics, and parts.
   D. Use headings and visuals, when appropriate, to make meaning clear.
III. The closing, usually brief, emphasizes particular aspects of the mechanism.
   A. Show how the individual parts work together.
   B. If applicable, mention variations of the mechanism, such as optional features, other types, and other sizes.
   C. If applicable, comment on the importance or significance of the mechanism.

PROCEDURE FOR A SPECIFIC DESCRIPTION OF A MECHANISM

I. The identification of the mechanism is usually simple and requires only a few sentences.
   A. Identify the mechanism by giving the brand name or model number.
   B. Tell the function or purpose of the mechanism.
   C. Tell who uses the mechanism, when it is used, and where.
   D. In a sentence, list the features or characteristics of the mechanism, or in a sentence, state that the mechanism possesses "unique features," "five specific characteristics," "the following desirable features," or some similar general phrase to introduce the main section.
II. The features or characteristics of the particular brand or model make up the main section of the description.
   A. Identify each feature or characteristic.
      1. Select information about the mechanism to set it apart from other similar mechanisms.
      2. Consider such features as size, shape, weight, material, overall appearance, available colors, cost, guarantee.
   B. Describe each feature or characteristic in detail.
   C. Use headings and visuals, when appropriate, to make meaning clear.
III. The closing, if included, is usually brief.
   A. The description may end after the discussion of the last feature or characteristic.
   B. The features or characteristics discussed may be summarized.
   C. Any variations of the mechanism, such as other models, different colors, other prices, or different designs, may be mentioned.

APPLICATION 1 DESCRIBING A MECHANISM

Sort the sentences below into three general groups under the following three headings: Function, Physical Characteristics, and Parts. Write the numbers of the sentences under the proper headings.

1. The jaws are made of cast iron and have removable faces of hardened tool steel.
2. The machinist uses a small stationary holding device called "the machinist's bench vise" to grip the work securely when performing bench operations.
3. For a firm grip on heavy work, serrated faces are usually inserted.
4. In addition to the typical bench vise described here, there are many other varieties and sizes.
5. It is essential for holding work pieces when filing, sawing, and clipping.
6. A vise consists of a fixed jaw, a movable jaw, a screw, a nut fastened in the fixed jaw, and a handle by which the screw is turned to position the movable jaw.
7. To protect soft metal or finished surfaces from dents and scratches, false lining jaws are often set over the regular jaws.
8. This holding device is about the size of a small grinding wheel and is fastened to the work bench in a similar manner.
9. These lining jaws can be made from paper, leather, wood, brass, copper, or lead.
10. A smooth face is inserted to prevent marring the surface of certain work pieces.

After sorting the sentences into three groups, arrange the sentences in logical order to form a paragraph. The reorganized paragraph thus would read:

Sentence   __2__ , ____, ____, __6__ , ____, ____, ____, ____, ____, __4__

Now write out the reorganized paragraph.

APPLICATION 2   DESCRIBING A MECHANISM

Write a general description of one of the following mechanisms or of a mechanism in your major field.

  a. Make a Plan Sheet like the one on pages 80–81, and fill it in.
  b. Write a preliminary draft.
  c. Revise.
  d. Write the final draft.

Describe:

1. A disk drive
2. A jack
3. A drill press
4. A power saw
5. A set of drawing instruments
6. A flashlight
7. A microphone
8. A wristwatch
9. A camera
10. A sprayer
11. A room air conditioner
12. A shotgun

13. A stapler
14. A washing machine
15. A lie detector
16. A diesel engine
17. A Geiger counter
18. An alternator
19. An antenna
20. A barometer
21. A sliding T bevel
22. A bicycle
23. An electric toaster or some other household appliance
24. A vaccinating needle
25. A calculator
26. A mechanical pencil
27. An autoclave
28. A dental unit
29. A stethoscope
30. An incubator

APPLICATION 3   DESCRIBING A MECHANISM

Give an oral description of a mechanism in Application 2 above. Ask your classmates to evaluate your speech by making an Evaluation of Oral Presentations sheet like the one on page 459 and filling it in.

APPLICATION 4   DESCRIBING A MECHANISM

From the list in Application 2, choose a mechanism and write a specific description of it. This time, however, describe a *specific* model or make, such as a Swingline 90 stapler, a 20-gauge Remington automatic shotgun, or a Zenith portable radio, model number 461.

   a. Make a Plan Sheet like the one on pages 82–83, and fill it in.
   b. Write a preliminary draft.
   c. Revise.
   d. Write the final draft.

APPLICATION 5   DESCRIBING A MECHANISM

Select a mechanism that you use in one of your lab courses. Follow this procedure:

   a. Make a Plan Sheet like the one on pages 80–81, and fill it in.
   b. Write a preliminary draft.
   c. Revise.
   d. Write the final draft.

Use appropriate information for audience and purpose to give the following three descriptions.

1. Describe this mechanism so that an employee can find it and put an inventory number on it.
2. Describe this mechanism for a new lab student who must use the mechanism.
3. Describe this mechanism for a technician who will repair or replace a broken part.

APPLICATION 6   DESCRIBING A MECHANISM

Choose a mechanism from the list in Application 2 or from your major field. Describe the mechanism at rest and in operation.

APPLICATION 7   DESCRIBING A MECHANISM

Give orally a specific description of a mechanism. Plan to use a visual of the mechanism, either a sample mechanism, a picture, or a line drawing, or arrange for the class to visit your shop or laboratory and view the mechanism. Ask your classmates to evaluate your speech by making an Evaluation of Oral Presentations sheet like the one on page 459 and filling it in.

APPLICATION 8   DESCRIBING A MECHANISM

Research a mechanism to find out all possible options. Then "create" your own mechanism by adding your choice of options to the basic mechanism. After studying a sampling of brochures and fliers advertising mechanisms, plan and present a sales brochure to advertise your mechanism. Use appropriate visuals (see Chapter 11).

PLAN SHEET
FOR A GENERAL DESCRIPTION OF A MECHANISM

Analysis of Situation Requiring a General Description of a Mechanism

What is the general mechanism to be described?

For whom is the description intended?

How will the description be used?

In what format will the description be given?

Analysis of the Mechanism

Definition, identification, and/or special features:

Function, use, or purpose:

Who uses:

When:

Where:

Physical characteristics:
   Size:

   Shape:

   Weight:

   Material:

Other:

Major parts and a description of each:

Part	Function	Physical characteristics

Operation Showing Parts Working Together

Variations or Special Features

Types and Subject Matter of Visuals to Be Included

Sources of Information

PLAN SHEET
FOR A SPECIFIC DESCRIPTION OF A MECHANISM

Analysis of Situation Requiring a Specific Description of a Mechanism

What is the specific mechanism to be described?

For whom is the description intended?

How will the description be used?

In what format will the description be given?

Analysis of the Mechanism

Who uses:

When:

Where:

Physical characteristics:
  Size:

  Shape:

  Weight:

  Material:

  Other:

Special features to be emphasized:

Variations available:

Types and Subject Matter of Visuals to Be Included

Sources of Information

CHAPTER 3

Definition: Explaining What Something Is

OBJECTIVES 85
INTRODUCTION 85
DEFINITION ADAPTED TO PURPOSE 85
WHEN TO DEFINE A TERM 87
EXTENT OF DEFINITION 88
HOW TO DEFINE A TERM 88
    Sentence Definition 88
     Inadequate Sentence Definitions 90
    Extended Definition 91
INTENDED AUDIENCE AND PURPOSE 96
    Definitions in General Reference Works 96
    Definitions in Specialized Reference Works 96
DEFINITION AS PART OF A LONGER COMMUNICATION 98
ORAL DEFINITION 98
VISUALS 98
GENERAL PRINCIPLES IN GIVING A DEFINITION 99
PROCEDURE FOR GIVING AN EXTENDED DEFINITION 99
APPLICATIONS 100

OBJECTIVES

Upon completing this chapter, the student should be able to:

- List the conditions under which a term should be defined
- Demonstrate the three steps in arriving at a sentence definition
- Give a sentence definition
- Give an extended definition
- State definitions according to their purpose and the knowledge level of the reader

INTRODUCTION

All too often in preparing a written or an oral presentation, the careless person dismisses the idea of including definitions in the presentation, apparently thinking, "Why bother with definitions? Aren't there dictionaries around for people who run into words they don't know?" Before evaluating this attitude, consider a common, frequently used word in the English language: *pitch*. Certainly, this is not a strange word to most people. A draftsperson writing about *pitch* for other draftspersons can be sure that they know the term refers to the slope of a roof, expressed by the ratio of its height to its span. An aeronautical technician, however, would automatically associate *pitch* with the distance advanced by a propeller in one revolution. A geologist would think of *pitch* as being the dip of a stratum or vein. A machinist thinks of *pitch* as the distance between corresponding points on two adjacent gear teeth or as the distance between corresponding points on two adjacent threads of a screw, measured along the axis. To the musician *pitch* is that quality of a tone or sound determined by the frequency or vibration of the sound waves reaching the ear. To the construction worker *pitch* is a black, sticky substance formed in the distillation of coal tar, wood tar, petroleum, and such, and used for such purposes as waterproofing, roofing, and paving. To the average layperson *pitch* is an action word meaning "toss" or "throw," as in "Pitch the ball." Such expressions as "It's *pitch* dark" or "I see the neighborhood's chief con man has a new *pitch*" illustrate other uses of *pitch*.

This one word illustrates quite well the importance of knowing when to define for different readers, and it implies that the writer or speaker must know *how* to define.

DEFINITION ADAPTED TO PURPOSE

Because in business and industry many words have precise, specific meanings, the need for defining a term frequently arises. You must be able to give a clear, accurate definition that is appropriate for the situation, you must know how and when to write a sentence definition and an extended definition, and you must know how to word these definitions for a particular purpose and according to the knowledge level of the audience. A mechanical technician or a draftsperson, for instance, has to be able to adapt the length and simplicity of the definition of a micrometer caliper according to need. Consider each of the three following definitions and the different occasions on which each would best serve the writer's purpose.

1. A micrometer caliper is an instrument for measuring very small distances.
2. A micrometer caliper is a precision measuring instrument graduated to read up to one ten-thousandth of an inch and sized to measure stock from one to twenty-four inches. There are three kinds of micrometers — the inside, the depth gauge, and the outside. The latter is the more common.
3. The micrometer caliper is a precision measuring instrument designed to use the decimal divisions of the inch. Some micrometers are graduated to read a thousandth part of an inch while others have verniers by which measurements of one ten-thousandth of an inch can be made.

   The micrometer has a U-shaped frame to which are fastened an anvil and a barrel, or hub (see the drawing). Inside the barrel are very fine threads (40 per inch) that make a nut and screw for the moving spindle and thimble. On the front of the barrel is a long line divided by short crosslines; the inch of space along the barrel is divided into parts. The first line, starting from 0, is .025 inch; the second, .050; the third, .075; and the fourth (the long crossline), .100 inch. The spindle turns inside the barrel; the thimble, attached to the spindle, fits over the barrel. Turning the thimble to the right or the left moves the spindle toward or away from the anvil. A complete turn moves the spindle one-fortieth of an inch, or .025 inch. The thimble has a beveled edge divided into 25 equal parts or thousandths with each division representing .001 inch (one-thousandth of an inch). Turning the spindle one complete turn (.025 inch) moves it 25 spaces on the beveled edge of the thimble. For every complete turn to the right, one more mark on the barrel is covered over.

   When the micrometer is closed, the zero line on the thimble and the zero line on the barrel coincide. Unscrewing the thimble one full turn will align the zero on the thimble with the horizontal line on the barrel and expose one space on the barrel. The micrometer has been opened one-fortieth of an inch, or 25 thousandths. Each complete turn of the thimble will expose one more mark on

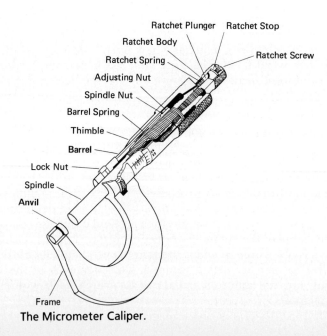

The Micrometer Caliper.

the barrel or an additional 25 thousandths. Also from a closed position the thimble can be turned so that the graduation next to zero on the beveled edge lines up with the horizontal line on the barrel, thus opening the micrometer one-thousandth of an inch. Every one-space turn of the thimble on the beveled edge opens the micrometer another one-thousandth. When the thimble has been turned 25 spaces along its beveled edge (one full revolution: 25 thousandths), the first line on the barrel is exposed.

The micrometer must be checked frequently for accuracy. To make the check, insert between the spindle and anvil a gauge block of known unit size, making sure both micrometer and gauge block are free from dirt and grit. The micrometer is accurate if the reading of the micrometer, with the block in place, is the same as the known size of the gauge block.

There are occasions on which each of the micrometer definitions is the most appropriate. The first definition, in its brevity, would be appropriate for a listing of precision measuring instruments and perhaps for a general desk dictionary. (A general desk dictionary does not include many of the specialized terms and meanings that technicians often need.) The second definition, which gives more detailed information, might be used in an introduction to a paper or an oral presentation describing the outside micrometer or in a paper or lecture describing the instruments a draftsperson should be familiar with. The extended definition would be appropriate for a textbook on machine shop tools, for a technical handbook or dictionary, or for a manufacturer to enclose with a micrometer.

You need to know when to define a term, to what extent to define it, and how to define it.

See also Jargon, pages 7–8.

WHEN TO DEFINE A TERM

A writer or speaker should define a term that (1) is unfamiliar to the audience, (2) has multiple meanings, (3) is used in a special way in a presentation.

First, a term should be defined when the audience might not know its meaning but should. An audience might need such a definition simply because they are unfamiliar with it. A metallurgist, communicating with a general adult audience, would probably have to explain the use of *anneal* or *sherardize;* or an electronics technician, writing a repair memorandum for a customer's information, would have to explain the meaning of *zener diode* or *signal-to-noise ratio.*

Second, a term that has multiple meanings should be defined. A term may not be clear to an audience because it has taken on a meaning different from that which the audience associates with it. For instance, if the company nurse instructs the carpenter to put a new "2 by 4" and "4 by 8" on the cuts on his leg each morning, the carpenter may leave in disbelief—and certainly in misunderstanding. To the nurse, of course, "2 by 4" and "4 by 8" are common terms for *gauze squares* in those inch dimensions used in dressing wounds. But to the carpenter "2 by 4" and "4 by 8" mean *boards* in those inch dimensions. If there is any possibility that the intended meaning of a term may be misunderstood, define it.

Finally, occasionally a writer or speaker gives a term or concept a special meaning within a presentation. The writer or speaker should then certainly let the reader know exactly how the term is being used.

EXTENT OF DEFINITION

The extent to which a term should be defined, thus the length of a definition, depends on the writer's or speaker's purpose and the knowledge level of the audience.

Sometimes merely a word or a phrase is sufficient explanation: "The optimum (most favorable) cutting speed of cast iron is 100 feet per minute." Notice the various ways in which the definitions are given in the following examples. "Consider, for instance, lexicographers—those who write dictionaries." "The city acquired the property by eminent domain, that is, the legal right of a government to take private property for public use."

At other times a definition may require a sentence or an entire paragraph. Occasionally a definition requires several paragraphs for a clear explanation, as when explaining an unfamiliar idea or item that is the central focus of a presentation.

Further, the extent to which a term should be defined depends on the complexity of the term. In a presentation for the general public, a definition of Ohm's law, for instance, undoubtedly would require more details than a definition of a Phillips screwdriver, because few readers or listeners would be familiar with the principles and terms of a specialized field like electronics and thus would have difficulty understanding the unfamiliar concept of Ohm's law. Most people, on the other hand, are familiar with a screwdriver; thus a definition of a Phillips screwdriver would be concerned only with how the Phillips is different from other screwdrivers. In addition, an abstract term like *Ohm's law* is usually more difficult to explain than a concrete item like *Phillips screwdriver*. The general knowledge and interest of the audience are certainly important in determining just how far to go in giving a definition. Most important of all, however, is the *purpose* for which the definition is given. In defining a term you must keep clearly in mind your purpose and a way to accomplish it. It may be that a definition is merely parenthetical. Or it may be that a definition is of major significance, as when an audience's understanding of a key idea hinges on the comprehension of one term or concept. And occasionally, though not often, an entire presentation is devoted to an extended definition.

HOW TO DEFINE A TERM

Once you decide that a term needs defining and decide whether it should be a brief or an extended definition, you can then follow these suggested procedures to prepare an adequate definition.

Sentence Definition

A well-established, three-step method for giving a sentence definition includes stating:

1. The term (species)
2. The class (genus)
3. The distinguishing characteristics (differentiae)

The term is simply the word to be defined. The class is the group or category of similar items in which the term can be placed. For instance, a *chair* is a "piece of furniture"; a *stethoscope* is a "medical listening instrument." The distinguishing characteristics are the essential qualities that set the term apart from all other terms of the same class; the distinguishing characteristics make the definition accurate and complete. A *chair* (term) is a "piece of furniture" (class). But there are pieces of furniture that are not chairs; thus the chair as a piece of furniture must be distinguished from all other pieces of furniture. The characteristic "that is used for one person to sit in" differentiates the chair from other items in the class. The sentence definition would be: "A chair is a piece of furniture that is used for one person to sit in."

Study the following examples.

Term	Class	Distinguishing Characteristics
Program	Set of organized instructions	To direct the performance of a computer
Rivet	Permanent metal fastener	Shaped like a cylinder and has a head on one end; when placed in position, the opposite head is formed by impact
Sprinkler system	Integrated system of underground and overhead piping	Designed in accordance with fire protection engineering standards

Thus, *program* (term) is "set of organized instructions" (class) "prepared to direct the performance of a computer" (distinguishing characteristics).

A *rivet* (term) is "a permanent metal fastener" (class) "that is shaped like a cylinder and has a head on one end. When placed in position, the opposite head is formed by impact" (distinguishing characteristics).

A *sprinkler system* (term) is "an integrated system of underground and overhead piping" (class) "designed in accordance with fire protection engineering standards" (distinguishing characteristics).

As these examples show, a sentence definition covers only one meaning of a word. Further, a sentence definition may actually be longer than just one sentence, as in the definition above of *rivet*. Two or more sentences may be needed in order to include all the essential distinguishing characteristics or for effective sentence structure.

When determining a class, be as precise and specific as possible. Placing a screwdriver in the class of "small hand tools" is much more specific than placing it in a class such as "objects, instruments, or pieces of hardware." The more specific the class is, the simpler it is to give the distinguishing characteristics, that is, the qualities that separate this term from all other terms in the same class. For instance, if, in defining *trowel*, the class is given simply as "a device," many distinguishing characteristics will have to be given to set a trowel apart from innumerable other devices (staple guns, rockets, tractors, phonographs, keys, pencil sharpeners, washing machines, etc.). If the class for *trowel* is given as "a hand-held, flat-bladed implement," then the distinguishing characteristics might be narrowed down to "having an offset handle and used to smooth plaster and mortar."

To avoid confusing peripheral information with the essential distinguishing characteristics, it is important to have an understanding of the *essence* of the term being defined. Essential to the nature of a brick, for instance, is that it is made out of baked clay. The color, methods of firing, size, shape, cost, and so on, would be peripheral information. Essential to the nature, the essence, of a refrigerator is that it preserves food by keeping it at a constant, cold temperature. Information that this large home appliance may be self-defrosting or that it may come in combination with a freezer would have no place, ordinarily, in a sentence definition.

Inadequate Sentence Definitions   The sentence definition, if it is to be adequate, must give the term, state the class as specifically as possible, and give characteristics that are really distinguishing. Such sentence definitions as "Scissors are things that cut" or "Slicing is something you ought not do in golf" or "Sterilization is the process of sterilizing" or "A stadium is where games are played" are inadequate if not completely useless. These definitions give little if any insight into what the term means.

The definition "Scissors are things that cut" equates scissors with razors, saws, drills, cookie cutters, plows, knives, sharp tongues, and everything else that cuts in any way. The definition is not specific in class ("things"), and the characteristic ("that cut") can hardly be called distinguishing. A more adequate definition might be "Scissors are a two-bladed cutting implement held in one hand. The pivoted blades are pressed against opposing edges to perform the cutting operation."

"Slicing is something you ought not do in golf" gives *no* indication of what slicing is. The so-called definition is completely negative. The class ("something") is about as nonspecific as it can be. Furthermore, there are no distinguishing characteristics ("you ought not do in golf" is meaningless—a golfer ought not slow down the players coming up behind, ought not bother other players' balls, ought not damage the green, ought not start at any hole except the first, ought not cheat on the score, etc.) A better definition is this: "Slicing is the stroke in golf that causes the ball to veer to the right."

"Sterilization is the process of sterilizing" as a definition is completely useless because the basic word *sterile* is still unexplained. If a person knows what sterilizing means, he or she has a pretty good idea of what sterilization means; however, if someone has knowledge of neither word, the stated "definition" is only confusing. This kind of definition, which uses a form of the term as either the class or the distinguishing characteristic, is called a circular definition because it sends the reader in circles—the reader never reaches the point of learning what the word means. Sterilization might more satisfactorily be defined as the following: "Sterilization is the hygienic process of getting rid of living microorganisms."

"A stadium is where games are played" is inadequate as a sentence definition because no class is given and the distinguishing characteristic is not specific. The "is where" or "is when" construction does not denote a class. Furthermore, only certain types of games—sports events—are typically associated with a stadium. An adequate sentence definition is this: "A stadium is a large, usually unroofed building where sports events are held."

Extended Definition

The extended definition gives information beyond stating the essence, or primary characteristic, of a term. The extended definition is concerned with giving enough information so the audience can gain a thorough understanding of the term. This definition in depth may contain such information as synonyms; origin of the term or item; data concerning its discovery and development; analysis of its parts; physical description; necessary conditions, materials, equipment; description of how it functions; explanation of its uses; instructions for operating or using it; examples and illustrations; comparisons and contrasts; different styles, sizes, and methods; and data concerning its manufacture and sale. The central focus in an extended definition is on stating what something is by giving a full, detailed explanation of it.

The extended definition is closely related to other forms of explanation, particularly instructions and process description (see Chapter 1) and description of a mechanism (see Chapter 2), and often includes them.

Following is an example of a student-written extended definition (including the Plan Sheet that was filled in before the paper was written). Marginal notes have been added to help in analyzing the paper.

Analysis of Situation Requiring Definition

What is the term to be defined?
airbrush

For whom is the definition intended?
classmates in Commercial Design and Advertising

How will the definition be used?
for their knowledge and understanding

In what format will the definition be given?
a written explanation with headings

Sentence Definition

Term:
airbrush

Class:
hand-held, precision paint sprayer

Distinguishing characteristics:
for applying color and shading where detail and control are essential.
Smooth, delicate tones and subtle blending are possible with an airbrush.

As Applicable

Synonyms:
omit

Origin of the term or item:
omit

Information concerning its discovery and development:
omit

Analysis of its parts:

Handle	*Head assembly*
Air hose connection	*Head*
Paint and air control	*Spray regulator*
Paint jar or cup	*Tip*

Physical description:
omit

Necessary conditions, materials, equipment:
Air supply (a compressor or carbon dioxide) needed. A wide range of inks, dyes, water soluble paints, ceramic underglazes, and acrylics can be used.

Description of how it functions:
omit

Explanation of its uses:
Coloring and shading drawings, prints, photographs; highlighting films; glazing ceramics, customizing vans, painting model planes, painting miniatures, spraying T-shirts; producing original artwork where extreme control is needed

Instructions for operating or using it:
omit

Examples and illustrations:
omit

Comparisons and contrasts:
omit

Different styles, sizes, methods:
Single action — one action (pushing down the paint and air control) releases a combination of air and paint
Double action — separate actions control the flow of air and the flow of paint
External mix — mixture of the paint and air occurs outside the head assembly
Internal mix — mixture of the paint and air occurs inside the head assembly; this provides thorough atomization of the paint and eliminates overspray

Data concerning its manufacture and sale:
Airbrushes that are double action and that are internal mix are the most expensive.

Other:
omit

Types of Subject Matter of Visuals to Be Included
drawing of an airbrush showing its parts

Sources of Information
class lecture in CDA, textbook in CDA, merchandise catalog, personal use of an airbrush

DEFINITION OF AN AIRBRUSH

A painting tool indispensable to the commercial artist, the photographer, and even the do-it-yourselfer is an airbrush (see Figure 1). An airbrush is a hand-held, precision paint sprayer for applying color and shading where detail and control are essential. An airbrush can be further defined by examining its uses, parts, and types.

Term to be defined
Reference to visual
Sentence definition
Kinds of additional information to be given

Uses

The airbrush of today has been refined so that almost anyone can use it effectively for a variety of jobs. The airbrush is used in coloring and shading drawings, prints, and photographs, and in supplying background and accentuating highlights in films. The airbrush is widely used in retouching photographs and for producing original artwork where extreme control or realism is needed. The airbrush is used for such jobs as glazing ceramics, customizing vans, painting model planes, painting miniatures, and painting designs on T-shirts.

Characteristics of airbrush work are smooth, delicate tones and subtle blending. Wherever these are needed, the airbrush is the appropriate tool.

Uses
Variety of jobs

Parts

The two main parts of an airbrush are the handle and the head assembly. See Figure 1. The handle, or barrel, is the housing for the internal parts. To the handle are attached the air hose connection, the paint and air control, the paint jar or cup, and the head

Parts
Two major parts
First major part, handle, discussed

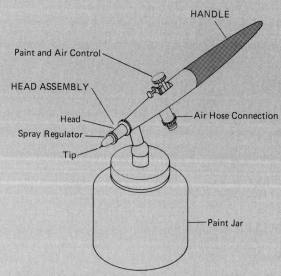

Figure 1. An airbrush.

assembly. The air hose connection is fitted with a coupling to connect the air supply (either a compressor or carbon dioxide) to the handle. The paint and air control regulates the amount of air and paint that are mixed to produce the desired effect. The paint jar or cup, made usually of either glass or metal, holds the paint to be sprayed in the airbrush operation. A wide range of inks, dyes, water soluble paints, ceramic underglazes, and acrylics can be used.

The head assembly consists of the head, spray regulator, and tip. The spray regulator can be adjusted and various tips can be interchanged to achieve the desired control, precision, and fine detailing.

Second major part, head assembly, discussed

Types

Types

Airbrushes can be classified as single action or double action and as external mix or internal mix. Single action means that when the paint and air control is pushed down, it releases a combination of air and paint. A needle adjuster on the back of the handle controls the amount of color and the width of the spray. In a single-action airbrush the user cannot change from a fine line to a broad spray pattern without stopping spraying and then rotating the needle adjuster. The double-action airbrushes are usually more expensive and are more versatile than the single-action types. In the double-action types, a variable spray is produced by the index finger pushing down on the paint and air control to regulate the air while at the same time pulling back on the control to release the desired amount of color. The most important feature of a double-action airbrush is that the width of the spray can be varied without stopping the spraying operation.

Classified by action and by mix
Single-action type discussed

Double-action type discussed

Airbrushes are either external mix or internal mix. On external mix airbrushes, mixture of the paint and air occurs outside the head assembly. External mix airbrushes are less complicated and less expensive than the internal mix airbrushes. In internal mix airbrushes, mixture of the paint and air occurs inside the head assembly, providing thorough atomization of the paint. This atomization eliminates overspray and provides for a smoother and more uniform coverage.

Mix
External mix type discussed

Internal mix type discussed

The choice of single action or double action and of internal or external mix depends on the user's experience and needs. For the beginning airbrush student, the inexpensive single action, external mix airbrush may be sufficient. However, whenever very fine detailing is required, the double action, internal mix airbrush is needed. The double-action, internal mix types are the ones that artists, illustrators, photograph retouchers, and automotive customizers use.

Choice of types

INTENDED AUDIENCE AND PURPOSE

Whether the definition involves one sentence, a paragraph, or several paragraphs, the writer or speaker must be aware of the audience to whom the communication is directed and the purpose of the communication.

Definitions in General Reference Works

Professional writers are keenly aware of who will be reading their material and why. Consider, for instance, lexicographers—those who write dictionaries. Lexicographers know that people of all ages and with varying backgrounds turn to the dictionary to discover or ascertain the meanings that most people attach to words. Lexicographers are aware that dictionary definitions must be concise, accurate, and understandable to the general reader. The following definition of *measles*, for instance, from a standard desk dictionary is adequate for its purpose.

> **mea·sles** /'mē-zelz/ *n pl but sing or pl in constr* [ME *meseles,* pl. of *mesel* measles, spot characteristic of measles; akin to **MD** *masel* spot characteristic of measles] (14c) **1a**: an acute contagious viral disease marked by an eruption of distinct red circular spots **b**: any of various eruptive diseases (as German measles) **2** [ME *mesel* infested with tapeworms, lit., leprous, fr. **OF**, fr. **ML** *misellus* leper, fr. L, wretch, fr. *misellus,* dim. of *miser* miserable]: infestation with or disease caused by larval tapeworms in the muscles and tissues°

Definitions in Specialized Reference Works

A specialized dictionary or encyclopedia, however, is not designed to give a concise definition for the general reader. The specialized reference book aims its information at a well-defined, select audience. The following entry, "Measles," from the *McGraw-Hill Encyclopedia of Science and Technology,* illustrates such a definition. Note the number of cross references suggested for the reader to see.

> **Measles**
>
> An acute, highly infectious viral disease, with cough, fever, and maculopapular rash. It is of worldwide endemicity. *See* ANIMAL VIRUS.
>
> The infective particle is an RNA virus about 100–150 nm in diameter, measured by ultrafiltration, but the active core is only 65 nm as measured by inactivation after electron irradiation. Negative staining in the electron microscope shows the virus to have the helical structure of a paramyxovirus with the helix being 18 nm in diameter. Measles virus will infect monkeys easily and chick embryos with difficulty; in tissue cultures the virus may produce giant multinucleated cells and nuclear acidophilic inclusion bodies. The virus has not been shown to have the receptor-destroying enzyme associated with other paramyxoviruses. Measles, canine distemper, and bovine rinderpest viruses are antigenically related. *See* EMBRYONATED EGG CULTURE; MYXOVIRUS; PARAMYXOVIRUS; TISSUE CULTURE; VIRAL INCLUSION BODIES.
>
> The virus enters the body via the respiratory system, multiplies there, and circulates in the blood. Prodromal cough, sneezing, conjunctivitis, photophobia,

---

° By permission. From *Webster's Ninth New Collegiate Dictionary* © 1983, by Merriam-Webster, Inc., publisher of the Merriam-Webster dictionaries.

and fever occur, with Koplik's spots in the mouth. A rash appears after 14 days' incubation and persists 5–10 days. Serious complications may occur in 1 of every 15 persons; these are mostly respiratory (bronchitis or pneumonia), but neurological complications are also found. Encephalomyelitis occurs, but it is rare. Permanent disabilities may ensue for a significant number of persons. Laboratory diagnosis (seldom needed since 95% of cases have the pathognomonic Koplik's spots) is by virus isolation in tissue culture from acute-phase blood or nasopharyngeal secretions, or by specific neutralizing, hemagglutination-inhibiting, or complement-fixing antibody responses.

In unvaccinated populations, immunizing infections occur in early childhood during epidemics which recur after 2–3 years' accumulation of susceptible children. Transmission is by coughing or sneezing. Measles is spread chiefly by children during the catarrhal prodromal period; it is infectious from the onset of symptoms until a few days after the rash has appeared. By the age of 20 over 80% of persons have had measles. Second attacks occur but are very rare. Treatment is symptomatic.

At one time, prevention was limited to use of gamma globulin, which protects for about 4 weeks, and can modify or prevent the disease. Prevention is advisable in infants 4–12 months of age or in sick children. However, if the disease has been prevented by administration of gamma globulin, the child develops no immunity, whereas the illness modified by gamma globulin may confer lasting immunity. *See* IMMUNOGLOBULIN.

Killed virus vaccine should not be used, as certain vaccinees become sensitized and develop local reactions when revaccinated with live attenuated virus, or a severe illness upon contracting natural measles.

Live attenuated virus vaccine can effectively prevent measles; vaccine-induced antibodies persist for years. Prior to the introduction of the vaccine, over 500,000 cases of measles occurred annually in the United States. Following mass immunization in 1966–1967, the number of cases decreased to 22,000 in 1968. Failure to immunize children from certain segments of the population resulted in 75,000 cases in 1971; however, with renewed emphasis on immunization, the number of cases declined to 32,000 in 1972, and by 1974 was again down to 22,000. In many areas of the United States, measles occurs in sporadic epidemics among nonimmunized children, in which the attack rate for immunized and nonimmunized children is about 2 and 34%, respectively. *See* BIOLOGICALS; HYPERSENSITIVITY; SKIN TEST.

Measles antibodies cross the placenta and protect the infant during the first 6 months of life. Vaccination with the live virus fails to take during this period, thus immunization is not recommended. Vaccination is not recommended also in persons with febrile illnesses, with allergies to eggs or other products used in production of the vaccine, and with congenital or acquired immune defects.

Measles virus appears to be responsible for subacute sclerosing panencephalitis (SSPE, Dawson's inclusion body encephalitis), a rare chronic degenerative brain disorder. The disease manifests itself in children and young adults by progressive mental deterioration, myoclonic jerks, and an abnormal EEG with periodic high-voltage complexes. The disease develops a number of years after the initial measles infection. A virus closely resembling measles virus, but not completely identical to it, has been isolated from brain tissue of patients. The virus is not localized only in brain tissues, since isolations have been made from lymph nodes. The presence of a latent intracellular measles virus in lymph nodes suggests a tolerant infection with defective cellular immunity.

Patients with SSPE have a functioning humoral attack system against cells which express surface measles virus antigens; cultured cells from the brain of a patient with SSPE have been lysed by the patient's own serum. Lysis occurs only when measles virus antigens are expressed on the cell surface, and is dependent on the presence of antibody to measles virus and complement. Lysis can also be induced by sera and cerebrospinal fluid from other SSPE patients, by sera from patients who have convalesced from normal measles virus infections, and by heterologous rabbit serum against measles virus. *See* VIRUS INFECTIONS, LATENT, PERSISTENT, SLOW.

A laboratory-produced, defective (temperature-sensitive) mutant of measles virus has caused hydrocephalus when inoculated intracranially into newborn hamsters; this finding shows the need for caution in use of experimentally induced virus variants.   [JOSEPH L. MELNICK]

Bibliography: P. Isacson and A. Stone, Allergic reactions associated with viral vaccines, *Progr. Med. Virol.*, 13:239–270, 1971; F. E. Payne, Measles virus associated with subacute sclerosing panencephalitis, *Progr. Med. Virol.*, vol. 22, 1976; J. J. Whitte, The epidemiology and control of measles, *Amer. J. Epidemiol.*, 100:77–78, 1974.°

DEFINITION AS PART OF A LONGER COMMUNICATION

Giving a definition may be the main purpose of a communication; perhaps more often, however, a definition is an integral part of a longer communication. Consider for instance, the paragraph definition of the term *report* on page 306 in Chapter 8, Reports. While the chapter, of course, is concerned with much more than definition, the definition of the focal term *report* serves as a framework for the entire chapter.

ORAL DEFINITION

In giving a definition orally, you would generally follow the procedures suggested for a sentence or extended definition. Suggestions for effective oral presentation of information are made in Chapter 10, Oral Communication.

VISUALS

Visuals are very helpful in definitions. For example, the definition of a micrometer on pages 86–87 is much clearer because of the included drawing of the micrometer; the drawing helps the reader to see what a micrometer looks like, to know its parts and where they are located, and to understand better how the micrometer is used. Similarly, the definition of an airbrush on pages 94–95 is made clearer with the drawing.

In defining concepts, visuals can be especially helpful. Consider, for instance, the following sentence definition of *horsepower*. Note how each of the three distinguishing characteristics (raising 33,000 pounds, distance of 1 foot, in 1 minute) is visually illustrated.

° Reprinted by permission from *McGraw-Hill Encyclopedia of Science and Technology*, Vol. 8 (New York: McGraw-Hill, 1982).

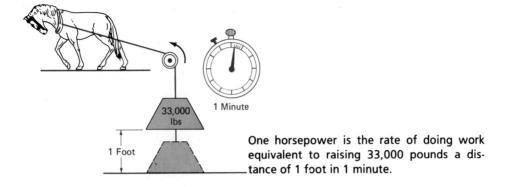

One horsepower is the rate of doing work equivalent to raising 33,000 pounds a distance of 1 foot in 1 minute.

Any time you can illustrate a term you are defining and thus help your audience understand it more easily and clearly, do so. For a discussion of types of visuals and guidance in preparing them, see Chapter 11, Visuals.

GENERAL PRINCIPLES IN GIVING A DEFINITION

1. *Knowing when to define a term is essential.* A term should be defined if: The audience does not know the meaning of a word but should, a word is used in a meaning different from that which the audience ordinarily associates with it, or a term is given a special meaning within a presentation.
2. *The extent to which a term should be defined depends on several factors.* It depends on the complexity of the term, the general knowledge and interest of the audience, and, primarily, the purpose for which the definition is given.
3. *A sentence definition has three parts: the term, the class, and the distinguishing characteristics.* The term is simply the word to be defined. The class is the group or category of similar items in which the term can be placed. The distinguishing characteristics are the essential qualities that set the term apart from other terms in the same class.
4. *An extended definition gives information beyond stating the essence, or the primary characteristic, of a term.* The extended definition includes such information as origin, development, analysis of parts, physical description, function, and so on.
5. *The crucial factor in giving a definition is understanding the essence of the term being defined.* The writer or speaker must understand the nature of the object or concept to define it accurately.

PROCEDURE FOR GIVING AN EXTENDED DEFINITION

An extended definition, whether it is one paragraph or several, or whether it is an independent presentation or part of a longer whole, usually has two distinct parts: identification of the term and additional information. A formal closing is unnecessary, although frequently the presentation ends with a comment or summarizing statement.

 I. The identification of the term is usually brief.
   A. State the term to be defined.
   B. Give a brief definition.
   C. Indicate the reason for giving a more detailed definition.
   D. State the kinds of additional information to be given.
 II. The additional information forms the longest part of the presentation.
   A. Select additional information (as applicable): synonyms; origin of the term or item; information concerning its discovery and development; analysis of its parts; necessary conditions, materials, equipment; description of how it functions; explanation of its uses; instructions for operating or using it; examples and illustrations; comparisons and contrasts; different styles, sizes, methods; and data concerning its manufacture and sale.
   B. Organize the selected additional information.
   C. Give the additional information, including whatever details are needed to give the audience an adequate understanding of the term.
   D. Use connecting words and phrases so that each sentence flows smoothly into the next and so that all the sentences in a paragraph hang together as a unit.
   E. Include visuals if their use will enhance understanding of the term defined.
 III. Generally there is no formal closing, although a comment or summarizing statement is often included.

APPLICATION 1   GIVING DEFINITIONS

By giving the distinguishing characteristics, complete the following to make general sentence definitions.

1. An orange is a citrus fruit. . .

2. A speedometer is a gauge. . .

3. A hammer is a hand tool. . .

4. Measles is a disease. . .

5. Smelting is the melting of metals. . .

6. Electricity is a form of energy. . .

7. Milk is a liquid food. . .

8. A molar is a tooth. . .

9. An anesthetic is a drug. . .

10. Arraignment is the first step in the formal trial process.   . .

APPLICATION 2 GIVING DEFINITIONS

Analyze the following definitions, noting their degree of accuracy and usefulness. Make whatever revisions are needed for adequate general sentence definitions.

1. A compass is for drawing circles.

2. A kerf is where you have sawed.

3. A T square, helpful in drawing lines, is a device used by draftspersons.

4. Immunity means to be <u>immune</u> to disease.

5. A crime is a violation of the law.

6. An anesthetic is a drug.

7. A board foot is a piece of material 1 inch thick, 12 inches long, and 12 inches wide.

8. Sterilization is the process of sterilizing.

9. A pictorial drawing is a drawing that is drawn from a drawing that was first drawn flat.

10. Airplanes without engines are called gliders.

APPLICATION 3 GIVING DEFINITIONS

Write a sentence definition of five of the following terms.

1. Architects' scale	21. Sawhorse
2. Diode	22. Depreciation
3. Solenoid valve	23. Terminal
4. Database	24. Thermometer
5. Coupling	25. Osmosis
6. Helix	26. Serum
7. Brazing	27. Coagulation
8. Leader	28. Antibiotic
9. Calipers	29. Conflagration
10. Dial indicator	30. Nutrition
11. Dowel	31. Enzyme
12. Flashing	32. Canister mask
13. Feedback	33. Lineup
14. Inductance	34. Disinfectant
15. Thermostat	35. Arrest
16. Bias	36. Metabolism
17. Traction	37. Anesthesia
18. Herbicide	38. Tort
19. Hydraulic lift	39. Tourniquet
20. Dividers	40. Gland

APPLICATION 4 GIVING DEFINITIONS

Name your major field. Then make a list of ten words from that field that you should be thoroughly familiar with. Write an adequate sentence definition of each of the words.

APPLICATION 5 GIVING DEFINITIONS

As an exercise in definition study, choose from your major field a term that can be found in each reference work specified below and note how it is treated in each of them. In giving the requested information, include the title of each reference work consulted. You may prefer photocopying a lengthy definition.

1. State the term.
2. Give the meaning of the term as stated in a standard desk dictionary.
3. Give the meaning as stated in a technical handbook or dictionary.
4. Give the meaning as stated in the *McGraw-Hill Encyclopedia of Science and Technology* and its yearbooks or a similar encyclopedia pertinent to your field. (Find the term in the index and then turn to the pages referred to.)

APPLICATION 6 GIVING DEFINITIONS

Read the following article, "Medical Laboratory Workers," from the *Occupational Outlook Handbook,* 1982–83 edition.

1. Write a sentence definition of a (a) medical technologist, (b) medical laboratory technician, and (c) medical laboratory assistant. Use your own wording; do not merely copy phrases from the article.
2. Write a paragraph definition of a medical laboratory worker. Use your own wording; do not merely copy phrases and sentences from the article.

Medical Laboratory Workers

Laboratory tests play an important part in the detection, diagnosis, and treatment of many diseases. Medical laboratory workers, often called clinical laboratory workers, include three levels of personnel: Medical technologists, technicians, and assistants. They perform laboratory tests on specimens taken from patients by other health professionals, such as physicians. They perform these tests under the general direction of pathologists (physicians who diagnose the causes and nature of disease) and other physicians, or doctoral scientists who specialize in clinical chemistry, microbiology, or the other biological sciences. Medical laboratory workers analyze blood, tissues, and fluids in the human body by using precision instruments such as microscopes and automatic analyzers.

Medical technologists, who usually have 4 years of postsecondary school training, perform complicated chemical, biological, hematological, microscopic, and bacteriological tests. These may include chemical tests to determine, for example, the blood cholesterol level, or microscopic examination of the blood to detect the presence of diseases such as leukemia. Technologists microscopically examine other body fluids; make cultures of body fluid or tissue samples to determine the presence of bacteria parasites, or other microorganisms; and analyze the samples for chemical content or reaction. They also may type and cross-match blood samples for transfusions.

Technologists in small laboratories perform many types of tests, while those in large laboratories usually specialize. Among the areas in which they can specialize are biochemistry (the chemical analysis of body fluids), blood bank technology (the laboratory work of a blood bank), cytotechnology (the study of human body cells), hematology (the study of blood cells), histology (the study of human and animal tissue), and microbiology (the study of bacteria and other microorganisms).

Most medical technologists conduct tests related to the examination and treatment of patients. Others do research, develop laboratory techniques, teach, or perform administrative duties.

Medical laboratory technicians, who generally have 2 years of postsecondary school training, perform tests and laboratory procedures that require a high level of skill but not the in-depth knowledge of highly trained technologists. Like technologists, they may work in several areas or specialize in one field.

Medical laboratory assistants, who generally have a year of formal training, assist medical technologists and technicians in routine tests and related work that can be learned in a relatively short time. In large laboratories, they may specialize in one area of work. For example, they may identify different types of blood cells on slides. In addition to performing less complex tests, assistants may store and label plasma; clean and sterilize laboratory equipment, glassware, and instruments; prepare solutions following standard laboratory formulas and procedures; keep records of tests; and identify specimens.

APPLICATION 7   GIVING DEFINITIONS

Choose a term in your major field for an exercise in writing extended definitions that serve different purposes.

  a. Make a Plan Sheet like the one on pages 105–106, and fill it in.
  b. Write preliminary drafts.
  c. Revise.
  d. Write the final drafts.

Write a paper to:

1. Define the term for a fifth grade class that noticed it in their *Weekly Reader.*
2. Define the term for your English teacher, who wants to understand the term well enough to judge the accuracy and completeness of students' sentence definitions of the term.
3. Define the term as if you were having an examination in your technical field and you were asked to write a paragraph definition of it.

APPLICATION 8   GIVING DEFINITIONS

Orally give the definitions you prepared for Application 7 above. Ask your classmates to evaluate your speech by making an Evaluation of Oral Presentations sheet like the one on page 459 and filling it in.

APPLICATION 9 GIVING DEFINITIONS

Write an extended definition (200–300 words) of a term or concept pertaining to your technical field.

  a. Make a Plan Sheet like the one on pages 105–106, and fill it in.
  b. Write a preliminary draft.
  c. Revise.
  d. Write the final draft.

EXAMPLES

heat treating, tolerance, orthographic projection, laminating, square foot cost estimating, inert-gas welding, magnetism, radio, amplifier, integrated circuit, blueprint, metabolism, hematology, anemia, library, farm recreation, modeling, proteins, pH meter, radiograph, holography

APPLICATION 10 GIVING DEFINITIONS

Give an oral extended definition of a term in Application 9 above. Ask your classmates to evaluate your speech by making an Evaluation of Oral Presentations sheet like the one on page 459 and filling it in.

PLAN SHEET
FOR GIVING AN EXTENDED DEFINITION

Analysis of Situation Requiring Definition

What is the term to be defined?

For whom is the definition intended?

How will the definition be used?

In what format will the definition be given?

Sentence Definition

Term:

Class:

Distinguishing characteristics:

As Applicable

Synonyms:

Origin of the term or item:

Information concerning its discovery and development:

Analysis of its parts:

Physical description:

Necessary conditions, materials, equipment:

Description of how it functions:

Explanation of its uses:

Instructions for operating or using it:

Examples and illustrations:

Comparisons and contrasts:

Different styles, sizes, methods:

Data concerning its manufacture and sale:

Other:

Types and Subject Matter of Visuals to Be Included

Sources of Information

CHAPTER 4

Analysis Through Classification and Partition: Putting Things in Order

OBJECTIVES   108
INTRODUCTION   108
DEFINITION OF CLASSIFICATION   109
ANALYSIS THROUGH CLASSIFICATION   109
    Items That Can Be Classified   111
    Characteristics of a Classification System   112
      Coordination   112
      Mutual Exclusiveness   112
      Nonoverlapping   112
      Completeness   113
    Bases for Classification   113
      Usefulness   113
      Purpose   113
    Order of Data Presentation   113
    Forms of Data Presentation   114
      Outline   114
      Verbal Explanation   115
      Visuals   121
      Combination   123
GENERAL PRINCIPLES IN GIVING AN ANALYSIS THROUGH CLASSIFICATION   125
PROCEDURE FOR GIVING AN ANALYSIS THROUGH CLASSIFICATION   125
APPLICATIONS   126
ANALYSIS THROUGH PARTITION   134
    Definition of Partition   134
    Characteristics of a Partition System   134
    Basis of Partition   144
    Order of Data Presentation   144
    Forms of Data Presentation   144
CONTRAST OF CLASSIFICATION AND PARTITION   145
GENERAL PRINCIPLES IN GIVING AN ANALYSIS THROUGH PARTITION   146
PROCEDURE FOR GIVING AN ANALYSIS THROUGH PARTITION   146
APPLICATIONS   147

OBJECTIVES

Upon completing this chapter, the student should be able to:

- Define classification
- State the basis of division into categories in a classification system
- Select for a classification system a basis of division that is useful and purposeful
- Set up a classification system whose categories are coordinate, mutually exclusive, nonoverlapping, and complete
- Present classification data in outlines, in verbal explanations, and in visuals
- Select an appropriate order for presentation of classification categories
- Give an analysis through classification
- Define partition
- State the basis of division in a partition system
- Select for a partition system a basis of division that is useful and purposeful
- Set up a partition system whose divisions are coordinate, mutually exclusive, nonoverlapping, and complete
- Present partition data in outlines, in verbal explanations, and in visuals
- Select an appropriate order for presentation of partition divisions
- Give an analysis through partition
- Give an analysis using both classification and partition
- Describe situations in which an employee would need to know how to give an analysis using classification or partition, or both

INTRODUCTION

Human beings try to make sense out of the world in which they live. They try to see how certain things are related to other things. They try to impose some kind of order on their environment. More specifically, the technical student tries to see how a skill in building trades or in engineering technology or health occupations is related to getting and keeping a good job and being able to support a family. Or perhaps the student is trying to devise a practical plan for getting enough money for college expenses.

Persons on the job try to make sense out of the industrial and business world in which they work. There are situations in which they need to put things in some kind of organized relationship. The situation may be a request from a superior for a list of parts that must be replaced in a machine. The situation may be a weekly report of the number of units produced in a particular department. The situation may be a memorandum to the division head on the problems encountered in a new manufacturing process. The situation may be a report to the doctor on the temperature changes of a patient.

All of these kinds of situations, whatever their nature and wherever they are experienced, call for analysis—looking at a subject closely so that it can be put into a useful, meaningful order. Establishing an order, or relationship, is the basic step in solving a problem, whether the problem is how to reduce air pollution, how to operate a blood bank more efficiently, or how to improve a variety of cotton.

The purpose of this chapter is to help an individual give order to information — to give order by classifying it into related groups or by partitioning it into its components.

DEFINITION OF CLASSIFICATION

Classification is a basic technique in organization, and thus in writing. It starts with the recognition that different items have similar characteristics and develops with the sorting of these items into related groups. In a letter of application, for instance, details about places of former employment, dates of employment, or names of supervisors all have similar characteristics in that they all have to do with work experience. In organizing the letter of application, items would be sorted into one group on the basis of work experience, into another group on the basis of education, and so on. Classification, then, is the grouping together, according to a specified basis, of items having similar characteristics.

For example, in preparing to explain how batteries generate power, batteries might first be broadly classified as primary and secondary types. The explanation might then be given as follows:

> Batteries are broadly classified as primary and secondary types. Primary batteries generate power by irreversible chemical reaction and require replacement of parts that are consumed during discharge (or, more commonly, the batteries are thrown away when discharged). Secondary batteries, on the other hand, involve reversible chemical reactions in which their reacting material will be restored to its original "charged" state by applying a reverse, or charging, current. In general, primary batteries provide higher energy density, specific energy, and specific power than do secondary batteries.

Classification is obviously the method used to organize the material in the paragraph.

ANALYSIS THROUGH CLASSIFICATION

Suppose that a newspaper reporter is visiting a campus to gather data from students for an informative article about the student body. During interviews with students she has jotted down some of their comments. The notes include the following:

> A lot of the students live at home and commute to college.
> Some students have real hangups, particularly when it comes to sex.
> There are more freshmen than sophomores.
> I'm a technical student in data processing. When I finish the two-year program here, I'll be able to get a good job in my specialized field.
> I'm not taking a full number of courses this semester because I work eight hours a day to support my family.
> Many students have a real money problem. Like my roommate. He's completely paying his own way.
> I chose this college because it's close to home.
> They say you gotta go to college to get anywhere. OK, here I am.
> Somehow I didn't do too well on my ACT score, so I can't take all the courses I want to take.
> Some students are lucky enough to have their own apartment.

The biggest thing I've had to cope with is finding enough time to study and to play—all in the same weekend.

This college is really growing. This year we have the biggest freshman class in the history of the college.

The newspaper reporter must put these items in order. Assist her in organizing the information into related groups so that she can write an article her readers can follow.

In sorting this information into meaningful categories, group together the items that are related in a specific way. In the sorting process, start with the first statement:

A lot of the students live at home and commute to college.

This has to do with student residence. Find other statements that have to do with where students live while attending college.

Some students are lucky enough to have their own apartment.

This is the one directly related item.

Further analysis of the reporter's notes shows that there are additional groupings of information. Several statements deal with problems of students, several with reasons for attending college, several with the status of the student according to the number of hours completed, and several with the status of the student according to the number of hours currently enrolled in, as shown below:

Residence of Students While Attending College:

A lot of the students live at home and commute to college.
Some students are lucky enough to have their own apartment.

Problems of Students:

Some students have real hangups, particularly when it comes to sex.
Many students have a real money problem. Like my roommate. He's completely paying his own way.
The biggest thing I've had to cope with is finding enough time to study and to play—all in the same weekend.

Reasons for Students' Attending College:

I'm a technical student in data processing. When I finish the two-year program here, I'll be able to get a good job in my specialized field.
I chose this college because it's close to home.
They say you gotta go to college to get anywhere. OK, here I am.

Status of Student According to Number of Hours Completed:

There are more freshmen than sophomores.
This college is really growing. This year we have the biggest freshman class in the history of the college.

Status of Student According to Number of Hours Currently Enrolled in:

I'm not taking a full number of courses this semester because I work eight hours a day to support my family.
Somehow I didn't do too well on my ACT score, so I can't take all the courses I want to take.

The process of organizing the newspaper reporter's notes into groups, or categories, is analysis through classification. This process of organization was not carried out haphazardly but logically. In the first place, it is clear that the subject being classified is the reporter's notes, not students or courses or factors affecting student achievement. Moreover, to help the newspaper reporter sort the notes into useful categories, you had to be knowledgeable about the various aspects of a student body.

Five different bases were used for sorting the information:

Residence of students while attending college
Problems of students
Reasons for students' attending college
Status of student according to number of hours completed
Status of student according to number of hours currently enrolled in

These bases are clear and logical. If, for instance, the last two bases had been considered as one basis, such as "Status of student," there would be confusion. The term *status of student* has two different meanings here, depending on whether reference is made to the student as a freshman, sophomore, or upper classman ("Status of student according to number of hours completed") or whether reference is made to the student as a full-time student, part-time student, probationary student, or whatever ("Status of student according to number of hours currently enrolled in").

In the example, the categories are coordinate; that is, they are all on the same level, with no confusion of major categories with subcategories. If, however, along with the five major categories there had been included "Students who have money problems," the major categories, or classes, would not be coordinate. They would no longer be on the same level because "Students who have money problems" is a subcategory, or subclass, of "Problems of students."

Each of the categories is mutually exclusive; that is, each of the five categories is composed of a clearly defined group that would still exist without the other categories. "Residence of students while attending college," for example, would be a valid category even if some or all of the other categories were unnecessary.

In the example, the categories do not overlap; an item can be placed in only one category. For instance, the item "I chose this college because it's close to home" can be placed in only one of the groups: "Reasons for students' attending college." The speaker of the "close to home" comment may live at home and commute to school, but the comment itself could not possibly be grouped under "Residence of students while attending college" or any of the groups except "Reasons for students' attending college."

Finally, in the classification of the reporter's notes into five categories, each item of information fits into a category; no item is left out.

Items That Can Be Classified

Any group of items *plural* in meaning may be classified. These items may be objects, concepts, or processes; the items may be classified into a variety of categories. Objects such as men's beach coats might be classified by size, style, fabric, color, and so on. Concepts or ideas, such as the causes of the Industrial

Revolution in England, may make use of the principles of classification; the causes, for instance, may be classified according to significance, origin, historical influences, and so forth. Processes frequently employ classification — methods of desalinizing water may be classified according to cost, required time, materials needed, and so on, or particular steps may be classified as one phase of a desalinization method.

Characteristics of a Classification System

The categories in a classification system, as illustrated in organizing the information about a student body, must be *coordinate, mutually exclusive, nonoverlaping*, and *complete*. A classification system must have all of these qualities if it is to be adequate.

Coordination The categories in a classification system must be coordinate, or parallel. The groups, or categories, that items are sorted into must be on the same level in grammatical form and content. For instance, classification of the refrigerators in Mr. Lee's appliance store, according to source of power, into the following categories would be inadequate: natural gas, butane gas, and electric. The error is in the grammatical form of the word *electric,* which here is an adjective; *natural gas* and *butane gas* here are nouns. These categories, however, would be adequate: natural gas, butane gas, and electricity.

Categories must be coordinate in content as well as in grammatical form. The classification of automobile tires as whitewall, blackwall, red stripe, and tubeless is not coordinate because *tubeless* does not refer to the same content, or substance, that *whitewall, blackwall,* and *red stripe* do. These three terms have to do with decorative coloring; *tubeless* does not.

See also Parallelism in Sentences, pages 501–502, and Coordinating Conjunctions, pages 492–493.

Mutual Exclusiveness The categories in a classification system must be mutually exclusive, that is, each category must be independent of the other categories in existence. A category must be composed of a clearly defined group that would still be valid even if any or all of the other categories were unnecessary or nonexistent. For instance, if a shipment of coats were being classified according to the amount of reprocessed wool each coat contained and the categories were designated "Coats in Group A," "Coats with more reprocessed wool than Group A," and "Coats with less reprocessed wool than Group A," the categories would be inadequate. Two of the categories depend upon "Group A" for their meaning, or existence. A more logical classification could be "Coats containing 40 to 60 percent reprocessed wool," "Coats containing more than 60 percent reprocessed wool," and "Coats containing less than 40 percent reprocessed wool." In this grouping, each category is independent, that is, mutually exclusive, of the other categories.

Nonoverlapping The categories in a classification system must be nonoverlapping. It should be possible to place an item into only *one* category. If an item, however, can reasonably be placed under more than one category, the categories should be renamed and perhaps narrowed. For instance, if the fabrics in a sewing shop were being classified as natural fibers, synthetics, or blends, how would a fabric that is part cotton and part wool be classified? The fabric is of natural fibers but it is also a blend. Thus the given categories are inadequate. More satisfactory would be categories such as these: fabrics of a pure natural fiber, fabrics of blended natural fibers, synthetic fabrics, and fabrics that have a blend of synthetic and natural fibers.

Completeness   The categories in a classification system must be complete. Every item to be classified must have a category into which it logically fits, with no item left out. For instance, the categories in a classification of American-made automobiles according to the number of cylinders would not be sufficient unless the categories were these: four cylinders, six cylinders, and eight cylinders. The omission of any one of the categories would make the classification system incomplete, for a number of automobiles then would have no category into which they would logically fit.

Bases for Classification

Usefulness   The bases on which classifications are made should be useful. Classification of trees according to bark texture or according to leaf structure would be of significance to one interested in botany. It would take a stretch of the imagination, however, to understand the usefulness of classifying trees according to the number of leaves produced and shed over a 50-year span.

Purpose   The usefulness of a classification system depends on its purpose. And according to this purpose, the writer or speaker, as classifier, will emphasize certain aspects of the subject. Suppose, for instance, that a salesperson in a garden center has three pieces of mail regarding lawn mowers that must be answered. There is a letter from a woman who wishes to purchase a lawn mower that she can start easily. She wants suggestions for such models. There is a letter from a meticulous gardener who gives certain motor, cutting blade, and attachment specifications. He would like suggestions for several models that most nearly meet his requirements. There is a memorandum from the store manager requesting a list of the best-selling lawn mowers. Obviously, each of the three persons is seeking quite different information for different purposes—but the information concerns the same group of lawn mowers, the lawn mowers that the garden center stocks. In order to meet each request, the salesperson must classify the lawn mowers according to at least three different bases: ease in starting (for the woman); motor, cutting blade, and attachment specifications (for the gardener); and popularity of sale (for the store manager).

Order of Data Presentation

The categories, or classes, in a classification system should be presented in the order that will best help to accomplish your purpose. In classifying steps in a process, probably a *chronological*, or *time*, *order* would be used. In classifying items such as breeds of cattle in the United States, it might be wise to use an *order of familiarity*, that is, to start with the best known or most familiar and go to the least known or least familiar. In classifying the qualities a nurse should have, the qualities might be listed in *order of importance.* At times, *order according to complexity,* that is, movement from the simple to the more difficult, might be best to use, as in classifying swimming strokes or in classifying casserole recipes. A *spatial order,* movement from one physical point to another (from top to bottom, inside to outside, left to right, etc.), may be the most practical arrangement, as in classifying the parts of an automobile engine or the furnishings in a house. If the categories are such that order is not important, an *alphabetical* or a *random presentation* may be used. The important thing to remember is this: use whatever order is appropriate for whatever you want to accomplish in your presentation.

Forms of Data Presentation

Classification may be the major organizing principle in a presentation or in a section of a presentation, or it may be the major organizing principle within a paragraph or in a part of a paragraph. In whichever way classification is used, there are several forms in which the data may be presented: in outlines, in verbal explanations, and in visuals.

Outline Outlines are particularly helpful for grouping items in an orderly, systematic arrangement. The outline may be purely for personal use in preparing information for presentation in a verbal explanation or in a visual. Or the outline may be the form selected for presentation of the information. The outline that others are to read should be clear, consistent, and logical. If the outline is to meet these requirements, certain accepted standards should be followed:

1. Choose either the traditional number-letter outline form or the decimal outline form. (Both outline forms are illustrated below.)
2. Make the outline either a topic outline (illustrated below) or a sentence outline (illustrated on pages 125–126). In a topic outline each heading is a word, phrase, or clause. In a sentence outline each heading is a complete sentence. *Do not combine both topics and sentences in an outline.* (Such a combination usually confuses the reader.)
3. Headings should be given an appropriate number or letter. In the traditional number-letter outline form, first-level, or major, headings are designated with Roman numerals (I, II, III, etc.); second-level headings have uppercase letters (A, B, C, etc.); third-level headings have Arabic numerals (1, 2, 3, etc.); and fourth-level headings have lowercase letters (a, b, c, etc.). In the decimal outline form a system of decimal points is used to designate the various levels of headings.
4. Headings should be indented to indicate the degree of subclassification.
5. Headings on a given level should keep the same grammatical structure. Nouns should be used with nouns, gerund phrases with gerund phrases, etc.
6. There should be at least two headings on each level. Each level is composed of divisions of the preceding heading. (If, however, a heading calls for a *list,* it is possible to have only one item in the list.)

TOPIC OUTLINES: CLASSIFICATION OF SAWS
Two Bases: Uses and Types

Traditional Number-Letter
Outline Form

I. Basic uses
   A. Crosscutting
   B. Ripping
II. Types
   A. Hand-operated saws
      1. Handsaw
      2. Backsaw
      3. Keyhole saw
      4. Coping saw
      5. Hacksaw
   B. Power saws
      1. Portable power saws
         a. Circular saw
         b. Saber saw
         c. Reciprocating saw
      2. Stationary power saws
         a. Radial arm saw
         b. Table saw
         c. Motorized miter saw

Decimal Outline Form

1. Basic uses
   1.1 Crosscutting
   1.2 Ripping
2. Types
   2.1 Hand-operated saws
      2.1.1. Handsaw
      2.1.2. Backsaw
      2.1.3. Keyhole saw
      2.1.4. Coping saw
      2.1.5. Hacksaw
   2.2 Power saws
      2.2.1. Portable power saws
         2.2.1.1. Circular saw
         2.2.1.2. Saber saw
         2.2.1.3. Reciprocating saw
      2.2.2. Stationary power saws
         2.2.2.1. Radial arm saw
         2.2.2.2. Table saw
         2.2.2.3. Motorized miter saw

A well-organized classification presentation can be easily outlined. For example, the student-written classification of Southern lawn grasses on pages 119–121 might be outlined as follows:

SOUTHERN LAWN GRASSES
I. Warm-season lawn grasses
   A. Bermuda grasses
   B. Zoysia grasses
   C. St. Augustine grass
   D. Centipede grass
II. Cool-season lawn grasses
   A. Bluegrasses
   B. Tall fescue grasses

Verbal Explanation Although the outline, as a presentation form of a classification system, may be used alone, it is more frequently accompanied by verbal explanation; sometimes it is used with a visual. Most often, however, a classification system is presented as a verbal explanation, as in the following classification system of Southern lawn grasses. Note that in the explanation, lawn grasses are divided into two broad categories. These two broad categories are divided into subcategories, which are still further divided. Note also the interrelationship of classification and definition. The Plan Sheet that the student filled in before writing the report is included, and marginal notes have been added to indicate the development of the classification system.

PLAN SHEET FOR GIVING AN ANALYSIS THROUGH CLASSIFICATION

Analysis of Situation Requiring Classification

What is the subject to be classified?
southern lawn grasses

For whom is the classification intended?
new home owners

How will the classification be used?
to decide on a lawn grass

In what format will the classification be given?
written report

Setting up the Classification System

Definition or identification of subject:
selection of lawn grass a major decision before preparing lawn

Basis (or bases) for classification:
planting season, varieties of grasses, characteristics, planting method, care

Significance or purpose of basis (or bases):
An attractive lawn increases the value of a house.

Categories of the subject, with identification of each category:
Warm-season lawn grasses — planted in spring (March – July)
  Bermuda
      Types — Tifgreen, Tiflawn, Tifway, Tidwarf, common
      *Characteristics — bright emerald to dark green; fine leaf texture; does
          not grow well in shade*
      *Planting method — common seeded (1 lb. per 1000 sq. ft.); other
          sprigs or plugs (10 - 12 inches apart, 10 - 12 inches between rows)*
      *Care — 2 - 3 lbs. nitrogen per 1000 sq. ft. in April – May, June – July,
          Aug. - Sept.; mowed regularly*
  Zoysia
      Types — Emerald, Japonica, Matrella, Meyer
      *Characteristics — grows well in shade; tolerant of low temperatures,
          frost*
      *Planting method — sprigs, or plugs; plants and rows 6 - 8 inches apart;
          plugs (2 in.) and rows, 6 inches apart*
      *Care — 2 lbs. nitrogen per 1000 sq. ft., April - May, June - July,
          Aug. - Sept.*

117

St. Augustine
　One type
　Characteristics — dark green, coarse textured; susceptible to insects, disease, weather. Grows in shade; tolerates salt spray.
　Planting method — no seed; springs or plugs, plants and rows 10 -12 inches apart
　Care — 2 lbs. nitrogen per 1000 sq. ft. April -May and June - July; 1 lb. Aug.-Sept.
Centipede
　One type
　Characteristics — light green; coarse leaf texture; needs warm temperatures; light shade. Tolerates insects and disease. Prefers slightly acid soil.
　Planting method — seed (1/4 to 1/2 lb. per 1000 sq. ft.; very expensive); sprigs, plants and rows 10 -12 inches apart
　Care — light fertilization, 1 lb. nitrogen per 1000 sq. ft. in April -May, June - July, Aug. - Sept.; little mowing
Cool-season lawn grasses — planted in fall (Sept. - Nov.)
　Bluegrasses
　　Types — Fylking, Kenblue, Park, Windsor·
　　Characteristics — medium green; fine leaf; reasonable growth in shade
　　Planting method — seed, 2- 3 lbs. per 1000 sq. ft; solid sodding
　　Care — 1 -2 lbs. nitrogen per 1000 sq. ft. in March; 2 -3 lbs. in Sept.
　Tall Fescue
　　Types — Kentucky 31, Kenwell
　　Characteristics — dark green; coarse texture; fair shade growth
　　Planting method — seed, 5 - 10 lbs. per 1000 sq. ft.
　　Care — 2 lbs. nitrogen per 1000 sq. ft. in March, 2 -3 lbs. in Sept.

Presentation of the System

Most logical order for presenting the categories:
random listing

Types and subject matter of visuals to be included:
omit

Sources of Information

The Pasture Book, World Book Encyclopedia, Cooperative Extension Service, county agent

CLASSIFICATION OF SOUTHERN LAWN GRASSES BY PLANTING SEASON

An attractive lawn increases the value of a house. But an attractive lawn does not develop by accident; it is carefully planned, prepared, and maintained. A major decision in the planning stage for a southern lawn is the selection of the right grass. Basically the selection of grass depends upon the season when planting will be done.

Subject identified
Importance of subject

There are two major planting seasons for southern lawn grasses: warm-season planting and cool-season planting. Warm-season grasses should be planted in the spring (March–July). Cool-season grasses should be planted in the fall (September–November).

Subject divided into two broad categories on basis of planting season

WARM-SEASON LAWN GRASSES

The possible selections of warm-season grasses include Bermuda grasses, Zoysia, St. Augustine, and Centipede. The choice of one of these grasses can be made after considering the available varieties, characteristics, planting method, and basic care.

First broad category divided on basis of selection of grasses

Each selection described by varieties, characteristics, planting method, care

Bermuda Grasses

The Bermuda grasses recommended for home lawn use in the South include Tifgreen, Tiflawn, Tifway, Tidwarf, and common Bermuda. The color of these grasses varies from a bright emerald green to a dark green. Generally Bermuda grasses have a fine leaf texture. Bermuda grasses do not grow well in the shade. Common Bermuda grasses can be seeded; all other varieties require vegetative planting, either by sprigs or plugs. Common Bermuda should be seeded 1 pound per 1000 square feet; other varieties should have sprigs or plugs placed 10–12 inches apart in rows 10–12 inches apart.

First selection described by varieties

by characteristics

by planting method

All varieties must be highly fertilized. Recommended fertilizer includes 2–3 pounds of nitrogen per 1000 square feet in April–May, June–July, and August–September. All varieties must be mowed regularly to look the very best.

by care

Zoysia Grasses

Zoysia grasses used for southern lawns are Emerald, Japonica, Matrella, and Meyer.

Second selection described by varieties

These grasses grow well in the shade and are tolerant of low temperatures, including even frost. They should be planted by sprigs or plugs. Sprigs should be placed 6–8 inches apart in rows 6–8 inches apart; 2–inch plugs should be placed 6 inches apart in rows 6 inches apart. Zoysia should be fertilized with 2 pounds of nitrogen per 1000 square feet in April–May, June–July, and August–September.

by characteristics
by planting method

by care

St. Augustine Grass

St. Augustine, a single variety, is dark green and coarse textured. It does not tolerate insects, diseases, or weather well. St. Augustine does grow in shade and is not affected by salt spray, making it a good choice for lawns in coastal areas.

Third selection described by characteristics

No St. Augustine seeds are available; the grass is established vegetatively by sprigs or plugs. Sprigs or plugs should be planted 10–12 inches apart in rows 10–12 inches apart. Nitrogen amounts to maintain healthy green grass are 2 pounds of nitrogen per 1000 square feet in April–May and June–July with 1 pound per 1000 square feet in August–September.

by planting method

by care

Centipede Grass

Centipede grass, a single variety, is light green with a coarse leaf texture. It prefers warm temperatures and will grow in lightly shaded areas. Not susceptible to insects or disease, centipede grows in most soils, although it prefers a slightly acid soil. This grass can be started from seed or sprigs, but the seeds are quite expensive. Each 1000 square feet requires the spreading of ¼ to ½ pound of seed; sprigs should be set 10–12 inches apart in rows 10–12 inches apart. Centipede requires little fertilization, 1 pound of nitrogen per 1000 square feet in April–May, June–July, and August–September. It also needs little mowing.

Fourth selection described by characteristics

by care

COOL-SEASON LAWN GRASSES

Two common cool-season lawn grasses are bluegrasses and tall fescue.

Second broad category divided on basis of selection of grasses

Bluegrasses

Improved varieties of Kentucky bluegrass are Fylking, Kenblue, Park, and Windsor. Bluegrass has a medium green color and a fine leaf texture. It will grow reasonably well in shaded areas. It can be grown from seed or by solid sodding. Seeding rate is 2–3 pounds per 1000 square feet. Nitrogen amounts recommended are 1–2 pounds per 1000 square feet in March and 2–3 pounds per 1000 in September.

First selection described by varieties

by characteristics
by care

Tall Fescue Grasses

Varieties of tall fescue include Kentucky 31 and Kenwell.

Second selection described by varieties

Tall fescue has a very coarse texture and is a dark green. This grass will grow fairly well in the shade. Tall fescue is established by seeding 5–10 pounds of seed per 1000 square feet. Nitrogen should be applied in March, 2 pounds per 1000 square feet, and in September, 2–3 pounds per 1000 square feet.

by characteristics

by care

The person planning a lawn in the South has a wide choice of grasses among the warm-season and the cool-season lawn grasses. For information concerning lawn care and maintenance, an excellent source is the Cooperative Extension Service personnel in each county.   Closing comment

Visuals In addition to presenting data in a classification system as an outline or as a verbal explanation, visuals may be used. Such visuals as charts, diagrams, maps, photographs, drawings, graphs, and tables frequently make a mass of information understandable. Study the bar chart on page 122. Determine the data being organized; then determine the bases on which the data are organized. Why are the data presented in this form?

Of course, the information in the chart might have been presented in outline form, as follows:

    I. Fiscal years 1974–1979
        A. Claims paid by U.S.: $55.3 million
        B. Amount collected from defaulters: $3.3 million
   II. Fiscal year 1980
        A. Claims paid by U.S.: $55.2 million
        B. Amount collected from defaulters: $4.2 million
  III. Fiscal year 1981
        A. Claims paid by U.S.: $71.7 million
        B. Amount collected from defaulters: $7.6 million
  IV. Fiscal year 1982 (15 mos.)
        A. Claims paid by U.S.: $105.5 million
        B. Amount collected from defaulters: $10 million
    V. Fiscal year 1983
        A. Claims paid by U.S.: $148.8 million
        B. Amount collected from defaulters: $8.7 million
  VI. Fiscal year 1984 (estimated)
        A. Claims paid by U.S.: $110 million
        B. Amount collected from defaulters: $15 million

Or the information might have been presented as a verbal explanation, as follows:

Since the inception of the Guaranteed Student Loan Program, amounts in claims paid by the U.S. Government have far exceeded amounts collected from defaulters. In the fiscal years 1974–1979 claims paid by the United States amounted to $55.3 million; the amount collected from defaulters totaled $3.3 million. In fiscal year 1980 the United States paid $55.2 million in claims and collected $4.2 million from defaulters. In fiscal year 1981 the United States paid $71.7 million in claims and collected $7.6 from defaulters. In fiscal year 1982 the United States paid out $105.5 million and collected $10 million. In fiscal year 1983 the United States paid claims of $148.8 million and collected $8.7 million from defaulters. The estimated amounts for fiscal year 1984 are that $110 million will be paid in claims and $15 million will be collected from defaulters.

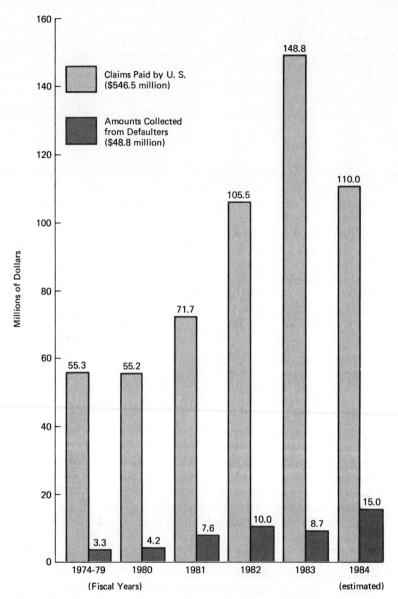

Defaulted Student Loan Claims. (Claims paid and collected by U.S. Office of Education from inception of Guaranteed Student Loan Program in 1974 through fiscal 1984.)

Of the three forms—chart, outline, and verbal explanation—used for presenting the data concerning money paid out through the student loan program, the chart is the clearest. The reader can easily comprehend the data because for each of the two items charted, money paid in claims and money collected from defaulters, there are light and dark bars representing each year, and because there is a monetary scale on the left. The comparison is visibly evident in the chart. In the outline, the comparison is somewhat evident, but the reader has to do more work to grasp the relationships that are so plainly reflected in the chart. In the verbal explanation, the comparison of monetary amounts and dates becomes wearisome after the first few figures. The reader has to do a great deal of work to comprehend the information and understand the relationships that the writer is trying to show.

Thus the data regarding student loan claims were presented in a chart because this form clearly communicates the information.

For further discussion of visuals, see Chapter 11, Visuals.

Combination Frequently a combination of outline, visual, and verbal explanation is used in presenting data. The following example from a report on the characteristics of burglary incidents, prepared by the U.S. Department of Justice, combines visual and verbal explanation.

Table 16 [below], which shows temporal characteristics of reported burglary incidents, indicates that residential burglaries were more likely to occur during the day

Table 16 Temporal Characteristics of Burglaries, by Type of Structure Burglarized (in percents)

| Temporal Characteristics | Type of Structure | | |
	Residential	Nonresidential	Total[a]
Time:			
Day	56	15	45
	(2,274)	(232)	(2,506)
Night	44	85	55
	(1,812)	(1,313)	(3,125)
Total	100	100	100
	(4,086)	(1,545)	(5,631)
Day:			
Weekday	70	58	67
	(3,681)	(1,348)	(5,029)
Weekend	30	42	33
	(1,568)	(959)	(2,527)
Total	100	100	100
	(5,249)	(2,307)	(7,556)
Season:			
Winter	33	32	32
	(1,858)	(765)	(2,623)
Spring–Autumn	33	33	33
	(1,883)	(818)	(2,701)
Summer	34	35	35
	(1,945)	(866)	(2,811)
Total	100	100	100
	(5,686)	(2,449)	(8,135)

[a] Total number of cases for each variable may vary because of missing cases.

(56 percent) and on weekdays (70 percent). Forty-four percent of all reported residential burglaries occurred during nighttime hours. Table 16 reveals few seasonal differences in the reporting of residential and nonresidential burglaries. Thirty-three percent and 32 percent of all residential and nonresidential burglaries, respectively, occurred during the winter months.

The material below classifying flow chart symbols also effectively combines verbal explanation and visuals.

Classification of Data Processing Flowchart Symbols

Data processing flowchart symbols may be classified into three groups, depending on their use: basic symbols, symbols related to programming, and symbols related to systems.

Basic Symbols

Any processing function

General input/output function; information for processing; recording processed information

Connector to show exit to or entry from another part of flowchart

Offpage connector; entry to or exit from a page

Flow; direction of processing

Symbols Related to Programming

Decision; determines which of several alternative directions is followed

Preparation; instruction modification to change a program

Predefined process; program steps or operations specified in a subroutine or other flowcharts

Terminal interrupt; a terminal point—start, stop, interrupt, delay, halt

Symbols Related to Systems

Punched card

A collection of related punched-card records

Magnetic tape

A collection of punched cards

Any paper document

Punched tape

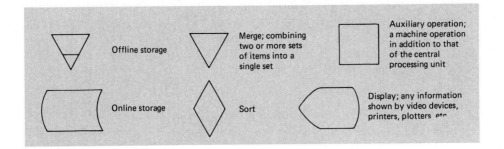

GENERAL PRINCIPLES IN GIVING AN ANALYSIS THROUGH CLASSIFICATION

1. *Classification is a basic approach in analysis.* It places related items into categories, or groups.
2. *Only a plural subject or a subject whose meaning is plural can be classified.* If a subject is singular, it can be partitioned but not classified.
3. *The categories in classification must be coordinate, or parallel.* All categories on the same level must be of the same rank in grammatical form and in content.
4. *The categories must be mutually exclusive.* Each category should be composed of a clearly defined group that would still exist without the other categories on the same level.
5. *The categories must not overlap.* An item can have a place in only one category.
6. *The categories must be complete.* There should be a category for every item, with no item left out.
7. *The data in a classification analysis may be presented in outlines, in verbal explanation, and in visuals.* The form or combination of forms that presents the data most clearly should be used.
8. *The basis on which classification is made should be clear, useful, and purposeful.*
9. *The order of presentation of categories depends on their purpose.* Among the possible orders are time, familiarity, importance, complexity, space, and alphabetical and random listing.

PROCEDURE FOR GIVING AN ANALYSIS THROUGH CLASSIFICATION

This kind of analysis is generally a part of a larger whole, as have been the other forms of communication discussed in the preceding chapters. Regardless of whether the classification analysis is a dependent or an independent communication, however, the structure of such an analysis is as follows:

I. The presentation of the subject and of the bases of division into categories is usually brief.
   A. State the subject that is to be divided into categories.
   B. Identify or define the subject.

    C. If applicable, list various bases by which the subject can be divided into categories.

    D. State explicitly the bases of the categories.

    E. Point out the reasons why the categories are significant and what purpose they serve.

  II. The listing and the discussion of the categories are the longest parts of the presentation.

    A. List the categories and, if any, the subcategories.

    B. Give sufficient explanation to clarify and differentiate among the given categories.

    C. Present the categories in whatever order best serves the purpose of the analysis.

    D. Divide the categories into subcategories wherever needed.

    E. Use outlines and visuals whenever they will help clarify the explanation.

  III. The closing (usually brief) depends on the purpose of the presentation.

    A. The closing may be the completion of the last point in the analysis.

    B. The closing may be a comment on the analysis or a summary of the main points.

APPLICATION 1 GIVING AN ANALYSIS THROUGH CLASSIFICATION

Some of the following classifications are satisfactory and some are not. Indicate the sentences containing unsatisfactory classifications. Rewrite them to make them satisfactory.

    1. The students on our campus can be classified either as blonds or as brunets.

    2. Automobiles serve two distinct functions: They are used either for pleasure or for business.

    3. Cattle may be classified as purebred, crossbred, or unbred.

    4. The courses a technical student takes at this college can be divided into technical courses, related courses, and general education courses.

    5. Structural material may be wood, brick, aluminum, steel, concrete blocks, or metal.

APPLICATION 2 GIVING AN ANALYSIS THROUGH CLASSIFICATION

Each of the following classification systems is lacking in *coordination, mutual exclusiveness, nonoverlapping,* and/or *completeness.* Point out the specific errors. Then make whatever changes are necessary for the outlines to be more adequate.

  I. Classification of Watches According to Shape

    A. Round

    B. Oblong

    C. Thin

    D. Oval

II. Classification of Phonograph Records According to Type of Music
   A. Classical
   B. Jazz
   C. Michael Jackson
   D. Western and country
   E. Instrumental
III. Classification of Mail According to Collection Time
   A. Day
      1. Weekdays
      2. Saturdays
      3. Holidays
   B. Hour
      1. A.M.
      2. Afternoons
IV. Classification of Television Shows
   A. Westerns
   B. Situation comedies
   C. Today Show
   D. NBC
V. Classification of College Students
   A. Academic classification
      1. Freshmen
      2. Sophomores
      3. Upperclassmen
   B. Residence
      1. Dormitory
      2. Local
      3. In state
      4. Out of state

APPLICATION 3 GIVING AN ANALYSIS THROUGH CLASSIFICATION

For each of the following groups of items, suggest at least three bases of classification.

EXAMPLE

Group of items: Books
Bases of classification: Subject matter, nationality of author, cost, date of writing, publisher, alphabetical listing by author

1. Metals
2. Office machines
3. Diseases
4. Buildings
5. Clothing

APPLICATION 4 GIVING AN ANALYSIS THROUGH CLASSIFICATION

For Application 3 above, choose one group of items and one basis of classification. For that basis of classification write an explanatory paragraph.

APPLICATION 5   GIVING AN ANALYSIS THROUGH CLASSIFICATION

Joe received the following injuries in an automobile accident: black eyes, broken nose, fractured ribs, crushed pelvis, broken thumb, twisted ankle, cuts on the forehead, teeth knocked out, dislocated knee, gash on the right leg, bruised shoulder, and tip of little finger cut off. Organize Joe's injuries into related groups. Use a formal outline.

APPLICATION 6   GIVING AN ANALYSIS THROUGH CLASSIFICATION

From the following list of words pick out at least four groups of related items and identify the relationship within the group. Use your dictionary to look up any unfamiliar words.

EXAMPLE

List of Words	*Word Group*	*Relationship*
Electrical pressure	Electrical pressure	Basic electric quantities
Magnets	Ohm	
Ohm	Ampere	
Ampere	Coulomb	
Copper wire		
Coulomb		

1. Gothic
2. Propeller
3. Airbrush
4. Dry cells
5. FORTRAN
6. Blood pressure
7. Horn
8. Nonphotographic pencil
9. Drawing board
10. Classifying
11. Drill press
12. Keyboard
13. Tractor
14. Dissecting microscope
15. Storing
16. Micrometer
17. COBOL
18. X-acto knife
19. Dial indicator
20. Plaintiff
21. Breathing
22. Ruling pen
23. Planer
24. Sorting
25. Text
26. Wing
27. Stirrup
28. Primary cells
29. Punched cards
30. RPG
31. Preserved specimen
32. Screen
33. Pulse
34. Arrest
35. Lathe
36. T square
37. Central processing unit
38. Slide
39. Magnetic tape
40. Updating
41. Dial caliper
42. Roman
43. Lead-acid storage cells
44. Reflexes
45. BASIC
46. Flexible disk
47. Printer
48. Witness
49. Strap
50. Shaper
51. Hay baler
52. Compass
53. Triangles
54. Seat
55. Italic
56. Vernier bevel protractor
57. PASCAL
58. Program
59. Drawing set
60. Combine

APPLICATION 7   GIVING AN ANALYSIS THROUGH CLASSIFICATION

Select one of the following subjects. Divide the subject into classes in accordance with at least four different bases; subdivide wherever necessary. Use outline form to show the relationship of divisions.

EXAMPLE

Automobiles

I. Body style
  A. Sedan
  B. Coupe
  C. Convertible
  D. Hard top
II. Body size
  A. Regular
  B. Intermediate
  C. Compact
  D. Subcompact
III. Kind of fuel
  A. Gasoline
  B. Diesel
  C. Gasohol
  D. Butane
  E. Propane
IV. Cost
  A. Inexpensive — under $10,000
  B. Average — $10,000 – $18,000
  C. Expensive — over $18,000

1. Computers
2. Farm machinery
3. Cattle
4. Hand tools
5. Drawing instruments
6. Scales
7. Precision measuring instruments
8. Building materials
9. Transistors
10. Muscles
11. Home air conditioners
12. Commercial aircraft
13. Typewriters
14. Clocks
15. Clothing
16. Food
17. Transportation
18. Tires
19. Trees
20. Meters
21. Furniture
22. Wrenches
23. Books
24. Radios
25. Paint
26. Flexible disks

APPLICATION 8   GIVING AN ANALYSIS THROUGH CLASSIFICATION

For the subject you chose in the preceding application (or another of the listed subjects), present the data in a written explanation.

  a. Make a Plan Sheet like the one on pages 132 – 133, and fill it in.
  b. Write a preliminary draft.
  c. Revise.
  d. Write the final draft.

APPLICATION 9 GIVING AN ANALYSIS
THROUGH CLASSIFICATION

Give an oral classification analysis of one of the topics in Application 7 above. Ask your classmates to evaluate your speech by making an Evaluation of Oral Presentations sheet like the one on page 459 and filling it in.

APPLICATION 10 GIVING AN ANALYSIS
THROUGH CLASSIFICATION

Modern automobiles can be bought with numerous options. List these options, and then group them into categories. Use outline form to show the relationship between divisions.

APPLICATION 11 GIVING AN ANALYSIS
THROUGH CLASSIFICATION

Present the data from Application 10 in a written explanation.

    a. Make a Plan Sheet like the one on pages 132–133, and fill it in.
    b. Write a preliminary draft.
    c. Revise
    d. Write the final draft.

APPLICATION 12 GIVING AN ANALYSIS
THROUGH CLASSIFICATION

Assume that an insurance company will give you an especially good rate if you will insure all your possessions with it. Prepare an *organized* list of your belongings so that the insurance company can suggest the amount of coverage you need.

APPLICATION 13 GIVING AN ANALYSIS
THROUGH CLASSIFICATION

From the statistics on the next page, select information and present it in another visual form, such as a pie chart (see pages 467–468) or bar chart (see pages 468–469).

APPLICATION 14 GIVING AN ANALYSIS
THROUGH CLASSIFICATION

Select a subject suitable for classification. Present the classification system in a visual.

Table 1 Carraway Community College
           Enrollment Summary 1983–1984

Session	Campuses			Total
Fall	*Sanders*	*Mayville*	*Rock Springs*	
Academic	2840	367	291	3498
Technical	1937	680	130	2747
Vocational	682	357	250	1289
Other	54	34	1196	1284
				8818
Spring				
Academic	2576	347	268	3191
Technical	1881	742	72	2695
Vocational	636	359	201	1196
Other	36	16	1147	1199
				8281
Summer				
Academic	1066	129	220	1415
Technical	538	156	58	752
Vocational	266	418	138	822
Other	27	66	58	151
				3140

PLAN SHEET
FOR GIVING AN ANALYSIS THROUGH CLASSIFICATION

Analysis of Situation Requiring Classification

What is the subject to be classified?

For whom is the classification intended?

How will the classification be used?

In what format will the classification be given?

Setting Up the Classification System

Definition or identification of subject:

Basis (or bases) for classification:

Significance or purpose of basis (or bases):

Categories of the subject, with identification of each category:

Presentation of the System

Most logical order for presenting the categories:

Types and subject matter of visuals to be included:

Sources of Information

ANALYSIS THROUGH PARTITION

Definition of Partition

Partition is analysis that divides a singular item into parts, steps, or aspects. Only *singular* subjects can be partitioned; plural subjects are classified. Partition breaks down into its components a concrete subject, such as a tree (parts: roots, trunk, branches, and leaves), or an abstract subject, such as how to build a herd of cattle (steps: select good stocker cows, select a good herd bull, breed the cows at the right time, keep the heifers, sell the bull calves, and sell the old cows), or such as inflation (aspects: causes, effects on consumers, etc.).

A partition system must have certain characteristics if it is to be adequate; a partition system may be presented in various forms; divisions may be made on various bases; and data may be presented in several orders. All these aspects of analysis through partition are similar to those of analysis through classification.

Characteristics of a Partition System

If a partition system is to be adequate, that is, if it is to fulfill its purpose, the divisions must have certain characteristics:

1. The divisions must be coordinate.
2. The divisions must be mutually exclusive.
3. The divisions must not overlap.
4. The divisions must be complete.

Consider the following partition of a concrete subject, a lamp socket, on the basis of its construction.

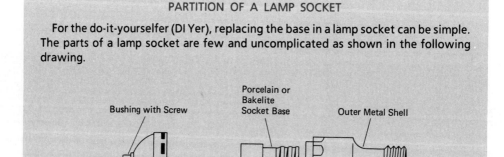

PARTITION OF A LAMP SOCKET

For the do-it-yourselfer (DI Yer), replacing the base in a lamp socket can be simple. The parts of a lamp socket are few and uncomplicated as shown in the following drawing.

Bushing with Screw

Porcelain or Bakelite Socket Base

Outer Metal Shell

Socket Cap

Fiber Insulating Shell

A lamp socket.

The lamp socket has an outer metal covering with an interlocking cap topped with a bushing and screw. Lodged inside in a fiber insulating shell is the socket base, usually made of porcelain or Bakelite. To replace the socket base, the Di Yer has only to disconnect the wires from the old base, remove that base, insert a new socket base, reconnect the wires, and pull the socket cap over the outer metal shell so that the lamp socket is one piece again.

The partition of the lamp socket is adequate. The divisions are coordinate: they are of equal rank in grammatical form and in content, as shown below:

LAMP SOCKET PARTITION

Outer parts } *First level of partition*
   Outer metal shell ⎫
   Socket cap   ⎬   *Second level of partition*
   Bushing with screw ⎭

Inner parts } *First level of partition*
   Fiber insulating shell ⎫
   Socket base   ⎬ *Second level of partition*

On each level, the divisions are mutually exclusive, that is, each division could exist without the other divisions. For instance, the outer metal shell could still exist even if there were no socket cap. The divisions do not overlap; a part has a place in only *one* division. The divisions are complete; every part of the lamp socket is accounted for and no part is left out.

Or, consider the claw hammer. It can be partitioned into two main parts: the handle and the head, as illustrated in the outline and the visual following.

  I. Handle
 II. Head
    A. Neck
    B. Poll
    C. Face
    D. Cheek
    E. Claw
    F. Adze eye

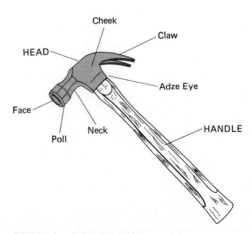

Figure 1. A claw hammer.

A carpenter would be concerned about the main parts and the subparts as they function in various ways when the hammer is in use.

The following student-written report is an analysis through partition of an abstract subject, a police department. The subject is given careful examination by separating it into its constituent parts so that, through individual consideration of each part, a better understanding of the whole can be achieved. The Plan Sheet that the student filled in before writing is included. The notes in the right-hand margin of the report have been added as an aid in studying the organization of the material.

BRENTSVILLE POLICE DEPARTMENT:
ORGANIZATION AND RESPONSIBILITIES

The city of Brentsville has an efficient, effective police department. This is possible largely because of the administrative organization. (See the accompanying organization chart.) The police department is administered by two persons: the Chief of Police and the Assistant Chief of Police. Various divisions and bureaus support one another as well as the police department as a whole by fulfilling specific responsibilities.

> Partition of police department on basis of administrative organization
>
> Two major administrators

All divisions within the department ultimately are responsible to the Chief of Police. However, only six divisions report directly to the Chief of Police, while four bureaus report directly to the Assistant Chief of Police.

DIVISIONS REPORTING TO THE CHIEF OF POLICE

> First major administrator

The following divisions report directly to the Chief of Police: Chaplain's Office, Internal Affairs, Intelligence Division, Administrative Assistant, Research and Development, and Legal Office. Their duties are varied.

> Divisions reporting directly to the Chief

Chaplain's Office

> First division explained

Personnel in the Chaplain's Office are in contact with all police department employees. They minister to individuals in any stress situation, either personal or professional.

Internal Affairs

> Second division explained

The Internal Affairs Division has as its major responsibility "policing" each member of the department. This division investigates any charges or questions from the public, other police officers, or independently developed sources about the activities or action(s) of any department member as to misconduct and criminality. This division enforces written policies, procedures, and rules to maintain discipline within the department.

Intelligence Division

> Third division explained

Finding and analyzing information is the task of the Intelligence Division. This information has to do with such matters as the activities of organized crime and radical groups. Usually this information is gathered from informants and by undercover personnel. Officers in this division are usually department veterans, experienced in investigation, with unquestionable integrity.

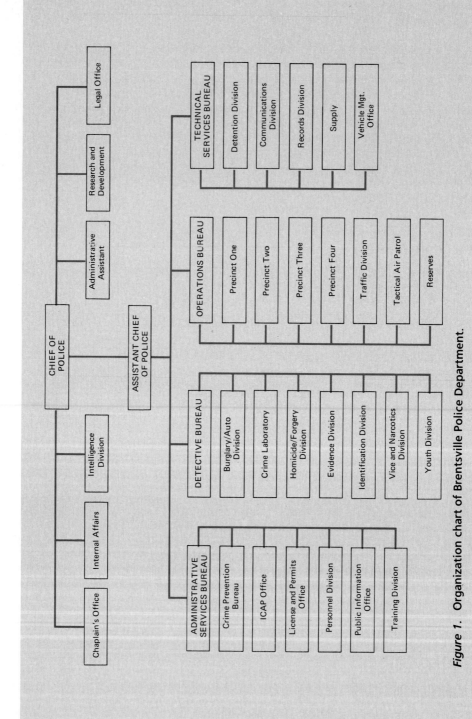

Figure 1. Organization chart of Brentsville Police Department.

Administrative Assistant

The Administrative Assistant is a go-between who listens to complaints, problems, concerns, and suggestions. The assistant screens all information, handles routine situations, and decides what information to pass on to the Chief of Police for handling.

Fourth division explained

Research and Development

The Research and Development group are planners for the police department. They anticipate future needs and prepare to meet those needs. For example, they would be aware of city growth and population shifts, determining when to increase or decrease the number of beats. Or they might determine that within 12 months the department will need to add six additional squad cars.

Fifth division explained

Legal Office

The Legal Office aids officers in the prosecution of criminal cases. This office serves in any capacity where legal assistance is needed; advises on policies, planning, internal hearings, and problems in criminal cases; and maintains liaison with the courts.

Sixth division explained

BUREAUS REPORTING TO THE ASSISTANT CHIEF

Reporting to the Assistant Chief of Police are four bureaus: the Administrative Services Bureau, the Detective Bureau, the Operations Bureau, and the Technical Services Bureau. Within each of these bureaus are numerous divisions to facilitate the responsibilities of each bureau.

Second major administrator

Bureaus reporting to the Assistant Chief

Administrative Services Bureau

The Administrative Services Bureau's tasks have long-term application; they are tasks performed for the benefit of the department as a whole.

Divisions within the bureau include the Crime Prevention Bureau, ICAP Office, License and Permits Office, Personnel Division, Public Information Office, and Training Division.

First bureau explained

Crime Prevention Bureau. The Crime Prevention Bureau controls, reduces, and prevents crime. Personnel concentrate on informing the public on ways to make crimes more difficult to carry out, such as improved security, better lighting, locks, and alarms.

ICAP Office. The Integrated Criminal Apprehension Program (ICAP) is concerned with crime analysis. Personnel collect reports, analyze the reports over a period of time, and determine needs.

For example, a study of accident reports might reveal a high-risk accident area during specific hours; additional patrol persons or traffic officers could then be assigned to the area during these hours.

License and Permits Office.   Any individual wishing to apply for licenses and permits for such activities as operating a dance hall, selling beer, or driving a taxi must make application through the License and Permits Office. Office personnel screen both the applicant and the location of the desired activity and review city ordinances to be sure carrying out the activity would not violate any ordinance.

Personnel Division.   Personnel Division employees oversee all tasks related to employees—recruitment, selection, assignment, transfer, promotion, termination, and labor relations.

Public Information Office.   The Public Information Office handles public relations and press relations; its major task is to keep the public informed on police activities through the various media— radio, television, newspapers, public lectures.

Training Division.   The Training Division meets the professional needs of police service. It provides, for example, in-class and on-the-job training, physical and mental training, theory and practice, recruit training, and in-service training.

Detective Bureau

Second bureau
explained

   The Detective Bureau is a collection of divisions that are directly involved in the daily operation of the department. These divisions include Burglary/Auto, Crime Laboratory, Homicide/Forgery, Evidence, Identification, Vice and Narcotics, and Youth.

Burglary/Auto Division.   Personnel in Burglary/Auto are skilled in investigating crimes of theft. A special division is set aside to handle such matters since theft is a very common crime.

Crime Laboratory.   Crime Laboratory personnel provide examination and classification of concrete evidence such as tire tracks, bloodstains, fingerprints, and fibers. Physical evidence has a major role in the prosecution of cases.

Homicide/Forgery Division.   This division's personnel are especially trained or experienced in investigating all crimes related to homicide and forgery. Often they must testify in follow-up court sessions.

Evidence Division.   Employees in the Evidence Division are responsible for the safekeeping of all evidence from a crime, accident, or other such occurrence. They must catalog the evidence and store it for easy access and make sure no one tampers with it.

Identification Division.   Identification Division personnel fingerprint and photograph suspects and prisoners. They must be skilled since they provide permanent records and investigate major crimes.

Vice and Narcotics Division.   The Vice and Narcotics Division enforces vice and drug laws. These laws have to do with such activities as illegal gambling, selling liquor illegally, obscene conduct, pornography, and sale of drugs.

Youth Division.   The Youth Division has the task of dealing with juveniles. The personnel must follow special legal and practical guidelines that pertain to minors. Frequently personnel become involved in such matters as child abuse, neglect, and runaways. The focus is on social welfare rather than on crime.

Operations Bureau

Third bureau explained

The Operations Bureau oversees activities carried out to directly assist the public. This bureau is the division of police work that the average person knows about. Its work includes such tasks as patrol, traffic, community relations, vice, and crime prevention. Precincts in strategic geographical locations throughout the city are "mini police departments" that oversee the carrying out of these tasks.

Three special divisions—Traffic Division, Tactical Air Patrol, and Reserves—also aid in implementing the tasks of the Operations Bureau.

Technical Services Bureau

Fourth bureau explained

Activities within the Technical Services Bureau directly support the other divisions within the police department. This bureau usually operates every hour, every day of the year. The divisions include Detention, Communications, Records, Supplies, and Vehicle Management.

Detention Division.   Detention personnel handle the confinement, usually temporary, of persons arrested and the needs of the confined persons.

Communications Division.   Communications employees are the link between the public and the police. They answer telephone calls from persons seeking help and they dispatch help.

Records Division. Records personnel collect, organize, and store data on wanted persons, on traffic accidents, on parking tickets, on arrests, and so forth. Using various report forms, records personnel keep reports on file on all types of information that would be useful to the department. Many records systems are on computer for quick, easy access. Record information is available 24 hours a day, every day.

Supply. Supply employees make sure that the department has everything necessary to function, everything from flashlight batteries, to parking ticket forms, to bullets. This division must keep an accurate inventory of supplies and make purchases as needed.

Vehicle Management Office. The Vehicle Management Office insures that all vehicles are maintained and "ready to roll."

Obviously the Brentsville Police Department is a complex organization. Its structure, however, allows it to function easily and effectively.   Closing comment

Basis of Partition

Partition, like classification, must be done on a useful, purposeful basis. A carpenter's partitioning, or dividing, the tasks in the construction of a proposed porch on the basis of needed materials would be useful and purposeful.

Order of Data Presentation

The order of data presentation in a partition system is determined by your purpose. As in classification, among the possible orders are time, familiarity, importance, complexity, space, and alphabetical and random listing. For example, the work of a general duty nurse could be partitioned, or divided, into what she does the first hour, second hour, and so on (time order), if the purpose of partition is to show how she spends each working hour. Or a light socket could be partitioned according to the outer and the inner parts (spatial order), if the purpose of the partition is to show the construction of the light socket.

Forms of Data Presentation

The forms of presentation of analyses through partition are the same as those for classification. Logical methods are outlines, verbal explanations, and visuals.

Look at the following floor plan of the nation's capitol (Figure 1). It partitions the building to show the design and layout and to show space utilization.

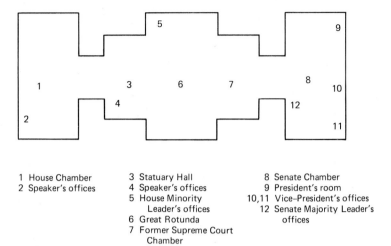

1 House Chamber
2 Speaker's offices

3 Statuary Hall
4 Speaker's offices
5 House Minority
   Leader's offices
6 Great Rotunda
7 Former Supreme Court
   Chamber

8 Senate Chamber
9 President's room
10,11 Vice-President's offices
12 Senate Majority Leader's
   offices

Figure 1. Floor plan of the U.S. Capitol.

The same information could be shown in outline form:

Floor Plan of the U.S. Capitol

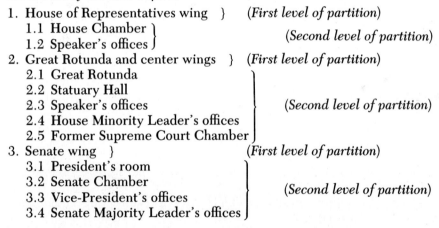

1. House of Representatives wing } *(First level of partition)*
   1.1 House Chamber
   1.2 Speaker's offices   *(Second level of partition)*
2. Great Rotunda and center wings } *(First level of partition)*
   2.1 Great Rotunda
   2.2 Statuary Hall
   2.3 Speaker's offices   *(Second level of partition)*
   2.4 House Minority Leader's offices
   2.5 Former Supreme Court Chamber
3. Senate wing } *(First level of partition)*
   3.1 President's room
   3.2 Senate Chamber
   3.3 Vice-President's offices   *(Second level of partition)*
   3.4 Senate Majority Leader's offices

Visuals are frequently used in verbal partition presentations, such as the organization chart in the preceding explanation of a police department. Other often used visuals include diagrams, flow charts, and drawings. (See Chapter 11 for a fuller discussion of visuals.)

CONTRAST OF CLASSIFICATION AND PARTITION

Both classification and partition are approaches to analyzing a subject, though for each the approach is from a different direction. Classification and partition differ in the number of the subject being analyzed, in the relationship of divisions, and in the overall result.

    Classification divides plural subjects into kinds or classes. The subject may be singular in form, but if the meaning is plural (such as mail, furniture, food) the subject is classifiable. Partition, on the other hand, divides a singular subject, or item, into its component parts.

In partition the parts do not necessarily have anything in common, other than being parts of the same item. For instance, the handle, shank, and blade of a screwdriver share no relationship beyond their being parts of the same item. In classification, however, all the items in a division have a significant characteristic in common. For example, in classifying typewriters as manual or electric, all manual typewriters use the typist as the source of energy, and all electric typewriters use electricity as the source of energy.

Classification and partition differ also in their end results. Since their purposes are different — the purpose of classification being to sort related items into groups and the purpose of partition being to divide an item into its parts — their outcomes are different. For instance, regardless of the category into which screwdrivers are classified (common, Phillips, spiral ratchet, powered, etc.), they are still screwdrivers. In the partition of a screwdriver, however, a part — whether the handle, blade, or shank — is still only a part of the whole.

GENERAL PRINCIPLES IN GIVING AN ANALYSIS THROUGH PARTITION

1. *Partition is a basic approach in analysis.* It divides a subject into parts, steps, or aspects so that through individual consideration of these, a better understanding of the whole can be achieved.
2. *Only a singular subject can be partitioned.* If a subject is plural it can be classified but not partitioned.
3. *The divisions in partition must be coordinate, or parallel.* All divisions on the same level must be of the same rank in grammatical form and in content.
4. *The divisions must be mutually exclusive.* Each division should be composed of a clearly defined group that would still exist without the other divisions on the same level.
5. *The divisions must not overlap.* A part can have a place in only *one* division.
6. *The divisions must be complete.* Every part must be accounted for, with no part left out.
7. *The data in a partition analysis may be presented in outlines, in verbal explanation, and in visuals.* The form or combination of forms that presents the data most clearly should be used.
8. *The basis on which partition is made should be clear, useful, and purposeful.*
9. *The order of presentation of divisions depends on their purpose.* Among the possible orders are time, familiarity, importance, complexity, space, and alphabetical and random listing.
10. *Classification and partition may be used together or separately.*

PROCEDURE FOR GIVING AN ANALYSIS THROUGH PARTITION

Analysis through partition is generally a part of a larger whole, as have been the other forms of communication discussed in the preceding chapters. Regardless of whether the partition analysis is a dependent or an independent communication, however, the structure of such an analysis is as follows:

I. The presentation of the subject and of the bases of partition is usually brief.
   A. State the subject that is to be partitioned.
   B. Identify or define the subject.
   C. If applicable, list various bases by which the subject can be partitioned.
   D. State explicitly the bases of the divisions.
   E. Point out the reasons why the divisions are significant and what purpose they serve.
II. The listing and discussion of the divisions are the longest parts of the presentation.
   A. List the divisions and, if any, the subdivisions.
   B. Give sufficient explanation to clarify and differentiate among the given divisions.
   C. Present the divisions in whatever order best serves the purpose of the analysis.
   D. Use outlines and visuals whenever they will help clarify the explanation.
III. The closing (usually brief) depends on the purpose of the presentation.
   A. The closing may be the completion of the last point in the analysis.
   B. The closing may be a comment on the analysis or a summary of the main points.

APPLICATION 1   GIVING AN ANALYSIS THROUGH PARTITION

Select one of the following for partition. First make a Plan Sheet like the one on pages 149–150, and fill it in; then give the partition in outline form.

1. Disk or magnetic tape
2. Resistor
3. House
4. A store (department, grocery, etc.)
5. Typewriter
6. Stapler
7. Clock
8. Telephone
9. Egg
10. A part of the body (ear, eye, heart, etc.)
11. Cash register terminal
12. Musical instrument (piano, trumpet, guitar, etc.)
13. Pocket calculator
14. Drafting table
15. Term of your own choosing from your major field

APPLICATION 2   GIVING AN ANALYSIS THROUGH PARTITION

For Application 1 above, give the partition as a verbal explanation.

APPLICATION 3   GIVING AN ANALYSIS THROUGH PARTITION

For Application 1 above, give the partition as a visual.

APPLICATION 4   GIVING AN ANALYSIS THROUGH PARTITION

Take the material you have prepared in Applications 1, 2, and 3 above and integrate them into one written presentation.

    a. Add or delete material, as needed, in the Plan Sheet filled out in Application 1 above.
    b. Write a preliminary draft.
    c. Revise.
    d. Write the final draft.

APPLICATION 5   GIVING AN ANALYSIS THROUGH PARTITION

Give an oral partition analysis of the topic from Application 4 above. Ask your classmates to evaluate your speech by making an Evaluation of Oral Presentations sheet like the one on page 459 and filling it in.

APPLICATION 6   GIVING AN ANALYSIS THROUGH PARTITION

Select a subject suitable for partition. Present the partition system in a visual.

APPLICATION 7   GIVING AN ANALYSIS THROUGH PARTITION

Select a business (store, industry, farm, etc.) that you are familiar with (or can become familiar with). Show how this organization functions by dividing it into departments or areas. Include an organization chart. Your presentation will be an explanation of a process; within this framework you will be relying heavily on analysis through classification and through partition.

    a. Make a Plan Sheet like the one on pages 149–150, and fill it in.
    b. Write a preliminary draft.
    c. Revise.
    d. Write the final draft.

APPLICATION 8   GIVING AN ANALYSIS THROUGH PARTITION

Give an oral partition analysis of the topic from Application 7 above. Ask your classmates to evaluate your speech by making an Evaluation of Oral Presentations sheet like the one on page 459 and filling it in.

PLAN SHEET
FOR GIVING AN ANALYSIS THROUGH PARTITION

Analysis of Situation Requiring Partition

What is the subject to be partitioned?

For whom is the partition intended?

How will the partition be used?

In what format will the partition be given?

Setting Up the Partition

Definition or identification of subject:

Basis (or bases) for partition:

Significance or purpose of basis (or bases):

Divisions of the subject, with identification of each division:

Presentation of the System

Most logical order for presenting the divisions:

Types and subject matter of visuals to be included:

Sources of Information

CHAPTER 5

Analysis Through Effect-Cause and Comparison-Contrast: Looking at Details

OBJECTIVES   152
INTRODUCTION   152
ANALYSIS THROUGH EFFECT AND CAUSE   152
EFFECT-TO-EFFECT REASONING   154
INTENDED AUDIENCE AND PURPOSE   155
RELATIONSHIP TO OTHER FORMS OF COMMUNICATION   155
ESTABLISHING THE CAUSE OF AN EFFECT   159
ILLOGICAL AND INSUFFICIENT CAUSES   161
    A Following Event Caused by a Preceding Event   161
    Hasty Conclusion   161
    Oversimplification   161
    Sweeping Generalization   161
CAUSE-TO-EFFECT ANALYSIS   162
PROBLEM SOLVING   162
    Recognition of the Real Problem   163
    Various Possible Solutions   163
    Merits of Each Possible Solution   163
    Choosing the Best Solution   163
    Determination to Succeed   164
GENERAL PRINCIPLES IN GIVING AN ANALYSIS THROUGH EFFECT
    AND CAUSE   164
PROCEDURE FOR GIVING AN ANALYSIS THROUGH EFFECT AND CAUSE   164
APPLICATIONS   166
ANALYSIS THROUGH COMPARISON AND CONTRAST   171
ORGANIZATIONAL PATTERNS OF COMPARISON-CONTRAST ANALYSIS   171
    Point by Point   171
    Subject by Subject   172
    Similarities/Differences   172
    Three Patterns Compared   173
RELATIONSHIP TO OTHER FORMS OF COMMUNICATION   178
GENERAL PRINCIPLES IN GIVING AN ANALYSIS THROUGH COMPARISON
    AND CONTRAST   178
PROCEDURE FOR GIVING AN ANALYSIS THROUGH COMPARISON
    AND CONTRAST   179
APPLICATIONS   180

OBJECTIVES

Upon completing this chapter, the student should be able to:

- Establish the cause of an effect
- Differentiate between an actual cause and a probable cause
- Differentiate between logical and illogical or insufficient causes of an effect
- List and explain the steps in problem solving
- Solve a problem
- Give an analysis through effect and cause
- List and explain three organizational patterns for a comparison and contrast analysis
- Give an analysis through comparison and contrast

INTRODUCTION

Analysis through effect and cause and through comparison and contrast involves an intense examination of details. This examination may be as extraordinary as Sherlock Holmes's solving a case or as ordinary as a technician troubleshooting an air conditioning unit. Both Mr. Holmes and the technician have the same problem: discovering the cause of a particular effect.

Similarly, a comparison-contrast analysis may be as complex as a scientist's comparison of life in Hiroshima before and after the atom bomb. Or a comparison-contrast analysis may be as pointed as a technician's explaining that a chip in a computer is like a note in a piece of music: remove one chip or one note and the whole is disrupted but not destroyed.

The purpose of this chapter is to help you develop skill in analyzing details through effect-cause and comparison-contrast and in reporting the results of these analyses.

ANALYSIS THROUGH EFFECT AND CAUSE

Trying to find the cause of a situation (given the effect) is a common problem. Not at all unusual are such questions as these: Why was production down last week? Why does this piece of machinery give off an unusual humming sound after it has been in operation a few minutes? Why didn't this design sell? Why does this hairspray make some customers' hair brittle? Why does this automobile engine go dead at a red light when the air conditioner is on? Why does this patient have recurring headaches?

When persons begin to answer these questions, they are using an investigative, analytical approach; they are seeking a logical reason for a situation, event, or condition. Explaining the cause of an effect is a kind of process; in this analysis, however, the concern is with answering *why* rather than *how*. In explaining the process of making a print by the diazo method, for example, the emphasis is on *how* the operation is done. In analyzing the effect-cause relationship in the diazo process, the concern might be *why* this particular process was used in reproducing a print and not another method, or the concern might be *why* exposed diazo film must be subjected to ammonia gas for development.

In the following report, condensed from a student's paper, the writer is analyzing the reasons for the loss of 1500 lives aboard the *Titanic*. The student wants to know *why* so many people perished in the tragedy. (Marginal notes have been added.)

WHEN THAT GREAT SHIP WENT DOWN

On the evening of 14 April 1912, on its maiden trip, the "unsinkable" luxury liner the Titanic struck an iceberg in the freezing waters of the North Atlantic. Within a few hours the ship sank, taking with it some 1500 lives. Why did so many people perish, particularly when there was another ship within ten miles? Subsequent investigation by national and international agencies showed that the Titanic crew was small and insufficiently trained, that the ship did not have sufficient lifesaving equipment, and that international radio service was inadequate.

Effect investigated

Actual causes (conclusions) established

Small and Insufficiently Trained Crew

One reason so many people perished in the Titanic tragedy was that the crew was small and insufficiently trained for such an emergency. In the face of grave danger, evidently the crew of the Titanic was simply not able to meet the situation. Many of the lifeboats left the ship only half full and others could have taken on several more people. The passengers were not informed of their imminent danger upon impact with the iceberg, investigation suggests, and the officers deliberately withheld their knowledge of the certain sinking of the ocean liner. Therefore, when lifesaving maneuvers were finally begun, many passengers were unprepared for the seriousness of the moment. Further indication of poor crew leadership is that when the Titanic disappeared into the sea, only one lifeboat went back to pick up survivors.

First cause explained in detail

Causes discussed in order of least to most important

Insufficient Lifesaving Equipment

Another reason so many people lost their lives was that the ship was not properly equipped with lifeboats. Although millions of dollars had been spent in decorating the ship with palm gardens, Turkish baths, and even squash courts, this most luxurious liner afloat was lacking in the vitally important essentials of lifesaving equipment. Records show that the Titanic carried only 16 wooden lifeboats, capable of carrying fewer than 1200 persons. With a passenger and crew list exceeding 2200, there were at least 1000 individuals unprovided for in a possible sea disaster—even if every lifeboat were filled to capacity.

Second cause explained in detail

Inadequate International Radio Service

Undoubtedly, however, the primary reason that so many of the persons aboard the <u>Titanic</u> were lost is that international radio service was inadequate. Within ten miles of the <u>Titanic</u> was the <u>Californian</u>, which could have reached the <u>Titanic</u> before she sank and could have taken on all of her passengers. When the <u>Titanic</u> sent out emergency calls, near midnight, the radio operator of the <u>Californian</u> had already gone to bed. A crew member, however, was still in the radio room and picked up the signals. Not realizing that they were distress signals from a ship in the immediate vicinity, the crew member decided not to wake up the radio operator to receive the message. At that time there were no international maritime regulations requiring a radio operator to be on duty around the clock. *Third cause explained in detail*

Had there been a more adequate international radio system, regardless of the <u>Titanic</u>'s small and insufficiently trained crew and its insufficient lifesaving equipment, probably those 1500 lives could have been saved when that great ship went down. *Comment on significance of causes*

In "When That Great Ship Went Down," the writer begins by identifying the topic and stating the circumstances. Next, the question is posed, "Why did so many people perish," with the crucial modification, "particularly when there was another ship within ten miles." Then the writer summarizes in one sentence the three main causes. In the following three paragraphs, each cause is explained in turn, with sufficient supporting details. The writer discusses the causes in the order of their significance, leading up to the most critical cause. Then the writer closes the analysis with a brief comment that includes a relisting of the three main causes and emphasis on the most critical cause.

EFFECT-TO-EFFECT REASONING

Analysis through effect and cause may involve a chain of reasoning in which the cause of an effect is the effect of another cause. In the following paragraph (from the *Occupational Outlook Handbook*) dealing with technological progress and labor, for instance, industrial applications of scientific knowledge and invention (cause) result in increased automation (effect). Increased automation (cause) calls for skilled machine operators and service people (effect). This (cause), in turn, results in occupational changes in labor (effect).

Technological progress is causing major changes in the occupational makeup of the nation's labor force. Rapid advances in the industrial applications of scientific knowledge and invention are making possible increasing use of automatic devices that operate the machinery and equipment used in manufacturing. Nonetheless, the number of skilled and semiskilled workers is expected to continue to increase through the 1980s, despite this rapid mechanization and automation of production processes. It is expected that our increasingly complex technology generally will require higher levels of skill to operate and service this machinery and related equipment.

INTENDED AUDIENCE AND PURPOSE

You must be aware of who will read the effect-cause analysis and why, for these two basic considerations determine the extent of the investigation and the manner in which the investigation will be reported. For instance, the analysis may be presented for the general adult reader who wants a general understanding of the topic or the analysis may be for a division manager who will base decisions and actions on the analysis.

RELATIONSHIP TO OTHER FORMS OF COMMUNICATION

Analysis through effect and cause is a method of thinking and of organizing and presenting material. The effect-cause analysis frequently includes other forms of communication, such as definition, description, process explanation, classification, and partition, as well as oral presentation and the use of visuals. (For discussion of oral communication, see Chapter 10; for discussion of visuals, see Chapter 11.) Several of these forms are found in the following student-written effect-cause analysis. Given first is the Plan Sheet that the student filled in before writing the analysis.

PLAN SHEET
FOR GIVING AN ANALYSIS THROUGH EFFECT
AND CAUSE

Analysis of Situation Requiring Effect-Cause Analysis

What is the subject to be analyzed?
causes and effects of Vitamin B Complex deficiency

For whom is the analysis intended?
the general public

How will the analysis be used?
hopefully, to help others realize the importance of the Vit. B Complex

In what format will the analysis be given?
a written explanation

Effect to Be Investigated

Lack of thiamin:
— loss of appetite
— loss of weight
— constipation
— fatigue

Lack of riboflavin:
— unhealthy skin
— dim vision
— rapid aging
— cheilitis

Lack of niacin:
— skin problems
— poor digestion
— pellagra

Significance of the Effect

All these effects are detrimental to a person's health.

Causes (as applicable)

Possible causes:
omit

Probable cause (or causes):
omit

Actual cause (or causes):
All these effects are caused by a deficiency of one or more of the members of the Vitamin B Complex: thiamin, riboflavin, or niacin.

Supporting Evidence or Information for the Probable or Actual Cause (or Causes)

Observable symptoms
These vitamins can be found in certain foods.

Organization of the Analysis

I will divide the Vitamin B Complex into thiamin, riboflavin, and niacin. Then I will state why each is needed. And then I will describe what happens when there is a deficiency.

Types and Subject Matter of Visuals to Be Included

Three sets of pictures: examples of food that contain each of the three types of Vitamin B, for preventing deficiency.

Sources of Information

Nutrition textbook
World Book Encyclopedia

THE EFFECTS OF VITAMIN B COMPLEX ON THE HUMAN BODY

Vitamins are a necessary part of human growth. One such type of vitamin is the Vitamin B Complex. Many health problems are caused by a deficiency in the Vitamin B Complex.

The Vitamin B Complex can be divided into three main vitamins: thiamin, riboflavin, and niacin. A deficiency in any of these vitamins has a detrimental effect on the human body.

Thiamin

Thiamin is sometimes called the appetite vitamin. It is needed for growth, for releasing energy from carbohydrates, and for proper functioning of the heart and nerves. Some of the best sources of thiamin are pork, potatoes, and milk. See Figure 1. When the human body does not get enough thiamin, certain symptoms develop. These symptoms are a loss of appetite, loss of weight, constipation, and fatigue. People who have a thiamin deficiency feel tired, irritable, and depressed.

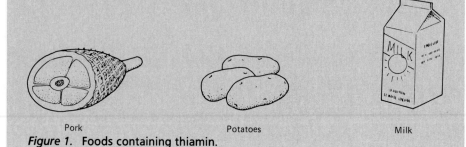

Pork   Potatoes   Milk

Figure 1. Foods containing thiamin.

Riboflavin

Riboflavin is sometimes called the "anti-old-age vitamin." It is necessary for growth, for the health of the skin, and for proper functioning of eyes. A diet rich in riboflavin helps to protect against disease and seems to prevent too rapid aging. Riboflavin is obtained from eggs, fowl, and green and leafy vegetables. These foods are shown in Figure 2. A lack of riboflavin in the body can cause dim vision and digestive disturbances. A disease known as cheilitis (cracks at the corner of the mouth) is caused by a riboflavin deficiency.

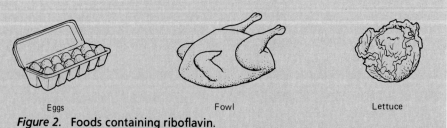

Eggs   Fowl   Lettuce

Figure 2. Foods containing riboflavin.

Niacin

Niacin is the third member of the Vitamin B Complex. It is essential for the health of the skin and nerves and for good digestion. The best sources of niacin are beans, peas, and cheese, as shown in Figure 3. A disease called pellagra is caused by a deficiency in niacin. This disease is marked by a slick, burning tongue; rough, red skin; sore eyeballs; digestive disturbances; and even mental disorders.

Beans   Peas   Cheese

Figure 3. Foods containing niacin.

A deficiency in any of these vitamins can be protected by a well-balanced diet that includes some of the foods mentioned above. Once a deficiency occurs, it can usually be corrected by an improved diet.

ESTABLISHING THE CAUSE OF AN EFFECT

A common problem is to discover the cause, or causes, of a given effect. Through reading, observation, consultation with knowledgeable people, and so on, an answer is sought. Why was there a high rate of absenteeism last week? Investigation shows that 97 percent of the absenteeism was due to a highly contagious virus. Why has the new paint already begun to peel on a car that was repainted only two months ago? Investigation shows that the cause is inferior paint, not an improper method of paint application or improper conditioning of the old finish, as at first suspected. In these two situations, it was possible to establish a definite or *actual cause*—one that evidence proves beyond question is the true cause.

Often, however, a definite cause cannot be established. A possible or *probable cause* must suffice. Why was the Edsel car a flop? Why is this patient antagonistic toward the nurses? Why is red hair associated with a quick temper? Why have sales this year more than tripled those of last year? Why is my roommate so popular? Although such questions as these cannot be answered with complete certainty, causes that answer them, nevertheless, need to be established.

In the process of establishing a probable cause, all the possible causes must be considered. After examining each possible cause, eliminate it entirely, keep it as merely a possibility, or decide that—all things considered—it is a probable cause. In the investigation of possible causes, the reasoning must be logical and relevant. Each possible cause must be logical and relevant. Each possible cause must be examined on the basis of reason, not on the basis of emotions or preconceived ideas; and each possible cause must *really* be a possible cause.

ESTABLISHING THE CAUSE: WHY SAM DIDN'T GET 100 BUCKS

Consider the plight of Sad Sam, who asks, "Why didn't I get the 100 bucks I asked my parents for to get new front tires on my car?" Perhaps – not on paper but at least mentally – Sam thinks of these possible reasons:

1. My parents don't love me.
2. They don't have the money.
3. They didn't receive my letter.
4. They mailed me a check but something happened to the letter.
5. They just don't realize what bad shape those front tires are in.
6. They think I should pay my car expenses out of the money I earn from my part-time job.

Sam turns over each possibility in his mind. He immediately dismisses possibility 1 (My parents don't love me). He knows this was only a childish reaction and that love cannot be equated with money. Sometimes parents who don't love their children send them money; and sometimes, for very good reasons, parents who love their children don't send them money.

There is a real possibility Sam's parents didn't have 100 dollars to spare (possibility 2). But Sam reasons if that is the cause, they would have asked him to wait a while longer or at least made some response.

Perhaps his parents did not receive his request (possibility 3). Maybe they mailed him a check but something happened to the letter (possibility 4). Either of the letters could have gotten lost in the mail. To his knowledge, however, none of his other letters have ever gotten lost.

Possibility 5 (They just don't realize what bad shape those front tires are in) could certainly be a true statement. But Sam realizes that his parents could be aware of the condition of the tires and still have reason not to send the money.

The more Sam considers possibility 6 (They think I should pay my car expenses out of the money I earn from my part-time job), the more this seems the likely reason. After all, Sam had promised his parents that if they would help him buy a car, he would keep it up. Furthermore, in his excitement of owning a car at long last, he had cautioned his parents to ignore any requests for car money, no matter how desperate they sounded.

So, as Sam carefully considers each possibility, he comes to the conclusion that the probable reason he did not receive the money is that his parents expect him to pay for his car expenses.

Whether the conclusion that is reached is the definite cause or the most probable cause of a situation, it must be arrived at through *logical* investigation, as in Sam's case. A conclusion, to be logical, must be based on reliable evidence, on relevant evidence, on sufficient evidence, and on an intelligent analysis of the evidence. Reliable evidence is the *proof* that can be gathered from trustworthy sources: personal experience and knowledge, knowledgeable individuals, textbooks, encyclopedias, and the like. Relevant evidence is information that directly influences the situation. Sufficient evidence means enough, or adequate, information with no significant facts that would alter the situation omitted. Evidence that is reliable, relevant, and sufficient must be analyzed intelligently. The meaning and significance of each individual piece of information and of all the pieces of information together must be considered if the most plausible conclusion is to be reached.

ILLOGICAL AND INSUFFICIENT CAUSES

In an investigation of the "why" of a situation, there are four pitfalls in reasoning to guard against especially, lest an illogical or insufficient cause be arrived at.

A Following Event Caused by a Preceding Event

This pitfall in reasoning assumes that a preceding event causes a following event, simply because of the time sequence. This fallacy in logic is called *post hoc, ergo propter hoc*, which literally means "after this, therefore because of this." Many superstitions are based on this false assumption. For instance, if a black cat runs across the street in front of Tom and later his automobile has a flat tire, blaming the cat is illogical. The two events (black cat running across street and flat tire) are not related in any way, except that they both concern the same person.

Hasty Conclusion

A common pitfall in effect-cause reasoning is jumping to a conclusion before all the facts are in. This results from not thoroughly investigating all aspects of a situation before announcing or indicating the cause. Consider this telephone call from a teenager to his parents:

> "Hello. Dad? I'm calling from City Drug Store. I've been in a slight automobile accident."
> "Automobile accident? Just how fast were you driving?"
> "I had stopped at a traffic light and this guy just rammed me from the rear."

Note the hasty conclusion that the son had caused the accident by driving too fast. The parent had jumped to a conclusion before all the facts were made known.

Oversimplification

Avoid the pitfall of oversimplifying a situation by thinking the situation has only one cause when it has several causes. If Mary says the reason she did not get a job she wanted is that she was nervous during the interview, she is oversimplifying the situation. She is not taking into consideration such possibilities as her training was inadequate, she lacked experience in the type of work, another applicant was better qualified, or she was not recommended highly enough.

Sweeping Generalization

All-encompassing general statements that are not supportable reflect illogical cause-effect thinking. Consider these statements:

> Labor unions are never concerned with consumer safety.
> Our products always completely satisfy the customer.

The two preceding statements are sweeping generalizations. They are broad statements that are difficult if not impossible to support with sufficient evidence. Be wary of using all-inclusive terms such as "never," "always," "completely," "everyone," and the like.

CAUSE-TO-EFFECT ANALYSIS

Thus far the discussion has centered around movement from a known or evident effect or situation to reasons explaining that effect or situation. Frequently there are occasions, however, when persons must approach this problem from the opposite end. That is, they are confronted with a cause and want to know what the effects are, or will be. For instance, if a piece of stock is not perfectly centered in a lathe (cause), what will happen (effect)? If a television antenna is not properly installed (cause), what will be the consequences (effect)? If the swelling of an injured foot (cause) is not attended to, what will happen to the patient (effect)? The following sample paragraph explains that aspirin (cause) has many advantages as well as some disadvantages (effects).

> Since its introduction in Germany 80 years ago, aspirin (the acetyl derivative of salicylic acid) has proved to be a miracle drug. Aspirin banishes headache, reduces fever, and eases pain. Not without its dangers, however, aspirin taken in excess will cause stomach upset, bleeding ulcer, and even death. Nevertheless, aspirin is responsible for more good than harm. It may even prevent heart attacks. According to current research, it is possible that aspirin contains anticoagulant properties that prevent thrombi, the blood clots that clog the coronary arteries, causing heart attacks.

Whether the occasion warrants approaching a problem by moving from effect to cause or by moving from cause to effect, the principles of logic are the same.

PROBLEM SOLVING

Closely related to answering the "why"—the effect/cause—of a situation is answering the "what should I do" in a situation. What courses should I take next semester? Should I drop out of school for a while until I can make some money? Should I continue in a technical program or should I switch to a baccalaureate degree program? Should I take another job that has been offered to me? Which tires should I buy?

All these questions indicate problems that people are trying to solve. Everyone has problems—some of them insignificant, some very significant—that must be faced and dealt with. Such problems as which shoes to wear today or which vegetables to choose at lunch or which movie to go to tonight require only a few moments consideration and, viewed a few days from now, are quite insignificant. But other problems, other decisions, require thoughtful consideration and will still be significant a few days or a few years from now. How does one go about solving such problems?

Problem solving is not easy; several suggestions, however, may help in reaching a more satisfactory decision:

1. Recognize the problem for what it is.
2. Realize that there are *various* possibilities for solution.
3. Consider *each* possibility on its own merits.
4. Decide which possibility is *really* best.
5. Determine to make the chosen course of action successful.

Recognition of the Real Problem

The first step in solving any problem is recognizing the problem for what it is. The student who wrote only three pages on a test and who thinks a classmate received an A because the classmate filled up ten pages is avoiding the *real* problem: what the pages contain, not how many pages there are. In looking at a problem for what it is, reason and logical thinking must prevail. Glorifying oneself as a martyr or exaggerating the circumstances is avoiding the real issue. Sometimes emotions and pressures from others cloud reason and thus camouflage the real problem.

Various Possible Solutions

Various choices, or possibilities, or answers are available for solving problems. Sometimes, in a hastily posed problem, there seem to be only two alternatives, thus an either-or situation. An example is the problem of the student who does not have money for college and says, "I'll either have to go so far in debt it will take me ten years to get a clear start in life, or I'll have to postpone college until I have enough money in the bank to see me through two years." This student is certainly not considering *all* the alternatives available. The student has not considered that many colleges have an agreement with various industries whereby the student goes to college for a semester and works for a semester. Or the possibility of evening school, through which the student can attend courses one or more evenings per week after work and earn college credit. Or the possibility of taking a part-time job to help defray most or all of the college expenses. Or the possibility of taking a reduced college load and working full time. Thus a problem that seemed to have only two possible solutions really has a number of possible solutions.

Merits of Each Possible Solution

The third step in solving a problem is considering each possible choice on its own merits. Each possible solution must be analyzed and weighed carefully from every angle. This may involve investigation: consulting with knowledgeable people, drawing upon the experiences of family and friends, turning to reference materials, and so forth.

Choosing the Best Solution

Once each of the possible choices has been given an honest, thoughtful consideration, it is time to decide which *one* choice is best. This is the most difficult step in problem solving, but if it is preceded by a mature analysis of the problem and all of its possible solutions, the final decision is more likely to be satisfactory even in a few weeks or in several years. Sometimes it may seem easier to let someone else make the decision; in that way, if things do not turn out as wished, someone else gets the blame. But shunning responsibility by avoiding making a decision goes back to the first step in problem solving: recognizing the problem for what it is.

Determination to Succeed

Finally, in problem solving there must be a determination to make the chosen course of action successful. This may involve acquainting others with the decision and the reasons for it and perhaps even persuading them to accept the decision. A positive, open-minded attitude toward a well-thought-out decision is the best assurance that the decision, after all, was the best one.

GENERAL PRINCIPLES IN GIVING AN ANALYSIS THROUGH EFFECT AND CAUSE

1. *The precise effect (situation, event, or conditions) being investigated must be made clear.* The focus is on gathering information that relates directly to that one effect.
2. *Awareness of who will read the analysis and why, is essential to the writer.* These two considerations — the who and the why — determine the extent of the investigation and the manner of reporting it.
3. *Additional forms of communication may be needed.* Definition, description, process explanation, classification, and partition — plus visuals — may help clarify the effect-cause analysis.
4. *If the actual cause can be established, sufficient supporting evidence should be given.* The evidence must be reliable, relevant, and sufficient.
5. *If the actual cause cannot be established, adequate support for the probable cause should be given.* The support must be reliable, relevant, and as sufficient as possible.
6. *A preceding event may or may not cause a particular following event.* It is the task of the effect-cause analyst to determine whether there is a causal relationship between two events.
7. *A hasty conclusion indicates lack of thorough analysis.* All aspects of a situation should be investigated and weighed carefully before reaching a conclusion.
8. *A situation may be oversimplified by attributing to it only one cause when it may have several causes.* Significant situations are usually more complex than they at first seem.
9. *Sweeping generalizations weaken a presentation because they are misleading and are often untrue.* Caution should guide the use of such all-inclusive terms as "never," "always," and "every person."
10. *Problem solving is a logical process.* The steps in problem solving are recognizing the problem for what it is, realizing that there are various possible solutions, considering each possible solution on its own merits, deciding which possibility is really best, and determining to make the chosen course of action successful.

PROCEDURE FOR GIVING AN ANALYSIS THROUGH EFFECT AND CAUSE

The analysis may be an independent presentation, or it may be a paragraph or a part of a presentation. Whichever the case, the procedure is the same and presents no unusual problems. (Although the procedure suggested here is for analyzing from effect to cause, the particular communication situation may call for analyzing from cause to effect.) Generally, the analysis should be divided into three sections:

I. Stating the problem usually requires only a few sentences.
   A. State the effect (situation, event, or condition) that is being analyzed.
   B. If applicable, give the scope and limitations of the investigation (as in reporting the causes of traffic accidents involving fatalities at the Highway 76-Justice Avenue intersection from January 1 to July 1).
   C. Give the assumptions, if any, on which the analysis or interpretation of facts is based (as in assuming that the new machine which is not working properly today was correctly installed and serviced last month).
   D. If applicable, give the methods of investigation used (reading, observation, consultation with knowledgeable people, etc.).
   E. Unless the order of the presentation requires otherwise, state the conclusions that have been reached.

II. Reporting the investigation of the problem is the longest section of the presentation.
   A. Consider in sufficient detail possible causes; eliminate improbable causes.
   B. If the actual cause can be established, give the cause and sufficient supporting evidence.
   C. If the actual cause cannot be established, give the probable cause and sufficient supporting evidence.
   D. Interpret facts and other information when necessary.
   E. If necessary, especially in a longer presentation, divide the subject into parts and analyze each part individually.
   F. Organize the information around a logical pattern or order.
      1. The topic may suggest moving from the less important to the more important, or vice versa.
      2. The topic may suggest using a time order of what happened first, second, and so on.
      3. The topic may suggest moving from the more obvious to the less obvious.
      4. The topic may suggest going from the less probable to the more probable.
      5. The nature of the presentation may suggest some other order.

III. The conclusion (usually brief) reflects the purpose of the analysis.
   A. If the purpose of the analysis is to give the reader a general knowledge of an effect-cause situation, summarize the main points or comment on the significance of the situation.
   B. If the analysis is a basis for decisions and actions, summarize the main points, comment on the significance of the analysis, *and* make recommendations.

APPLICATION 1 GIVING AN ANALYSIS THROUGH EFFECT AND CAUSE

Each of the following statements contains an illogical or insufficient cause for an effect. Point out why the stated or implied cause is inadequate.

1. The reason my cow died is that I didn't go to church last Sunday.
2. Strikes occur because people are selfish.
3. Mr. Smith's television appearance on election eve won him the election.
4. Automobile insurance rates are higher for teenagers than for adults because teenagers are poorer drivers.
5. Susan isn't dependable. She was supposed to turn in a report today but she hasn't shown up.
6. The atom bomb won World War II.
7. If I were you, I wouldn't switch kinds of drinks at a party. I did so last night, and this morning I have a terrible headache.
8. I can't stand pizza. I ate some once and it was as soggy as a wet dishrag.
9. Most successful businessmen have large vocabularies. If I develop a large vocabulary, I'll be successful in business.
10. "I joined the Confederacy for two weeks. Then I deserted. The Confederacy fell."—Mark Twain

APPLICATION 2 GIVING AN ANALYSIS THROUGH EFFECT AND CAUSE

In each of the following situations, indicate whether a probable cause or an actual cause is the more likely to be established. Point out why.

1. I thought that I had a B for sure in history, but the grade sheet shows a D. Why did I get a D?
2. This is the fourth time that the same jaw tooth has been filled. Why won't the filling stay in?
3. For the third night in a row I have asked my neighbors to please be a little quieter. Tonight they have the stereo turned up even higher. Why won't they be quieter?
4. In the 1980 presidential election the Republican candidate won. Why did he receive more votes than the Democratic candidate?
5. Every time my mother eats a lot of tomatoes, she breaks out in a rash. Why?

APPLICATION 3 GIVING AN ANALYSIS THROUGH EFFECT AND CAUSE

Make a list of five problems regarding your schoolwork, job, vocation, and so on, that require thoughtful consideration. Choose one of these problems and solve it by listing:

1. The real problem
2. Various possibilities for solution

3. Consideration of each possible solution
4. The solution
5. Ways to assure that the chosen course of action will be successful

APPLICATION 4 GIVING AN ANALYSIS THROUGH EFFECT AND CAUSE

Choose one of the general subjects below (or one that is similar). Restrict the subject to a specific topic.

EXAMPLE OF SUBJECT RESTRICTION

General subject: Decrease or increase of students in certain majors
Specific topic: Increase in students majoring in building trades

a. Make a Plan Sheet like the one on pages 169–170, and fill it in.
b. Write a preliminary draft.
c. Revise.
d. Write the final draft.

Cause (or causes) of:

1. Improper functioning of a mechanism
2. A mishap of national importance
3. A decrease or increase in jobs in your city, county, or state
4. Variations in fringe benefits with different companies
5. A decrease or increase in sales during a particular period of time
6. Factors in a company's consideration of a plant site

APPLICATION 5 GIVING AN ANALYSIS THROUGH EFFECT AND CAUSE

Give an oral effect-to-cause analysis of a topic from Application 4 above. Ask your classmates to evaluate your speech by making an Evaluation of Oral Presentations sheet like the one on page 459 and filling it in.

APPLICATION 6 GIVING AN ANALYSIS THROUGH EFFECT AND CAUSE

Write an explanation of the cause (or causes) in one of the topics below.

a. Make a Plan Sheet like the one on pages 169–170, and fill it in.
b. Write a preliminary draft.
c. Revise.
d. Write the final draft.

Explain:

1. Why an automobile engine starts when the ignition is turned on
2. Why a light comes on when the switch is turned on
3. Why water and oil do not mix
4. Why computer literacy is important

5. Why two houses on adjacent lots and with the same floor space may require different amounts of electricity for air conditioning or for heating
6. Why an earthquake occurs
7. Why a diesel engine is more economical to operate than a gasoline engine
8. Why artificial breeding has become a popular practice among ranchers
9. Why extreme care should be taken in moving an accident victim
10. Why different fabrics (such as silk, cotton, wool, linen) supposedly dyed the same color may turn out to be different shades
11. Why proper insulation decreases heating and cooling costs
12. Why an appliance wired for alternating current will not operate on direct current
13. Why a dull saw blade should be attended to
14. Why a stain should not be applied over a varnish
15. Why the Rh factor is important in blood transfusions and in pregnancy
16. Why the blood bank insists on having complete identification in a patient sample of blood
17. Why a new book in the library does not appear on the shelf immediately after it is received
18. Why computer documentation is essential
19. Why vitamins are essential in human growth
20. A topic of your own choosing from your major field

APPLICATION 7 GIVING AN ANALYSIS THROUGH EFFECT AND CAUSE

Give an oral effect-to-cause explanation of a topic from Application 6 above. Ask your classmates to evaluate your speech by making an Evaluation of Oral Presentations sheet like the one on page 459 and filling it in.

PLAN SHEET
FOR GIVING AN ANALYSIS THROUGH EFFECT
AND CAUSE

Analysis of Situation Requiring Effect-Cause Analysis

What is the subject to be analyzed?

For whom is the analysis intended?

How will the analysis be used?

In what format will the analysis be given?

Effect to Be Investigated

Significance of the Effect

Causes (as applicable)

Possible causes:

Probable cause (or causes):

Actual cause (or causes):

Supporting Evidence or Information for the Probable or Actual Cause (or Causes)

Organization of the Analysis

Types and Subject Matter of Visuals to Be Included

Sources of Information

ANALYSIS THROUGH COMPARISON AND CONTRAST

A basic method of looking at things closely is comparison and contrast, that is, showing how two or more things are alike and how they are different. Comparison or contrast may be used singly, of course, but most often they are used together; further, the term *comparison* is commonly used to encompass both likenesses and differences.

Frequently, comparison-contrast is used to explain the unfamiliar. For instance, an airbrush looks like a pencil and is held like one; a computer terminal resembles a typewriter keyboard.

Often, too, comparison-contrast is used to highlight specific details. Llamas, for instance, are related to camels but are smaller and have no hump. *Approve* and *endorse,* though synonyms, have slightly different meanings: *approve* means simply to express a favorable opinion of, and *endorse* means to express assent publicly and definitely.

Analysis through comparison-contrast is a part of the life of every consumer: Should I buy Brand A or Brand B tires; which is the better buy in a color TV set — Brand X or Brand Y; which of these hospital insurance plans is better? Comparison of products is such an important aspect of the economy that some periodicals, such as *Consumers' Research, Consumer Reports,* and *Changing Times,* are devoted to test reports and in-depth comparisons.

ORGANIZATIONAL PATTERNS OF COMPARISON-CONTRAST ANALYSIS

An analysis developed by comparison and/or contrast must be carefully organized. The writer must decide in what order the details will be presented. Although various organizational patterns are possible, three are particularly useful.

Point by Point

In this pattern, sometimes called "comparison of the parts," a point (characteristic, quality, part) of each subject is analyzed, then another point of each subject is analyzed, and so on. The report below on a comparison of two electronics technology programs is organized point by point. The first point of comparison is cost. Cost details are given for each subject — Stevens College and Tinnin Community College. Then the next point, lab equipment, is analyzed for each program; and then the last point, instruction, is analyzed for each program. The point-by-point pattern can be delineated in this way:

    Point A (cost) of Subject I (Stevens College)
    Point A (cost) of Subject II (Tinnin Community College)

    Point B (lab equipment) of Subject I (Stevens College)
    Point B (lab equipment) of Subject II (Tinnin Community College)

    Point C (instruction) of Subject I (Stevens College)
    Point C (instruction) of Subject II (Tinnin Community College)

The point-by-point organizational pattern is usually preferred if the entire analysis is complex; that is, if the comparison is longer than a paragraph or two or if the analysis treats in depth more than two or three points.

Subject by Subject

This organizational pattern, sometimes referred to as "comparison of the whole," gives all the details concerning the first subject, then all the details concerning the next subject, and so on. The report below on a comparison of two electronics technology programs could be reorganized around the subject-by-subject pattern: all the details concerning the first subject, Stevens College (cost, lab equipment, and instruction), could be given first. Then would follow all the details concerning the second subject, Tinnin Community College (cost, lab equipment, and instruction). The subject-by-subject pattern can be delineated in this way:

Subject I (Stevens College)
   Point A (cost)
   Point B (lab equipment)
   Point C (instruction)
Subject II (Tinnin Community College)
   Point A (cost)
   Point B (lab equipment)
   Point C (instruction)

Similarities/Differences

In this pattern, a comparison of the similarities of the subjects is given first, followed by a contrast of differences between the subjects. Again, the report below on a comparison of two electronics technology programs could be reorganized. If the similarities/differences pattern were used, the similarities between Stevens College and Tinnin Community College would be given, and then the differences between the two colleges would be given. The similarities/differences pattern can be delineated in this way:

Similarities of Subjects I and II (Stevens College and Tinnin Community College)
   Point A (cost)
   Point B (lab equipment)
   Point C (instruction)
Differences between Subjects I and II (Stevens College and Tinnin Community College)
   Point A (cost)
   Point B (lab equipment)
   Point C (instruction)

The similarities/differences (or differences/similarities) organizational pattern is particularly effective when positive and negative emphases are desired. The subject or emphasis presented last makes the greatest impression.

Three Patterns Compared

These three organizational patterns can be delineated as follows (of course, there can be any number of points and any number of subjects; here it is assumed that two subjects are being compared/contrasted on three points):

Point by Point	*Subject by Subject*	*Similarities/Differences*
Point A of Subject I	Subject I	Similarities of Subjects I and II
Point A of Subject II	Point A	Point A
	Point B	Point B
Point B of Subject I	Point C	Point C
Point B of Subject II	Subject II	Differences between Subjects I and II
	Point A	Point A
Point C of Subject I	Point B	Point B
Point C of Subject II	Point C	Point C

The following student-written report is an analysis through comparison-contrast. Note that the report is organized around three points of comparison: cost, lab equipment, and instruction. The Plan Sheet that the student filled in before writing is included. Marginal notes have been added to show how the student developed and organized the paper.

PLAN SHEET
FOR GIVING AN ANALYSIS THROUGH
COMPARISON AND CONTRAST

Analysis of Situation Requiring Comparison-Contrast Analysis

What are the subjects to be analyzed?
the electronics technology program at Stevens College and the electronics technology program at Tinnin Community College

For whom is the analysis intended?
prospective electronics students

How will the analysis be used?
to decide which college the student should attend

In what format will the analysis be given?
a written report

Major Points (Characteristics, Qualities, Parts) to Be Compared/Contrasted

cost, lab equipment, instruction

Details Concerning the Major Points of Each Subject

Stevens College   *Tinnin Community College*

I. Cost

Tuition $4600.00   *Tuition ($250 a*
No charge for books   *semester). . .$1000*
                                     Books (after reselling for 1/2 price)
                                     $300

II. Lab Equipment

15 . . . Power supply. 50
12 . . . Digital multimeter 40
4 . . . Microprocessor trainer. 12
6 . . . Sine-square wave generator. 25
0 . . . Transmitter curve tracer . . . 1
0 . . . Decade box. 40
4 . . . Digital trainer 20

```
 4 . . . Function generator . . . . . . . 30
10 . . . Oscilloscope . . . . . . . . . . . . 34
 1 . . . Personal computer system . .  4
```

Value:
$50,000

Value:
over $150,000

III. Instruction

1 Instructor
A.A.S. from Stevens, taught 3
yrs at Stevens, worked 2 yrs
in industry (IBM)

3 Instructors
Instructor A: B.S., taught at 1
other college, taught 5 yrs,
worked in industry 3 yrs
Instructor B: B.S., taught in 1
other college, taught 7 yrs,
worked in industry 4 yrs and
alternate summers
Instructor C: M.S., taught in 2
other colleges, taught 18 yrs,
worked in industry 7 yrs

Classes 8-12, 1-2, M-Th
Electronics lectures 8-10:30, lab
10:30-12
A.A.S. degree: Eng 1 & 11,
Bus. Law 1 & 11, Soc., Math for
Electronics, Digital Math,
Computer Math, Basic
Electronics, Fund of Elec,
Digital Circuits, Semiconductors,
Transistor Circuits

Variable schedules 8-3, M-F
Electronics — usually 2-hr block

A.A.S. degree: Tech Writing 1
& 11, soc. sc., P.E., Ind. Psy.,
Tech Math 1 & 11, Tech
Physics 1 & 11, Fund of
Drafting, Elec for Electronics,
Electron Devices & Circuits,
4 sophomore-level electronics
courses, 1 elective

Organization of the Analysis

Point by point. First I'll discuss the cost of attending each college. Then
I'll talk about the lab equipment in each, and finally, the instruction in
each.

Types and Subject Matter of Visuals to Be Included

table showing the cost of tuition and books for each college
table showing the major pieces of lab equipment for each college

Sources of Information

catalog from each college; chairman of the electronics technology dept. at
each college

A COMPARISON OF TWO ELECTRONICS TECHNOLOGY PROGRAMS: STEVENS COLLEGE AND TINNIN COMMUNITY COLLEGE

A comparison of the electronics technology program at Stevens College and at Tinnin Community College indicates that the Tinnin program has more to offer the student. This conclusion is based on a thorough examination of the catalog from each college and a visit to each college for a personal interview with the chairman of the electronics technology department. This investigation shows that the Tinnin program costs less, has more lab equipment, and possibly has better instruction.

Subjects compared
General conclusion reached

Sources of information

Specific conclusions and points of comparison

COST

The cost of tuition and books for each college is as follows:

First point of comparison for each subject

Stevens College

Tuition (18-month program)	$4600.00
Books — included with tuition	-0-
	$4600.00

Table visually depicts supporting information

Tinnin Community College

Tuition (4-semester program) $250.00 per semester	$1000.00
Books (about $150.00 per semester)	300.00

4 semesters × $150.00 = $600.00
resale value = 300.00
$300.00

$1300.00

The Stevens program costs $3300.00 more than the Tinnin program. This large difference in cost is due primarily to Stevens being a private college and Tinnin being a public community college.

Interpretation of information

LAB EQUIPMENT

Each college has these major pieces of lab equipment:

Second point of comparison for each subject

Equipment	Stevens	Tinnin
Power supply	15	50
Digital multimeter	12	40
Microprocessor trainer	4	12
Sine-square wave generator	6	25
Transistor curve tracer	0	1

Table visually depicts supporting information

Equipment	Stevens	Tinnin
Decade resistance/ capacitance box	0	40
Digital trainer	4	20
Function generator	2	30
Dual-trace oscilloscope	5	34
Personal computer system	1	4

The total value (approximate retail value) of the Stevens equipment is approximately $50,000. The total value of the Tinnin equipment is well over $150,000.

Supporting details

The program at Tinnin Community College has more kinds and more pieces of each kind of lab equipment than does Stevens College.

Interpretation of information

INSTRUCTION

The programs in both colleges differ in three aspects of instruction: qualifications of the instructors, daily class schedule, and required courses. Stevens College has one electronics instructor. He has an Associate in Applied Science degree from Stevens, has taught three years (all at Stevens), and has worked two years in industry (at IBM). Tinnin Community College has three electronics instructors. Two of them have Bachelor of Science degrees and the other has a Master of Science degree. Each has taught in at least one other college, has taught at least five years, and has worked in industry at least three years. One instructor works in industry every other summer.

Third point of comparison— instruction— for each subject divided into three aspects

First aspect of instruction (instructors) compared for both subjects

The daily class schedule is set up differently at each school. At Stevens, the students are in class from 8:00 A.M. until 12:00 noon and from 1:00 P.M. to 2:00 P.M. Monday through Thursday (there are no classes on Friday). For the electronics courses, the students have lecture from 8:00 to 10:30 and lab from 10:30 to 12:00. The afternoon hour is for a nonelectronics course. At Tinnin, the students have variable schedules from 8:00 A.M. to 3:00 P.M. five days a week, with electronics courses typically in two-hour blocks. The distribution of lecture and lab time is at the discretion of the instructor.

Second aspect of instruction (schedule) compared for both subjects

Both Stevens and Tinnin offer an Associate in Applied Science degree upon successful completion of their programs. Requirements for the associate degree differ slightly at the two schools. At Stevens, the required courses are College English I and II, Business Law I and II, Sociology, Math for Electronics, Digital Mathematics, Computer Mathematics, Basic Electronics, Fundamentals of Electricity, Digital Circuits, Semiconductors, and Transistor Circuits. At Tinnin the required courses are Technical Writing I and II, any course in social science, Physical Education, Industrial Psychology, Technical Mathematics I and II, Technical Physics I and II, Fundamentals of Drafting, Electricity for Elec-

Third aspect of instruction (courses) compared for both subjects

tronics, Electron Devices and Circuits, any four additional sopho-more-level electronics courses, and one elective. Both programs offer the same amount of classroom instruction — 18 months — but the Stevens program does not have a three-month summer break.

Thus, the instructors at Tinnin may be better qualified than the instructor at Stevens, the daily class schedule is more flexible at Tinnin, but the requirements for graduation are similar in both colleges.

Summarizing statement about the third (and lengthiest) point of comparison

CONCLUSIONS

A person planning to specialize in electronics technology should thoroughly explore the programs in prospective colleges. This report shows that two colleges (both in the same city) vary widely in their electronics programs. The electronics technology program at Tinnin Community College costs less, has more lab equipment, and possibly has better instruction than does the electronics technology program at Stevens College.

Comment

Summary of main points

RELATIONSHIP TO OTHER FORMS OF COMMUNICATION

Comparison-contrast analyses are closely related to other forms of communication, especially to description, definition, classification, and partition, and often involve them. Often, too, the comparison-contrast analysis is given orally. (For a discussion of oral communication, see Chapter 10.)

Various kinds of visuals — drawings, diagrams, tables, graphs, charts — are particularly helpful in showing comparison-contrast. (For a discussion of visuals, see Chapter 11.) The table on the following page, for instance, shows the average annual energy use and annual cost of home appliances in a typical American home. Note how the arrangement of information makes it easy for the reader to see similarities and differences.

GENERAL PRINCIPLES IN GIVING AN ANALYSIS THROUGH COMPARISON AND CONTRAST

1. *Comparison-contrast can be used to explain the unfamiliar or to highlight specific details.*
2. *The comparison-contrast analysis must be carefully organized.* Various organizational patterns are possible.
3. *The point-by-point organizational pattern can be used.* In this pattern, a point of each subject is analyzed, then another point of each subject, and so on.
4. *The subject-by-subject pattern can be used.* In this pattern, all the details concerning the first subject are presented, then all the details about the next subject, and so on.

Table 1 Home Appliance Annual Energy Use and Cost

Use of electricity is stated in the number of kilowatt-hours (kwh) used per year. Cost is based on an average charge by utilities of 9¢ per kwh.

Electric Appliance	Annual Energy Use	Annual Cost
Air conditioner	2000 kwh	$180.00
Can opener	1 kwh	.09
Clock	17 kwh	1.53
Clothes dryer	1200 kwh	108.00
Coffee maker	100 kwh	9.00
Dishwasher	350 kwh	31.50
Floor furnace	480 kwh	43.20
Freezer (16 cu. ft.)	1200 kwh	108.00
Frying pan	240 kwh	21.60
Hair dryer	15 kwh	1.35
Hot plate	100 kwh	9.00
Iron	150 kwh	13.50
Lighting	2000 kwh	180.00
Radio	20 kwh	1.80
Radio-phonograph	40 kwh	3.60
Range	1500 kwh	135.00
Refrigerator (12 cu. ft.)	750 kwh	67.50
Shaver	1 kwh	.09
Television (black and white)	400 kwh	36.00
Television (color)	550 kwh	49.50
Toaster	40 kwh	3.60
Vacuum cleaner	45 kwh	4.05
Washer (clothes)	100 kwh	9.00
Water heater (all electric)	4200 kwh	378.00

5. *The similarities/differences pattern can be used.* In this pattern, a comparison of similarities of the subjects is given, followed by a contrast of differences between the subjects.

PROCEDURE FOR GIVING AN ANALYSIS THROUGH COMPARISON AND CONTRAST

The comparison-contrast analysis may be independent or it may be part of a longer presentation. Whichever the case, the analysis is typically divided into three sections.

    I. Stating the subjects and points to be compared and contrasted requires only a few sentences.

        A. State the subjects that are being compared and contrasted.

        B. State the points (characteristics, qualities, parts) by which the subjects are being compared and contrasted.

        C. Give any needed background information.

      D. If applicable, give the source of information or methods of investigation used (reading, observation, consultation with knowledgeable people, etc.).

      E. Unless the order of the presentation requires otherwise, state the conclusions that have been reached.

  II. Reporting the details is the longest section of the presentation.

      A. Give sufficient supporting details for each point of each subject.

      B. When needed, subdivide the major points.

      C. Interpret facts and other information when necessary.

      D. Use visuals if they will help clarify the analysis.

      E. Organize the information around a logical pattern or order.

 III. The conclusion (usually brief) reflects the purpose of the analysis.

      A. If the purpose of the analysis is to give the reader a general knowledge of the subjects, summarize the main points or comment on the significance of the comparison.

      B. If the analysis is a basis for decisions and actions, summarize the main points, comment on the significance of the analysis, *and* make recommendations.

APPLICATION 1 GIVING AN ANALYSIS THROUGH COMPARISON AND CONTRAST

Compare and contrast your program of study at your institution with a similar program in another institution.

  a. Make a Plan Sheet like the one on pages 182–183, and fill it in.

  b. Write a preliminary draft.

  c. Revise.

  d. Write the final draft.

APPLICATION 2 GIVING AN ANALYSIS THROUGH COMPARISON AND CONTRAST

Choose one of the topics below for a comparison-contrast analysis.

  a. Make a Plan Sheet like the one on pages 182–183, and fill it in.

  b. Write a preliminary draft.

  c. Revise.

  d. Write the final draft.

Analyze:

1. Two brands of a product (Examples: an RCA and a Zenith color television set, a John Deere and a Massey-Ferguson tractor, Levi and Dickey blue jeans, a Chrysler Cordoba and a Ford Thunderbird)

2. Two synonyms (Examples: job-career, technician-technologist, education-training, friend-acquaintance)

3. Before-and-after situations (Examples: a piece of furniture or a building before and after renovation, an engine before and after overhauling, efficiency before and after using a new procedure)

4. A topic of your own choosing

APPLICATION 3 GIVING AN ANALYSIS THROUGH COMPARISON AND CONTRAST

Give an oral comparison-contrast explanation of Application 1 or of a topic from Application 2 above. Ask your classmates to evaluate your speech by making an Evaluation of Oral Presentations sheet like the one on page 459 and filling it in.

PLAN SHEET
FOR GIVING AN ANALYSIS THROUGH
COMPARISON AND CONTRAST

Analysis of Situation Requiring Comparison-Contrast Analysis

What are the subjects to be analyzed?

For whom is the analysis intended?

How will the analysis be used?

In what format will the analysis be given?

Major Points (Characteristics, Qualities, Parts) to Be Compared/Contrasted

Details Concerning the Major Points of Each Subject

Organization of the Analysis

Types and Subject Matter of Visuals to Be Included

Sources of Information

CHAPTER 6

The Summary: Getting to the Heart of the Matter

OBJECTIVES 185
INTRODUCTION 185
PURPOSE AND INTENDED AUDIENCE 185
UNDERSTANDING THE MATERIAL TO BE SUMMARIZED 186
WAYS TO SHORTEN THE ORIGINAL 188
    Summary by Condensation 188
    Summary by Abridgment 189
FORMS OF SUMMARIES 189
    Descriptive Summary 189
    Informative Summary 192
    Evaluative Summary 197
ACCURACY OF FACT AND EMPHASIS 199
DOCUMENTATION 200
    Placement of Bibliography 200
GENERAL PRINCIPLES IN GIVING A SUMMARY 200
PROCEDURE FOR GIVING A SUMMARY 201
APPLICATIONS 201

OBJECTIVES

Upon completing this chapter, the student should be able to:

- Define the terms *descriptive summary, informative summary,* and *evaluative summary*
- List the specific purposes that each form of summary may serve
- Prepare each form of summary
- Give bibliographical information for a summary
- Describe specific situations in which a student and an employee would need to know and use the preceding skills

INTRODUCTION

Why do you, a student, need to know how to give a summary, a digest of the main points of an original presentation? Of what importance is this to you? First, because you are a *student,* you should be able to give a summary orally and in writing. As a student, for example, you must be able to grasp the main points in a reading assignment for a course. One very effective way of studying textbook material is to write down the significant points, the important facts, in the lesson. Writing summaries of class lectures and of textbook assignments helps to clarify information and makes it stick in the mind longer.

This practice is quite helpful not only in day-to-day preparations but also in reviewing for tests. Pulling the main points and ideas from pages and pages of textbook material and class notes and then writing them down coherently and understandably is a sound approach to studying for tests. Since tests cannot possibly cover everything a student is supposed to learn in a course, test questions usually concentrate on major points and aspects of the subject.

Often a class requirement is to make a report or review (a summary) of reading assignments. Usually the only directions that are given have to do with what sources are to be read and how long the report should be. Rarely is the student told *how* the report should be presented.

Thus, for very practical reasons of immediate importance, you need to know how to give a summary.

There are occasions, too, in which giving summaries is part of a person's work, such as condensing reports, articles, speeches, or discussions for a superior too busy to read or hear the original. Further, people *read* summaries, and thus should be able to recognize a summary for what it is.

PURPOSE AND INTENDED AUDIENCE

The first consideration in giving a summary is *why* it is being written, what purpose it will serve. The purpose may be to *describe* very briefly, perhaps in only a sentence or two, what the article or situation is about. The purpose may be to *inform,* to present, in general, the principal facts and conclusions given in the original work. Or the purpose may be to *evaluate,* to judge the accuracy, completeness, and usefulness of the work.

Closely related to the purpose is the intended audience. If it is a study aid, the audience may be the student writing the summary. If the summary is an assignment, the audience may be an instructor. Or the audience may be a business executive who wants only the main points and conclusions of an original work. Or the audience may be a student trying to determine what sources would be most helpful for a research paper.

In other words, the direction that a summary takes is not haphazard; you must have clearly in mind the purpose of the summary and the intended audience.

UNDERSTANDING THE MATERIAL TO BE SUMMARIZED

You must have a thorough understanding of the material before you can summarize it. Since summary concerns main ideas, you must be able to distinguish main ideas from minor ideas and supporting details. To do this, you have to understand the material.

The first step in understanding the material to be summarized is to scan it. In looking over the material, note the title, introductory matter, opening and closing paragraphs, headings, marginal notes, major topics, organization, and method of presentation. This scant familiarity with the material is preparation for reading it closely.

Now read the material very carefully. Underline or jot down on a separate sheet of paper (particularly if the work belongs to someone else) the key ideas. Think through the relationship of these key ideas to get the overall significance of the material.

To illustrate the procedure for reading material to be summarized, an article from the January 1982 *Congressional Digest* follows. The article discusses debate over the Clean Air Act. Assume that a summary of the main points is to be written for a general adult reader. In scanning the article, note that the opening sentence is the central idea of the article. The material following identifies specific aspects of the Clean Air Act controversy.

Key points and ideas are printed in boldface italic type, and marginal notes explain how to determine what information to include and what to omit in a summary.

OMIT IN A
SUMMARY

Controversy Over the Clean Air Act

INCLUDE IN A
SUMMARY

Air quality policy has long involved complex economic, geographic and scientific factors.

Controlling idea
or the main point
of the article

Air pollution control was an early component of the industrial revolution of the 19th Century, the first emission control ordinance in the United States having been adopted in Pittsburgh around 1815. Anti-smoke and anti-odor ordinances were later enacted in a number of other industrial cities. Pollution abatement technology was also developed that improved the level of cleanliness in some areas. Much later, the shift from coal to oil and gas for urban electric power and industrial production, and office and home heating, contributed significantly to

Beginning of air
pollution control

Supporting
details
omitted

OMIT IN A
SUMMARY

Explanation
of smog
omitted

Historical
data
omitted

Explanation of
reason for
debate omitted

Temporary
measures
omitted

Recap of central
debate omitted

cleaner air, as did the change from coal to diesel oil for railroads.

By the 1950's the growth and shifting patterns of population combined with pollution research to add a new dimension to the subject of air quality. Los Angeles, with comparatively little heavy industry, saw a combination of smoke and fog, popularly called *smog,* develop when a weather condition known as an "inversion" existed. An upper layer of cold air prevented the dirty warm air from rising and dissipating. *The major source of such pollution was identified as the automobile.*

By 1970 the Congress had provided a program leading to national control of automobile emissions and support for State efforts to improve air quality.

The 1970 amendments to the *Clean Air Act* established the basic form of the present program. This Act, as amended in 1977, *provides for the establishment of national ambient (surrounding) air quality standards.*

The objective of achieving clean air enjoys generally universal support. The controversy centers on the tradeoff between costs and level of air purity necessary to ensure general health safety.

The thrust of the Clean Air Act is that economic considerations must not be predominant. For some time there has been debate over whether the jobs and tax base of an area should be weighed against having strict air quality standards. Complicating the problem of setting Federal policy for often localized situations are scientific factors described in generally unfamiliar technical language.

Committees in both the House and Senate are currently reviewing the entire Clean Air Act. *Attention has centered on two major basic industries* which are considered to be having financial difficulties — *steel* (a "stationary" source of pollution), and *automotive* (a "mobile" source).

In July 1981 a bill was enacted by the Congress extending on a case-by-case basis the steel industry's compliance requirements under the Clean Air Act. Mobile sources of emissions, notably automotive, later became the focus of testimony in the committee hearings.

The discussion of emission standards, which are measured in "grams per mile" of pollutants, involves some technical terminology. The basic issue, however, centers on the cost/benefit relationship of the existing standards. Those supporting legislation to ease the existing emission standards believe that the added costs outweigh the gains achieved in the

INCLUDE IN A
SUMMARY

New dimension
to air quality

Key word

Major source of
new pollution

Key term

Purpose of Clean
Air Act

Center of
controversy

Focus of Clean
Air Act

Attention on
steel and
automotive
industries

additional improvement of air quality, which they
maintain is slight. Opponents take the position that
relaxing emission standards would mean that some
areas could not meet the good air quality standards.

Automobiles and trucks not only constitute a
major pollution source, but *the underlying issue of*
economics touches most aspects of the controversy
over the Clean Air Act. *The financial condition of
the U.S. auto industry,* however, *is a special element*
in the debate over the control of mobile pollution
sources in the current Congress.

WAYS TO SHORTEN THE ORIGINAL

A summary is a shorter, briefer version of an original work. It may be a
condensation or it may be an abridgment of the main points in the original work.
The summary omits introductory matter, details, examples, and illustrations —
everything except the major ideas and facts.

Summary by Condensation

A summary that results from the condensation of the original material presents
the main content (a digest) of the original, rephrased. That is, the writer or
speaker has carefully read the original and then restated the details in his or her
own words.

The summary may sometimes include direct quotations from the original
work. The quoted material may be a phrase, a sentence, a paragraph, or perhaps
an even longer section. Quoted material should be put in quotation marks.
Sometimes page or chapter numbers for quotations are helpful for reference.
Footnotes are unnecessary, since only one source is involved and that source is
identified.

Below is a paragraph from *Machine Shop: Operations and Setups* (Chicago:
American Technical Society, 1977), page 1. Following the original paragraph is
a paragraph summarized through condensation.

ORIGINAL PARAGRAPH

How much a nation produces determines how well its people live. First, we must
produce enough food, clothing, and shelter. Only then can we produce the other
benefits of civilization. A society's standard of living is in direct proportion to the
amount it produces. People know that their own interests are served best when
their society produces the greatest good for the greatest number. The greatest
good for the greatest number means many things, but first and foremost it means
the greatest amount of goods or material things for the greatest number of people.
To produce these goods has required a steady increase in the quality of tools.

PARAGRAPH SUMMARIZED BY CONDENSATION

Production determines standards of living. After basic needs are met, other benefits
occur through producing the most goods for the most people. Such production has
resulted from better tools.

Summary by Abridgment

A summary produced by abridgment retains the essential content of a work in the original wording. Supporting details and supplementary matter are omitted.

Below is a paragraph from *Machine Shop: Operations and Setups;* lines mark out the supporting matter, leaving the essential content of the paragraph.

ORIGINAL PARAGRAPH WITH SUPPORTING MATTER MARKED OUT

Man's progress has been governed by the tools he has developed. . . . In ~~the~~ earliest times, man was limited by the movements his hands and arms were capable of making. ~~Craftsmen worked metal with muscular effort and handtools.~~ Today, ~~metal workers use~~ powered machine tools ~~to~~ shape and form ~~the~~ myriad parts ~~which, when assembled, comprise our modern world of machinery. Piece parts are assembled~~ into every conceivable product to satisfy our needs and wants. These products or ~~piece parts all have certain standard forms and shapes which may be classified as solid concentric, flats and flanges, cups or cones, nonconcentric, and spiral repetitive. All of these forms and shapes~~ require shape refinement to close tolerance and finishes by basic machine tools.

PARAGRAPH SUMMARIZED BY ABRIDGMENT

Man's progress has been governed by the tools he has developed. In earliest times, man was limited by the movements his hands and arms were capable of making. Today, powered machine tools shape and form myriad parts into every conceivable product to satisfy our needs and wants. These products require shape refinement to close tolerance and finishes by basic machine tools.

FORMS OF SUMMARIES

Depending on the writer's primary purpose, the summary can take various forms. It may be:

- A descriptive summary
- An informative summary
- An evaluative summary

Descriptive Summary

A summary may describe; it may state what a work is about in a very general way. The descriptive summary simply indicates the main topics that are discussed. It is usually very brief, sometimes only one or two sentences in length.

Descriptive summaries frequently occur in the headings to chapters in books, in the headings to magazine articles, on the table of contents pages in magazines, in publicity for new books and pamphlets, and in annotated bibliographies.

The following excerpt from a table of contents from *Data Management* illustrates a common use of the descriptive summary:[*]

14 **Data Base Machines — what and why** *Terry Bridges, CDP, describes the role this new equipment is playing in DBMS*

[*] Used by permission of *Data Management* (November 1982).

18 **Cutting corners in the IBM second market** *A question and answer article telling how companies are saving time and money by buying used hardware*

20 **Federal regulatory reform: Its day has finally arrived** *Joseph L. Nellis takes a look at recent rumblings in Washington dealing with regulation and control over business*

22 **How a properly structured Career Plan can attract and keep the real pros** *Mark H. Johnson tells how one large organization successfully planned and implemented a program to retain its highly valued employees*

24 **A manager's guide to making quality control circles work** *Looking for a way to increase productivity and boost morale of employees? According to Woodruff Imbermann, PhD, QCCs are the answer*

This excerpt from the table of contents page of *FDA Consumer* (December 1982–January 1983) illustrates fuller descriptive summaries.

A Physician's Spyglass for Looking Inward   4
Doctors can inspect many parts of the body's interior these days, and can identify and correct many irregularities without X-ray or incision. It's made possible by fiber optics—bundles of fine, flexible glass strands that are inserted into various body openings and transmit views of trouble spots to the doctor.

Handmade Antibodies That Go Forth and Multiply   7
Monoclonal antibodies are the offspring that result from fusing an antibody-producing white blood cell with a tumor cell. This hybrid, called a hybridoma, is painstakingly created in the laboratory. The hybrid in turn produces endless supplies of antibodies that are proving useful in diagnosis and research and may be used to treat diseases.

Of Hangovers and Love Potions   10
There's no product yet to prevent a hangover, though some will help ease the symptoms, according to an FDA advisory panel. Nor were any over-the-counter products found that would work as aphrodisiacs, or any safe or effective remedy for treating an enlarged prostate. Products for ingrown toenails, thumb sucking and upset stomach were among other areas covered in OTC panel reports.

Another use of the descriptive summary is the *descriptive abstract*. An abstract is a brief presentation of the essential contents of a document. The descriptive abstract frequently serves as an indicator of the usefulness of the original material.

Descriptive abstracts are very important to technicians who want to keep abreast of what is going on in their field. So invaluable are these descriptive abstracts in determining whether or not some particular article is pertinent to a specific interest that entire books and periodicals—for instance, *Chemical Abstracts, Nuclear Science Abstracts*, and *Biological Abstracts*—are devoted to descriptive abstracts of what is being written in particular fields. Persons interested in the field can read the abstracts to determine whether they want or need to obtain and read copies of the original works.

Other professional journals include within each issue a section for abstracts. These may be abstracts of papers presented at meetings of professional groups or they may be of articles appearing in related literature. Again, the abstract serves as an indicator of usefulness, directing persons to articles of concern and interest.

The first example below is a descriptive abstract of a report prepared for the U.S. Department of Agriculture, Economic Research Service.

> "The Electronic Scanner Checkout and Item Price Removal." Charlene C. Price and Charles Handy. (202) 447-6363

> Electronic scanner checkout is here to stay. This report focuses on the benefits of scanning, its effect on item pricing, the pros and cons of item price removal, and state legislation affecting price marking. The conclusion reached is that the question to be answered is how should item price information be provided.

The following sample abstract is from *Fire Technology.*°

> **KEY WORDS:** abrasion resistance, burn injury, clothing, fabrics, fire fighting, heat protection, insulation, physical properties, tensile strength, turnout coats.

> **ABSTRACT:** Several fabrics commonly used in the outer shells of structural fire fighters' turnout coats were subject to a variety of laboratory tests. These included breaking and tearing strength tests as well as several kinds of abrasion tests. The fabrics were also subjected to radiant heat ($8.4 kJ/m^2s = 2.0 kcal/m^2s$) and flames ($84 kJ/m^2s$), and their resistance to heat deterioration and insulative characteristics were measured. The flame exposure tests were also conducted on assemblies of outer shell fabric, vapor barrier and innerliner. It should be emphasized that the results were obtained on one piece of each material and that they cannot be generally applied to all fabrics of the same or similar description.

> **REFERENCE:** "Performance Evaluation of Fabrics Used in Fire Fighters' Turnout Coats," J. F. Krasny, R. W. Singleton, and J. Pettengill, *Fire Technology*, Vol. 18, No. 4 (November 1982), pp. 309–318.

The descriptive summary or descriptive abstract is an essential part of a report. It brings together in one section the major points discussed in the report. (For a detailed discussion of the summary or abstract in reports, see Chapter 8, Reports, pages 310 and 311. See also the abstract included with a library research report on page 415.)

The summary that follows appeared in a student-written report "Police Work as an Occupation."

> The continued need for police officers is obvious. The opportunities are not overwhelming, but they can be found by the qualified applicant. It is an occupation with a long history and tradition and is continuously being upgraded. It provides a secure job even though the salaries are not as high as those in other occupations requiring similar qualifications.

In the classroom, instructors frequently mention standard resource materials in particular fields and suggest that students become familiar with them. The student who examines the material and jots down several facts about the kind and manner of presentation of information is writing an annotation, a kind of descriptive summary, as in the following:

> *The McGraw-Hill Encyclopedia of Science and Technology,* 1982 edition, from McGraw-Hill, 15 volumes, including an index. Updated by yearbooks. Specialized encyclopedia written for knowledgeable persons with a high reading level. Includes drawings, diagrams, and schematics. Long, detailed, highly technical articles.

Descriptive summaries are often used to publicize books, pamphlets, brochures, catalogs, and the like, as in this excerpt from the Bookshelf column in the Spring 1982 *Water Spectrum* (published by the U.S. Corps of Engineers):

> **The Bight of the Big Apple,** by Donald F. Squires, traces the history of the New York bight from wilderness to thriving commerce center to current disuse. The author discusses how the bight — the big stretch of ocean between New Jersey and Long Island — influenced the development of metropolitan New York City and offers some projections for its future. The illustrated 84-page paperback is available for $3.00 from New York Sea Grant Institute, State University of New York and Cornell University, 411 State St., Albany, NY 12246.

Informative Summary

The primary purpose of an informative summary is to inform; that is, it is designed to present the principal facts and conclusions given in the original work. When most people use the word *summary,* they are probably referring to the informative summary. No personal feelings or thoughts are injected; the main points of the material are presented objectively. Unlike the descriptive summary that tells *about* the work in only a few sentences, the informative summary tells what is *in* the work in a paragraph to several pages, depending on the length of the original.

Given below are two examples of the informative summary. The first is from *Public Health Reports* (September–October 1982), a publication that includes with each report a synopsis (informative summary).

> VERBRUGGE, LOIS M. (University of Michigan): *Sex differentials in health. Public Health Reports, Vol. 97, September–October 1982, pp. 417–437.*
>
> Health status and health behavior of males and females in the United States are compared; the data employed in the analysis are from community studies and the surveys of the National Center for Health Statistics. Females generally show a higher incidence of acute conditions, higher prevalence of minor chronic conditions, more short-term restricted activity, and more use of health services (especially outpatient services) and medicines. By contrast, males have higher prevalence rates for life-threatening chronic conditions, higher incidence of injuries, more long-term disability, and after about age 50, higher rates of hospitalization. These sex differences appear at all ages, except for early childhood when boys have a worse health profile than girls.
>
> The following interpretations are consistent with the data; they are hypotheses rather than demonstrated facts. Women are more frequently ill than men, but with relatively mild problems. By contrast, men feel ill less often, but their illnesses and injuries are more serious. These morbidity differences help to explain sex differentials in health behavior; frequent symptoms lead to more restricted activity, physi-

cian and dentist visits, and drug use for women; severe symptoms lead to more permanent limitations and hospitalization for men.

But attitudes about symptoms, medical care, drugs, and self-care are also extremely important. Males may be socialized to ignore physical discomforts; thus, they are unaware of symptoms that females feel keenly. Also, men may be less willing and able to seek medical care for perceived symptoms. When diagnosis and treatment are finally obtained, men's conditions are probably more advanced and less amenable to control. Finally, men may be less willing and able to restrict their activities when ill or injured.

Four important factors that underlie sex differentials in health are discussed: inherited risks of illness, acquired risks of illness and injury, illness and prevention orientations, and health reporting behavior.

Statistics show that women ultimately have lower mortality rates than men — despite women's more frequent morbidity and possibly because of more care for their illnesses and injuries. The apparent contradiction between sex differences in morbidity and mortality (females are sicker but males die sooner) is explored.

The following student-written summary (with filled-in Plan Sheet) is informative. The length of the original article was approximately 1500 words; the length of the summary is approximately 300 words.

Analysis of Situation Requiring Summary

What type of summary is this to be?
informative

For whom is the summary intended?
students in communications class

How will the summary be used?
for conveying main points of original article

In what format will the summary be given?
a written explanation

Identification of Work (Bibliographical Information) as Applicable

Title:
"Videotex: Ushering in the Electronic Household"

Author:
John Tydeman

Date:
February, 1982

Type of material (magazine article, book, report, etc.):
magazine article

Title of publication:
The Futurist

City of publication and publishing company:
omit

Volume number:
omit

Page numbers:

Other:

Key Facts and Ideas in the Work

Change through electronics technology by home information services
Two systems: teletext (a one-way flow of information)
               videotex (a two-way flow of information)
Uses of videotex: news, advertising/shopping, ordering
Future possibilities: added services to existing TV coverage, entertainment
  and game potential, retrieval of information by libraries, telephone
  directories, message sending
Most popular use of teletext: information retrieval
Most popular use of videotex: probably information retrieval,
  computer-based gaming, and transactions
Projected users: 30-40% of all households by 2000
Effects on society: living facilities, places of employment, home shopping,
  electronically controlled schooling, new careers in information
  management
Relatively slow development because of no infrastructure
Move toward electronic household to continue

AN INFORMATIVE SUMMARY OF "VIDEOTEX: USHERING IN THE
ELECTRONIC HOUSEHOLD"

John Tydeman. "Videotex: Ushering in the Electronic Household." The Futurist,
February 1982, pp. 54–61.

Electronics technology has brought about tremendous change in the world. One
aspect of this electronic technology change is in the home information service,
teletext and videotex, "systems that primarily disseminate verbal and pictorial
information by wholly electronic means, for visual display or printing under the
control of the user."

Teletext is a one-way flow of information that utilizes television signals. With the
necessary equipment, a keypad, an individual can choose information to appear on
the TV screen. In contrast, videotex is a two-way flow of information through such
existing equipment as telephone networks, some cable TV systems, or "a one-way
cable into the home with a normal telephone link out."

Home Applications

Videotex is in the trial state in the United States. It offers such things as news,
weather, and sports information from newspapers and wire services. The systems
also provide advertising and shopping information; the user of some systems can
not only see the advertised products but can also order the products through the
system.

Possible future uses of videotex systems include adding services to video programs covering such events as elections or sports, or the system could provide
services for the hearing impaired or multilingual television audience.

In addition to providing "pages" of information to the home user, "both teletext
and videotex have entertainment and game potential as well." Also retrieval of
information is made possible through electronic retrieval services offered by specialized libraries and information banks. Telephone directories could be delivered
electronically with a more frequent update on yellow pages than the current annual
update. Another possible use is message sending, such as community bulletin board
information access; health, gardening, and weather tips; and financial information.

The Household Market

Of the potential uses for teletext, market surveys indicate it would probably be
used for information retrieval. Videotex systems are in such a state of evolution, it is
difficult to identify the most popular applications; more than likely "information
retrieval, computer-based gaming, and transactions (including home-based shopping) will be the driving applications." The many potential uses may be classified
into five areas of application: information retrieval, transaction, messaging, com-
puting, and telemonitoring.

Projected users of these systems include 30–40% of all households by 2000. The
systems' use will develop because bankers, retailers, manufacturers, wholesalers are
realizing that these systems can offer their services more economically than can
conventional ways.

<u>Where to Next?</u>

The systems today are in very early stages. Those of the future will little resemble current systems. As they evolve, the systems will also bring about many changes in society. These include:

- Living facilities (home, apartment) will become the place of employment, changing the structure and the location of these facilities.
- Shopping from the home; consumers' orders will result in "production on demand," thus controlling manufacturing processes.
- Schooling will be influenced, if not controlled, electronically.
- The need for information management will create new careers.

<u>Videotex: Ready or Not?</u>

Compared to the speed of development of radio and television, videotex perhaps more closely resembles the development of radio. "There is no infrastructure in place." Further, the product(s) of videotex is not clearly defined. "Is it information retrieval, is it transactions, is it messaging, or is it all of these things?" The one thing that can be stated with certainty is "the move toward the electronic household is irrevocable."

Evaluative Summary

A summary may evaluate; it may be the primary purpose of the summary to analyze the accuracy, completeness, usefulness, appeal, and readability of a piece of writing. In the evaluative summary you include your own comments and reactions, your thoughts and feelings regarding the material. The evaluative summary emphasizes assessment of the original material.

The evaluative summary should contain sufficient information to show that you thoroughly understand the work being evaluated. Include specific main points from the original and make specific references to the original work.

In the following student-written evaluative summary, evaluative comments are underlined. Read the summary, skipping the underlined comments; then read the entire summary. The inclusion of the evaluative comments makes the summary an evaluative rather than an informative summary.

EVALUATIVE SUMMARY: "CLEAR ONLY IF KNOWN"

The <u>well-written, clearly illustrated</u> article "Clear Only If Known," by Edgar Dale*, answers the question, "Why do people give directions poorly and sometimes follow excellent directions inadequately?"

In answering the first half of the question, "Why do people give directions poorly?" Dale states six specific reasons.

* Edgar Dale, "Clear Only If Known," reprinted in Nell Ann Pickett and Ann Laster, *Technical English*, 4th ed. (New York: Harper & Row, 1984), pp. 524–526.

1. People do not always understand the complexity of the directions they attempt to give.
2. People give overly complex directions that include unnecessary elements.
3. People overestimate the experience of the person asking directions.
4. People make explanations more technical than necessary.
5. People are unwilling to say, "I don't know."
6. People use the wrong medium for giving directions.

Each reason is easily identified because Dale uses words like "First of all," "Another frequent reason," and "Another difficulty in communicating directions" as introductory phrases. Further, each reason is explained in detail, as Dale gives at least one excellent illustration for each reason.

The last half of the article briefly answers the second part of the question, "Why do people sometimes follow excellent directions inadequately?" Dale gives two reasons:

1. People don't understand directions but think they do.
2. People often are in too big a hurry when they ask for directions.

In closing, Dale emphasizes the need for clear communication, saying that "clarity in the presentation of ideas is a necessity."

Anyone reading this article will have a clear understanding of why the communication process often breaks down.

The book review is a popular form of evaluative summary. (See also Reading Report, pages 313–321.) The following example was written by John O. Coleman, mathematical statistician, Bureau of Labor Statistics, and appeared in *Labor Review*, February 1983. Compare the length of the original work, 128 pages, to the length of the evaluative summary, some 400 words. Clearly the purpose of this review is to evaluate the usefulness of the book as well as to tell what it contains.

> *Managing Conflict—A Complete Process-Centered Handbook.* By Roy W. Pneuman and Margaret E. Bruehl. Englewood Cliffs, N.J., Prentice-Hall, Inc. Publishers, 1982. 128 pp. $6.95.

Whether you are a rank novice or seasoned professional, you are likely to experience some anxiety when confronted with a situation involving conflict. The main reason for this is probably the time-honored perception of conflict situations, that is, as strictly win or lose propositions. But what if this isn't necessarily true? What if it's possible to have a conflict situation in which nobody loses? If this idea is new to you or you are tired of reacting to conflict situations by hiding, fighting, submitting, or running away, a careful reading of Roy W. Pneuman's and Margaret E. Bruehl's "Managing Conflict" is likely to reward your effort. Beginning with the first paragraph, it's as though the authors have taken a seat beside you and are urging, probing, and guiding your thought processes.

Unlike most publications on management, collective bargaining, and tactics, this book is geared toward problem-solving rather than gamesmanship. Although the authors start with the premise that conflict is inevitable, they argue that it can and should be searched out, respected, encouraged, and managed. Toward that end, they have developed a general model for dealing with conflict situations and have provided step-by-step instructions to follow as we work through some managerial, personal, or other conflict situation. Of special help are the conflict source checklist, critical (that is, strategic) issues analysis form, viable choices evaluation form, capsule outline of the entire process, and an abundance of anecdotes and illustrations (graphic and narrative) sprinkled throughout the text.

The book fails to provide information on what to do when the preventive measures fail. However, that deficiency is somewhat compensated for by the fact that the authors' illustrations and anecdotes portray the type of real-life situations to which we can relate.

For example, the point is made that, as individuals, a significant shortcoming is our tendency to assume that the way we see things is the way they are and, therefore, others see (or should see) them the same way. To illustrate the point, they relate the following story: A high relationship-oriented, low task-oriented young minister accepted a position on the staff of a large church. During the first year, she found much satisfaction in developing relationships among the people with whom she worked, but neglected a number of her important tasks and goals. The senior minister, who related positively to the young minister, was both relationship-oriented and task-oriented. So, he kindly called her to accountability for her neglected tasks. At her annual evaluation, she was shocked when the church council was highly critical of her performance. She claimed that throughout the year, no one had told her they were dissatisfied. She later recognized that she had "projected" her own views onto the senior minister and, therefore, when he called her to accountability, she experienced only his kindness and failed to notice the call to be responsive to assigned goals and tasks.

The authors place strong emphasis on the communication process and the role it plays in the creation and escalation of conflict. To assist the reader in understanding this interaction, they discuss and illustrate problems created by the message sender, the media by which the message is transmitted, and the receiver of the message. In this regard, the following story is both entertaining and instructive. Alice, a clinical psychologist, when trying to help a counselee understand the connection between a current behavior and the words used to describe it, would often ask, "Where are you?" This is a jargon they understood and found helpful. One evening at home, her 10-year-old son, Brian, began a long, rambling, and unclear, but highly emotional tale. Finally, Alice asked, "Brian, where are you?" Brian's quick, but quizzical, reply was, "Mom, I'm right here in the kitchen."

As previously noted, this book is problem-solving oriented. Like all treatises concerned with problem-solving methodologies and techniques, it uses as its framework the following basic steps: (1) recognizing, that is, identifying the problem; (2) understanding and classifying the problem; (3) analyzing and evaluating the problem; (4) deciding whether to attempt to solve the problem; (5) devising a plan for solving the problem; (6) carrying out the plan, and (7) checking the results. Thus, it provides a model that, with some relatively minor modifications, should prove useful in many problem situations, whether or not they involve conflict as traditionally perceived.

ACCURACY OF FACT AND EMPHASIS

A summary must agree with the original material in two ways: in the presentation of factual information and in the emphasis given the information.

The misrepresentation of factual information may occur through careless error, as in omitting a digit or a decimal point in a number. Through the process of cutting out words, misleading information may be given. Consider this sentence: "Wood posts can be expected to last at least 30 years *if they have been pressure treated and handled properly.*" The last half of the sentence is essential; omission of the *if* qualification changes the meaning of the entire sentence. The sentence might be condensed as follows: "Pressure-treated and properly handled wood posts last at least 30 years."

Misrepresenting the emphasis placed on information in the original material may occur because of overemphasizing or underemphasizing information. If a one-page summary of a ten-page report on a new weed killer stresses the possible danger to animals when this was only a minor point in the original report, the summary has misrepresented the emphasis. A summary must agree in emphasis with the original; the intended audience of the summary should get the same impression that the intended audience of the original should get.

DOCUMENTATION

Material being summarized should be cited, that is, be completely identified. Such an identification is referred to as documentation. Documentation is complete bibliographical information on the original material. In addition to author and title, it includes facts about publication (place, publisher, and date). See pages 410–411 for examples of bibliographical forms. Depending on the purpose of the summary, documentation may also include such information as price, number of pages, and availability in paper or cloth binding. See pages 406–411 for a discussion of documentation.

Placement of Bibliography

The placement of bibliographical information may vary. Although the bibliographical information may be given within the summary, it appears more often as a formal bibliographical entry at the beginning (or the end) of the summary.

A summary that includes the bibliographical information within its content might begin: "In 'The Gene Idea,' an article by Julie Ann Miller (*Science News*, March 13, 1982, pages 180–182), the author. . . ." For examples of bibliography given as a separate entry at the beginning or the end of a summary, see pages 191, 192, 196, 197, and 198.

Also, the arrangement of information and the punctuation in an entry may vary, although the information itself does not vary.

GENERAL PRINCIPLES IN GIVING A SUMMARY

1. *The emphasis of a summary is determined by the purpose and the intended audience.* The primary purpose may be to describe, to inform, or to evaluate.
2. *Summarizing requires a thorough understanding of the material.* Scanning, reading carefully, and underlining or taking notes are important in comprehending the material and thus in distinguishing which information to include in the summary and which to omit.

3. *A descriptive summary states what the material is about in a very general way.* Frequently only a few sentences are required to indicate the major concern of the material.

4. *An informative summary states objectively what is in the material.* The principal facts and conclusions given in the original are presented in a paragraph to several pages, depending on the length of the original.

5. *An evaluative summary emphasizes assessment of the material.* The accuracy, completeness, and usefulness of the information are judged. Include your own reactions, thoughts, and feelings along with a report of the main facts and ideas in the original.

6. *A summary is accurate in fact and in emphasis.* Unintentional distortion of the original may occur through careless error, through omitting essential information, or through unequal treatment of ideas presented as equally significant in the original.

7. *The material being summarized should be identified.* The identification may be given as a formal bibliographical entry at the beginning (or end) of the summary, or within the summary.

PROCEDURE FOR GIVING A SUMMARY

1. Decide whether the primary purpose of the summary is to describe what the work is about; to inform by presenting the principal facts and conclusions given in the original work; or to evaluate the accuracy, completeness, and usefulness of the work.

2. Look over the work. Note the opening and closing paragraphs, the major concern of the work, the organization, and the method of presentation.

3. Read the work very carefully. Underline or jot down on a separate sheet of paper (particularly if the work does not belong to you) the key ideas. Think through the relationship of these key ideas; be sure that you understand what the writer is trying to communicate.

4. Identify the original material specifically by author, work, and date. This information may be given within the summary or as a formal bibliographical entry at the beginning or end of the summary. (See pages 410–411 for bibliographical forms.)

5. Write a draft of the summary, giving the author's main ideas in the order presented.

6. Reread the original work; then check the summary for accuracy of fact and emphasis, and for completeness.

APPLICATION 1   GIVING A SUMMARY

Bring to class two *descriptive* summaries, as explained on pages 189–192, written by others. State the specific sources.

APPLICATION 2   GIVING A SUMMARY

Write a two-to-three sentence *descriptive* summary of "Controversy Over the Clean Air Act" on pages 186–188.

APPLICATION 3   GIVING A SUMMARY

Write a *descriptive* summary of any five works (specialized encyclopedias, dictionaries, etc.) related to your major field of study. Before you can write the summary, you need to become familiar with each book. Examine its physical characteristics (size, soft or hard binding, one volume or several), organization (table of contents, index, illustrations), content (chapter or entry headings, kind and extent of information, intended reader), and publishing information (publisher, year of publication, method of updating information).

APPLICATION 4   GIVING A SUMMARY

In the library find two books, two periodicals, and two other sources (pamphlets, reports, bulletins, audiovisual materials, etc.) that relate to your technical field. Write a *descriptive* summary of each.

APPLICATION 5   GIVING A SUMMARY

Give orally the descriptive summaries you wrote in Application 2, 3, or 4 above. Ask your classmates to evaluate your speech by making an Evaluation of Oral Presentations sheet like the one on page 459 and filling it in.

APPLICATION 6   GIVING A SUMMARY

Write two *descriptive* summaries of a book of your selection. First, write a descriptive summary for a librarian who will order the book; second, write a descriptive summary for a student who will use the book for reference.

APPLICATION 7   GIVING A SUMMARY

Write an *informative* summary of the following excerpt from the *Occupational Outlook Handbook*.

a. Make a Plan Sheet like the one on pages 208 – 209, and fill it in.
b. Write a preliminary draft.
c. Revise.
d. Write the final draft.

Programmers

(D.O.T. 020.162-014,   167-018,   167-022,
187-010,   187-014; and 219.367-026)

Nature of the Work

Computers can process vast quantities of information rapidly and accurately, but only if they are given step-by-step instructions to follow. Because the machines cannot think for themselves, computer programmers must write detailed instructions called programs that list in a logical order the steps the machine must follow to organize data, solve a problem, or do some other task.

Programmers usually work from descriptions prepared by systems analysts who have carefully studied the task that the computer system is going to perform — perhaps organizing data collected in a survey or estimating the stress on portions of a building during a hurricane. These descriptions contain a detailed list of the steps the computer must follow, such as retrieving data stored in another computer, organizing it in a certain way, and performing the necessary calculations. (A more detailed description of the work of systems analysts is contained elsewhere in the *Handbook*.) An applications programmer then writes the specific program for the problem, by breaking down each step into a series of coded instructions using one of the languages developed especially for computers.

Some organizations, particularly smaller ones, do not employ systems analysts. Instead, workers called programmer-analysts are responsible for both systems analysis and programming.

Programs vary with the type of problem to be solved. For example, the mathematical calculations involved in payroll accounting procedures are different from those required to determine the flight path of a space probe. A business applications programmer developing instructions for billing customers would first take the company records the computer would need and then specify a solution by showing the steps the computer must follow to obtain old balances, add new charges, calculate finance charges, and deduct payments before determining a customer's bill. The programmer then codes the actual instructions the computer will follow in a high-level programming language, such as COBOL.

Next, the programmer tests the operation of the program to be sure the instructions are correct and will produce the desired information. The programmer tries a sample of the data with the program and reviews the results to see if any errors were made. If errors did occur, the program must be changed and rechecked until it produces the correct results. This is called "debugging" the program.

Finally, an instruction sheet is prepared for the computer operator who will run the program. (The work of computer operators is described in the statement on computer operating personnel.)

Although sample programs can be written in a few hours, programs that use complex mathematical formulas or many data files may require more than a year of work. In some cases, several programmers may work together in teams under a senior programmer's supervision.

Applications programmers are usually business oriented, engineering oriented, or science oriented. A different type of specialist, the systems programmer, maintains the general instructions (called software) that control the operation of the entire computer system. These workers make changes in the sets of instructions that determine the allocation of the computer's resources among the various jobs it has been given. Because of their knowledge of operating systems, systems programmers often help applications programmers determine the source of problems that may occur with their programs.

Working Conditions

Programmers work about 40 hours a week, but their hours are not always from 9 to 5. Once or twice a week programmers may report early or work late to use the computer when it is available; occasionally, they work on weekends. When a new program is being tested, programmers may get calls from computer operators asking for advice at all hours of the day or night.

Training, Other Qualifications, and Advancement

There are no universal training requirements for programmers because employers' needs vary. Most programmers are college graduates; others have taken special courses in computer programming to supplement their experience in fields such as accounting or inventory control.

Employers using computers for scientific or engineering applications prefer college graduates who have degrees in computer or information science, mathematics, engineering, or the physical sciences. Graduate degrees are required for some jobs. Very few scientific organizations are interested in applicants who have no college training.

Although some employers who use computers for business applications do not require college degrees, they prefer applicants who have had college courses in data processing or who are experienced in computer operation or payroll accounting but who have no college training. However, they need additional data processing courses to become fully qualified programmers. Although it may be preferred, prior work experience is not essential for a job as a programmer; in fact, about half of all entrants to the occupation have little or no work experience.

Computer programming is taught at public and private vocational schools, community and junior colleges, and universities. Instruction ranges from introductory home study courses to advanced courses at the graduate level. High schools in many parts of the country also offer courses in computer programming.

An indication of experience and professional competence at the senior programmer level is the Certificate in Computer Programming (CCP). This designation is conferred by the Institute for Certification of Computer Professionals upon candidates who have passed a basic five-part examination. In addition, individuals may take another section of the exam in order to specialize in business, science, or systems applications.

In hiring programmers, employers look for people who can think logically and are capable of exacting analytical work. The job calls for patience, persistence, and the ability to work with extreme accuracy even under pressure. Ingenuity and imagination are particularly important when programmers must find new ways to solve a problem.

Beginning applications programmers usually spend their first weeks on the job attending training classes. After this initial instruction, they work on simple assignments while completing further specialized training programs. Programmers generally must spend at least several months working under close supervision before they can handle aspects of their job. Because of rapidly changing technology, programmers must continue their training by taking courses offered by their employer and software vendors. For skilled workers, the prospects for advancement are good. In large organizations, they may be promoted to lead programmers and be given supervisory responsibilities. Some applications programmers may become systems programmers. Both applications programmers and systems programmers often become systems analysts or are promoted to managerial positions.

Job Outlook

Employment of programmers is expected to grow faster than the average for all occupations through the 1980's as computer usage expands, particularly in firms providing accounting, business management, and computer programming services, and in organizations involved in research and development. In addition to jobs resulting from increased demand for programmers, many openings will arise each year from the need to replace workers who leave the occupation. Because many programmers are relatively young, few openings will result from retirements or deaths. However, many vacancies will be created as experienced workers transfer into jobs as systems analysts or managers.

The demand for applications programmers will increase as many more processes once done by hand are automated, but employment is not expected to grow as rapidly as in the past. Improved software, such as utility programs that can be used by other than data processing personnel, will simplify or eliminate some programming tasks. More systems programmers will be needed to develop and maintain the complex operating programs made necessary by higher level computer languages, as well as to link or coordinate the output of different computer systems.

Job prospects should be excellent for college graduates who have had computer-related courses, particularly for those with a major in computer science or a related field. The number of persons with computer skills is not expected to keep pace with rising demand. Graduates of 2-year programs in data processing technologies also should have good prospects, primarily in business applications.

Earnings

Average weekly earnings of programmer trainees in private industry ranged from $250 to $330 in 1980, according to surveys conducted in urban areas by the Bureau of Labor Statistics and firms engaged in research on data processing occupations. In general, programmers earn about twice as much as the average earnings of all nonsupervisory workers in private industry, except farming. Systems programmers generally earn more than applications programmers, and lead programmers earn more than either systems or applications programmers. For example, experienced systems programmers averaged about $470 a week compared to $400 for applications programmers. Average weekly salaries for lead systems programmers were $505, compared to $430 for lead applications programmers. In the Federal civil service, the entrance salary for programmers with a college degree was about $200 a week in early 1981.

Programmers working in the North and West earned somewhat more than those working in the South. Those working for data processing services and public utilities had higher earnings than programmers employed in banks, advertising, or educational institutions.

Related Occupations

Other workers in mathematics, business, and science who solve detailed problems include systems analysts, mathematicians, statisticians, engineers, financial analysts, actuaries, mathematical technicians, and operations research analysts.

APPLICATION 8   GIVING A SUMMARY

Write an *informative* summary of this chapter in your textbook.

    a. Make a Plan Sheet like the one on pages 208–209, and fill it in.
    b. Write a preliminary draft.
    c. Revise.
    d. Write the final draft.

APPLICATION 9 GIVING A SUMMARY

Write an *informative* summary of a reading assignment in one of your other courses or of an article in a recent issue of a periodical relating to your major field.

    a. Make a Plan Sheet like the one on pages 208–209, and fill it in.
    b. Write a preliminary draft.
    c. Revise.
    d. Write the final draft.

APPLICATION 10 GIVING A SUMMARY

Give orally the informative summary you wrote in Application 7, 8, or 9 above. Ask your classmates to evaluate your speech by making an Evaluation of Oral Presentations sheet like the one on page 459 and filling it in.

APPLICATION 11 GIVING A SUMMARY

In a paragraph of approximately 75 words, write an *evaluative* summary of "Controversy Over the Clean Air Act" on pages 186–188.

    a. Make a Plan Sheet like the one on pages 210–211, and fill it in.
    b. Write a preliminary draft.
    c. Revise.
    d. Write the final draft.

APPLICATION 12 GIVING A SUMMARY

Write an *evaluative* summary of a reading assignment in one of your other courses, or of an article in a recent issue of a periodical relating to your major field.

    a. Make a Plan Sheet like the one on pages 210–211, and fill it in.
    b. Write a preliminary draft.
    c. Revise.
    d. Write the final draft.

APPLICATION 13 GIVING A SUMMARY

Give orally the evaluative summary you wrote in Application 11 or 12 above. Ask your classmates to evaluate your speech by making an Evaluation of Oral Presentations sheet like the one on page 459 and filling it in.

APPLICATION 14 GIVING A SUMMARY

Find and attach to your paper an example of a descriptive summary, of an informative summary, and of an evaluative summary. Write a one-page report on what is accomplished in the summaries. Be sure to include in your report specific identification on the source of each summary, the form of each summary, the purpose of each, and any other pertinent information.

APPLICATION 15 GIVING A SUMMARY

Select a piece of writing, such as a magazine article, pamphlet, or chapter in a book, relating to your major field. For the selection, write:

- A descriptive summary
- An informative summary
- An evaluative summary

a. Make a Plan Sheet like the one on pages 210–211, and fill it in.
b. Write the preliminary drafts.
c. Revise.
d. Write the final drafts.

PLAN SHEET
FOR GIVING AN INFORMATIVE SUMMARY

Analysis of Situation Requiring Summary

What type of summary is this to be?

For whom is the summary intended?

How will the summary be used?

In what format will the summary be given?

Identification of Work (Bibliographical Information), as Applicable

Title:

Author:

Date:

Type of material (magazine article, book, report, etc.):

Title of publication:

City of publication and publishing company:

Volume number:

Page numbers:

Other:

Key Facts and Ideas in the Work

PLAN SHEET
FOR GIVING AN EVALUATIVE SUMMARY

Analysis of Situation Requiring Summary

What type of summary is this to be?

For whom is the summary intended?

How will the summary be used?

In what format will the summary be given?

Identification of Work (Bibliographical Information), as Applicable

Title:

Author:

Date:

Type of material (magazine article, book, report, etc.):

Title of publication:

City of publication and publishing company:

Volume number:

Page numbers:

Other:

Key Facts and Ideas in the Work

My Evaluative Comments

CHAPTER 7

Memorandums and Letters: Sending Messages

OBJECTIVES   214
INTRODUCTION   214
MEMORANDUMS   214
    Heading   215
    Body   215
BUSINESS LETTERS   218
    The "You" Emphasis   218
    The Positive Approach   219
    Natural Wording   219
FORM IN LETTERS   220
    Format   220
      Paper   220
      Handwriting or Typewriting   220
      Appearance   220
      Layout Forms   220
    Parts of a Business Letter   221
      Regular Parts   221
      Special Parts   225
    The Envelope   227
      Regular Parts   227
      Special Parts   228
TYPES OF LETTERS   229
    Letter of Inquiry   229
    Order Letter   232
      Printed Order Forms   237
    Sales Letter   239
    Claim and Adjustment Letters   243
    Collection Letters   248
    Letter of Application   253
      Purpose of the Letter   253
      Background Information   253
      Request for an Interview   253
      Letter of Application — No Resumé   253
    Resumé (Data Sheet or Vita)   254
      Information in a Resumé   254
      Types of Resumés   255

Examples of Letters of Application   255
Examples of Resumés   263
Job Application Form   270
Application Follow-Up Letters   273
GENERAL PRINCIPLES IN WRITING MEMORANDUMS AND LETTERS   278
APPLICATIONS   278

OBJECTIVES

Upon completing this chapter, the student should be able to:

- List and define the two regular parts of a memorandum
- Set up a heading for a memorandum
- Write a memorandum
- Analyze the form and content of a letter
- Show and identify by label the three most often used layout forms
- Head a second page properly
- List, define, label, and write an example of the six regular parts of a letter
- List, define, label, and write an example of seven special parts of a letter
- List, define, label, and write an example of the two regular parts on the envelope
- Write a letter of inquiry or request
- Write an order letter
- Write a sales letter
- Write a claim letter and an adjustment letter
- Write a collection series
- Write a job application letter
- Write a resumé
- Fill out a job application form
- Write application follow-up letters

INTRODUCTION

Being able to write effective memorandums and letters, according to business people and industrialists, is one of the major writing skills that an employee needs. These employers say that the employee must be able to handle the aspects of work that involve correspondence, such as communicating with fellow employees, making inquiries about processes and equipment, requesting specifications, making purchases, answering complaints, and promoting products. Over half of all business is conducted in part or wholly by correspondence. Thus it is impossible to overemphasize the importance of effective business correspondence.

Too, memorandums and letters are business records; copies show to whom messages have been written and why. Since more than one message frequently is required in settling a matter, copies become a necessity for maintaining continuity in the correspondence. Even now you should begin to develop the habit of keeping a copy of every memorandum and letter you send.

Whether or not you get a job may be determined by your application materials (letter of application, resumé, application form). Employers, particularly personnel managers, are concerned that often a potentially good worker does not get the job desired because the application materials do not make a good impression.

MEMORANDUMS

Memorandums are communications typically between persons in the same company. The correspondents may be in the same building or in different branch offices of the company. Memorandums are used to convey or confirm information. They serve as written records for transmittal of documents, policy statements, instructions, meetings, and the like. Although the term *memorandum* formerly was associated with a communication of only a temporary nature, usage of the term has changed. Now a memorandum is regarded as a communication that makes needed information immediately available or that clarifies information.

The memorandum, unlike the business letter, has only two regular parts: the heading and the body. The formalities of an inside address, salutation, complimentary close, and signature usually are omitted. (Some companies, however, prefer the practice of including either a complimentary close with signature or simply the signature, as in the memorandum on page 217.) If there is no signature at the end of the memo, as illustrated in the memorandum on page 218, the memorandum is usually initialed in handwriting following the typed "From" name. This initialing (or signature at the end) indicates official verification of the sender. As in business letters, an identification line (see page 226) and a copy line (see pages 226–227) may be used, if appropriate.

See also Memorandum in Chapter 8, Reports, pages 308–309.

Heading

The heading in a memorandum is a concise listing of:

- *To* whom the message is sent
- *From* whom the message comes
- The *subject* of the message
- The *date*

For ease in reading, the guide words To, From, Subject, and Date usually appear on the memorandum. (These guide words are not standardized as to capitalization, order, or placement at the top of the page.) Most companies use a memorandum form, printed with the guide words and the name of the company. It is perfectly permissible, however, to make your own memorandum form by simply typing in the guide words, as illustrated in the memo on page 217.

Body

The body of the memorandum is the message. It is written in the same manner as any other business communication. The message should be clear, concise, complete, and courteous. If internal headings will make the memo easier to read, insert them (see Headings, pages 4–5 and 313).

In the following two examples of memorandums, note how the messages serve different purposes. The first memorandum, with a filled-in Plan Sheet, explains the reason for an industrial manufacturing error and sets forth a new procedure to eliminate the problem; the second memorandum explains a change in company policy concerning annual leave.

PLAN SHEET
FOR WRITING A MEMORANDUM

Heading

To:
Anna Shulermann, Quality Control Manager

From:
Henry J. McCord, Fabrication Superintendent

Subject:
Weld failure on pull rod

Date:
March 22, 1985

Body

The purpose of this memorandum is:
to explain why the pull rod failed on the Charlesworth Power & Light circuit breaker and to set forth a procedure to eliminate the problem

I need to include this information:
Cause of pull rod failure: inadequate weld penetration because of incorrect machine setting
New procedure: weld current and voltage to be recorded by shop operator on routing card
Routing card to be checked by Quality Control before the pull rod goes to next work station
Correct machine settings to be sent to Quality Control

Special Parts

This memorandum requires these special parts:
signature — Henry J. McCord

Memorandum with Typed-In Guide Words

TO: Anna Shulermann, Quality Control Manager

FROM: Henry J. McCord, Fabrication Superintendent

SUBJECT: Weld failure on pull rod

DATE: March 22, 1985

Manufacturing Engineering has determined that the pull rod
failure on the Charlesworth Power and Light circuit
breakers was due to inadequate weld penetration, caused by
incorrect machine setting.

To provide a check on future pull rod welds, Manufacturing
Engineering has recommended that the weld current and
voltage used on pull rod welds be recorded by the shop
operator on the shop routing card.

This card will be checked by the Quality Control inspector
before the pull rod goes to the next work station.

Correct machine settings established by Manufacturing
Engineering will be provided the Quality Control inspector.

Henry J. McCord

Memorandum on Printed Form

THE NATIONAL BANK OF AMERICA
IN JEFFERSON PARISH (LOUISIANA)

MEMORANDUM   DATE: _July 1, 1984_

FOR _All employees_____

FROM _Donald S. Milton, President_____   *Dsm*

Effective January 1, 1985, requests for annual leave of
three or more consecutive days must be presented in writing
to your immediate supervisor at least three weeks in
advance.

BUSINESS LETTERS

The basic principles of composition apply to letters as they do to any other form of writing. The writer should have the purpose of the letter and its intended reader clearly in mind and should carefully organize and write the sentences and paragraphs so that they say what the writer wants them to say.

Business letters are usually not very long; therefore, sentences and paragraphs tend to be short. Often the first and last paragraphs each contain only a single sentence and seldom more than two sentences. Other paragraphs may contain from two to five sentences. In letters that are longer than average, paragraphs are likely to be longer. The longer paragraph should stay on a single topic, and the sentences should be clearly related one to another.

Study the sample letters throughout this chapter, noting sentence and paragraph length and development.

One of the main differences between the business letter and other forms of writing discussed in previous chapters is that in the business letter there is a specific reader who is named and to whom the communication is directly addressed.

The "You" Emphasis

Since the business letter is directed to a named reader, it becomes more personal; courtesy becomes important. To achieve a personal, courteous tone, stress the "you."

Focus on qualities of the addressee and minimize references to "I," "me," "my," "we," and "us." For example,

> We were pleased to receive your order for ten microscopes. We have forwarded it to the warehouse for shipment.

can easily be rephrased to:

> Thank you for your order for ten microscopes. You should receive the shipment from our warehouse within two weeks.

The first sentence is writer centered; the rephrased sentence is reader centered.

The Positive Approach

The "you" emphasis helps the writer attain a positive approach. For example, the negative statement

> We regret that we cannot fill the order for ten microscopes by December 1. It is impossible to get the shipment out of our warehouse because of a rush of Christmas orders.

can be rephrased to:

> Your order for ten microscopes should reach you by December 10. Your bill for the microscopes will reflect a 10% discount to say thank you for accepting a delayed shipment caused by a backlog of Christmas orders.

The negative statement rewritten to emphasize "you" becomes a positive statement. The letter writer should follow the admonition of a once-familiar popular song: "Accentuate the positive; eliminate the negative."

Natural Wording

The wording of a letter should be as natural and normal as possible. Jot down thoughts or organize them in your mind so that they can be presented clearly and naturally. Consider the following wording:

> Pursuant to your request of November 10 that I be in charge of the program at the December DECA meeting, I regret to inform you that my impending departure for a holiday tour of Europe will prevent a positive response.

This sentence probably resulted from a writer trying to sound impressive. The result is stilted, awkward wording. The same information might be clearly and naturally worded:

> I am sorry I cannot be in charge of the DECA program for December. I will be leaving on December 5 for a holiday tour of Europe.

As you write a business letter, keep your reader in mind. How will the letter sound to the reader? Have I presented the information in a natural, normal way so that the content is clear?

FORM IN LETTERS

Learning about the form of a letter includes becoming familiar with standard formats and with the parts of a letter and their arrangement.

Format

There are standard practices concerning paper, typewriting, appearance, and layout. Failure to follow these standards shows poor taste, reflects the ignorance of the writer, and invites an unfavorable response. In business correspondence, there is no place for unusual or "cute" stylistic practices. (A specialized type of business letter, the sales letter, sometimes uses attention-getting gimmicks. Follow-up sales letters, however, tend to conform to standard practices.)

Paper   Use unruled, good-quality, standard-size paper. Do not use notebook paper.

Handwriting or Typewriting   Letters should be typewritten or produced on a word processor because the printed word is neater and easier to read. If a letter is handwritten, only black, blue, or blue-black ink should be used.

Appearance   The general appearance of a letter is very important. A letter that is neat and pleasing to the eye invites reading and consideration much more readily than one that is unbalanced or has noticeable erasures. The letter should be like a picture, framed on the page with margins in proportion to the length of the letter. Allow at least a 1½-inch margin at the top and bottom, and a 1-inch margin on the sides. Short letters should have wide margins and be appropriately centered on the page. As a general rule, single space within the parts of the letter; double space between the parts of the letter and between paragraphs. It is always a wise investment to spend the extra time to retype a letter if there is even the slightest doubt about its making a favorable impression on the reader. (See the letter on page 225 for proper spacing.)

Layout Forms   Although there are several standardized layout forms for letters, three seem to be preferred by most firms: the block (see pages 232, 237, 246, 247), the modified block (see pages 262, 277), and the full block (see pages 242, 249, 252, 258–259). Another layout form gradually gaining favor is the simplified block form (see page 236).

> *Block Form.* In the block form, the inside address, salutation, and paragraphs are flush, or even, with the left margin. The heading, complimentary close, and signature are to the right half of the page.
>
> *Modified Block Form.* The modified block differs from the block in only one respect: each paragraph is indented.
>
> *Full Block Form.* In the full block form *all* parts of the letter are even with the left margin. Open punctuation is sometimes used with the full block

form; that is, no punctuation follows the salutation and the complimentary close.

Simplified Block Form. The parts of the letter in the simplified block form are the heading, the inside address, the subject line, the body, and the signature. The salutation and the complimentary close are omitted. Like the full block, all parts begin at the left margin.

Parts of a Business Letter

The parts of a business letter follow a standard sequence and arrangement. The six regular parts in the letter include: heading, inside address, salutation, body, complimentary close, and signature (these are illustrated in the letter on page 225). In addition, there may be several special parts in the business letter. On the envelope, the two regular parts are the outside address and the return address (these are illustrated on page 229).

Regular Parts

1. *Heading.* Located at the top of the page, the heading includes the writer's complete mailing address and the date, in that order, as shown below. The longest line in the heading is flush, or even, with the right margin. As elsewhere in standard writing, abbreviations should generally be avoided. (Note that the heading does *not* include the writer's name.)

   Route 12, Box 758   704 South Pecan Circle
   Elmhurst, IL 60126   Hanover, PA 17331
   July 25, 1984   9 April 1984

   In writing the state name, you may use the two-letter abbreviation suggested by the postal service.

   TWO-LETTER ABBREVIATIONS FOR STATES

Alabama	AL	Florida	FL
Alaska	AK	Georgia	GA
Arizona	AZ	Hawaii	HI
Arkansas	AR	Idaho	ID
California	CA	Illinois	IL
Colorado	CO	Indiana	IN
Connecticut	CT	Iowa	IA
Delaware	DE	Kansas	KS
District of Columbia	DC	Kentucky	KY
Louisiana	LA	Ohio	OH
Maine	ME	Oklahoma	OK
Maryland	MD	Oregon	OR
Massachusetts	MA	Pennsylvania	PA
Michigan	MI	Rhode Island	RI
Minnesota	MN	South Carolina	SC
Mississippi	MS	South Dakota	SD

Missouri	MO	Tennessee	TN
Montana	MT	Texas	TX
Nebraska	NB	Utah	UT
Nevada	NV	Vermont	VT
New Hampshire	NH	Virginia	VI
New Jersey	NJ	Washington	WA
New Mexico	NM	West Virginia	WV
New York	NY	Wisconsin	WI
North Carolina	NC	Wyoming	WY
North Dakota	ND		

Note that each abbreviation is written in all capitals and that no periods are used.

Letterhead Stationery. Many firms use stationery that has been especially printed for them with their name and address at the top of the page. Some firms have other information added to this letterhead, such as the names of officers, a telephone number, or a slogan. The letterhead on stationery is always put there by a printer. Thus, the writer of a business letter, whether a student or an employee, never makes his or her own letterhead by typing, writing, or drawing one in.

 If letterhead stationery is used, the address is already printed on the paper; only the date must be added. Letterhead paper is used for the first page only. (See the letters on pages 237, 242, 246, 247, 249, 252.)

2. *Inside Address.* The inside address is placed even with the left margin and at least two spaces below the heading. It contains the full name of the person—including a proper title such as *Mr., Ms., Dr.,* and the like—or firm being written to and the complete mailing address, as in the following illustrations:

Mr. Ronald M. Benrey	Kipling Corporation
Electronics Editor, *Popular Science*	Department 40A
355 Lexington Avenue	P.O. Box 127
New York, NY 10017-0127	Beverly Hills, CA 90210

 Preface a person's name with a title of respect if you prefer; and when addressing an official of a firm, follow the name with a title or position. Write a firm's name in exactly the same form that the firm itself uses. Although it may be difficult to find out the name of the person to whom a letter should be addressed, it is always better to address a letter to a specific person rather than to a title, office, or firm. In giving the street address, be sure to include the word *Street, Avenue, Circle,* and so on. Remember: No abbreviations.

3. *Salutation.* The salutation, or greeting, is two spaces below the inside address and is even with the left margin. The salutation typically includes the word *Dear* followed by a title of respect plus the person's last name or by the person's full name: "Dear Ms. Badya:" or "Dear Maron Badya." In addressing a company, acceptable forms include "Dear Davidson, Inc.:" or simply "Davidson, Inc."

 Usually the salutation is followed by a colon. Other practices include using a comma if the letter is a combination business-social

letter, and, in the full block form, the option of omitting the mark of
punctuation after both the salutation and the complimentary close.

4. *Body.* The body, or the message, of the letter begins two spaces below
the salutation. Like any other composition, it is structured in paragraphs. Generally it is single spaced within paragraphs and double
spaced between paragraphs. The paragraphs may or may not be indented, depending on the layout form used (see pages 220–221).

Second Page. For letters longer than one page, observe the same margins
as used for the body of the first page. The second-page top margin
should be the same as that of the sides of the second page. Be sure to
carry over a substantial amount of the body of the letter (at least two
lines) to the second page.

Although there is no one conventional form for the second-page
heading, it should contain (*a*) the name of the addressee (the person to
whom the letter is written), (*b*) the date, and (*c*) the page number. The
following illustrate two widely used forms:

Mr. Thomas R. Racy	May 22, 1984	Page 2

or

Mr. Thomas R. Racy
May 22, 1984
Page 2

5. *Complimentary Close.* The complimentary close, or closing, is two
spaces below the body. It is a conventional expression, indicating the
formal close of the letter. Of the numerous possible expressions, "Yours
truly," "Yours very truly," "Very truly yours," "Sincerely," and "Sincerely yours" are commonly used. "Cordially" may be used when the
writer knows the addressee well. "Respectfully" or "Respectfully
yours" indicates that the writer views the addressee as an honored
individual or that the addressee is of high rank.

Capitalize only the first word, and follow the complimentary close
with a comma. (In the full block form using open punctuation, the
comma is omitted after both the salutation and the complimentary
close.)

6. *Signature.* Every letter should have a legible, handwritten signature in
ink. Below this is the typewritten signature. If the entire letter is
handwritten, of course there is only one signature.

If a person's given name (such as Dale, Carol, Jerry) does not
indicate whether the person is male or female, the person may want to
include a title of respect (Ms., Miss, Mrs., Mr.) in parentheses to the left
of the typewritten signature (see the letter on page 236). In a business
letter, a married woman uses her own first name, not her husband's first
name. Thus, the wife of Jacob C. Andrews signs her name as Thelma S.
Andrews. In addition, she may type her married name in parentheses
(Mrs. Jacob C. Andrews) below her own name (see page 237).

The name of a firm as well as the name of the individual writing the
letter may appear as the signature (see the letters on pages 237, 247).

In this case, responsibility for the letter rests with the name that appears first.

Following the typewritten signature there may be an identifying title indicating the position of the person signing the letter; for example: Estimator; Buyer, Ladies Apparel; Assistant to the Manager, Food Catering Division. (See pages 242, 246, 247, 249, 252).

Regular Parts of a Typical Business Letter and Their Spacing

At least 1½-inch margin at top

HEADING

Longest line
determines left
margin of heading

Route 12, Box 75B
Elmhurst, IL 60126
July 25, 1984

Double space or more, depending on length of letter

**INSIDE
ADDRESS**

Mr. Ronald M. Benrey
Electronics Editor, Popular Science
355 Lexington Avenue
New York, NY 10017-0127
Double space

Same as address on
envelope

SALUTATION

Dear Mr. Benrey: Followed by colon

Double space

BODY

In an electronics laboratory I am taking as a part of my
second-year training at Midwestern Technical College,
Elmhurst, Illinois, I have developed a six-sided hi-fi
speaker system. The speaker system is inexpensive (the
materials cost less than $50), light-weight, and quite
simple to construct. The sound reproduction is excellent.

**At least 1-inch
margin on
each side**

Double space

My electronics instructor believes that other hi-fi
enthusiasts may be interested in building such a speaker
system. If you think the readers of Popular Science would
like to look at the plans, I will be happy to send them to
you for reprint in your magazine.
Double space

**COMPLIMENTARY
CLOSE**

Closing and
signature
slightly left
of center

Yours truly,

Followed by comma; first
word capitalized

SIGNATURE

Thomas G. Stein

4 to 6 spaces for
handwritten signature

Thomas G. Stein

At least 1½-inch margin at bottom

Special Parts In addition to the six regular parts of the business letter, some-times special, or optional, parts are necessary. The main ones, in the order in which they would appear in the letter, are the following.

1. *Attention Line.* When a letter is addressed to a company or organization rather than to an individual, an attention line may be given to help in mail delivery. An attention line is never used when the inside address

contains a person's name. Typical are attention lines directed to: Sales Division, Personnel Manager, Billing Department, Circulation Manager; the attention line may also be an individual's name. The attention line contains the word *Attention* (capitalized and sometimes abbreviated) followed by a colon and name of the office, department, or individual.

Attention: Personnel Manager   *or*   Attn: Mr. Robbin Carmichael

The name written after the word *attention* is not used in the salutation; the salutation includes the name from the first line of the inside address. The attention line appears both on the envelope and in the letter. On the envelope, it is generally two spaces below and an inch to the left of the address; frequently it is underlined. In the letter, the attention line is even with the left margin and is usually two spaces below the inside address. (See page 258.) Since a letter addressed to an individual is usually more effective than one addressed simply to a company, the attention line should be used sparingly.

2. *Subject, or Reference, Line.* The subject, or reference, line saves time and space. It consists of the word *Subject* or *Re* (a Latin word meaning "concerning") followed by a colon and a word or phrase of specific information, such as a policy number, account number, or model number.

Subject: Policy No. 10473A   *or*   Re: Latham Stereo Tape Deck Model 926

The position of the subject line is not standardized. It may appear to the right of the inside address or salutation; it may be centered on the page several spaces below the salutation. (See pages 236, 247.)

3. *Identification Line.* When the person whose signature appears on the letter is not the person who typed the letter, there is an identification line. Current practice is to include in the line only the initials (in lowercase) of the typist. The identification line is two spaces below the signature and is even with the left margin of the letter. (See pages 237, 246, 247.)

4. *Enclosure.* When an item (pamphlet, report, check, etc.) is enclosed with the letter, an enclosure line is usually typed two spaces below the identification line and even with the left margin. If there is no identification line, the enclosure line is two spaces below the signature and even with the left margin. The enclosure line may be written in various ways and may give varying amounts of information.

Enclosure
Enclosures: Inventory of supplies, furniture, and equipment
                Monthly report of absenteeism, sick leave, and vacation
                    leave
Encl.: Application of employment form
Encl. (2)

(See pages 236, 237, 249, 262.)

5. *Copy.* When a copy of a letter is sent to another person, the letter *c* (usually lowercase) or the word *copy* followed by a colon and the name

of the person or persons to whom the copy is being sent is typed one space below the identification line and even with the left margin of the letter. (See page 247.) If there is no identification line, the copy notation is two spaces below the signature and even with the left margin.

c: Mr. Jay Longman
copy: Joy Minor

6. *Personal Line.* The word *Personal* or *Confidential* (capitalized and usually underlined) indicates that only the addressee is to read the letter; obviously, this line should appear on the envelope. It usually appears to the left of the last line of the outside address. The personal line may be included in the letter itself, two spaces above the inside address and even with the left margin.
7. *Mailing Line.* If the letter is sent by means other than first class mail, a notation may be made on both the letter and the envelope. The mailing line in the letter is even with the left margin and appears after all other notations.

Delivered by Messenger
Certified Mail

The Envelope

The U.S. Postal Service has established guidelines for sizes of and addresses on envelopes. These guidelines allow an Optical Character Reader (OCR), an automated device that reads the address and sorts the mail by ZIP code, to operate efficiently.

Regular business envelopes should be a minimum of $3\frac{1}{2}$ inches high and 5 inches long and a maximum of $6\frac{1}{8} \times 11\frac{1}{2}$ inches. Mailable thickness is 0.007 to 0.25.

Envelope sizes regularly used by businesses are classified as All-Purpose ($3\frac{5}{8} \times 6\frac{1}{4}$ inches), Executive ($3\frac{7}{8} \times 7\frac{1}{2}$ inches), and Standard ($4\frac{1}{8} \times 9\frac{1}{2}$ inches). Larger manila envelopes are available in three standard sizes: $6\frac{1}{2} \times 9\frac{1}{2}$ inches, 9×12 inches, and $11\frac{1}{2} \times 14\frac{5}{8}$ inches.

Regular Parts The two regular parts on the envelope, the outside address and the return address, are explained and illustrated on page 229.

1. *Outside Address.* The outside address on the envelope is identical with the inside address. The postal service prefers single spacing, all uppercase letters, and no punctuation marks for ease in sorting mail by an OCR. For obvious reasons, the address should be accurate and complete. For large-volume mailing the postal service encourages using the nine-digit zip code to facilitate mail delivery.
2. *Return Address.* Located in the upper left-hand corner of the envelope, not on the back flap, the return address includes the writer's name (without "Mr.," etc.) plus the address as it appears in the heading. The ZIP code should be included.

Special Parts In addition to the two regular parts on the envelope, sometimes a special part is needed. The main ones are the attention line and the personal line.

1. *Attention Line.* An attention line may be used when a letter is addressed to a company rather than to an individual. The wording of the attention line on the envelope is the same as that of the attention line in the letter. On the envelope, the attention line is generally two spaces below and about an inch to the left of the outside address; frequently it is underlined.

2. *Personal Line.* The word *Personal* or *Confidential* (capitalized and usually underlined) indicates that only the addressee is to read the letter. The personal line usually appears to the left of the last line of the outside address.

Regular Parts of the Envelope and Their Spacing

RETURN ADDRESS	Thomas G. Stein Route 12, Box 75B Elmhurst, IL 60126	**Except for name and date, same as heading in letter**
		Begin outside address slightly left of center
OUTSIDE ADDRESS	**Content same as in inside address in letter**	MR RONALD M BENREY ELECTRONICS EDITOR POPULAR SCIENCE 355 LEXINGTON AVENUE NEW YORK NY 10017-0127

TYPES OF LETTERS

There are many, many types of letters. There are numerous books devoted wholly to discussions of letters. This chapter discusses some of the common types of letters written by businesses and individuals: inquiry, order, sales, claim and adjustment, collection, job application, and application follow-up. (See also Chapter 8, Reports, for further discussion of letters, page 309, and the letter of transmittal, pages 310 and 412.)

Letter of Inquiry

A letter to the college registrar asking for entrance information, a letter to a firm asking for a copy of its catalog, a letter to a manufacturing plant requesting information on a particular product — each is a letter of inquiry, or request. Such a letter is simple to write if these directions are followed:

1. State clearly and specifically what is wanted. If asking for more than two items or bits of information, use an itemized list.
2. Give the reason for the inquiry, if practical. Remember: if you can show clearly a direct benefit to the company or person addressed, you increase your chances of a reply.
3. Include an expression of appreciation for the addressee's consideration of the inquiry. Usually a simple "Thank you" is adequate.
4. Include a self-addressed, stamped envelope with inquiries sent to individuals who would have to pay the postage themselves to send a reply.

On the next page is a Plan Sheet filled in by a student preparing to write a letter of inquiry. The letter follows.

PLAN SHEET
FOR WRITING A LETTER OF INQUIRY

Layout Form (block, modified block, full block, simplified block)

I will use:
block

Heading

My mailing address is:
P.O. Box 0863
Jackson, MS 39218

The date is:
April 25, 1985

Inside Address

The person (or firm) to whom I am writing (including any identifying title after the name) is:
Pella, Inc.

The complete mailing address is:
209 Madison Avenue
New York, NY 10022

Salutation

I will use:
Pella, Inc.:

Body

Through this letter I am seeking:
information on manufacture, materials, and cost of casement windows

The reason for my inquiry is:
I am employed in the drafting department of a construction company. Like to be aware of new materials in construction.

230

To make my inquiry clear and specific, I need to include this information:
saw advertisement in *Architectural Forum*, *March, 1985, issue*

Complimentary Close

I will use:
Sincerely,

Signature (including, if applicable, the name of the firm and identifying title)

I will use:
Karen Gore

Special Parts

This letter requires the following special parts:
omit

Letter of Inquiry in Block Form

```
                                          P. O. Box 0863
                                          Jackson, MS 39218
                                          April 24, 1985

        Pella, Inc.
        209 Madison Avenue
        New York, NY 10022

        Pella, Inc.:

        The March, 1985, issue of Architectural Forum contained an
        advertisement of your casement windows. The article indi-
        cated that further information was available upon request.

        Would you please send me information on manufacture, ma-
        terials, and cost of these windows.

        As an employee in the drafting department of a construction
        firm, I like to be aware of new materials used in con-
        struction.

        Thank you.

                                  Sincerely,

                                  Karen Gore

                                  Karen Gore
```

Order Letter

The order letter, as the term implies, is a written communication to a seller from a buyer who wishes to make a purchase. For the transaction to be satisfactory, the terms of the sale must be absolutely clear to both. Since in the order letter it is the writer (purchaser) who is requesting certain merchandise, it is the writer's responsibility to state clearly, completely, and accurately exactly what is wanted, how it will be paid for, and how it is to be delivered.

In writing an order letter:

1. State clearly, completely, and accurately what is wanted. If ordering two or more different items, use an itemized list format. Include the exact name of the item, the quantity wanted, and other identifying information such as model number, catalog number, size, color, weight, and finish.
2. Give the price of the merchandise and the method of payment: check, money order, credit card (give name, number, and expiration date), COD, charge to account if credit is established (give account name and number).
3. Include shipping instructions with the order. Mention desired method for shipment of the merchandise: parcel post, truck freight, railway express, air express, or the like. If the date of shipment is important, say so.

As the two following order letters indicate, the general principles for writing an order letter are the same, whether the order be for a small or a large amount, or from an individual or a company. The first order letter has a filled-in Plan Sheet, which shows the thinking that the student did before writing the letter.

Layout Form (block, modified block, full block, simplified block)

I will use:
simplified form

Heading

My mailing address is:
Route 7, Box 148
Browning, TX 77020

The date is:
June 1, 1985

Inside Address

The person (or firm) to whom I am writing (including any identifying title after the name) is:

The complete mailing address is:
Arlington Manufacturing Company, Inc.
1149 Seventh Avenue
Deevers, OH 44109

Salutation

I will use:
not used in simplified block form

Body

The items I am ordering and their identification (model number, catalog number, size, color, weight, finish, etc.) are:

Item	Quantity	Identification	Cost
Flat cutting blade for lawn mower	*1*	*19-inch blade for a series "W" lawn mower*	*$18.25*

The manner of payment (check, money order, credit card, COD, charge, etc.) is:
check

The method of shipping (parcel post, truck freight, railway freight, air express, etc.) is:
air express; cost includes shipping

Other information or instructions:
omit

Complimentary Close

I will use:
not used in simplified block form

Signature (including, if applicable, the name of the firm and identifying title)

I will use:
Lynn Reed

Special Parts

This letter requires the following special parts:
Subject: 19-inch flat cutting blade (Subject line required in simplified block form)
Enclosure: Check for $18.25

Order Letter in Simplified Form

Route 7, Box 148
Browning, TX 77020
June 1, 1985

Arlington Manufacturing Company, Inc.
1149 Seventh Avenue
Deevers, OH 44109

Subject: 19-inch flat cutting blade

Please mail me a 19-inch flat cutting blade for a series
"W" lawn mower. Enclosed is a check for $18.25 for the
blade. I understand that the price includes shipping
charges.

Since the mower is not usable without the new blade and
since my summer work is mowing lawns, please send the
blade immediately, by air express.

Lynn Reed

(Ms.) Lynn Reed

Enclosure: Check for $18.25

Order Letter in Block Form on Letterhead Stationery

the ANDREWS COMPANY

432 FIELDING AVENUE
YOUNGSTOWN, OREGON 97386

May 1, 1985

Woodfield Wholesale Company
300 N. State Street
Braxton, CA 90318

Woodfield Wholesale:

Please send by railway express the following items advertised in your spring sale catalog.

Quan-tity	Catalog No.	Item	Unit Price	Amount
5	77X1628	Chain Saw, 5 H.P. engine	$195.00	$975.00
10	32W5602	Bow and Arrow Set	22.00	220.00
100	11R7487	Golf Club Pac	36.00	3,600.00
			Total	$4,795.00

I am enclosing a check for one-fourth the amount
($1,198.75), and the balance ($3,596.25) plus shipping
charges will be paid within 30 days after the merchandise
arrives.

Yours very truly,
The Andrews Company

Thelma S. Andrews

Thelma S. Andrews
(Mrs. Jacob C. Andrews)

msw
Enclosure: Check for $1,198.75

Printed Order Forms Many companies provide a printed order form for
ordering merchandise. These forms indicate specific information needed and
provide spaces to fill it in, and they usually give directions for filling in the form.
An example of a filled-in order form is shown on page 238.

Sears

You can count on

DAY	ORDERS	# LINES	SOURCE OF-SALE	TYPE SALE	METHOD SHIPMT.	CASH	DISCT.	TAX EXMT	SPEC CODE	SPECIAL INFORMATION (DO NOT TRANSMIT DASHES)
			5							

		TERMS TABLE	NO. OF MONTHS

Satisfaction Guaranteed or Your Money Back

My SearsCharge number is:

Direct Mail Order Blank

NAME AND PRESENT ADDRESS

NAME (first, middle initial, last) Please use the same name on ALL orders from your household

M I K E S G I T A N O

MAILING ADDRESS | APT. NO.

3 7 1 R O S E S T

CITY STATE | ZIP CODE 3 5 9 0 3

G A D S D E N A L

AREA CODE   PHONE NUMBER   TODAY'S DATE

2 0 5   9 3 8 2 0 0 6   2 2 5 8 5

METHOD OF PAYMENT

☐ Add to my SearsCharge account

My SearsCharge signature: _____

☒ CASH: (check or money order payable to Sears, Roebuck and Co.)

☐ PLEASE OPEN AN ACCOUNT. Completed credit application enclosed.

☐ Amount enclosed to be applied to my Sears Credit Account $ _____

NOTE: ✔ PLEASE GIVE COMPLETE DELIVERY INFORMATION
Be sure to give complete mailing address at left filling in the correct information, on the lines provided, including telephone number.
  ✔ PLEASE MAIL ALL INQUIRIES NOT DIRECTLY RELATED TO THIS ORDER UNDER SEPARATE COVER
  ✔ C.O.D. ORDERS NOT ACCEPTED BY DIRECT MAIL

PLEASE DO NOT WRITE IN THIS SPACE

IF YOUR ADDRESS HAS CHANGED since your last order, please give your old mailing address here:

FORMER ADDRESS | APT. NO.

CITY/STATE | ZIP CODE

SHIP TO ANOTHER ADDRESS? If you want this order shipped to another person or to a different address, freight or express station, give address here:

NAME (first, middle initial, last)

MAILING ADDRESS | APT. NO.

CITY/STATE | ZIP CODE

See Yellow Pages in General Catalog for shipping information

If the merchandise you are ordering exceeds postal limitations, it is usually more economical to ship your order to our store nearest your home for pickup. Please indicate the Sears store most convenient for you

Store Name and Location: _____

	CATALOG NUMBER	HOW MANY	Color NO.	SIZE	Name of Item	PRICE EACH	Dollars	Cents	Code	Special Instructions	Lbs.	Oz.	PAGE NO.
1	34 E 68928	— 1			CORN POPPER	17.99	& 17	99		CR LF	6	2	426
2	33 E 56515 F	2 PR		XL	GLOVES	15.00	& 30	00		CR LF		10	194
3	96 BR 3796 H	3		542	TOWELS	9.99	& 29	97		CR LF	3	6	79
4		—	—				&			CR LF			
5		—	—				&			CR LF			
6		—	—				&			CR LF			
7		—	—				&			CR LF			

◄ To order additional items, use other side

TAX: Please be sure to add correct state, county, city and local taxes applicable.

*SHIPPING AND HANDLING: Figure separate charges for weight of each individual item ending in a "C" or "L" as each of these items must be shipped separately. Do not add the weight of multiples of same item together, figure each separately. Calculate on reverse side. See Big Book for information on items ending with an "N".

F6015   3.82   Printed in U.S.A.   Sears, Roebuck and Co.

Reprinted by permission of Sears, Roebuck and Co.

Fill in spaces below on CASH ORDERS only

	Dollars	Cents		
TOTAL FOR GOODS	77	96	Total Pounds	Total Ounces
SHIPPING, HANDLING*	3	45	9	18
TAX (See at left)	3	12	Total Weight* in Pounds	
Amount I owe Sears on previous order		—	11	
TOTAL CASH PRICE	84	53	*thank you* for shopping at Sears	
AMOUNT ENCLOSED Sears Checks				
Money Order or Check	84	53		

Send Mail Orders to the nearest Sears Catalog Distribution Center listed below
ATLANTA, GA 30395
BOSTON, MA 02215
CHICAGO, IL 60607
COLUMBUS, OH 43228
DALLAS, TX 75295
GREENSBORO, NC 27480
JACKSONVILLE, FL 32297
KANSAS CITY, MO 64127
LOS ANGELES, CA 90051
MEMPHIS, TN 38140
MINNEAPOLIS, MN 55440
PHILADELPHIA, PA 19132
SEATTLE, WA 98184

Sales Letter

The sales letter is a specialized kind of business letter requiring careful planning if it is to serve its purpose: to convince the reader to buy a particular product or service. (See also "Basic Considerations in Persuasion," pages 440–441.)

A successful letter gets the reader's attention and arouses interest. The "you" attitude is especially important and should be particularly emphasized in the sales letter. Since the letter is directed toward the *reader's* interests and needs, references to what *"I"* the writer can do or think are kept to a minimum. Emphasis is on the reader and the benefits from the product.

The good sales letter is positive and sincere in approach. The writer must be thoroughly familiar with the product and its capabilities and limitations. Rather than trying to sell by downgrading a competitor, it is wiser to present the product on its own merits. The description of the product should be truthful and should avoid misleading and sensational promises.

The reader must be convinced of personal need for the product. Tactfully, yet concisely and forcefully, the reader must be shown the relationship between the product and good business and the ways in which the product will be of profit or benefit. Finally, the effective sales letter leads to the purchase of the product. The sales letter is successful if the reader immediately begins (whether by a plan presented in the letter or by one devised by the reader) to make arrangements to use the product.

In writing a sales letter

1. Appeal to the reader through something that is important: home, family, business, community involvement, prestige, or some other area of importance.
2. Identify and describe, accurately and honestly, the product or service offered.
3. Make clear the reader's need for the product or service.
4. State confidently the action you want the reader to take.

On the following pages is a filled-in Plan Sheet for a sales letter, followed by the letter.

PLAN SHEET
FOR WRITING A SALES LETTER

Layout Form

The layout form (block, modified block, full block, simplified block) that I will use is:
full block

Heading

My mailing address is:
letterhead

The date is:
February 22, 1985

Inside Address

The person (or firm) to whom I am writing (including any identifying title after the name) is:
Mr. W. D. Adams

The complete mailing address is:
Adams Service Center
4102 Green Street
Jackson, CO 80172

Salutation

I will use:
Dear Mr. Adams:

Body

To get the reader's attention and arouse interest, I will:
mention that automobiles need special care in the spring and summer and then mention particular products

The product (or service) I am selling is:
a new consignment program for automotive supplies

The product can be described in this way:
We will stock your shelves with a complete supply of Autoright supplies. You pay us for only what you sell. After four months if you are not satisfied with the plan, you may discontinue it.

The product will benefit or profit the reader in these ways:
It will help you give even better service to your customers. A participating station cannot lose money.

The plan that I will present whereby the reader can immediately begin to use the product is:
I will call on you at your station on March 2.

Complimentary Close

I will use:
Yours truly,

Signature (including, if applicable, the name of the firm and identifying title)

I will use:
E. C. Pace
Jackson Area Distributor

Special Parts

This letter requires the following special parts:
omit

Sales Letter in Full Block Form

AUTORIGHT

2829 CHARLOTTE DRIVE
DENVER, COLORADO 80213
TEL. 303-269-3313

February 22, 1985

Mr. W. D. Adams
Adams Service Center
4102 Green Street
Jackson, CO 80172

Dear Mr. Adams:

With spring approaching, you and your customers will be
thinking of special automotive needs for the spring and summer.
And you will be checking your stock of radiator hoses, summer
coolants, plugs, points, condensers, and fan belts.

As the Autoright distributor for the Jackson area, may I
introduce you to our new consignment program for automotive
supplies. We will stock your shelves with Autoright parts, at
no cost to you. You will have on hand a complete supply of parts
for automobiles and trucks of all makes and models. You will
not pay for the parts until you sell them. If, after four
months, you are not entirely satisfied with the program, I will
pick up the parts and issue full credit. With a program of this
kind you have all to gain and nothing to lose.

You are already familiar with the high quality of Autoright
products and their competitive prices. We believe our new
consignment plan will help you not only maintain but increase
the efficient service you want to give your customers.

I would like to call on you at your station on March 4. If you
have any questions, I will be more than glad to answer them.

Yours truly,
E. C. Pace
E. C. Pace
Jackson Area Distributor

WE CARRY EVERYTHING AUTOMOTIVE

Claim and Adjustment Letters

Claim (complaint) and adjustment letters are in some ways the most difficult letters of all to write. Frequently the writer is angry or annoyed or extremely dissatisfied, and the first impulse is to express those feelings in a harsh, angry, sarcastic letter. But the purpose of the letter is to bring about positive action that satisfies the complaint. A rude letter that antagonizes the reader is not likely to result in such positive action. Thus, above all in writing a claim or an adjustment letter, be calm, courteous, and businesslike. Assume that the reader is fair and reasonable. Include only factual information, not opinions; and keep the focus on the real issue, not on personalities.

In writing a claim letter:

1. Identify the transaction (what, when, where, etc.). Include copies (not the originals) of substantiating documents — sales receipts, canceled checks, invoices, and the like.
2. Explain specifically what is wrong.
3. State the adjustment or action that you think should be made.
4. Remember that reputable companies are eager to have satisfied customers and that most respond favorably to justifiable complaints.

In writing an adjustment letter:

1. Respond to the claim letter promptly and courteously.
2. Refer to the claim letter, identifying the transaction.
3. State clearly what action will be taken. If the action differs from that requested in the claim letter, explain why.
4. Remember to be fair, friendly, and firm.

The following claim letter, with its filled-in Plan Sheet, illustrates a common complaint: the purchaser feels there has simply been an oversight, or error, in the shipment of goods he has ordered. The second letter is an adjustment letter, replying to the first.

PLAN SHEET
FOR WRITING A CLAIM OR AN ADJUSTMENT LETTER

Layout Form (block, modified, full block, simplified block)

I will use:
block

Heading

My mailing address is:
letterhead

The date is:
February 20, 1985

Inside Address

The person (or firm) to whom I am writing (including any identifying title after the name) is:
Middleton Manufacturing Company

The complete mailing address is:
Alton, IL 60139

Salutation

I will use:
Middleton Manufacturing Company

Body

Identification of the transaction (items purchased, date, invoice number, model number, style, size, etc.):
ten refrigerators, invoice 479320

Statement of the problem or complaint:
Supposed to include five ice trays for each refrigerator.
No trays received.

Desired action or action that will be taken:
Send trays by air express.

Complimentary Close

I will use:
Sincerely yours,

Signature (including, if applicable, the name of the firm and identifying title)

I will use:
John A. Manuel, Manager
Appliance Department

Special Parts

This letter requires the following special parts:
Identification line — jph

Claim Letter in Block Form on Letterhead Stationery

appleton's, inc.

4636 MOCKINGBIRD EXPRESSWAY
BATON ROUGE, LOUISIANA 70806

February 20, 1985

Middleton Manufacturing Company:
Alton
Illinois 60139

Middleton Manufacturing Company:

Thank you for your prompt delivery of the ten refrigerators, invoice #479320.

Your catalog indicated that each refrigerator contains
five ice trays. None of these were included in the order
we received. Since your invoice does not show a back order
or a separate delivery of the trays, we believe there may
have been an error in filling the order.

Since we are having to delay our sales promotion until we
receive the trays, please ship them by air express.

Sincerely yours,

John A. Manuel

John A. Manuel, Manager
Appliance Department

jph

Adjustment Letter in Block Form on Letterhead Stationery

Middleton   ALTON, ILLINOIS 60139

Manufacturing

Company

25 February 1985

Mr. John A. Manuel, Manager
Appliance Department
Appleton's, Inc.
4636 Mockingbird Expressway
Baton Rouge, LA 70806

    Subject: Refrigerators
           Serial Nos. WS-802945 through WS-802954

Dear Mr. Manuel:

Your letter of February 20, concerning ice trays, has been
directed to my attention. The trays are being sent to you
by air express today.

We regret the omission of the ice trays when the appliances
were shipped. This was due to a slight difference in the
assembly schedule caused by the new formula coating on the
ice trays, your refrigerators being the first to have these
improved trays.

We apologize for the inconvenience this has caused you and
we appreciate your understanding.

           Very truly yours,
           MIDDLETON MANUFACTURING COMPANY

           Patrick Beasley

           Patrick Beasley
           Supervisor, Shipping Division

jm
c: J. T. Reeves, Sales Division, Middleton Manufacturing
Company

Collection Letters

Collection letters are used to collect overdue accounts. They must be firm yet friendly to cause the customer to pay up yet keep the customer's goodwill.

Often collection letters are form letters and often they are a series of letters, starting with a reminder letter and moving through various appeal letters to an ultimatum letter, depending on the response of the customer.

A reminder letter, written early in a collection series, might mention that the unpaid balance is overdue and appeal to the customer's pride. It might include the sentence: "If you have already mailed your payment, please disregard this reminder."

An appeal letter, written later in a collection series, might:

1. Ask for payment.
2. Ask about possible problems. Suggest the customer call (include a toll-free number) to discuss any such problems.
3. Remind the customer of the value of good credit.
4. Enclose a return envelope to make payment easier.

A sample letter on page 249 illustrates this type of appeal letter.

The ultimatum letter is the last resort. It may:

1. State that payment must be received, often by stating a deadline.
2. Mention previous notices sent.
3. State what action will be taken if payment is not received by the deadline, such as turning the account over to a collection agency or a lawyer.

The sample letter on page 252 is an example of the ultimatum letter. The Plan Sheet used to organize the letter is included.

Collection Letter in Full Block Form

February 8, 1985

Mr. Walter O. Casey
5701 Honda Lane
Forsyth, GA 39129

Dear Mr. Casey:

We are concerned about your overdue account of $161. During the
past 90 days we have sent three statements, reminding you of this
problem. Since you have always paid bills promptly, we believe
some special circumstances may have caused this delay.

If you need to make special arrangements for paying your
account balance, we will be happy to work out a satisfactory
payment plan. Or, by sending us a check today for the $161, you
can preserve your excellent credit rating. A good credit
rating is of inestimable value.

Please use the enclosed postpaid envelope to mail us your check
or call us at 800-601-0043 to discuss your account.

Sincerely,

James W. Malley

James W. Malley
Credit Manager

Enc: postpaid envelope

Layout Form (block, modified block, full block, simplified block)

I will use:
full block

Heading

My mailing address is:
letterhead

The date is:
March 11, 1985

Inside Address

The person (or firm) to whom I am writing (including any identifying title after the name) is:
Walter O. Casey

The complete mailing address is:
5701 Honda Lane
Forsyth, GA 39129

Salutation

I will use:
Dear Mr. Casey:

Body

Appeal to customer:
Why not preserve your heretofore excellent credit rating and avoid an unpleasant situation by mailing your check for $161 today.

Reference to balance due and payment:
You have been given every opportunity to pay your overdue balance of $161. We do not feel we can permit any further delay in payment.

Problem(s) preventing payment:
omit

Action the company owed has taken:
omit

Action the company owed will take:
If payment is not received immediately, we will be forced to turn your account over to a collection agency.

Complimentary Close

I will use:
Sincerely,

Signature (including, if applicable, the name of the firm and identifying title)

I will use:
James W. Malley
Credit Manager

Special Parts

This letter requires the following special parts:
omit

Collection Letter in Full Block Form

M&P APPLIANCES
HWY 15S
ALBANY, GA 31707
(912)601-0043

March 11, 1985

Mr. Walter O. Casey
5701 Honda Lane
Forsyth, GA 39129

Dear Mr. Casey:

You have been given every opportunity to pay your overdue
balance of $161. We do not feel that we can permit any further
delay in payment.

If payment is not received immediately, we will be forced to
turn your account over to a collection agency.

Why not preserve your heretofore excellent credit rating and
avoid an unpleasant situation by mailing your check for $161
today.

Sincerely,

James W. Malley

James W. Malley
Credit Manager

Letter of Application

The most important letter you ever write may well be a letter of application for a job. As a college student, you may want to apply for a part-time job or a summer job. As a family breadwinner, you may be seeking employment. Since there are usually several applicants for a position, the letter may be the decisive factor, particularly in determining whether or not an interview is granted; the letter is successful if it results in an interview.

The letter of application has three sections: purpose of the letter, background information, and request for an interview. The background information may be included entirely within the letter itself or, more often, it is given on a separate page, referred to as a resumé, data sheet, vita, or some similar title. Regardless of how the background information is presented, however, the purpose of the letter is stated in the first paragraph, and an interview is requested in the closing.

The following suggestions for writing a letter of application are given, assuming that a resumé will be included.

Purpose of the Letter   In the first paragraph, state that you are applying for a position (better to apply for a specific position). Tell how you found out about the job (if in a periodical or newspaper, give name and date; if from a person, give name), and explain the reason for wanting it. If you have special qualifications for the job, state those qualifications.

Background Information   From the resumé, select those facts that qualify you for the job. State that a resumé with more complete information is included, and, of course, make the proper "enclosure" notation. If you refer to yourself, do so modestly. Don't undersell yourself, however. You want to convince the potential employer that you are the person to hire, that your skills and knowledge will be an asset to the company.

Request for an Interview   Any firm interested in employing an applicant will want a personal interview. In the closing paragraph of the letter of application, therefore, request an interview at the prospective employer's convenience. However, should there be restrictions regarding time, such as classes or work, say so. If distance makes an interview impractical (living in Virginia and applying for a summer job in Yellowstone National Park), suggest some alternative, such as an interview with a local representative or sending a tape recording if speaking ability is essential to the job.

Be sure to include in the closing paragraph how and when you may be reached.

Letter of Application — No Resumé   A letter of application may be written to contain all necessary information, without including a resumé. Information included in the letter is selected from the resumé; it may cover personal information, education, experience, and references. Emphasize the information that shows you are qualified for the job.

As in a resumé, the education information begins with the most recent and works backward. The section on experience begins with current employment or the last employment and works backward.

The closing paragraph seeks an interview. It includes how and when you may be reached.

Resumé (Data Sheet or Vita)

In the letter of application, background information is frequently given on a separate sheet of paper headed "Resumé," "Data Sheet," or "Vita." (See pages 266–267, 268, and 269 for examples of resumés.) By whatever name, this organized listing of background information on a separate page(s) keeps the letter from being overly long and makes locating specific details easier. The resumé is a *full* listing of information concerning the applicant. The accompanying letter, as in the general letter without a resumé, or the cover letter with an application form, focuses attention on facts relevant to the prospective job.

It is a good idea to keep the resumé as short as possible since busy employers are interested in necessary information only. If possible, keep the resumé to one page. After you have had considerable work experience, the resumé may be longer.

Information in a Resumé The information in a resumé may include the following:

1. *Job or career objective.* State your immediate employment objective. For example, Computer Programmer. You may also state your ultimate career goal. For example, Manager Trainee with future opportunity to become a buyer.
2. *Heading.* Includes name, address, telephone number. May include salary expected. Some experts advise against mentioning a salary; you might have been paid more, or if you mention too high a figure, you may not even get an interview.
3. *Education.* College education and high school education may be sufficient. After gaining considerable experience, you may want to include highest level of college education only. If you include several levels of education, begin with your most recent education and work backward.
4. *Experience.* Experience on a job of almost any kind is valuable; do not hesitate to mention any job you have had. If you have a listing of several job experiences, you might divide the information into two sections: experience related to job objective and general or other experience. In listing experience begin with current or most recent employment and work backward.
5. *Personal data.* You may want to include statistics on age, height, weight, health, and so on, particularly if these statistics are important to the job objective. Also you may mention hobbies or leisure interest activities as well as memberships in organizations.
6. *References.* Select three to five individuals who can speak knowledgeably about your qualifications and character. A student with little or no experience might select a friend of long standing, a teacher, or a community leader. Give the name, occupation, business address, and telephone number of each individual. If not obvious, explain your relationship to the individual. If you do not wish to list references, you may state: "References supplied upon request."
7. *Special Qualifications.* List any special qualifications, awards, honors, and the like. Include these in a properly headed section.

Types of Resumés A resumé follows no standard form. Once you have jotted down facts under the topics listed above, you can then decide on the headings you will use and the arrangement of the information. The sections of a resumé may be arranged in several different ways with different headings.

One way is to include the sections listed above, with the headings "Education," "Experience," "Personal Data," and "References," as illustrated in the sample resumé on page 264. Arrange the headings so that the most impressive details will appear near the top of the page. This type of resumé is called a *traditional* or a *chronological resumé.*

Another arrangement of sections of the resumé emphasizes functions you can perform or skills you have. For example, you might use headings such as "Communication Skills," "Supervisory Skills," "Budgetary Skills," "Machine Operating Skills," "Personnel Skills," "Research Skills," and the like. Following the headings give a summary of activities that helped you become competent at performing a function or helped you develop a skill.

You may also include traditional headings such as "Education," "Personal Data," and "References." The heading "Experience" may also be included if you do not cover experience in the function or skills section, or the heading "Experience" may be used to introduce the function or skills section.

This type of resumé may be called a *skills* or a *functional resumé.* See the sample resumé on pages 268–269.

A good rule of thumb: Select the type of resumé and arrange the information on the page to show your qualifications as a potential employee in the best possible way.

Examples of Letters of Application On the following pages are two letters of application. The first letter, written by a student, includes a filled-in Plan Sheet. The letter is self-contained, that is, it includes all the necessary information within the letter itself and thus has no accompanying resumé. Note that in this general letter of application only the qualities that are relevant to the particular job, that is, the items that really *qualify* the applicant, are included.

The second letter, written by an experienced technician, has an accompanying skills resumé. The letter has a filled-in Plan Sheet. (See pages 266–269 for the skills resumé with filled-in Plan Sheet.)

PLAN SHEET
FOR WRITING A LETTER OF APPLICATION
WITHOUT A RESUMÉ

Layout Form (block, modified block, full block, simplified block)

I will use:
full block

Heading

My mailing address is:
516 Madison Street
Jackson, MS 39207

The date is:
February 4, 1985

Inside Address

The person (or firm) to whom I am writing (including any identifying title after the name) is:
Ratliff Construction Company

The complete mailing address is:
P.O. Box 401
Union, TN 38014

Salutation

I will use:
Ratliff Construction Company

Body

Job applied for is:
general construction worker

I learned about it:
from Tom Spengler, a former employee

The reason I want the job is:
Company specializes in apartment construction

I want to emphasize the following:
physical strength; interest in apartment design and construction

Education (starting with the most recent experience, give name and location of high school and/or college, date of graduation, degree, major, subjects related to prospective job, awards, activities):

Metropolitan Community College, Jackson, MS, June 1986—planned
    graduation; drafting major
North High School, Jackson, MS, June 1982
    lettered in football

Experience (list each job, beginning with most recent, or present):

1981 present   stock boy   Grant's Grocery
    (part-time)   and clerk   903 North Madison Street
                                  Jackson, MS 39207
                                  Mr. Douglas R. Grant

Personal data:

Age: 19   Height: 5'10"   Weight: 175 lbs.   Health: Excellent

Other:
names and addresses of references

I would like an interview on:
any time during spring holidays or perhaps a Saturday

I can be reached by:
4:00 p.m. to 7:30 a.m. at (601) 254-7613

Complimentary Close

I will use:
Yours truly,

Signature

I will use:
Albert L. Livingston

Special Parts

This letter requires the following special parts:
Attention: Personnel Manager

Letter of Application in Full Block Form

516 North Madison Street
Jackson, MS 39207
February 4, 1985

Ratliff Construction Company
P. O. Box 401
Union, TN 38014

Attention: Personnel Manager

Ratliff Construction Company:

Through Tom Spengler, who worked for your company last summer,
I have learned that you are hiring a number of college students
for summer work. I would like to apply for a job as a general
construction worker.

Your company, I understand, specializes in the construction of
apartment buildings. The courses related to apartment design
that I am taking are making me aware of the importance of
accuracy and of adherence to specifications in apartment
construction. A freshman drafting and design technology major
at Metropolitan Community College, I plan to graduate in June
1986 with an Associate in Applied Science degree.

I am in excellent health and am amble to do strenuous physical
work. In high school I lettered in football two years.

I am 19 years old, 5 feet 10 inches tall, and weight 175 pounds.
On Saturdays and during the summer for the past four years I
have worked in a neighborhood grocery store. Mr. Douglas R.
Grant, owner of Grant's Grocery, 903 North Madison Street,
Jackson, Mississippi 39207, told me he would be happy to write
a letter of recommendation for me. If you wish a further
reference, please contact Mr. Charles A. Wadman, Instructor of
Drafting and Design Technology, Metropolitan Community
College, Jackson, Mississippi 39203.

My education, physicl stamina, and experience in handling
responsibility will make me a dependable employee for Ratliff
Construction Company. I would like to work for you company. And
I would like to come to Union for an interview. Our spring
holidays are only a few weeks away, March 11 - 15, and I could

Ratliff Construction Company
February 4, 1985
Page 2

very conveniently come any day during that period. Or if I knew
at least two weeks ahead of time so that I could make
arrangements about my work at the grocery, I could drive up any
Saturday. I can usually be reached at my home address before
7:30 A.M. and after 4:00 P.M., telephone (601) 254-7613. I look
forward to hearing from you.

Yours truly,

Albert L. Livingston

Albert L. Livingston

PLAN SHEET
FOR WRITING A LETTER OF APPLICATION WITH A RESUMÉ

Layout Form (block, modified block, full block, simplified block)

I will use:
modified block

Heading

My mailing address is:
1045 Drake Place
Ellisville, MA 01047

The date is:
March 27, 1985

Inside Address

The person (or firm) to whom I am writing (including any identifying title after the name) is:
Mr. Adrian M. Mantee, Director of Personnel

The complete mailing address is:
Blackwell Manufacturing Company
Plattsburg, IN 47401

Salutation

I will use:
Dear Mr. Mantee:

Body

Job applied for is:
supervisor in quality control

I learned about it:
March issue What's New in Manufacturing

The reason I want the job is:
desire to return to Indiana. Parents ill.

From the resumé I want to emphasize:

Education:
formal education in mechanical technology

Experience:
Presently employed as assistant supervisor of quality control at Barron Enterprises, Engineering Division. Have other experience in mechanical technology.

Personal data:
*Have always liked working with machinery.
Current supervisor knows of this application.*

Other:
none

I would like an interview on:
at convenience of Mr. Mantee, with a week's notice

I can be reached by:
mailing address given in heading

Complimentary Close

I will use:
Yours very truly,

Signature (including, if applicable, the name of the firm and identifying title)

I will use:
Thomas D. Davis

Special Parts

This letter requires the following special parts:
Enclosure: Resumé

Letter of Application, with Resumé, in Modified Block Form

1045 Drake Place
Ellisville, MA 01047
March 27, 1985

Mr. Adrian M. Mantee
Director of Personnel
Blackwell Manufacturing Company
Plattsburg, IN 47401

Dear Mr. Mantee:

In the March issue of What's New in Manufacturing, I
read your advertisement seeking supervisory personnel for
your multimillion-dollar plant expansion program. Please
consider this letter as my application for a supervisory
position in Quality Control.

Presently I am Assistant Supervisor of Quality Control
at Barron Enterprises, Engineering Division. My work here
is pleasant and I enjoy it, but my wife and I want to move
back to Indiana because of the failing health of our
parents, who live there.

The enclosed resumé gives a brief outline of my skills and
experience. From my earliest job while a sophomore in high
school, I have liked working with machines of any kind. This
keen interest, developed by my formal education and experience
in various aspects of mechanical technology, has given me a
background that should be of immense value to a supervisor.

I will be happy to supply any additional information
concerning my background or present employment. My
immediate supervisor here at Barron Enterprises is aware
that I am looking for a supervisory position with a
company in the Midwest and why I am doing so. I would like
to have an interview with you, and, although distance is
an important factor, I would be glad to fly out at your
convenience, if I had at least a week's notice.

Yours very truly,

Thomas D. Davis

Thomas D. Davis

Enclosure: Resumé

Examples of Resumés Following are three examples of resumés. The first two examples illustrate student-written traditional resumés. The third example, a skills resumé written by an experienced technician, includes a filled-in Plan Sheet.

An Example of a Traditional Resumé

APPLICATION FOR POSITION OF COMPUTER PROGRAMMER

ALICE M. RYDEL

3621 Bailey Drive   Spring 1985
Big Rapids, MI 39207
(579) 456-2156

Education

1982-1984: Will receive AAS degree in Computer Programming, John Williams Community College, Big Rapids, Michigan. Related Courses: RPG Programming, Systems Analysis and Design, Principles of Management, Accounting.

1978-1982: Murrah High School, Jackson, Michigan. Took college preparatory courses and basic business courses.

Experience

1982-present: Part-time assistant to Tom Lewis, Director of Data Processing, John Williams Community College.

1982-present: Part-time (summers and holidays) night supervisor in Data Processing Department, Midwestern Bell Telephone Company, Big Rapids, Michigan.

Personal Data

Age: 22. Weight: 120 pounds. Height: 5' 6". Leisure activities: sports, reading.

References

Mr. Tom Lewis, Director of Data Processing, John Williams Community College, Big Rapids, Michigan 39207. Telephone: (579) 456-9596

Ms. Lauren Watson, Supervisor of Data Processing Department, Midwestern Bell Telephone Company, Big Rapids, Michigan 39207. Telephone: (579) 467-3271

Dr. Edith Rodgers, Professor of English, John Williams Community College, Big Rapids, Michigan 39207. Telephone: (579) 456-9512

An Example of a Traditional Resumé

JAMES E. BROWN, JR.

206 Davis Drive
Jackson, Mississippi 39209
601-948-7660

MARITAL STATUS: Single   HEIGHT: 6'1"
AGE: 27   WEIGHT: 190 pounds

JOB OBJECTIVE

To begin work in the technical department of a company dealing
with electronics with the purpose of qualifying for full
management responsibilities. No geographic limitations.

EDUCATION

Louisiana State University

Class: May 1982   Minor: Speech
Degree: B.S.   G.P.A.: 3.40 Overall
Major: Industrial   3.31 in major
         Management   field of study

HONORS

Dean's List, Beta Gamma Sigma National Honor Society in
Business Administration, Associated Students Service and
Leadership Award, Member of Who's Who Among American Colleges
and Universities.

ACTIVITIES

Station Manager and Head Engineer of college radio station
KERS-FM, member of the Society for the Advancement of Management,
Vice-President of the Young Republicans.

EXPERIENCE

United States Air Force, Electronics-Communications, 6/74 to
9/78. Duties and Responsibilities: Shift Chief Long-Haul
Transmitter Site (supervised 3 persons in operation of 52
transmitters and 2 microwave systems). Team Chief Group
Electronics Engineering Installation Agency (supervised 3 persons
on installing weather and communications equipment), Tech-Writer
(wrote detailed maintenance procedures for electronic equipment
manuals). Instructor in Electronic Fundamentals (continuous 3-month
classes of 10 persons each).

Resumé   James E. Brown, Jr.   page 2

    Summer and Part—Time: Manager, Campus Apartments; Disc Jockey
of KXOA and KXRQ; Laboratory Assistant for Radio—TV Speech
Department, Stage Technician.
    Special Qualifications: Federal Communications Commission
First Class Radio Telephone License. Top Secret Clearance for
Defense Work.

<u>PERSONAL INTERESTS</u>
    Interested in water skiing, computer games, jazz, and building
hi—fi equipment.

<u>REFERENCES</u>
    References available upon request.

PLAN SHEET
FOR WRITING A RESUMÉ

Type of Resumé (traditional or skills) I will use: *skills*

Heading

Name: *Thomas D. Davis*   Telephone: *521-363-2371*
Address: *1045 Drake Place*
             Ellisville, Massachusetts 01047

The date is: *omit*

Job Sought   *Supervisor in Quality Control*

Education

College	Location	Date(s) of Attendance
Cain Community College	*Cain, IN*	*1965–1968*

Degree (or degree sought):   Major Field:
AAS degree   *mechanical technology*

Subjects related to prospective job: *omit*

Special training:
Massachusetts Technical Institute
   1980 Quality Control with Computers (45 clock hours)
   1978 New Materials in Industry (45 clock hours)
   1976 Production Planning and Problems (45 clock hours)

Activities: *omit*

High School	Location	Date of Graduation
omit		

Areas of emphasis or of particular interest: *omit*

Awards or special recognition and/or activites: *omit*

Work Experience (beginning with the most recent or present employment)

Date of Employment	Specific Work	Name and Address of Firm	Full Name of Supervisor
1972 present	*Asst Supervisor and Processing Foreman*	*Barron Enterprises Engineering Division Ellisville, Massachusetts 01047*	*Omit*

1967-1972	Quality-control, Parts Inspector, Layout/Design Asst	Always Electric Company Pattison, Indiana 47312
1965-1967	Assembly line	Bickman Manufacturing Cain, Indiana 47315
1963-1965	Machinist	U.S. Navy

Personal Data

| Age: | Born 14 June 1946 | Weight: | omit |
| Height: | omit | Other: | omit |

References (give full name and complete business address)

Mr. G. Harris Carmel, Supervisor of Quality Control, Barron Enterprises, Engineering Division, Ellisville, Massachusetts 01047. (302) 571-3828

Dr. Harold C. Mantiz, Professor of Mechanical Engineering, Massachusetts Technical Institute, 3429 Elkins Avenue, Boston, Massachusetts 02107. (302) 495-3172

Mr. Alfred Leake, Chief Inspector, Always Electric Company, Pattison, Indiana 47321. (523) 340-5689

Skills

Skills I will list and supporting details:
Supervisory—directed crew of 20 workers
        determined work assignments on priority
        solved shop production problems
Communications—Orally passed orders to workers
        Prepared monthly reports: department, budget
        Prepared daily reports: discrepancies in product conformity
Personnel—Interviewed and recommended hiring new personnel
        Conducted performance evaluations
        Made recommendations for raises and promotions
Budgetary—Prepared and monitored spending of half-million
Machine—Can operate common machine shop tools: lathes, milling machines, grinding machines
        Can use related measuring tools and gauges

An Example of a Skills Resumé

Thomas D. Davis
1045 Drake Place
Ellisville, MA 01047
(521) 363-2371

Birthdate: 14 June 1946

POSITION SOUGHT: SUPERVISOR IN QUALITY CONTROL

SKILLS

Supervisory. Directed a crew of 20 workers. Determined work assignments based on priorities. Found solutions to shop production problems.

Communications. Orally passed on orders to workers. Prepared monthly written reports, such as departmental report to an immediate supervisor, report on budget variances. Prepared daily written reports, such as reports on discrepancies in product conformity.

Personnel. Interviewed and made recommendations for hiring new personnel. Conducted performance evaluations and made recommendations for raises and promotions.

Budgetary. Have prepared and monitored the spending of a half-million-dollar department budget.

Machine. Can operate all common machine shop tools, such as lathes, milling machines, grinding machines. Can use related measuring tools and gauges.

EXPERIENCE

1972-present: Barron Enterprises, Engineering Division, Ellisville, MA 01047. Assistant Supervisor of Quality Control and Processing Supervisor

1967-1972: Always Electric Company, Pattison, IN 47312. Quality-Control Checker, Parts Inspector, Layout and Design Assistant

1965-1967: Bickman Manufacturing Company, Cain, IN 47315. Assembly line worker

1963-1965: U.S. Navy. Machinist

Resumé   Thomas D. Davis   page 2

EDUCATION 1965 - 1968: Cain Community College, Cain, IN. AA
       degree. Major in Mechanical Technology

SPECIAL   Massachusetts Technical Institute
TRAINING   1980 Quality Control with Computers (45 clock
       hours)
      1978 New Materials in Industry (45 clock hours)
      1976 Production Planning and Problems (45
       clock hours)

REFERENCES Mr. G. Harris Carmel, Supervisor of Quality
      Control, Barron Enterprises, Engineering
      Division, Ellisville, MA 01047.
      Telephone: (302) 571-3828
     Dr. Harold C. Mantiz, Professor of Mechanical
      Engineering, Massachusetts Technical
      Institute, 3429 Elkins Avenue, Boston, MA 02107.
      Telephone: (302) 495-3172
     Mr. Alfred Leake, Chief Inspector, Always
      Electric Company, Pattison, IN 47312.
      Telephone: (523) 340-5689

Job Application Form

Many companies provide printed forms, such as the one on pages 271–272, for job applicants. The form is actually a very detailed data sheet. In completing the form, use a pen or typewriter, be neat, and answer every question. Some companies suggest that applicants put a dash (—), a zero (0), or NA (not applicable) after a question that does not pertain to them. Doing so shows that the applicant has read the question and not overlooked it.

The completed forms of many applicants look very similar. Therefore, it is the accompanying letter that gives you an opportunity to make the application stand out. For this letter, follow the suggestions for a letter of application with a resumé, given earlier in this chapter.

Following is a sample application form from the K mart Corporation.°

° Used by permission of the K mart Corporation, Troy, Michigan. K mart is a trademark of the K mart Corporation, registered with the United States Patent and Trademark Office and in other countries.

APPLICATION FOR EMPLOYMENT

A K mart Corporation Store is truly a pleasant place to work. An expression of Customer Appreciation is expected from all employees by promoting the feeling of friendliness and warmth to each customer who visits our store. Details of the "TYFSAK" program will be explained during indoctrination.

A Corporation Policy . . . "No relatives are permitted to work in the same store."

DATE	**19**	PERSONAL (Please print using ball point pen)	

FULL NAME	First *MARIA*	Middle *CLARA*	Last *MENDEL*	Social Security Number *429 71 0311*

| PRESENT ADDRESS | Street *126 E LEAF* | City *LEMANS* | State *FLORIDA* | Zip *32611* | How long *10 YRS* | Telephone No. *(305) 912-6204* |

If no phone how may we contact you?

Are you 18 years of age or older? X Yes   No

List activities or committments that may interfere with attendance requirements.   *NONE*

List handicaps, health problems or prior work injuries that should be considered in job placement.   *NONE*

Have you ever applied for employment to the K mart Corp. or a subsidiary before?	☐ Yes ☒ No	If "yes" where?	Approx. Date Mo. ___ Yr. ___	How referred to us?

Have you ever been convicted of a felony?	☐ Yes ☒ No	If "yes" when? Mo. ___ Yr. ___	Explain:

CITIZENSHIP

If requested, can proof of Citizenship, Visa, or Alien Registration be provided?   ☒ Yes ☐ No

Will Visa or immigration status prevent lawful employment?   ☐ Yes ☒ No

EMPLOYMENT INTERESTS AND SKILLS

WORK SCHEDULE DESIRED   ☐ FULL TIME ☒ PART TIME   ☐ DAYS ☒ EVENING   ☒ SATURDAY ☒ SUNDAY   ☐ SEASONAL

DATE AVAILABLE FOR WORK— *NOW*   TOTAL HOURS PER WEEK DESIRED— *20-30*   SALARY EXPECTED— *OPEN*

TYPE OF WORK PREFERRED	EXAMPLES: General Merchandise Register Operator Food Dept. Apparel (Women's-Mens-Children) Specialty Mdse. Mechanic Stockroom, etc.	1. Position desired *APPAREL - WOMEN'S*	Years experience in this work *1 SUMMER*
		2. *REGISTER OPERATOR*	*—*
		3.	

EDUCATION

SCHOOLS	NAME AND ADDRESS OF SCHOOL OR COLLEGE	Dates Attended From	To	MAJOR STUDIES	Last Grade Completed	Graduation Date
HIGH SCHOOL	*LEMANS HIGH, LEMANS, FL 32611*	*1980*	*1983*	*BUSINESS*	*12*	*MAY 1983*
COLLEGE TRADE OR BUSINESS SCHOOL	*MARIN COLLEGE, GALUME, FL 31721*	*1983*		*PRES RETAILING*	*FRESHMAN*	*—*

THE CIVIL RIGHTS ACT OF 1964 PROHIBITS DISCRIMINATION IN EMPLOYMENT PRACTICE BECAUSE OF RACE, COLOR, RELIGION, SEX OR NATIONAL ORIGIN.

(An Equal Opportunity Employer)

U. S. MILITARY

Branch of Service	Date of Entry	Date Released	Active Duty Date		Type of Duty
			Mo. Yr.	Mo. Yr.	

What specialized training did you receive?

EMPLOYMENT EXPERIENCE

GIVE PAST EMPLOYMENT AS COMPLETELY AS POSSIBLE, STARTING WITH YOUR PRESENT OR LATEST EMPLOYER. INCLUDE SUMMER EMPLOYMENT. FOR ANY UNEMPLOYED OR SELF EMPLOYED PERIODS, SHOW DATES AND LOCATIONS.

	MO.	DAY	YR.	EMPLOYER'S NAME & ADDRESS - CITY STATE ZIP	Name & Title of Immediate Superior	Last Position Held & Salary	Reason for Leaving
				Present or Last Employer	ANNA G. BROWN	FILE CLERK	RETURN TO
From	5	15	84	OLD LINE INSURANCE COMPANY	OFFICE MANAGER	TYPIST	COLLEGE
				Address		$4.65 hr	
To	PRESENT			ADAMS, GA 31620			
				Employer	OPHELIA LAWLER	SALES-	GO TO
From	5	20	83	LAWLER'S DRESS SHOP		PERSON	COLLEGE
				Address	OWNER-MANAGER	$4.00 hr	
To	8	15	83	LEMANS, FL 32611			
				Employer			
From							
				Address			
To							
				Employer			
From							
				Address			
To							

REFERENCES

GIVE NAME OF THREE PERSONS YOU ARE NOT RELATED TO AND BY WHOM YOU HAVE NOT BEEN EMPLOYED. THESE PEOPLE SHOULD HAVE KNOWN YOU FOR SEVERAL YEARS.

NAME – (INITIALS, LAST NAME)	ADDRESS STREET, CITY, STATE, ZIP	OCCUPATION	YEARS OF ACQUAINTANCE
A.L. WRIGHT	LEMANS HIGH SCHOOL LEMANS, FL 32611	COUNSELING	4
B.E. BURKHEAD	MARIN COLLEGE, GALUME, FL 31721	TEACHING (RETAILING)	1/2
W.M. HELIOS	142 E LEAF, LEMANS, FL 32611	RETIRED (PLUMBING)	10

GIVE NAME OF ANY RELATIVES, AND/OR ACQUAINTANCES, EMPLOYED BY K mart CORPORATION OR A SUBSIDIARY:

NAME	POSITION	LOCATION	RELATIONSHIP
G.M. BOENG	ASSISTANT MANAGER	BIRMINGHAM, AL	HUSBAND'S COUSIN

ADDITIONAL INFORMATION FOR PLACEMENT CONSIDERATION

CONCEPTS AND INFORMATION LEARNED IN MY MAJOR (RETAILING) WILL HELP ME BE AN ASSET TO K-MART. THIS LEARNING INCLUDES THE IMPORTANCE OF ATTRACTIVELY DISPLAY-ING MERCHANDISE, HANDLING SUSPECTED SHOPLIFTERS LEGALLY AND COPING WITH EMERGENCIES.

I authorize investigation of all statements on this application. It is further understood that misrepresentation or omission of facts called for hereon will result in cancellation of this application or dismissal from the Corporation's service if I have been employed. Upon employment I will submit a certified birth certificate or other satisfactory evidence of birthplace and citizenship.

This application is considered current for 30 days. If you wish to be considered for later employment you must renew your application in person and in writing. It is understood that no position with K mart Corporation is guaranteed for any length of time and either the employee or the Company can terminate the relationship at will at any time.

APPLICANT SIGNATURE	DATE SIGNED
Maria Clara Mendel	August 19, 1985

CODE 94-45-10—Pads 100's—(Rev. 7/81)—S—Litho in U.S.A.

Application Follow-up Letters

Frequently, after writing and mailing a letter of application (pages 255–262), filling out and submitting a job application form (pages 270–272), and possibly after completing an interview (pages 449–454), you may need to write a follow-up letter. The content of the follow-up letter is determined by events occurring after the application or interview.

The follow-up letter may be a request for a response from the prospective employer. This letter may be written if you were promised a response by a certain date but have not received a response by that date. This letter may also be written if you have sent an application for a job you hope will be available.

A letter requesting a response may resemble the sample letter on page 277. The Plan Sheet used for planning and organizing the letter is also included.

The letter may simply thank the interviewer, remind the person of your qualifications, and indicate a desire for a positive response. The body of such a letter appears below:

> The interview with you on Wednesday, June 10, was indeed a pleasant, informative experience. Thank you for helping me feel at ease.
>
> After hearing the details about the World Bank's training program and opportunities available to persons who complete the program, I am eager to be an employee of World Bank. I believe my experience working with People's Bank and my associate degree in Banking and Finance Technology provide a sound background for me as a trainee.
>
> I look forward to hearing from you that I have been accepted as a trainee in the World Bank's training program.

See also pages 229 and 454, 455.

The follow-up letter may reaffirm the acceptance of a job and your appreciation for the job. The letter may also ask questions that you have thought of since getting the job, mention the date you will begin work, and make a statement about looking forward to working with the company. The body of such a letter may include the following:

> Thank you for your offer to hire me as consulting engineer for Wanner, Clare, and Layshock, Inc. I eagerly accept the offer. The confidence you expressed in my abilities to help the firm improve workers' safety certainly motivates me to be as effective as possible.
>
> I look forward to beginning work on Tuesday, July 10, ready to demonstrate that I deserve the confidence expressed in me.

A follow-up letter may be needed if you decide to refuse a job offer. The body of such letter may be written as follows:

> Thank you for offering me a place in the World Bank's training program. The opportunities available upon completion are enticing.
>
> Since my interview with you, the president of People's Bank, where I have worked part-time while completing my associate degree in banking and finance, has offered me permanent employment. The bank will pay for my continued schooling, allow me to work during the summers, and guarantee me full-time employment upon completing an advanced degree.

By accepting this offer from People's Bank, I can live near my aging parents and help care for them.

I appreciate your interest in me and wish continued success for World Bank.

The follow-up application letter is simply a courteous response to events following the application or interview.

On the following pages are a Plan Sheet, filled in by the student before writing, and a follow-up letter requesting a response from a prospective employer.

PLAN SHEET
FOR WRITING AN APPLICATION FOLLOW-UP LETTER

Layout Form (block, modified block, full block, simplified block)

I will use:
modified block

Heading

My mailing address is:
2121 Oak Street
Fort Collins, CO 80521

The date is:
July 19, 1985

Inside Address

The person (or firm) to whom I am writing (including any identifying title after the name) is:
Mr. William Hatton, Personnel Director

The complete mailing address is:
World Bank
20 East 53rd Street
New York, NY 10022

Salutation

I will use:
Dear Mr. Hatton:

Body

The purpose of the letter is (check one):

_____X_____ to request a response from a prospective employer
_____ to thank the interviewer
_____ to reaffirm acceptance of a job
_____ to refuse a job offer

The opening statement(s) I will use is:
On June 10 I was interviewed by Mr. John Salman, your representative, for a place in the World Bank's training program. Mr. Salman told me that I

would be notified about my application by July 1. Although it is the middle of July, I have not received a response.

I will explain the purpose of the letter by:
Since I must make certain decisions by August 1, could I please hear from you about my employment possibilities with World Bank.

The closing statement(s) I will include is:
I am, of course, quite eager to become an employee of World Bank and would appreciate a response.

Complimentary Close

I will use:
Sincerely,

Signature (including, if applicable, the name of the firm and identifying title)

I will use:
Jayne T. Mannos

Special Parts

This letter requires the following special parts:
omit

Application Follow-Up Letter in Modified Block Form

2121 Oak Street
Fort Collins, CO 80521
July 19, 1985

Mr. William Hatton, Personnel Director
World Bank
20 East 53rd Street
New York, NY 10022

Dear Mr. Hatton:

On June 10 I was interviewed by Mr. John Salman, your representative, for a place in the World Bank's training program. Mr. Salman told me that I would be notified about my application by July 1. Although it is the middle of July, I have not received any reponse.

Since I must make certain decisions by August 1, could I please hear from you about my employment possibilities with World Bank.

I am, of course, quite eager to become an employee of World Bank and hope that I will receive a positive response.

Sincerely,

Jayne T. Mannos

Jayne T. Mannos

GENERAL PRINCIPLES IN WRITING MEMORANDUMS AND LETTERS

1. *Memorandums are typically used for written communication between persons in the same company.* Memorandums are used to convey or confirm information.
2. *A memorandum has only two regular parts: the heading and the body.* The heading typically includes the guide words TO, FROM, SUBJECT, and DATE plus the information. The body of the memorandum is the message. The writer usually initials the memo immediately following the typed "From" name; some writers prefer to give their signature at the end of the memo.
3. *An effective business communication is written on good quality stationery, is neat and pleasing to the eye, and follows a standardized layout form.*
4. *The six regular parts of a business letter are the heading, inside address, salutation, body, complimentary close, and signature.* The parts follow a standard sequence and arrangement.
5. *A letter may require a special part.* Among these are an attention line, a subject line, an identification line, an enclosure line, a copy line, a personal line, and a mailing line.
6. *The envelope has two regular parts: the outside address and the return address.* A special part, such as an attention line or a personal line, may also be needed.
7. *The content of an effective letter is well organized, stresses the "you" attitude, uses natural wording, and is concise.*
8. *Among the most common types of letters written by businesses and individuals are letters of inquiry, order, sales, claim and adjustment, collection, job application and job application follow-up.* Each type of letter requires special attention as to purpose, inclusion of pertinent information, and consideration of who will be reading the letter and why.
9. *Job application materials present the qualifications of the applicant, including education, work experience, personal information, and references.* This information may be presented in a letter, as a resumé, on a printed job application form, or in a combination of these.

APPLICATION 1   WRITING MEMORANDUMS AND LETTERS

Make a collection of at least ten memorandums and letters of various types and bring them to class. For each communication, answer these questions:

1. What layout form is used?
2. Is a letterhead used? What information is given in the letterhead?
3. Is the communication neat and pleasing in appearance? Explain your answer.
4. What special parts of a memorandum or letter are used?
5. What is the purpose of the communication?
6. Does the communication have the "you" attitude? Explain your answer.

APPLICATION 2   WRITING MEMORANDUMS AND LETTERS

Select one of the communications you collected for the preceding application. Evaluate the item according to the General Principles in Writing Memorandums and Letters, above, and any special instructions for this type of communication. Hand in both the communication and the evaluation.

APPLICATION 3   WRITING MEMORANDUMS AND LETTERS

Assume that you are the president of an organization. The date and the location of the next regular meeting have been changed. You need to send this information to the members of the organization.

    a. Make a Plan Sheet for Writing a Memorandum like the one on page 284, and fill it in.
    b. Write a preliminary draft of the memorandum.
    c. Revise.
    d. Write the final draft of the memorandum.

APPLICATION 4   WRITING MEMORANDUMS AND LETTERS

Assume that you are an employee in a company. You have an idea for improving efficiency that should lead to a larger margin of profit for the company. Present this idea in writing to your immediate supervisor. State the idea clearly and precisely, and give substantiating data.

    a. Make a Plan Sheet for Writing a Memorandum like the one on page 284, and fill it in.
    b. Write a preliminary draft of the memorandum.
    c. Revise.
    d. Write the final draft of the memorandum.

APPLICATION 5   WRITING MEMORANDUMS AND LETTERS

Examine the content and form of the following body of a letter addressed to *Popular Science Digest*. Point out every item that keeps the paragraph from being clear.

> In regard to your article a while back on how to make a home fire alarm system in *Popular Science Digest*, which was very interesting. I would like to obtain more information. Would also like to know the names of people who have had good results with same. Give me where they live, too.

APPLICATION 6   WRITING MEMORANDUMS AND LETTERS

Rewrite the body of the letter in Application 5.

APPLICATION 7   WRITING MEMORANDUMS AND LETTERS

Prepare a letter to a person such as a former employer or a former teacher asking permission to use the person's name as a reference in a job application.

    a. Make a Plan Sheet for Writing a Letter of Inquiry like the one on pages 285–286, and fill it in.
    b. Write a preliminary draft of the letter.
    c. Revise.
    d. Write the final draft of the letter.

APPLICATION 8   WRITING MEMORANDUMS AND LETTERS

Write a letter to the appropriate official in your college requesting permission to take your final examinations a week earlier than scheduled. Be sure to state your reason or reasons clearly and effectively.

    a. Make a Plan Sheet for Writing a Letter of Inquiry like the one on pages 285 – 286, and fill it in.
    b. Write a preliminary draft of the letter.
    c. Revise.
    d. Write the final draft of the letter.

APPLICATION 9   WRITING MEMORANDUMS AND LETTERS

Prepare an order letter for an item you saw advertised in a newspaper or magazine.

    a. Make a Plan Sheet for Writing an Order Letter like the one on pages 287 – 288, and fill it in.
    b. Write a preliminary draft of the letter.
    c. Revise.
    d. Write the final draft of the letter.

APPLICATION 10   WRITING MEMORANDUMS AND LETTERS

Assume that you are the instructor in one of your lab courses and you have been given the responsibility of ordering several new pieces of equipment.

    a. Make a Plan Sheet for Writing an Order Letter like the one on pages 287 – 288, and fill it in.
    b. Write a preliminary draft of the letter.
    c. Revise.
    d. Write the final draft of the letter.

APPLICATION 11   WRITING MEMORANDUMS AND LETTERS

Find a printed order form and make out an order on it. It is usually wise to write out the information on a sheet of paper and then transfer it to the order form.

APPLICATION 12   WRITING MEMORANDUMS AND LETTERS

Assume that you work part-time as a salesclerk in a clothing store and that you are paid on a commission basis. Write a sales letter to be sent to a number of people you know.

    a. Make a Plan Sheet for Writing a Sales Letter like the one on pages 289 – 290, and fill it in.
    b. Write a preliminary draft of the letter.
    c. Revise.
    d. Write the final draft of the letter.

APPLICATION 13   WRITING MEMORANDUMS AND LETTERS

Write a sales letter, to be distributed to students on campus, telling about a special sale in the campus bookstore.

a. Make a Plan Sheet for Writing a Sales Letter like the one on pages 289–290, and fill it in.
b. Write a preliminary draft of the letter.
c. Revise.
d. Write the final draft of the letter.

APPLICATION 14   WRITING MEMORANDUMS AND LETTERS

Assume that you ordered an item, such as a pair of shoes, a set of wheel covers, a ring, or a bowling ball, and the wrong size was sent to you. Write a claim letter requesting proper adjustment.

a. Make a Plan Sheet for Writing a Claim or an Adjustment Letter like the one on pages 291–292, and fill it in.
b. Write a preliminary draft of the letter.
c. Revise.
d. Write the final draft of the letter.

APPLICATION 15   WRITING MEMORANDUMS AND LETTERS

Write a claim letter requesting an adjustment on a piece of equipment, a tool, an appliance, or a similar item that is not giving you satisfactory service. You have owned the item two months and it has a one-year warranty.

a. Make a Plan Sheet for Writing a Claim or an Adjustment Letter like the one on pages 291–292, and fill it in.
b. Write a preliminary draft of the letter.
c. Revise.
d. Write the final draft of the letter.

APPLICATION 16   WRITING MEMORANDUMS AND LETTERS

Write an adjustment letter in response to Application 14.

a. Make a Plan Sheet for Writing a Claim or an Adjustment Letter like the one on pages 291–292, and fill it in.
b. Write a preliminary draft of the letter.
c. Revise.
d. Write the final draft of the letter.

APPLICATION 17   WRITING MEMORANDUMS AND LETTERS

Write an adjustment letter in response to Application 15.

a. Make a Plan Sheet for Writing a Claim or an Adjustment Letter like the one on pages 291–292, and fill it in.

b. Write a preliminary draft of the letter.
c. Revise.
d. Write the final draft of the letter.

APPLICATION 18   WRITING MEMORANDUMS AND LETTERS

As credit manager of the local college bookstore, write a series of collection letters to be mailed to students with accounts delinquent for varying periods of time.

a. Make a Plan Sheet for Writing Collection Letters like the one on pages 293–294, and fill it in.
b. Write a preliminary draft.
c. Revise.
d. Write the final draft of the letter.

APPLICATION 19   WRITING MEMORANDUMS AND LETTERS

Write a self-contained letter of application (without an accompanying resumé) for a summer, a part-time, or a full-time job for which your present experience and training qualify you. Remember that in the application letter you should concentrate on the *relevant* qualities.

a. Make a Plan Sheet for Writing a Letter of Application Without a Resumé like the one on pages 295–296, and fill it in.
b. Write a preliminary draft of the letter.
c. Revise.
d. Write the final draft of the letter.

APPLICATION 20   WRITING MEMORANDUMS AND LETTERS

Prepare a traditional resumé or a skills resumé or both, as directed by your instructor.

a. Make a Plan Sheet for Writing a Resumé like the one on pages 297–298, and fill it in.
b. Write a preliminary draft of the resumé.
c. Revise.
d. Write the final draft of the resumé.

APPLICATION 21   WRITING MEMORANDUMS AND LETTERS

Write a letter of application answering an advertisement in the "Help Wanted" section of a newspaper. Include with your letter one of the resumés you prepared in the preceding application. Remember that although the resumé is a full listing, the accompanying letter stresses information to the specific job.

a. Make a Plan Sheet for Writing a Letter of Application with a Resumé like the one on pages 299–300, and fill it in.
b. Write a preliminary draft of the letter.
c. Revise.
d. Write a final draft of the letter.

APPLICATION 22 WRITING MEMORANDUMS AND LETTERS

Secure a job application form. (The form used by the U.S. Government is especially thorough.) Fill in the form neatly and completely. It is usually wise to write out the information on a separate sheet of paper and then transfer it to the application form.

APPLICATION 23 WRITING MEMORANDUMS AND LETTERS

Write an application follow-up letter in which you accept the job applied for in Application 19.

   a. Make a Plan Sheet for Writing an Application Follow-up Letter like the one on pages 301–302, and fill it in.
   b. Write a preliminary draft of the letter.
   c. Revise.
   d. Write the final draft of the letter.

APPLICATION 24 WRITING MEMORANDUMS AND LETTERS

Write an application follow-up letter in which you refuse the job offered as a result of the Application 19 letter.

   a. Make a Plan Sheet for Writing an Application Follow-up Letter like the one on pages 301–302, and fill it in.
   b. Write a preliminary draft of the letter.
   c. Revise.
   d. Write the final draft of the letter.

PLAN SHEET
FOR WRITING A MEMORANDUM

Heading

To:

From:

Subject:

Date:

Body

The purpose of this memorandum is:

I need to include this information:

Special Parts

This memorandum requires these special parts:

PLAN SHEET
FOR WRITING A LETTER OF INQUIRY

Layout Form (block, modified block, full block, simplified block)

I will use:

Heading

My mailing address is:

The date is:

Inside Address

The person (or firm) to whom I am writing (including any identifying title after the name) is:

The complete mailing address is:

Salutation

I will use:

Body

Through this letter I am seeking:

The reason for my inquiry is:

To make my inquiry clear and specific, I need to include this information:

Complimentary Close

I will use:

Signature (including, if applicable, the name of the firm and identifying title)

I will use:

Special Parts

This letter requires the following special parts:

PLAN SHEET
FOR WRITING AN ORDER LETTER

Layout Form (block, modified block, full block, simplified block)

I will use:

Heading

My mailing address is:

The date is:

Inside Address

The person (or firm) to whom I am writing (including any identifying title after the name) is:

The complete mailing address is:

Salutation

I will use:

Body

The items I am ordering and their identification (model number, catalog number, size, color, weight, finish, etc.) are:

Item	Quantity	Identification	Cost

The manner of payment (check, money order, credit card, COD, charge, etc.) is:

The method of shipping (parcel post, truck freight, railway freight, air express, etc.) is:

Other information or instructions:

Complimentary Close
I will use:

Signature (including, if applicable, the name of the firm and identifying title)
I will use:

Special Parts
This letter requires the following special parts:

PLAN SHEET
FOR WRITING A SALES LETTER

Layout Form (block, modified block, full block, simplified block)

I will use:

Heading

My mailing address is:

The date is:

Inside Address

The person (or firm) to whom I am writing (including any identifying title after the name) is:

The complete mailing address is:

Salutation

I will use:

Body

To get the reader's attention and arouse interest, I will:

The product (or service) I am selling is:

The product can be described in this way:

.

The product will benefit or profit the reader in these ways:

The plan that I will present whereby the reader can immediately begin to use the product is:

Complimentary Close

I will use:

Signature (including, if applicable, the name of the firm and identifying title)

I will use:

Special Parts

This letter requires the following special parts:

PLAN SHEET
FOR WRITING A CLAIM OR AN ADJUSTMENT LETTER

Layout Form (block, modified block, full block, simplified block)

I will use:

Heading

My mailing address is:

The date is:

Inside Address

The person (or firm) to whom I am writing (including any identifying title after the name) is:

The complete mailing address is:

Salutation

I will use:

Body

Identification of the transaction (items purchased, date, invoice number, model number, style, size, etc.):

Statement of the problem or complaint:

Desired action or action that will be taken:

Complimentary Close

I will use:

Signature (including, if applicable, the name of the firm and identifying title)

I will use:

Special Parts

This letter requires the following special parts:

PLAN SHEET
FOR WRITING A COLLECTION LETTER

Layout Form (block, modified block, full block, simplified block)
I will use:

Heading
My mailing address is:

The date is:

Inside Address
The person (or firm) to whom I am writing (including any identifying title after the name) is:

The complete mailing address is:

Salutation
I will use:

Body
Appeal to customer:

Reference to balance due and payment:

Problem(s) preventing payment:

Action the company owed has taken:

Action the company owed will take:

Complimentary Close

I will use:

Signature (including, if applicable, the name of the firm and identifying title)

I will use:

Special Parts

This letter requires the following special parts:

Layout Form (block, modified block, full block, simplified block)

I will use:

Heading

My mailing address is:

The date is:

Inside Address

The person (or firm) to whom I am writing (including any identifying title after the name) is:

The complete mailing address is:

Salutation

I will use:

Body

Job applied for is:

I learned about it:

The reason I want the job is:

I want to emphasize the following:

Education (starting with the most recent experience, give name and location of high school and/or college, date of graduation, degree, major, subjects related to prospective job, awards, activities):

Experience (list each job, beginning with most recent, or present):

Personal data:

Other:

I would like an interview on:

I can be reached by:

Complimentary Close
I will use:

Signature
I will use:

Special Parts
This letter requires the following special parts:

PLAN SHEET
FOR WRITING A RESUMÉ

Type of Resumé (traditional or skills) I will use:

Heading

Name:
Address: Telephone:

The date is:

Job Sought

Education

College   Location   Date of Graduation

Degree (or degree sought)   Major Field

Subjects related to prospective job:

Special training:

Activities:

High School   Location   Date of Graduation

Areas of emphasis or of particular interest:

Awards or special recognition and/or activities:

Work Experience (beginning with the most recent or present employment)

Date of Employment	Specific Work	Name and Address of Firm	Full Name of Supervisor

Personal Data

Age: Weight:
Height: Other:

References (give full name and complete business address)

Skills

Skills I will list and supporting details:

PLAN SHEET
FOR WRITING A LETTER OF APPLICATION WITH
A RESUMÉ

Layout Form (block, modified block, full block, simplified block)

I will use:

Heading

My mailing address is:

The date is:

Inside Address

The person (or firm) to whom I am writing (including any identifying title after the name) is:

The complete mailing address is:

Salutation

I will use:

Body

Job applied for is:

I learned about it:

The reason I want the job is:

From the resumé I want to emphasize:

Education:

Experience:

Personal data:

Other:

I would like an interview on:

I can be reached by:

Complimentary Close
I will use:

Signature (including, if applicable, the name of the firm and identifying title)
I will use:

Special Parts
This letter requires the following special parts:

Layout Form (block, modified block, full block, simplified block)

I will use:

Heading

My mailing address is:

The date is:

Inside Address

The person (or firm) to whom I am writing (including any identifying title after the name) is:

The complete mailing address is:

Salutation

I will use:

Body

The purpose of the letter is (check one):

_____ to request a response from a prospective employer
_____ to thank the interviewer
_____ to reaffirm acceptance of a job
_____ to refuse a job offer

The opening statement(s) I will use is:

I will explain the purpose of the letter by:

The closing statement(s) I will include is:

Complimentary Close
I will use:

Signature (including, if applicable, the name of the firm and identifying title)
I will use:

Special Parts
This letter requires the following special parts:

CHAPTER 8

Reports: Conveying Needed Information

OBJECTIVES 305
INTRODUCTION 305
SCOPE OF REPORT WRITING 305
DEFINITION OF "REPORT" 306
    Qualities of Report Content 306
      Accuracy 306
      Clarity 306
      Conciseness 306
      Objectivity 307
SCHOOL REPORTS AND PROFESSIONAL REPORTS 307
FORMAT OF THE REPORT 308
    Print Form 308
    Memorandum 308
    Letter 309
    Conventional Report Format 309
      Nonformal Reports 309
      Formal Reports 309
        Parts 309
        Organization 312
    Oral Report 312
VISUALS 312
HEADINGS 313
LAYOUT AND DESIGN 313
COMMON TYPES OF REPORTS 313
    Reading Report 313
      Purpose 313
      Uses 314
      Main Parts 314
      Organization 316
    Periodic Report 322
      Purpose 322
      Uses 322
      Main Parts 322
      Organization 322
    Progress Report 327
      Purpose 327

Uses   327
Main Parts   327
Organization   327
Laboratory Report   333
Purpose   333
Uses   333
Main Parts   333
Organization   333
Field Report   341
Purpose   341
Uses   341
Main Parts   341
Organization   341
Research Report   353
GENERAL PRINCIPLES IN GIVING A REPORT   354
PROCEDURE FOR GIVING A REPORT   354
APPLICATIONS   354

OBJECTIVES

Upon completing this chapter, the student should be able to:

- Write a definition of reports
- Explain the difference between school reports and professional reports
- Select and use appropriate formats for presenting reports
- Use headings in reports
- Use effective layout and design in reports
- List and identify common types of reports
- Give a reading report
- Give a periodic report
- Give a progress report
- Give a laboratory report
- Give a field report

INTRODUCTION

The word *report* covers numerous communications that fulfill many purposes. You may be concerned about your monthly financial report (a bank statement) or the grade report that you will receive at the end of the term. Or you may be busy polling students about dormitory hours to support your committee's recommendations to the housing council. You may face a due date for a supplementary reading report, or a laboratory report, or a project report.

In the business, industrial, and governmental worlds, too, reports are a vital part of communication. A memorandum to the billing department, a weekly production report to the supervisor, a requisition for supplies, a letter to the home office describing the status of bids for a construction project, a performance report on the new computer, a sales report from the housewares department, a report on the availability of land for a housing project, a report to a customer on an estimate for automobile repairs: these are but a few examples of the kinds of reports and the functions they serve.

SCOPE OF REPORT WRITING

Although report writing is becoming a firmly established part of the curriculum for students who plan to enter business, industry, and government, difficulties arise in deciding on the specifics to be taught in the classroom. For one thing, there is no uniformity in report classifications. Depending upon the business, the industry, the particular branch of government, or the textbook, reports may be classified on one or more bases, such as subject matter, purpose, function, length, frequency of compilation, type of format, degree of formality, or method by which the information is gathered. Similarly, there is a lack of uniformity in terminology.

These difficulties underscore the aliveness, the contemporary pace, the elasticity of report writing. Only when report writing has become a relic — serving no practical usefulness — will actual reports fall into well-defined categories.

It is unrealistic, therefore, to draw sharp boundary lines between types of reports or to try to cover all the situations and problems involved in report writing. However, it is quite realistic and practical for you to:

- Become acquainted with the general nature of report writing.
- Develop self-confidence by learning basic principles of report writing. Thus, when you are given the responsibility for writing a report, you can analyze the need and then fulfill your assignment efficiently.
- Study and practice writing several common types of reports that you are most likely to encounter as a student and as a future employee.

DEFINITION OF "REPORT"

A very basic definition of a report might be: a report is technical data, collected and analyzed, and presented in an organized form. Another definition: a report is an objective, organized presentation of factual information that answers a request or supplies needed data. The report usually serves an immediate, *practical* purpose; it is the basis on which decisions are made. Generally, the report is requested or authorized by one person (such as a teacher or employer) and is prepared for a particular, limited audience.

Reports may be simple or complex; they may be long or short; they may be formal or informal; they may be oral or written. Characteristics such as these are determined mainly by the purpose of the report and the intended audience.

Qualities of Report Content

Reports convey exact, useful information. That information, or content, should be presented with accuracy, clarity, conciseness, and objectivity.

Accuracy A report must be accurate. If the information presented is factual, it should be verified by tests, research, documentary authority, or other valid sources. Information that is opinion or probability should be distinguished as such and accompanied by supporting evidence. Dishonesty and carelessness are inexcusable.

Clarity A report must be clear. If a report is to serve its purpose, the information must be clear and understandable to the reader. The reader should not have to ask: *What does this mean?* or *What is the writer trying to say?* The writer helps to ensure clarity by using exact, specific words in easily readable sentence patterns, by following conventional usage in such mechanical matters as punctuation and grammar, and by organizing the material logically.

Conciseness A report must be concise. Conciseness is "saying much in a few words." Unnecessary wordiness is eliminated, and yet complete information is transmitted. Busy executives appreciate concise, timesaving reports that do not compel them to wade through bogs of words to get to the essence of the matter. Note the example that follows.

> WORDY: After all is said and done, it is my honest opinion that the company and all its employees will be better satisfied if the new plan for sick leave is adopted and put into practice.

CONCISE: The company should adopt the new sick leave plan.

Revise a report until it contains no more words than those needed for accuracy, clarity, and correctness of expression. For further discussion of conciseness, see pages 8–9 and 219.

Objectivity A report must be objective. Objectivity demands that logic rather than emotion determine both the content of the report and its presentation. The content should be impersonal, with no indication of the personal feelings and sentiments of the writer. For instance, a report on the comparison of new car warranties for six makes of automobiles should not reveal the writer's preference among the six or the make of automobile he or she drives. The report must be organized logically and its appeal aimed at understanding.

Essential to objectivity is the use of the denotative meaning of words — the meaning that is the same, insofar as possible, to everyone. Denotative meanings of words are found in a dictionary; they are exact and impersonal. Such meanings contrast with the connotative meanings, which permit associated, emotive, or figurative overtones. The distinction between the single denotative meaning and the multiple connotative meanings of a word can be illustrated by examples:

WORD:	war
DENOTATIVE MEANING:	open, armed conflict
CONNOTATIVE MEANING:	death, injustice, Vietnam, freedom, cruelty, necessary evil, God vs. Satan, draft, soldiers, high taxes, destruction, bombing, orphans
WORD:	work
DENOTATIVE MEANINGS:	employment, job
CONNOTATIVE MEANINGS:	paying bills, happiness, curse of Adam, accomplishment, 9 to 5, satisfaction, adulthood, alarm clock, fighting the traffic, income, new car, sweat, sitting at a desk, nursing

For further discussion of denotation and connotation, see pages 5–6.

SCHOOL REPORTS AND PROFESSIONAL REPORTS

Reports can be classified according to the function they serve: school reports, which are a testing device for students; and professional reports, which are used in business, industry, and government.

Both school reports and professional reports are important to you — but in different ways and for different reasons. School reports, of course, are of more immediate concern simply because you are a student and because making reports is a widely used learning technique. In the school report it is you the student who is important; emphasis is on you as a learner and as a developer of potential skills. The report shows completion of a unit of study; it reflects the understanding, thoroughness, and intelligence with which you have carried out an assignment. The school report also gives you practice in presenting the kinds of reports that your future job may require. Such practice can be invaluable in helping you prepare to meet on-the-job demands.

Professional reports — the reports used in business, industry, and govern-ment — serve a different function from that of school reports. In professional reports, emphasis is on the information that the report contains and on serving the needs of the recipient. The crucial question is this: How well does the report satisfy the needs of the person to whom the report is sent? On the other hand, the instructor who assigns the school report ordinarily neither needs nor will use the information; the instructor is interested in the report only insofar as it reflects the educational progress of the writer.

In both school and professional reports, desirable qualities are accuracy, clarity, conciseness, and objectivity. But you should understand that some of the information given in a school report is not needed in a professional report. For example, in a student laboratory report, your instructor may require information on conventional theory and procedure (to be sure that you understand and can explain them). In business, industry, and government, such information ordinarily would be unnecessary because it is taken for granted that you are knowledgeable about recognized theories and accepted procedures.

FORMAT OF THE REPORT

Most reports (even those presented orally) are put in writing to record the information for future reference and to ensure an accurate, efficient means of transmitting the report when it is to go to several people in different locations. A report may be given in various formats: on a printed form, as a memorandum, as a letter, in a conventional report format, or as an oral report. The format may be prescribed by the person or agency requesting the report; it may be suggested by the nature of the report; or it may be left entirely to the discretion of the writer.

Printed Form

Printed forms are used for many routine reports, such as sales, purchase requests, production counts, general physical examinations, census information, delivery reports. Printed forms call for information to be reported in a prescribed, uniform manner, for the headings remain the same, and the responses —usually numbers or words and phrases—are expected to be of a certain length.

Printed forms are especially timesaving for both the writer and the reader. The writer need not be concerned with structure and organization; the reader knows where specific information is given and need not worry about omission of essential items. However, printed forms lack flexibility: they can deal with only a limited number of situations. Further, they lack a personal touch that provides an opportunity for the writer to express his or her individuality.

In making a report that uses a printed form, the primary considerations are accuracy, legibility, and conciseness. (See the report on page 323.)

Memorandum

Memorandums and report letters are used in similar circumstances, that is, if the report is short and contains no visual materials. Unlike a report letter, however, the memorandum is used primarily within a firm. (For a detailed discussion of memorandums, see pages 214–218.)

A report memorandum is illustrated on page 326.

Letter

As with the memorandum, the letter is often used for a short report (not more than several pages) that does not include visual materials. The letter is almost always directed to someone *outside* the firm.

The report letter should be as carefully planned and organized as any other piece of writing and should observe basic principles of letter writing. (See Chapter 7, Memorandums and Letters.) The report letter follows conventional letter writing practices concerning heading, inside address, salutation, and signature; however, the conventional complimentary close of a report letter is "Respectfully submitted." A subject line is usually included. The report letter often is longer than other business letters and may have internal headings if needed for easier readability. The degree of formality varies, depending on the intended reader and purpose.

Although report letters are widely used, some firms discourage their use to avoid the possible difficulty occasioned if they are filed with ordinary correspondence.

A report given in a letter format is illustrated on page 344.

Conventional Report Format

Conventional report formats include both *nonformal* and *formal* reports. Nonformal and formal, vague though often used terms, refer in actual practice to report length and to the degree to which the report is "dressed up."

Nonformal Reports The nonformal, or informal, report usually is only a few pages in length, is designed for circulation within an organization or for a named reader, and includes only the essential sections of the report proper:

> Introduction (or purpose)
> Body (procedure, discussion of results)
> Conclusions and recommendations

The preliminary matter and end matter of the formal report are omitted. Examples of nonformal reports appear on pages 319–321, 328, 331–332, 336, 337–340, and 345–346.

Formal Reports The formal report has a stylized format evolving from the nature of the report and the needs of the reader. Often the formal report is long (eight to ten pages, or more), is designed for circulation outside an organization, and will not be read in its entirety by each person who examines it.

PARTS Conventional parts of the formal report have developed to improve reporting efficiency and to increase readability. These parts, in their layout and organization, are simply tools or devices for aiding the communication process;

therefore, the writer should combine, omit, or vary them to accommodate the purpose and the intended audience of the report. The conventional parts may be listed as follows:

Preliminary matter:	Transmittal memorandum or letter
	Title page
	Table of contents
	Lists of tables and figures
	Summary or abstract
Report proper:	Introduction
	Body (procedure, discussion of results)
	Conclusions and recommendations
End matter:	Appendix
	Bibliography

1. *Preliminary Matter.* This includes the transmittal memorandum or letter, title page, table of contents, list of illustrations, and summary or abstract.

   The **transmittal memorandum** (if the report is delivered within a company) **or transmittal letter** (if the report is mailed) affords the writer an opportunity to make needed comments on the report; for instance, identification of the report, reason for the report, how and when the report was requested, problems associated with the report, or reasons for emphasizing certain items. The length of this covering memorandum or letter varies, depending on the circumstances. The communication may be as simple as: "Enclosed is the report on customer parking facilities, which you asked me on July 5 to investigate"; or it may be several pages in length. (For further discussion, see Chapter 7: Memorandums and Letters.)

   The **title page** contains a listing of the title of the report (as exact, specific, and complete as possible), the name of the person or organization for whom the report is made, the name of the person making the report, and the date. The arrangement of these items on the page should be pleasing to the eye.

   The **table of contents,** which functions as an outline, is a valuable part of any report of more than a few pages. It shows the reader at a glance the scope of the report, the specific points (headings) that are covered, the organization of the report, and page numbers. Indentation is used to indicate the interrelations of subdivisions and main divisions. Wording of headings in the contents should be exactly as they are in the report.

   If needed, separate **lists of tables and figures** follow the table of contents. (Tables are referred to as tables; graphs, charts, drawings, maps, and other illustrations are usually referred to as figures.) The lists are helpful if more than five or six tables and figures are used, or if they form a significant part of the body of the report. All captions are typed exactly as they appear in the text, with the beginning page for each table or figure. The usual practice is to capitalize only the first letter of the words *table* and *figure* and to use arabic numerals (1, 2, 3, etc.) for numbering. Quite acceptable, however, are the decimal system of numbering, and the use of all capitals for the word *table* and roman numerals: TABLE IV.

The **summary or abstract** (which may precede the table of contents) appears on a separate page. It is very important, especially when the report is to be passed upward through a chain of command. It gives the content of the report in a highly condensed form; it is a brief, factual pulling together of the essential, or central, points of the report. Included are an explanation of the nature of the problem; the procedure used in studying the problem; and results, conclusions, and recommendations. The summary, in length no more than 10 percent of the whole, should represent the *entire* report. (For further discussion, see Informative Summary, pages 192–197).

2. *Report Proper.* The report proper consists of three or four parts: introduction, body, and conclusions and recommendations (conclusions and recommendations may be treated separately or together).

The **introduction,** depending on the nature of the report, may be simply an introductory paragraph or an expanded formal introduction with a separate heading. A simple introductory paragraph gives an overview of the subject. In addition, the introduction may indicate the general plan and organization of the report (especially if no table of contents is provided), give a summary of the report (if no formal summary or abstract is included), provide background information, and explain the reason for the report. The formal introduction, usually entitled "Introduction," typically deals with aspects of reporting, not of subject matter: name of the person or group authorizing the report, function the report will serve, purpose of the investigation, nature of the problem, significance of the problem, scope of the report, historical background (previous study of the problem), plan or organization of the report, definition or classification of terms, and methods and materials used in the investigation.

The **body** is the major section of the report; it presents the information. The body includes an explanation of the theory on which the investigative approach is based, a step-by-step account of the procedure, a description of materials and equipment, the results of the investigation, and an analysis of the results.

The **conclusions and recommendations** complete the report proper—unless the report is purely informational, in which case the paper may conclude with a summary of the main points. Ordinarily, however, a formal technical paper is investigative in nature. Thus the conclusions (deductions or convictions resulting from investigation) and recommendations (suggested future activity) are a very significant part of the report. In fact, in some reports they may be *the* most significant part and as such should precede rather than follow the body of the report. The basis on which the conclusions were reached should be fully explained, and conclusions should clearly derive from evidence given in the report. The conclusions, stated positively and specifically, usually are listed numerically in the order of importance. The recommendations parallel the conclusions. Depending on the nature of the report, the conclusions and recommendations may be together in one section or they may be listed separately under individual headings.

3. *End Matter.* An **appendix** and a **bibliography** may or may not be needed, depending on the nature of the paper. An appendix should include supporting data or technical materials (tables, charts, graphs, questionnaires, etc.) in which most readers are not primarily interested. It includes information that supplements the text but if given in the text would interrupt continuity of thought. A bibliography lists the references used in writing the report, including both published and unpublished material. Unlike literary reports, the items in scientific and technical reports may be numbered and listed sequentially, that is, in the order in which they are first mentioned in the report. (For a discussion of bibliographical forms, see pages 406–411.)

ORGANIZATION   The various parts of the formal technical report may be combined or rearranged, depending on the needs of the writer and reader and on the nature of the report. The report is divided into sections, each with a heading. The headings are listed together to form the table of contents.

Examples of formal reports appear on pages 347–353 and 412–424.

Oral Report

As a student you may be assigned a report, such as a book report, to give as an oral presentation only. However, because of the nature and purpose of reports, most reports will first exist in written form, which allows them to be filed for future reference.

Often reports may be presented in both written and oral forms, the oral presentation emphasizing the major aspects of the report. For example, the treasurer of a small organization might give the latest treasury report orally; the report might include the amount of money in the treasury at the beginning of the previous accounting period, additional income, amount of expenditures, and the total remaining for the next period. The written report, prepared as a record, would probably include these same figures, as well as an itemized listing of sources and amounts of money received and creditors and amounts of money paid out. This written report might be handwritten or typed. However, large corporations send out printed reports, often lengthy and sometimes elaborate, showing profits and/or losses, dividends paid to stockholders, and decisions regarding future payments of dividends. At the stockholders' convention significant aspects of the report may be presented orally by one or more members of the corporation.

Suggestions for giving an oral presentation are made in Chapter 10, Oral Communication.

VISUALS

Frequently visuals make information clearer, more easily understood, and more interesting. If a report, therefore, can be made more meaningful through visual materials, decide what kinds can be used most effectively, and use them.

For a detailed discussion of visuals, see Chapter 11, Visuals.

HEADINGS

Headings are important in a report. They are an integral part of the layout and design of the report and contribute to readability and comprehension of the content. More specifically:

- Headings give the reader a visual impression of major and minor topics and their relation to one another.
- Headings reflect the organization of the report.
- Headings remind the reader of movement from one point to another.
- Headings help the reader retrieve specific data or sections of the report easily.
- Headings make the page more inviting to read by dividing what otherwise would be a solid page of unbroken print.

To be effective, headings must be visually obvious; they must clearly reflect the distinction between major sections and minor supporting sections.

Study the use of headings in the reports on pages 326, 328, 331–332, 336, 337–340, 344, 345–346, and 347–353. For additional discussion of headings, see pages 4–5. (For a discussion of headings in an outline, see pages 114–115.)

LAYOUT AND DESIGN

Critical to the effectiveness of a report are its layout and design. Layout pertains to how the material is laid out, or placed, on the page. There must be ample white space so that the text will be visually receptive. Just as importantly, material to be emphasized should be indicated through such techniques as uppercase (capital) letters, underlining, color, boxes, and the like. (For detailed discussion, see pages 1–2 and 23–25.)

Design has to do with the principles of visual composition. Careful attention should be given to such matters as report format, choice of visuals, spacing, and kinds and sizes of typefaces. (For further discussion, see pages 2–4 and 23–25.)

COMMON TYPES OF REPORTS

Among the common types of reports that you as a student and as a future technician may encounter are the reading report, the periodic report, the progress report, the laboratory report, the field report, and the research report. The following discussion examines each of these types of reports (except the research report, which is discussed separately in the next chapter) as to purpose, uses, main parts, and organization. Both student and professional reports illustrating the different types are given in several formats (on a printed form, as a memorandum, as a letter, and in the various conventional report formats).

Reading Report

Purpose A reading report on an article or book describes the general nature of the work, summarizes, analyzes, and evaluates it.

The reading report is one form of the evaluative summary (see Chapter 6, The Summary, especially pages 197–199).

Uses A reading report indicates an individual's comprehension, appreciation, and reaction to a work. In looking at the reading report, the intended audience looks for the answers to several questions: How thoroughly has the individual read the original work? How well does he or she understand it? Can he or she intelligently discuss its significant aspects? How well does he or she appreciate its literary qualities? How valid is his or her evaluation of the work?

Main Parts Whether the requested report is on a work of imaginative literature (novels, plays, short stories, poems) or on an informative work of nonfiction is immaterial. The report usually has four main parts: (1) identification of author and work, (2) summary, (3) analysis, (4) evaluation.

1. *Identification of Author and Work.* In no more than two or three sentences, give such information as the author's name and any helpful comments about him/her (such as relationship to a particular period or school of thought); publishing information (for a book, publishing company and date of publication; for an article, title of periodical, volume, date, and page numbers); audience; and the work in literary and historical perspective.

   Note: The publishing (bibliographical) information may also be given as a separate entry preceding or following the reading report. See Chapter 6, The Summary, especially page 200, and Chapter 9, The Research Report, especially pages 409, 410–411.

2. *Summary.* Keep the summary brief—no more than one-fifth of the entire report. For a nonfiction work, give the subject, scope (extent of coverage), theme or central idea, and method of presenting the material. For a work of fiction, give the setting (time and place) and atmosphere, characters, plot, and theme or central idea.

   If the work has divisions, such as parts, chapters, or stanzas, take them into consideration. Use short, strategic quotations, if needed, to help convey the flavor or tone of the work.

3. *Analysis.* Analysis, the process of dividing a subject into parts in order to understand the whole better, forms the largest section of the report. Show that you have read the work thoughtfully and carefully and can discuss it intelligently. The intended audience will seek answers to: Does this report reflect an alert reader? What insights have been gained from reading the original work?

   Analysis of a work should contain discussions on:

   Meaning—What particular ideas or group of related ideas does the author emphasize? What is the relationship of these ideas to the work as a whole, that is, how do they relate to the organization and style of the work? How sound are these ideas?

   Structure—What is the form or organization of the work? Why is the organization as it is? Is it satisfactory, or could it have been improved?

   Style—What particular stylistic devices (such as dialogue, irony, understatement) are used? How would you describe the vocabulary and word choice? What are the main characteristics of the sentence patterns? Is the style straightforward and literal, or figurative? What adjective best describes the style (e.g., lively, dull, wordy, scholarly, simple, etc.)? Is the style appropriate to the content? Or should the author have used different levels of language, vocabulary, sentence patterns, and the like?

4. *Evaluation.* This part usually comprises about one-fifth of the report and gives your reasoned reactions to the work. Did the work succeed in fulfilling its purpose? Was the work objective? Biased? How did the work affect you? Would you recommend it to others to read? Did you enjoy or like the work? Why or why not?

Give your honest opinions regarding the work; at the same time, however, be fair in placing the blame: Was the failure in the work itself or was it in you? As you become a more disciplined reader, you will find that you also become more skillful in evaluating.

Organization   A reading report, or any other piece of writing, should be coherent and permit the reader to go smoothly from one part to another. Begin the report with a brief introductory paragraph that helps the reader to understand the organization of your report and the aspects of the subject that are emphasized. This introductory paragraph may be combined with the first main part, identification of author and work. Then give the other main parts: summary, analysis, evaluation. Use transitions between sentences and paragraphs to give continuity.

The following reading report (with Plan Sheet) responds to an assignment in a career exploration class.

PLAN SHEET
FOR GIVING A READING REPORT

Analysis of Situation Requiring a Report

What is the subject of the report?
article, "What Career Education Means for the Community College"

For whom is the report intended?
instructor

How will the report be used?
to evaluate a class assignment

In what format will the report be given?
conventional report format

When is the report due?
Aug. 2, 1985

Identification of Author and Work

Amo de Bernadis, "What Career Education Means for the Community College," Community and Junior College Journal (May, 1973) 43: 9–13, 42

Summary

The article has 11 subdivisions: Dignity for Programs, Balance in Programs, Realistic Programs, Counseling and Advising, High School Articulation, Coordination of Facilities and Programs, General Education, Placement and Follow-up, Taking Education to the People, Innovation and Demonstration, and The Challenge. Much emphasis on the open-door policy and dignity of career education. The community college must respond to all who "want the opportunity to enter one of the many current occupational fields." Career programs require "informal and comprehensive counseling in the occupational fields through feedback of information . . . from business and industry." "Facilities and programs are expensive when compared with other college programs." The community college must be attuned to the economy.

Analysis

Author writes convincingly; uses factual presentation of statistics. Style — scholarly, straightforward, literal (appropriate for the intended audience). Seems to know his subject, to be genuinely interested in education, and to be ready to help others initiate career-education programs.

Evaluation

Author is successful in presenting his concerns and views. However, some needless repetition of phrases and ideas. The article is informative, educational, and "eye-opening." I recommend the article.

Types and Subject Matter of Visuals to Be Included in the Report

omit

Reading Report

Reading Report:

"What Career Education Means for the Community College"

Susan L. Gaulding
English 1123, Section 91
August 2, 1985
Instructor: Ms. Benson

Reading Report:

"What Career Education Means for the Community College"

"What Career Education Means for the Community College,"
by Amo de Bernadis, is published in <u>Community and Junior
College Journal</u>, Volume 43 (May, 1973), pages 9-11 and 42.
De Bernadis, President of Portland (Oregon) Community
College, served on a presidential committee on
occupational education.

The article, encompassing all aspects of career education
in the community college, is organized through 11
subdivisions: Dignity for Programs, Balance in Programs,
Realistic Programs, Counseling and Advising, High School
Articulation, Coordination of Facilities and Programs,
General Education, Placement and Follow-up, Taking
Education to the People, Innovation and Demonstration, and
The Challenge. The organization helps the reader follow
with ease the main idea of each subdivision as these main
ideas are thoroughly examined from both points of view,
the needs of the college and the needs of the community.
Much emphasis is placed on the open-door policy of
community colleges and on the dignity of career-oriented
education. These ideas are conveyed by a factual
presentation of statistics and projections of future
needs.

De Bernadis stresses the importance of the responsibility
of the community college to all persons who "want the
opportunity to enter one of the many current occupational
fields." The shift in our economy to a greater percentage
of job openings in service industries necessitates a
change in community college programs. These programs must
continue to respond to the needs of business and industry;
however, they must also respond to the needs of service
industries, which now provide two-thirds of the jobs in
our nation.

These career education programs require "informal and comprehensive counseling in the occupational fields through feedback of information . . . from business and industry." Because of the highly technical aspect of career education, "facilities and programs are expensive when compared with other college programs." Community college students should be encouraged to study in general fields as well as within their occupational field. A community college should be active in job placement and in on-the-job training. The community college can fulfill its purpose through close involvement with industry, business, labor, and community organizations. Above all, it must be aware of, and change with, the demands of the economy.

De Bernadis uses a scholarly style, straightforward and literal, quite appropriate to the subject of education and the probable audience of educators. He writes as one who knows his subject, who is genuinely interested in education, and who is ready to help initiate career education programs in all community colleges.

De Bernadis is successful in presenting his concerns and views of the purpose of the community college and its place in the community. There is, however, some repetition of phrases and ideas that could have been avoided, especially in the light of the educational level of the intended readers. The article is founded on provable concepts and statistics. I recommend it to all persons interested in career education, whether they are students or educators. The article is informative, educational, and "eye-opening." Until now I had never stopped to consider the important role career education can play in my own community.

Periodic Report

Purpose A periodic report gives information at stated intervals, such as daily, weekly, monthly, or annually, or upon completion of a recurring action.

Uses A daily report of absentees, weekly payroll reports, income tax returns, inventories, a sales report upon coverage of a particular geographical area, budget requests, semester grade reports, monthly bank statements — these are but a few examples of the specific uses that periodic reports serve in practically all phases of business activity.

Main Parts In its simpler, more common forms, the periodic report primarily gives specific measurable quantities, brief responses, and explanations. Data usually are given on a printed form, although the report form may vary from a memorandum or a letter to a full-scale, formal report, such as a large corporation's annual report to its stockholders. The periodic report, whatever its form, specifies the period of time covered, the subject dealt with, and the pertinent data concerning the subject.

Organization The organization of a periodic report usually presents little difficulty because of the nature of the material. Typically, the information is presented by categories or chronologically (time order in which events occurred). In a firm, the special-purpose periodic report tends to settle into a uniform pattern since it covers the same or similar items each time (thus it permits the use of timesaving printed forms).

An example of a periodic report on a printed form is given on the next page. Then follows a periodic report in the form of a memorandum (with Plan Sheet), written by a student employed on a part-time basis in a bank records center.

Periodic Report on Printed Form

MONTHLY ABSENTEE REPORT

FOR VOCATIONAL STUDENTS

Student # *428-54-0721*

C # *85751*

Name of Student ___*Brown*___ ___*James*___ ___*Oliver*___
                 Last   First   Middle

Program or Course ___*VBH 1100*___

Attendance from ___*March*___ ___*1*___ ___*1985*___ to ___*March*___ ___*31*___ ___*1985*___
             Month   Day   Year   Month   Day   Year

Length of Course (Hours) ___*1500*___ Total Accumulated Hours from Previous Month ___*500*___

Time: ☑ Full (30 Hours) ☐ ¾ (22½ Hours) ☐ ½ (15 Hours).

INSTRUCTIONS

Below, under each day of the month, write the number of hours attended or absent that day.
X-out Saturdays and Sundays.
Write C for each day school is officially closed.

DATE	1	2	3	4	5	6	7	8	9	10	11	12	13	14	15	16	17	18	19	20	21	22	23	24	25	26	27	28	29	30	31	TOTAL HOURS
HOURS ABSENT		X	X			8			X	X						X	X						X	X						X	X	8
HOURS ATT.	8			8	8		8	8			8	8	8	8	8			8	8	8	8	8			8	8	8	8	8			160

Total Accumulated Hours ___*660*___

Satisfactory ___✓___ Unsatisfactory _____

Remarks ___*James is doing outstanding work in razor cutting.*___

Units of Instruction	Total Hours	Units of Instruction	Total Hours
Haircutting	*60*		
Shaving	*20*		
Shampooing	*20*		
Facials	*10*		
Tonics	*10*		
Skin diseases	*20*		
Barber implements	*20*		

Signed ___*James O. Brown*___ Signed ___*Leslie McDonald*___
          Student   Instructor

Analysis of Situation Requiring a Report

What is the subject to be reported?
COM operator's night work

For whom is the report intended?
night supervisor

How will the report be used?
to keep a record of each operator's weekly activities

In what format will the report be given?
memorandum

When is the report due?
March 29, 1985

Type of Periodic Report (daily, weekly, monthly, etc.)

weekly

Dates covered:
March 24 - 28 (Sunday through Thursday nights)

Information to Be Reported

Work Date/Time:

Sunday, March 24
9:30 p.m. – 8:00 a.m.

Work Completed:

131 fiche; 20,224 frames; reruns: 1 fiche, 8 frames
Total: 132 fiche; 20,232 frames
Duplicates: 696; 103 reruns
Total duplicates: 799

Monday, March 25
11:30 p.m. – 8:00 a.m.

109 fiche; 28,320 frames; reruns: 1 fiche, 178 frames
Total: 110 fiche; 28,498 frames
Duplicates: 920; 67 reruns
Total duplicates: 987

Tuesday, March 26
11:30 p.m. – 8:00 a.m.

73 fiche; 12,378 frames
Duplicates: 322; 83 reruns
Total duplicates: 405

Wednesday, March 27   96 fiche; 14,956 frames; reruns: 4 fiche, 200
11:30 p.m.–8:00 a.m.   frames
                             Total: 100 fiche; 15,156 frames
                             Duplicates: 445; 150 reruns
                             Total duplicates: 595

Thursday, March 28   187 fiche; 43,409 frames; reruns: 19 fiche, 3001
11:30 p.m.–8:00 a.m.   frames
                             Total: 206 fiche; 46,410 frames
                             Duplicates: 944; 175 reruns
                             Total duplicates: 1119

Types and Subject Matter of Visuals to Be Included in the Report

omit

Sources of Information

daily work log

Periodic Report in Memorandum Form

To: Rich Melmein, Night Supervisor

From: Bob Kersh, COM Operator *BK*

Date: March 29, 1985

Subject: Weekly report on COM operator's work, March 24-28

Work Date/Time	Work Completed
Sunday, March 24 9:30 p.m.—8:00 a.m.	131 fiche--20,224 frames Reruns: 1 fiche--8 frames Total: 132 fiche--20,232 frames 696 duplicates Reruns: 103 Total duplicates: 799
Monday, March 25 11:30 p.m.—8:00 a.m.	109 fiche--28,320 frames Reruns: 1 fiche--178 frames Total: 110 fiche--28,498 frames 920 duplicates Reruns: 67 Total duplicates: 987
Tuesday, March 26 11:30 p.m.—8:00 a.m.	73 fiche--12,378 frames Reruns: None 322 duplicates Reruns: 83 Total duplicates: 405
Wednesday, March 27 11:30 p.m.—8:00 a.m.	96 fiche--14,956 frames Reruns: 4 fiche--200 frames Total: 100 fiche--15,156 frames 445 duplicates Reruns: 150 Total duplicates: 595
Thursday, March 28 11:30 p.m.—8:00 a.m.	187 fiche--43,409 frames Reruns: 19 fiche--3001 frames Total: 206 fiche--46,410 frames 944 duplicates Reruns: 175 Total duplicates: 1119

Progress Report

Purpose The progress report gives information concerning the status of a project currently under way.

Uses Students and employees use a progress report to describe investigations to date, either at the completion of each stage or as requested by a supervisor. For the student, the progress report can signal the teacher that assistance or direction is needed. In industry and business, the progress report keeps supervisory personnel informed so that timely decisions can be made accordingly.

Main Parts The progress report (1) describes briefly previous work on the project, (2) discusses in detail the specific aspects that are currently being dealt with, and (3) often states plans for the future. Unexpected developments or problems encountered in the investigation are collected in one section or at the points in other parts of the report where they logically arise.

Organization The three parts of the report (previous work, current work, future plans) form a natural, sequential order for presenting the information. For easier readability, a heading may be used for each part.

If several progress reports are to be made on the same project, they should all be organized similarly.

Two examples of a progress report follow. The first describes the status of repair of a washing machine. The second report (with Plan Sheet) was written by a student to assess progress toward his educational goals.

Progress Report

STATUS OF REPAIR OF WASHING MACHINE WM 307
For CUSTOMER SERVICE MANAGER from SHOP FOREMAN
March 7, 1985

Background

On Monday, March 4, a General Electric washing machine
was brought into the shop. It was tagged WM 307. The
customer was told that the machine, if possible, would be
repaired and ready for pickup by Friday afternoon,
March 8.

Repairs as of Thursday, March 7

Examination showed that repairs were probably needed on
the transmission, pump, and tub drain hose.

The transmission was removed and disassembled with a
check for defects in the gears and gear housing. There
were none. The transmission housing and gears were soaked
in solvent and checked again for defects. Still no defects
were found. New seals, however, were installed in the
unit; then it was reassembled and placed back into the
machine.

The pump was pulled from the machine and disassembled.
Then the impeller was removed from the pump and was
visually inspected. It was found to be defective, with
three broken teeth. This part was ordered from May and
Jackson Company on West Capitol Street. Upon delivery of
the new impeller the next day, it was installed along with
new pump seals. There were no leaks in the pump, so it was
reinstalled in the machine.

The tub drain hose was taken off the machine. This part
was beyond repair; thus a new hose was placed on the
washer and sealed with rubber glue at the base of the
hose. This is a sealant type of glue and requires 24 to 30
hours to dry.

Remaining Work

The glue will not be sufficiently set for the machine
to be hooked up and run through a complete cycle by
closing time tomorrow (Friday). The customer should be
notified that the machine will not be ready for pickup
until Monday afternoon, March 11.

PLAN SHEET
FOR GIVING A PROGRESS REPORT

Analysis of Situation Requiring a Report

What is the subject to be reported?
work as a student at HCC

For whom is the report intended?
major adviser

How will the report be used?
to evaluate progress toward educational goals

In what format will the report be given?
conventional report format

When is the report due?
May 1, 1985

Purpose of the Project

to acquire an Associate in Applied Science degree in electronics technology from HCC

Work Completed; Comments

Semester 1, 1984 – 85

ENG 1113	*Eng Comp I (technical)*
TEL 1356	*Electricity for Electronics*
TDR 1553	*Fund of Dft*
TRS 1613	*Tech Math I*
HPR 1111	*PE*

GPA   3.0. I really enjoyed the electronics course. All the courses were harder than I expected.

Work in Progress; Comments

Semester 11, 1984 – 85

ENG	1123	Eng Comp 11 (technical)
TEL	1376	Electronic Devices and Circuits
TRS	1623	Tech Math 11
TRS	1813	Tech Applied Phy 1
HPR	1121	PE

"B" average so far. Total work to be completed by the end of spring' semester, 32 semester hours. Possible 98 quality points.

Work to Be Completed; Comments

Semesters 1 and 11, 1985 – 86

TRS 1223	Ind Psy	3
Electronics		24
Social studies		3
Physics		3

I will need help from my faculty adviser in choosing most of the specific courses. At end of year should have completed 65 semester hours and 175–200 quality points.

Types and Subject Matter of Visuals to Be Included in the Report

Table showing work completed 1st sem., 1984 – 1985
Table showing work completed 2nd sem., 1984 – 1985
Table showing work to be completed in 1985 – 1986

Sources of Information

college catalog, my grade reports for each semester

Progress Report

My Work as a Student at Haws Community College--
Purpose, Progress, and Projections

Robert Lewis, May 1, 1985

In August of 1984 I enrolled in Haws Community College
to attain skills in electronics technology and to acquire
an Associate in Applied Science degree in that field. The
program requires 65 semester hours and 130 quality points
for completion. Now in the second semester of the
four-semester program, I am finding my courses very
satisfying. The courses are harder than I expected, but I
feel that I am learning valuable information and that I am
accomplishing my goal.

1984 - 1985

Semester I. During the first semester of the 1984 - 1985
academic year I completed these courses with the following
hours, grades, and quality points.

COURSES		HOURS	GRADE	QUALITY POINTS
ENG 1113	English Composition I (Technical)	3	C	6
TEL 1356	Electricity for Electronics	6	A	24
TDR 1553	Fundamentals of Drafting	3	C	6
TRS 1613	Technical Mathematics I	3	B	9
HPR 1111	Physical Education	1	A	4
	Total	16		49

These were the required courses for the first semester
of the two-year course in electronics technology. My
quality point average for the semester was 3.0 on a 4.0 scale. I
am proud of this average and I had to work hard for it,
especially for the A in Electricity for Electronics. Perhaps
the main reason that I experienced such success in this course
was that I really liked it (it was the only actual electronics
course I took this semester). Too, it met every day; thus I had
to study every day. The course that I found most difficult was
Fundamentals of Drafting; the course that I found most
challenging was freshman English.

Semester II. During the second semester of the 1984 - 1985
academic year I am currently enrolled in the following courses.

COURSES		HOURS
ENG 1123	English Composition II (Technical)	3
TEL 1376	Electronic Devices and Circuits	6
TRS 1623	Technical Mathematics II	3
TRS 1813	Technical Applied Physics I	3
HPR 1121	Physical Education	1
		16

These are all required courses. Thus far in the second semester I have maintained a "B" average, and I am still experiencing the most success with the electronics-related courses.

At the end of this school year, I should have completed 32 semester hours and acquired a possible 98 quality points.

1985 - 1986

Semesters I and II. During the 1985 - 1986 academic year I plan to take the additional courses and hours required for graduation in electronics technology. These include one specified course and my choice of courses in several areas.

COURSES		HOURS
TRS 1223	Industrial Psychology	3
Technical electronics		24
Social studies		3
Physics		3
		33

Except for Industrial Psychology, I will need help from a faculty adviser in choosing the specific courses. At this point, I think I want to take Digital Fundamentals (6 hours) and Linear Integrated Circuits (6 hours). I am considering taking Digital Integrated Circuits (6 hours), Introduction to Microprocessors (6 hours), and Programming Fundamentals (3 hours).

Upon completion of the sophomore year, I plan to have the required 65 semester hours of work plus many more than the 130 minimum quality points required.

The End Result

It is my aim to graduate from Haws Community College with an Associate in Applied Science degree in electronics technology. Upon completion of this program of study, I expect to be qualified to enter the field of high technology as a microelectronics technician.

Laboratory Report

Purpose   A laboratory report presents results of investigation, research, or testing done in a laboratory. The laboratory may be connected with any field of study — business, chemistry, physics, data processing, home economics, fire science, electronics, nursing, and so on.

Uses   This is a common kind of report for both students and on-the-job workers. It may simply report the results of tests, the purpose for the tests being implicit in their nature (such as a blood type test). Some types of laboratory reports, however, are very involved: they not only give test results but also the results are applied to specific problems or situations. Recommendations may be included as well.

Main Parts   For most laboratory reports, a basic, fairly well established form may be used. Its typical parts are as follows:

Title page
Object (also called Purpose)
Theory
Method (also called Procedure)
Results
Discussion of Results (also called Comments)
Conclusions
Appendix
Original Data

Organization   The various divisions may be combined or rearranged to suit the needs of the writer and the reader. For assignments, use the division headings listed above, unless another form of presentation has been specified.

Study the two examples of student-written laboratory reports that follow. The first report (with Plan Sheet) is concerned with testing two body fillers in an auto body and fender repair shop. The next report concerns an electronic experiment (this report is reprinted courtesy of the Mississippi State Department of Education).

PLAN SHEET
FOR GIVING A LABORATORY REPORT

Analysis of Situation Requiring a Report

What is the subject to be reported?
testing of two types of body filler

For whom is the report intended?
shop instructor, Mr. McPhillip

How will the report be used?
to determine whether the shop should use the less expensive body filler

In what format will the report be given?
conventional report format

When is the report due?
July 16, 1985

Object or Purpose of the Experiment

to compare two types of body filler to see if the $3.21 filler is as good as the $4.55 filler

Apparatus

the two types of body filler, several repair jobs of varying difficulty

Theory

The cheaper body filler may be just as good as the body filler we use now.

Method or Procedure

For two weeks the cheaper body filler was used under the same conditions that the more expensive body filler was used.

Results; Observations; Comments

The cheaper body filler cuts more easily, is more flexible, and has fewer pinholes than the other filler.

Conclusions; Recommendations

We should start using the cheaper filler. It's better and it can save the shop about $188.00 per month. The shop uses about 140 cans of body filler a month.

Types and Subject Matter of Visuals to Be Included in the Report

omit

Laboratory Report

AUTO BODY AND FENDER REPAIR

Report written by Warren Daniels
for Instructor Herbert C. McPhillip

July 16, 1985

OBJECT.   To compare Type I body filler that costs $4.55 per can with Type II body filler that costs $3.21 per can.

THEORY.   The less expensive Type II body filler may be just as good as the more expensive Type I body filler, which is used in the shop. A representative of the company that manufactures Type I claims that Type II has more talcum and is therefore less desirable.

METHOD.   For two weeks, Type II filler, rather than Type I, was used in the shop. It was tried on several jobs of varying difficulty. Each time it was mixed in the same way that Type I had been mixed. The same kind of primer was also used to cover the filler.

CONCLUSIONS.   Type II body filler cuts more easily, is more flexible, and has fewer pinholes than Type I. Type II is not only as good as Type I, it is better. Since the shop uses about 140 cans of body filler per month, the shop will save approximately $188.00 per month.

$$140 \times \$4.55 = \$637.00$$
$$140 \times \$3.21 = \underline{\quad 449.40}$$
$$\$187.60$$

RECOMMENDATIONS.   1. Only Type II body filler should be used in the shop.
2. The money that can be saved by using the less expensive body filler should be placed in a fund to purchase new shop equipment.

Laboratory Report

LABORATORY REPORT: EMITTER FOLLOWER

Elicia Longe

TEL 1326-02

Electronic Circuits I

Instructor: H. J. Johnson

February 8, 1985

<u>Purpose</u>: The purpose of this experiment was to design, construct, and test an emitter follower circuit which might be used as an impedance matching device. An approximation technique was employed in formulating the design characteristics.

<u>Procedure</u>: The circuit utilized is shown in Figure 1. For construction, standard 10% resistor values, nearest to those calculated, were used. Measurements were made with a digital multimeter and recorded. An audio signal of 1 kHz was fed to the input of the emitter follower and the output waveforms were observed on an oscilloscope. The input signal level was adjusted to provide maximum undistorted output. Input and output signal levels were measured and recorded. The input audio frequency was lowered until the output voltage across R_L dropped to .707 of the 1 kHz level. The resultant reading was recorded as the lower 3 dB frequency limit. The input audio frequency was then increased to a point above 1 kHz where .707 reading was obtained, and this reading was recorded as the upper 3 dB frequency limit. The audio signal generator was then reset to 1 kHz. The multimeter was placed in series with the audio signal generator in the input circuit, and the signal current was measured and recorded.

    See Table 1.

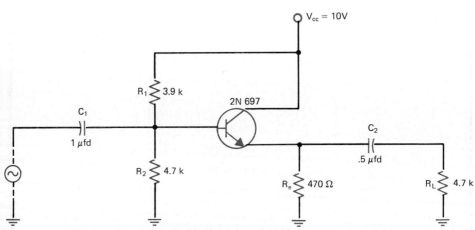

Figure 1 Emitter follower circuit used in experiment

Design

1. $V_{ce} = .5 \times 10 = 5V$

2. $R_e = Z_{out} = 500\Omega$ (470Ω standard value)

3. $I_e = \dfrac{10 - 5}{470} = \dfrac{5}{470} = 10.6mA$

4. $V_b = 5 + .7 = 5.7V$

5. Stability Factor (S) $\simeq 10 = \dfrac{R_z}{470\Omega}$

6. $I_2 \simeq \dfrac{5.7V}{4.7k\Omega} = 1.21mA$ (where $I_1 \simeq I_2$)

7. $R_1 \simeq \dfrac{10V - 5.7V}{1.23mA} = \dfrac{4.3V}{1.23mA} = 3.5k\Omega$

8. $A_v \simeq \alpha = \dfrac{80}{81} = .987$

9. $R_b = \dfrac{3.5k(4.7k)}{3.5k + 4.7k} = \dfrac{16.45M}{8.2k} = 2.24k\Omega$

10. $C = \dfrac{1}{6.28(100)\ (4.7k\Omega)} = .71\mu fd$

11. $C_2 = \dfrac{1}{6.28(100)\ (4.7k\Omega)} = .338\mu fd$

Table 1   Measurements

Bias Conditions Pertaining to all Measurements $V_{be} = .62V$ $V_{ce} = 4.9V$ $I_e = 10.9mA$			
Voltage Gain	Maximum undistorted output at 1khz = 8.1V p–p = 2.86V rms	Maximum input–8.65V p–p 3.05V rms	$A_v \simeq \dfrac{8.1}{8.6}$ $A_v \simeq .942$
3 dB Roll–off Frequencies	Voltage at roll–off points = .707 of voltage at 1kHz point = .707 × 8.1 = 5.72V	Lower roll–off freq. = 84 hZ	Upper roll–off freq. = 230 kHz
Signal input current and Impedance	Signal current = 1.58mA	$Z_{in} = \dfrac{V_{in}}{I_{in}}$	$Z_{in} = \dfrac{3.05V_{rms}}{1.58\ mA}$ $Z_{in} = 1.93k\Omega$

Observations

1. Bias Considerations

	Design	Achieved	% Error
Vce	5V	4.9V	2%
Vbe	.7V	.62V	11.4%
Ie	10.6mA	10.9mA	2.83%

   Comparison of the achieved Vce, Vbe and Ie shows the achieved conditions were very close to the design values.

2. Gain Characteristics

   Theoretical $A_v \simeq \alpha = .988$
   Achieved $A_v = .942$ or $.936$
   % Error = 4.56%

3. Frequency Response
   The achieved low 3dB roll-off point was 84Hz instead of the design 100Hz. This resulted from using coupling capacitors which had values larger than the design values. This lowered the low frequency cutoff point.

4. Input Impedance
   The theoretical and calculated input impedance differed by 13.8%.

5. Transistor Beta
   A transistor with a lower Beta will have little effect on dc bias conditions because the circuit is Beta independent. If the Beta falls off too much, the voltage gain could possibly suffer.

6. Stability
   Increasing the input to output impedance ratio would decrease the stability of the circuit.

Field Report

Purpose   The field report gives the results of a visit to a particular location or site. Major sources of information for the field report are personal observation, experience, and knowledgeable people. (See Chapter 10, Oral Communication, pages 454–455, for how to conduct an informational interview.)

Uses   Field reports are used in many ways. For example, they are important in estimating the value of real estate or the cost of repairing a house; establishing insurance claims for damage from a tornado or blizzard; improving production methods in a department or a firm; choosing a desirable site for a building, a highway, a lake; or serving as an educational experience for a prospective employee or interested layman. The field report gives an accurate, objective explanation and analysis of a situation so that appropriate action can be taken.

Main Parts   Since the field report has a variety of uses and includes various kinds of information, it has no established divisions or format. The report may include such parts as a review of background information, an account of the investigation, an analysis and commentary, and conclusions and recommendations. For a student (or any other interested person), a field report on a visit to a company might include a description and explanation of its physical layout; the personnel, materials and equipment involved; the individual activities that comprise the major function of the company; and comments.

Organization   At the beginning of the report, state the purpose of the report, the specific site or facility or division observed, and the aspects of the subject to be presented. Then give the results of the investigation, followed by conclusions and recommendations. If the report is more than a paragraph or two, use headings. Include sketches, diagrams, charts, and other visual materials when they make explanation and description simpler or clearer.

Three examples of field reports follow. The first (with Plan Sheet) is a report in the form of a letter on an inspection of a communication site. The second is a report of a student's visit to a business related to her major field of study, electronic data processing. The third report — tending to be formal with the preliminary matter of a transmittal letter, title page, and summary — concerns the field inspection of a pond dam.

PLAN SHEET
FOR GIVING A FIELD REPORT

Analysis of Situation Requiring a Report

What is the subject to be reported?
inspection of communication site at Pensacola, FL

For whom is the report intended?
Cole-Meyers Electric Company

How will the report be used?
to determine efficiency of present operation

In what format will the report be given?
letter

When is the report due?
Nov. 28, 1985

Site Visited

communication site at Pensacola

Purpose of Visit

to inspect power supply, equipment room, and control room

Methods Used for Gathering Data

on-site, personal investigation; standard tests and checks made on equipment

Background Information

inspection requested by letter, Oct. 31, 1985

Facts, Details, and Results of the Investigation

Transformers operating at peak operating condition. Automatic switchover equipment working properly. Converter equipment output has less than 3% distortion. No major outage since Oct. 2, 1980. Multiplex equipment is adequate; one branch operating on auxiliary power with no backup. This to be corrected by end of November. Control room well supervised and efficiently operated.

Conclusions; Recommendations

Communication site at Pensacola is one of the best in the Southeast. Personnel are satisfied. Sum of average outages: 30 min. per week.

Types and Subject Matter of Visuals to Be Included in the Report

omit

Field Report in Letter Form

Electric Troubleshooters, Inc.

810 Fourth Avenue
Waterbury, Connecticut 01836
P.O. Box 817
203-902-8165

November 28, 1985

Cole—Meyers Electric Company
1521 East Second Street
Great Neck, NY 10120

Attention: Mr. R. M. Rothchild

Cole—Meyers Electric Company:

In accordance with your letter of instructions of October 31,
1985, I have made a personal inspection of the communication site
at Pensacola, Florida, and submit the following report.

Power Supply

Transformers. The transformers are in peak operating condition.
According to the log, two transformers are operating at the same
time. One supplies the power, and the other is a standby.
Automatic Switchover. The automatic switchover equipment is
working properly. Standard tests were performed, and not once did
the signal lose phase from one transformer to another.

Equipment Room

Converters. The converter equipment has an output with less than
3% distortion. A routine check for distortion is made every hour
and recorded according to regulations. Very little outage is
recorded, and no major outage has been recorded since the cable
cut of October 2, 1980.
Multiplex. The multiplex equipment is adequate with one exception.
The second branch is operating on auxiliary power with no backup.
A power supply has been ordered and should arrive November 28.

Control Room

The control room is supervised, and everyone is well trained in
control facilities. The outage record and the logs are kept
accurately and up to date.

Conclusion

The site at Pensacola is one of the best in the Southwest. The
personnel are satisfied and no complaints were filed. The average
outages add up to about 30 minutes a week, which is the best
record in the Southeast.

Very truly yours,

J. M. Black

J. M. Black

Field Report

VISIT TO THE COMPUTER CENTER
TERRY, MINNESOTA
Sheila Foley
March 29, 1985

By telephone I made an appointment for March 22, 1985,
at 3:00 P.M. to visit Mr. Rayford Butler, Manager of the
Computer Center, Terry, Minnesota. The purpose of the
visit was to discuss and observe the operations and
techniques involved in running the business. Mr. Butler
and I discussed the qualifications needed to get a job at
the Center and the beginning positions there. Then I was
allowed to view the setup of the computer system and to
observe and take part in the operating of one of the
computers.

QUALIFICATIONS

To be even considered for a job at the Computer Center,
a person must have a background in either data processing
or some type of office work that involved such skills as
typing, bookkeeping, or filing. The more experienced a
person is in data processing, the better the chances are
of getting a job at the Center.

BEGINNING POSITIONS

A new employee with no data processing work experience
would probably start at the Computer Center with a job in
keypunch. This job involves the punching of data onto
cards that are run through the computer. Very often this
job includes a lot of night work, especially for the
beginner. As an employee masters certain skills, the
chances for a higher position in the company increase. The
new employee with experience or specialized training can
within a few months move into a responsible, high-paying
position.

OBSERVATION OF EQUIPMENT AND OPERATIONS

The Computer Center has such a large load of work that it is equipped with two IBM System 3 computers. Companies bring in raw data, which are programmed and processed by the computer, and the results are returned to the companies. The computers handle jobs such as preparing bank statements for local and area banks; keeping records for several large industries; doing the bookwork for a dozen or so insurance companies and oil corporations; and also keeping records for a number of certified public accountants.

I was given the opportunity to take part in and observe the execution of a program. I was asked to keypunch my full name on the 80-column punch cards. Then I observed how to remove and replace a disk pack and how to place the programmed punch cards in the computer and start the computer. I watched as the information programmed printed out a message: THIS COMPUTER WILL SELF-DESTRUCT IN 10 SECONDS. ALL PERSONNEL PLEASE EVACUATE THE AREA. . . . 10 9 8 7 6 5 4 3 2 1 BANG!! and then my name, as I had punched it on the cards, printed out. (The computer didn't self-destruct.) I was given the program and name cards, which I have included at the end of this report [omitted].

CONCLUSIONS AND RECOMMENDATIONS

My visit to the Computer Center was very interesting and worthwhile. Mr. Butler encouraged me to continue my education in data processing and to get as much out of the courses as I could because that knowledge would help me to get a good job and to advance. He asked me to be sure to apply for employment at the Computer Center when I completed my college studies.

I would recommend that anyone interested in data processing visit a company using a computer and observe its operation. The visit led me to feel secure in the belief that there is a very bright future for me in the field of data processing—if I get good training and if I apply myself.

Formal Field Report
Letter of Transmittal

1135 Combs Street
Jackson, MS 39204
6 April 1985

Mr. Harry F. Downing
4261 Marshall Road
Jackson, MS 39212

Dear Mr. Downing:

Attached is the field inspection report of the pond dam on your property. The dam is considered to be in stable physical condition although some minor seepage and erosion were discovered. Recommendations for correcting these are included in the report.

It has been a pleasure to work with you on this project.

Sincerely yours,

Paul Kennedy

Paul Kennedy

FIELD INSPECTION REPORT
OF
HARRY F. DOWNING DAM

Paul Kennedy

6 April 1985

SUMMARY

    On 2 April 1985 an unofficial inspection of the dam of
the Harry F. Downing Pond was conducted by Paul Kennedy.
    This dam is considered to be in stable physical
condition although some minor seepage and erosion were
discovered. This conclusion was based on visual
observations made on the date of the inspection.

FIELD INSPECTION REPORT

HARRY F. DOWNING POND
HINDS COUNTY, MISSISSIPPI
PEARL RIVER BASIN
CANY CREEK TRIBUTARY

PURPOSE

The purpose of this inspection was to evaluate the
structural integrity of the dam of the Harry F. Downing
Pond, which is identified as MS 1769 by the National Dam
Inventory of 1973.

DESCRIPTION OF PROJECT

Location. Downing Pond is located two miles SE of
Forest Hill School, Jackson, Mississippi, in Section 23,
Township 6, Range 1 East (see Figure 1).

Hazard Classification. The National Dam Inventory lists
the location of Downing Pond as a Category 3 (low-risk)
classification. Personal observation of areas downstream
confirm this classification since only a few acres of
farmland would be inundated in the case of a sudden total
failure of the dam.

Description of Dam and Appurtenances. The dam is an
earth fill embankment approximately 200 feet in length
with a crown width of 6 to 10 feet. The height of the dam
is estimated to be 16 feet with the crest at Elevation
320.0 M.S.L. (elevations taken from quadrangle maps). Maximum
capacity is 47 acre feet. The only discharge outlet for
the pond is an uncontrolled overflow spillway ditch in the
right (east) abutment. The spillway has an entrance crest
elevation of 317.0 M.S.L. and extends approximately 150
feet downstream before reaching Cany Creek. The total
intake drainage area for the pond is 30 acres of gently
rolling hills.

Design and Construction History. No design information
has been located. City records indicate that the dam was

constructed in 1940 to make a pond for recreational purposes.

FINDINGS OF VISUAL INSPECTION

Dam. Apparently the dam was constructed with a 1V or 2H slope. This steep downstream slope is covered with dense vegetation, which includes weeds, brush, and several large trees. These trees range from 15 to 20 feet in height (see photos 1 and 2). These trees have not likely affected the dam at the present time, but decaying root systems may eventually provide seepage paths.

A normal amount of underseepage was observed about halfway along the toe of the dam (see Photo 3). This seepage was not flowing at the time of the inspection but should be watched closely during high-water periods. The upstream face of the dam has several spots of erosion near the water's edge due to the lack of sod growth. Apparently topsoil was not placed after construction.

Overflow Spillway. The uncontrolled spillway shows no signs of erosion and is adequately covered with sod growth (see Photo 4).

RECOMMENDATIONS

It is recommended that the owner:
1. Periodically inspect the dam (at least once a year).
2. Prevent the growth of future trees on the downstream slope.
3. Install a gage and observe the flow of underseepage as compared to pool levels.
4. Fill areas of erosion and place topsoil and sod to prevent future erosion.

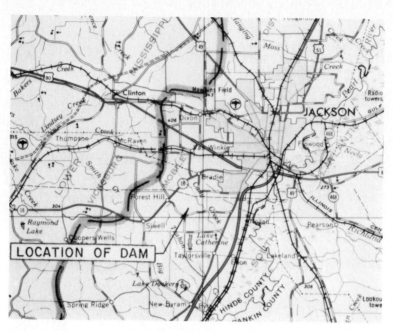

Figure 1. Location of Harry F. Downing Dam. (Map courtesy of
U.S. Corps of Engineers Waterways Experiment Station at
Vicksburg)

Photo 1. View looking east from left (west) abutment. Note large trees on dam at left.

Photo 2. View looking north at dam from inlet area. Note large trees on dam in background.

Photo 3. View looking west along toe of dam. Note seepage at left.

Photo 4. View looking upstream of uncontrolled overflow spillway ditch. Note adequate sod growth.

Research Report

The research report, prepared after a careful investigation of all available resources, is similar to what some students refer to as the research paper or term paper. The research report requires note-taking, documentation, and the like. For a full discussion, see Chapter 9, The Research Report.

GENERAL PRINCIPLES IN GIVING A REPORT

1. *A report must be accurate, clear, concise, and objective.*
2. *Reports may be classified according to the function they serve.* They may be school reports, which are a testing device for students. They may be professional reports, which are used in business, industry, and government.
3. *Reports may be given in various formats.* These formats include printed forms, memorandums, letters, conventional report formats (nonformal or formal), and oral presentations.
4. *Reports frequently include visuals.* Visuals may make information clearer, more easily understood, and more interesting.
5. *Reports usually include headings.* Headings reflect the major points of the report and their supporting points.
6. *Layout and design are integral aspects of effective reports.*
7. *Common types of reports include the reading report, the periodic report, the progress report, the laboratory report, the field report, and the research report.*

PROCEDURE FOR GIVING A REPORT

1. *Determine the audience and the purpose of the report.* It is essential to know who will be reading or listening to the report and why. Plan the report accordingly.
2. *Review the common types of reports.* Think about whether the report you are preparing might be classified as a reading report, a periodic report, a progress report, a laboratory report, a field report, a research report, or a combination of two or more of these types.
3. *Investigate and research the subject, being careful to take accurate notes and list sources used.* Make use of all available sources—print and nonprint materials, knowledgeable people, experiments, observation.
4. *Select an appropriate format for the report.* Decide whether the report will be oral or written or both. Decide whether to use a printed form, a memorandum, a letter, or a conventional report format.
5. *Organize the report, using headings.* Arrange the material in a logical order, as determined by audience, purpose, and subject matter.
6. *Plan and prepare visuals.* Decide which information should be given in visuals and what type of visuals to use. Then carefully prepare the visuals and place them in the report where they are most effective.
7. *Plan the layout and design of the report.* Think through how the text and the visuals can be most effectively placed on the page, and think through how you want each page and the report as a whole to visually appeal to the reader.
8. *Remember that a report should be accurate, clear, concise, and objective.*

APPLICATION 1   GIVING REPORTS

In a standard desk dictionary, look up the word *report;* list all the meanings that are given. Indicate the meanings that you think are related to report writing.

APPLICATION 2   GIVING REPORTS

Interview at least four people who are employed in business, industry, or government. Find out the kinds of writing they must do. Determine which of these kinds of writing could be classified as report writing. Present your findings in a one-page report.

APPLICATION 3   GIVING REPORTS

Make a collection of at least five reports. Using the criteria of accuracy, clarity, conciseness, and objectivity, analyze the reports. Present your analysis in a one-page report.

APPLICATION 4   GIVING REPORTS

Make a reading report on a chapter in one of your textbooks.

    a. Make a Plan Sheet like the one on pages 358–359 and fill it in.
    b. Write a preliminary draft.
    c. Revise.
    d. Write the final draft.

APPLICATION 5   GIVING REPORTS

Find an article in a current periodical related to your major field of study. Make a reading report on the article.

    a. Make a Plan Sheet like the one on pages 358–359 and fill it in.
    b. Write a preliminary draft.
    c. Revise.
    d. Write the final draft.

APPLICATION 6   GIVING REPORTS

Write a daily periodic report on your activities in office, field, shop, or laboratory. Then expand this report to a weekly periodic report on your activities in office, field, shop, or laboratory. Write the report in the form of a memorandum.

    a. Make a Plan Sheet like the one on pages 360–361 and fill it in.
    b. Write a preliminary draft.
    c. Revise.
    d. Write the final draft.

APPLICATION 7   GIVING REPORTS

Assume that you have an annual scholarship of $1800 from a company related to your major field of study. Every three months you must report how you have spent any or all of the money and how you intend to spend any remaining portion. Write the report in the form of a letter.

    a. Make a Plan Sheet like the one on pages 360–361 and fill it in.

b. Write a preliminary draft.
c. Revise.
d. Write the final draft.

APPLICATION 8   GIVING REPORTS

Write a report showing your progress toward completing a degree or receiving a certificate in your major field.

a. Make a Plan Sheet like the one on pages 362–363 and fill it in.
b. Write a preliminary draft.
c. Revise.
d. Write the final draft.

APPLICATION 9   GIVING REPORTS

Write a weekly progress report on your work in a specific course or project (math, science, research, specific technical subject). Using the same course or project, write a monthly progress report on your work.

a. Make a Plan Sheet like the one on pages 362–363 and fill it in.
b. Write a preliminary draft.
c. Revise.
d. Write the final draft.

APPLICATION 10   GIVING REPORTS

Write a laboratory report on an experiment or test.

a. Make a Plan Sheet like the one on pages 364–365 and fill it in.
b. Write a preliminary draft.
c. Revise.
d. Write the final draft.

APPLICATION 11   GIVING REPORTS

Assume that you have been experimenting with three different brands of the same product or piece of equipment in an effort to decide which brand name you should select for your home, shop, or lab. Write a report to be sent to all three manufacturers.

a. Make a Plan Sheet like the one on pages 364–365 and fill it in.
b. Write a preliminary draft.
c. Revise.
d. Write the final draft.

APPLICATION 12 GIVING REPORTS

Visit a business or industry related to your major field of study, a governmental office or department, or an office or division of your college, to survey its general operation. Write a report on your visit.

    a. Make a Plan Sheet like the one on pages 366–367 and fill it in.
    b. Write a preliminary draft.
    c. Revise.
    d. Write the final draft.

APPLICATION 13 GIVING REPORTS

Write a field report including conclusions and recommendations on one of the topics below or on a similar topic of your own choosing.

    a. Make a Plan Sheet like the one on pages 366–367 and fill it in.
    b. Write a preliminary draft.
    c. Revise.
    d. Write the final draft.

Write a field report on:

1. Parking problems on campus
2. Need for purchasing new equipment for a laboratory or shop
3. Rearrangement of equipment in a laboratory or shop
4. A color scheme and furnishings for lounges in a college union building
5. Recreational facilities for a town of 10,000
6. Selection of a site for an industry
7. On-the-job training for laboratory technicians or persons in other health-related occupations
8. Condition of a structure (building, dam, fire tower, etc.) or piece of equipment
9. Efficiency of the registration process on campus
10. Conditions at a local jail, prison, hospital, rehabilitation facility, mental institution, or other public institution
11. The present work situation of last year's graduates in your major field of study
12. Employment opportunities in your major field of study
13. A landscaping plan, a type of air conditioning system, an interior decorating plan (or some other area related to your major field of study) for a housing project
14. A system of emergency exit patterns and directions for several campus buildings
15. Services by an organization such as the Better Business Bureau or the Chamber of Commerce

APPLICATION 14 GIVING REPORTS

As directed by your instructor, adapt the reports you prepared in the applications above for oral presentation. Ask your classmates to evaluate your speech by making an Evaluation of Oral Presentations sheet like the one on page 459 and filling it in.

PLAN SHEET
FOR GIVING A READING REPORT

Analysis of Situation Requiring a Report

What is the subject of the report?

For whom is the report intended?

How will the report be used?

In what format will the report be given?

When is the report due?

Identification of Author and Work

Summary

Analysis

Evaluation

Types and Subject Matter of Visuals to Be Included in the Report

PLAN SHEET
FOR GIVING A PERIODIC REPORT

Analysis of Situation Requiring a Report

What is the subject to be reported?

For whom is the report intended?

How will the report be used?

In what format will the report be given?

When is the report due?

Type of Periodic Report (daily, weekly, monthly, etc.)

Dates covered:

Information to Be Reported

Types and Subject Matter of Visuals to Be Included in the Report

Sources of Information

PLAN SHEET
FOR GIVING A PROGRESS REPORT

Analysis of Situation Requiring a Report

What is the subject to be reported?

For whom is the report intended?

How will the report be used?

In what format will the report be given?

When is the report due?

Purpose of the Project

Work Completed; Comments

Work in Progress; Comments

Work to Be Completed; Comments

Types and Subject Matter of Visuals to Be Included in the Report

Sources of Information

Analysis of Situation Requiring a Report

What is the subject to be reported?

For whom is the report intended?

How will the report be used?

In what format will the report be given?

When is the report due?

Object or Purpose of the Experiment

Apparatus

Theory

Method or Procedure

Results; Observations; Comments

Conclusions; Recommendations

Types and Subject Matter of Visuals to Be Included in the Report

PLAN SHEET
FOR GIVING A FIELD REPORT

Analysis of Situation Requiring a Report

What is the subject to be reported?

For whom is the report intended?

How will the report be used?

In what format will the report be given?

When is the report due?

Site Visited

Purpose of Visit

Methods Used for Gathering Data

Background Information

Facts, Details, and Results of the Investigation

Conclusions; Recommendations

Types and Subject Matter of Visuals to Be Included in the Report

The Research Report: Becoming Acquainted with Resource Materials

OBJECTIVES 370
INTRODUCTION 370
LOCATING MATERIALS 370
SOURCES OF INFORMATION 371
    Personal Observation or Experience 371
    Personal Interviews 371
    Free or Inexpensive Materials 371
    Library Materials 372
      Systems of Classifying Books 372
      Public (Card) Catalog 374
      Library of Congress Subject Headings 377
    Indexes 379
      Magazine Index 379
      Readers' Guide to Periodical Literature 381
      Applied Science & Technology Index 382
      Business Periodicals Index 383
      Other Indexes to Professional Journals 384
      Indexes to Newspapers 384
      Indexes to Government Publications 385
      Essay Index 385
    Other "Helps" in Library Research 385
      Computer-Aided Search 386
      NewsBank 386
      Social Issues Resources Series 387
      Audiovisual Materials 387
      Periodicals Holdings List 388
      Reference Works 388
        Encyclopedias 388
        Dictionaries 388
        Books of Statistics 388
        Almanacs 389
        Bibliographies 389
        Handbooks 389
        Yearbooks 390

         Guides to Reference Works   390
            Periodicals   390
            Books   390
         Vertical File   390
PLANNING AND WRITING A RESEARCH REPORT   390
      Selecting a Subject and Defining the Problem   391
         Selecting a Subject   391
         Defining the General Problem   392
         Defining the Specific Problems   392
      Finding the Facts   392
      Recording and Organizing the Facts   393
         Evaluating Resource Material   393
            Primary and Secondary Sources   393
            Fact and Opinion   393
            Nontextual Qualities   393
         Compiling a Working Bibliography   393
            Bibliography Card for a Book   393
            Bibliography Card for an Essay in a Book   394
            Bibliography Card for an Article in a Journal   395
            Bibliography Card for an Article in a Popular Magazine   396
            Bibliography Card for an Item in a Newspaper   396
            Bibliography Card for an Item from NewsBank   397
            Bibliography Card for an Item Reprinted from Another Source   398
            Bibliography Card for an Encyclopedia Article   398
            Bibliography Card for a Pamphlet   399
            Bibliography Card for a Personal Interview   400
         Taking Notes   400
            General Directions for Taking Notes   400
            Types of Note Cards   401
               Direct Quotation   401
               Paraphrase and Summary   402
         Stating the Central Idea and Constructing a Formal Outline   403
         Arranging the Note Cards to Fit the Outline   404
REPORTING THE FACTS   404
      Writing the First Draft   404
         Introduction and Conclusion   404
         Quotations and Paraphrases   404
          A Note About Plagiarism   405
         Documentation   405
         Revising the Outline and First Draft   405
      Writing the Final Draft   406
      Documentation   406
         Four Styles of Documentation   407
         Citations List and Bibliography   409
         Examples of Citations   410
A SAMPLE RESEARCH REPORT   411
APPLICATIONS   425

OBJECTIVES

Upon completing this chapter, the student should be able to:

- Select an appropriate subject for a research report
- State the general problem being investigated in a report
- Divide the general problem into specific problems or questions (preliminary outline)
- Make a working bibliography
- Use the public (card) catalog
- Use periodical indexes
- Locate source materials for a research report
- Write a direct quotation note card
- Write a paraphrase note card
- Write a summary note card
- Formulate the central idea of a research report
- Make an outline for a research report
- Document a research report
- Write a complete research report

INTRODUCTION

Some of the writing and speaking you will do as a student — term papers, book reviews, reports on various topics, speeches — will require research. Also, assignments you may be given as an employee in business or industry — feasibility reports, proposals, process explanations, or even a speech to a local civic club — may require research. The information gathered through research can be organized into a final presentation to accomplish a stated purpose for a specific audience.

To research a topic thoroughly, you need to know the possible sources of information and how to use these sources effectively.

This chapter provides a general guide to library research, one type of research that can be used to prepare and write a research report. It does not attempt, however, to deal with the more intricate points in library research or with the methods used in pure research or in scientific investigation, two other types of research. It does not attempt to present every acceptable method and form for writing a research report. It does attempt to present in a logical, step-by-step sequence a procedure for researching and writing a successful report.

The first part of the chapter explains basic library research, and the second part outlines and explains the procedure for writing a research report.

LOCATING MATERIALS

Materials about a subject are usually located by a systematic, organized search of available sources. Therefore, to begin research, you must first have some idea of possible sources of information and know how to make a systematic search of the sources.

SOURCES OF INFORMATION

Possible sources of information can be classified as:

1. Personal observation or experience
2. Personal interviews
3. Free or inexpensive materials
4. Library materials

An investigation of these general sources will help you to compile a list of specific sources — books, periodicals, people, agencies, companies — that can supply needed information about a subject or topic.

Personal Observation or Experience

Personal observation or experience can make writing more realistic and vivid, and sometimes this observation or experience is essential. If writing, for instance, about the need for more up-to-date laboratory equipment in local technical education centers, personal inspections would be quite helpful.

Do not be misled, however, by surface appearances. Remember that the same conditions and facts may be interpreted in an entirely different way by another person. For this reason, do not depend completely on personal observations or personal experiences for information. Every statement given as fact in a research presentation must unquestionably be based on validated information.

Personal Interviews

Interviewing persons who are knowledgeable about a topic lends human interest to the research project. Talking with such people may also prevent chasing up blind alleys and may supply information unobtainable elsewhere.

Since methods of getting facts through interviews require almost as much thought as the methods involved in library work, interviewing should be carried out systematically. The first thing to remember is courtesy. In seeking an appointment for an interview, request cooperation tactfully. Secondly, give thoughtful preparation to the interview. Be businesslike in manner and prepare your questions in advance. Finally, keep careful notes of the interview. In quoting the person interviewed, be sure to use his or her exact words and intended meaning. And remember, although the personal interview is a valuable source of information, it offers only one person's opinions. (See Chapter 10, Oral Communication, pages 454 – 455, for a discussion of how to conduct an informational interview.)

Free or Inexpensive Materials

Many agencies distribute free or inexpensive pamphlets, documents, and reports that contain much valuable information. The U.S. Government Printing Office, the various departments of the United States Government, state and local agencies, industries, insurance companies, labor unions, and professional organizations are just a few of the sources that may supply excellent material on a subject.

Not at all unusual is the case of a student writing about Teflon who requested information from the DuPont Company. In his letter he stated that as a student in mechanical technology he was writing a library research paper about industrial uses of Teflon. Within a few days the student received a packet of extremely helpful materials. Some of the material was so new that it was months before it began to appear in periodicals. Some of the material consisted of reprints of magazine articles that the student did not have access to. And some of the individual pieces of material he received would never appear in magazine or book form.

In seeking material from various agencies, make the request specific. For instance, a student writing a research report about aluminum as a structural building material might be disappointed in the response to a request to Alcoa for "information about aluminum." Such a request is difficult if not impossible for the company to fill because the particular need of the writer is not specified. A request for "information about aluminum as a structural building material," however, specifies the subject and thus encourages a more satisfactory response.

In requesting materials, consider the time element. Do not assume that all materials will arrive immediately or that all or even most of the information for a research report will come from these requested materials. Depending too much on material to arrive before the due date of the report could be disastrous.

Library Materials

Much research is carried out in a library, whether a school library, a public library, or a specialized library such as a medical library, a business library, or a law library. The library contains a wealth of information in printed materials—books, newspapers, and periodicals—and in audiovisual materials—tapes, films, microforms, recordings. But this information is useless to the researcher until it is found and used to accomplish a purpose.

To simplify finding specific materials within the total library collection, which may be thousands or even millions of items, libraries use a system of cataloging and indexing information. With a knowledge of the system and a little curiosity, the researcher is well on the way to finding needed information.

Systems of Classifying Books Libraries classify books according to one of two systems: the Dewey Decimal Classification or the Library of Congress Classification.

The more common system, the one that most libraries follow, is the Dewey Decimal Classification, which uses numbers to divide all books into ten basic groups:

    000   General works
    100   Philosophy and related disciplines
    200   Religion
    300   Social sciences
    400   Language
    500   Pure sciences
    600   Technology (Applied sciences)
    700   The arts

800 Literature (Belles-lettres)
900 General geography, biography, history

These basic groups are divided and then subdivided numerous times.

In addition to the books in the first group, 000 General works, the books that the technical student will be using most often are those in the 500s, 600s, and 700s. The major divisions of these groups are as follows:

500 Pure sciences
    510 Mathematics
    520 Astronomy and allied sciences
    530 Physics
    540 Chemistry and allied sciences
    550 Sciences of earth and other worlds
    560 Paleontology
    570 Life sciences
    580 Botanical sciences
    590 Zoological sciences
600 Technology (Applied sciences)
    610 Medical sciences
    620 Engineering and allied operations
    630 Agriculture and related technologies
    640 Home economics and family living
    650 Management and auxiliary services
    660 Chemical and related technologies
    670 Manufactures
    680 Manufacture for specific uses
    690 Buildings
700 The arts
    710 Civic and landscape art
    720 Architecture
    730 Plastic arts and sculpture
    740 Drawing, decorative and minor arts
    750 Painting and paintings
    760 Graphic arts and prints
    770 Photography and photographs
    780 Music
    790 Recreational and performing arts

The Library of Congress Classification uses letters of the alphabet to divide all books into 20 basic groups. These basic groups have many divisions, designated by a letter-number combination. The main classes are these:

A General works
B Philosophy, psychology, religion
C History, auxiliary sciences
D History and topography (except America)
E and F American history
G Geography, anthropology
H Social sciences
J Political science

K   Law
L   Education
M   Music
N   Fine arts
P   Languages and literature
Q   Science
R   Medicine
S   Agriculture, plant and animal industry
T   Technology
U   Military science
V   Naval science
Z   Bibliography, library science

The following example shows how the book *Lasers and Their Applications* would be classified using the Library of Congress and the Dewey Decimal designations.

Library of Congress: TK7872.L3S7
Dewey Decimal: 621.329

Public (Card) Catalog   The single most useful item in the library is the public, or central, catalog, formerly called the card catalog. The public catalog, once available only in the form of 3- by 5-inch cards, is increasingly being made available in such electronic forms as a computer-output-microform (COM) catalog and/or on-line computer systems.

Microfiche, usually referred to as fiche, is a sheet of microfilm typically 4 by 6 inches and capable of accommodating and preserving a considerable number of pages in reduced form. One 4- by 6-inch fiche can, on the average, accommodate the information from 1600 3- by 5-inch cards in the card catalog. The COM catalog is produced in this way: the information contained in the public catalog is input and stored in a computer to which new acquisitions are routinely added. Periodically, a computer tape of the entire catalog is retrieved and reproduced on either microfiche or microfilm. An on-line computer system makes available quickly and accurately millions of items of information stored in a central computer. A terminal links the user to the computer.

The entries in the public (card) catalog are arranged alphabetically according to the first important word in the heading (first line) on the entry. The heading of each entry is determined by the type of entry: subject entry, author entry, or title entry. Only the heading for each entry differs; the other information is the same.

A typical entry in the public (card) catalog contains the following information (see the corresponding colored numbers on the last sample entry on page 376):

1. Call number. (This is the designation used for classifying and shelving the book.)
2. Heading. (This is a subject entry; therefore the subject, usually typed in red if on a card, is on the first line.)
3. Author's name, usually followed by year of birth and year of death. (A dash—indicates that the author was still living at the time the card was printed.)

4. Complete title of book
5. City of publication. (If New York were not a well-known city, the state would also have been given.)
6. Publishing company
7. Date of publication
8. Number of pages in the book. (Roman numeral indicates pages of introductory material.)
9. Height in centimeters (a centimeter is 0.4 inch)
10. International Standard Book Number
11. Cost of the book
12–13. Other ways in which the book is cataloged
14. Library of Congress catalog card number

As you begin looking in the public (card) catalog for books containing information on your subject, you may not know any authors or titles to consult. Therefore, look for subject entries. Suppose you were writing a paper entitled "Medical Applications of the Laser." If you do not know any title or authors concerning the subject, first look in the "L" section for "Laser." However, do not stop after looking under the one subject heading, "Laser"; look also under other related subject headings. Some of your most important information might be cataloged under such subjects as "Medicine" or "Surgery" or "Physics." (See the excerpt from *Library of Congress Subject Headings,* on pages 378–379.)

Sample Author, Title, and Subject Entries

Author Entry

```
309.262
C93t    Currie, Lauchlin Bernard.
             Taming the megalopolis: a design for
        urban growth/by Lauchlin Currie.--2nd
        ed.--Oxford; New York: Pergamon Press,
        c1983.
             ix, 127 p.; 26 cm.
```

Title Entry

```
309.262    Taming the megalopolis.
C93t    Currie, Lauchlin Bernard.
              Taming the megalopolis: a design for
         urban growth/by Lauchlin Currie.--2nd
         ed.--Oxford; New York: Pergamon Press,
         c1983.
              ix, 127 p.; 26 cm.
```

Subject Entry
(Numbers in color added for explanation; see corresponding list of items on pages 374–375.)

```
1 309.262   2 Cities and towns-Planning-1945-
  C93t 3 Currie, Lauchlin Bernard.
            4 Taming the megalopolis: a design for
       urban growing/by Lauchlin Currie.--2nd
       ed.--Oxford;5 New York:6 Pergamon Press,
       7 c1983.  8          9
            ix, 127 p.; 26 cm.
                                    11
         10 ISBN 0-08-020980-7: $14.10

     12 13    1. Cities and towns-Planning-1945-
         I. Title.
                              14 83-6848
                              MARC
```

Subject Entry Printed from Microfiche Card

```
Poynter, Den,
    Word processors and information
processing: a basic manual on what
they are and how to buy/by Den
Poynter. 2nd ed., rev. Santa
Barbara, CA: Para Pub., 1982.
    172 p.: ill.; 21 cm. m08726892
    0915516314
    1. Word processing (Office practice)
2. Word processing equipment. I.
Title.
651.8 P87w2 RAY VKB
```

Note that the call number, rather than appearing in the upper left-hand corner, is given at the end of the entry (RAY and VBR indicate locations in the library system that have one or more copies of the book).

Library of Congress Subject Headings   Particularly useful in looking up subject entries is the *Library of Congress Subject Headings* (and its supplements). This book gives subject descriptors used by the Library of Congress, and subsequently by most other libraries. An excerpt indicating the subject descriptors for "Laser" and "Lasers" is given on the next page.

Excerpt from *Library of Congress Subject Headings*

Laser anemometer
    See Laser Doppler velocimeter
Laser beam cutting
    x Cutting, Laser beam
    xx Cutting
        Metal-cutting
Laser beams
    x Beams, Laser
        Laser radiation
 —Diffraction   *(QC446.2)*
 —Scattering
Laser coagulation
    sa Lasers in surgery
    x Laser photocoagulation
    xx Lasers in surgery
        Light coagulation
Laser communication systems
    sa Astronautics—Optical
        communication systems
        Optical radar
    x Coherent light communication
        systems
        Communication systems, Optical
        (Laser-based)
        Light communication systems,
        Laser-based
        Optical communication systems,
        Laser-based
    xx Telecommunication
 —Patents
Laser Doppler velocimeter   *(TA357)*
    x Anemometer, Laser
        Doppler velocimeter, Laser
        Flowmeter, Laser
        Laser anemometer
        Laser flowmeter
        Velocimeter, Laser Doppler
    xx Fluid dynamic measurements
Laser flowmeter
    See Laser Doppler velocimeter
Laser gyroscopes
    See Optical gyroscopes
Laser materials *(Engineering, TK871.3:*
        Physics, QC374)
    sa Optical materials
    xx Optical materials
 —Defects
 —Radiation effects
    See Laser   materials,   Effect   of
    radiation on
Laser materials, Effect of radiation on
        (QC374)
    x Laser materials—Radiation effects
    xx Radiation
Laser photocoagulation
    See Laser coagulation
Laser photography
    See Holography
Laser radar
    See Optical radar

Laser radiation
    See Laser beams
Laser spectroscopy
    xx Lasers in chemistry
        Spectrum analysis
Laser welding
    xx Welding
Lasers
    sa Astronautics—Optical
        communication systems
        Atmosphere—Laser observations
        Chemical lasers
        Gas lasers
        Negative temperature
        Nonlinear optics
        Semiconductor lasers
        Solid-state lasers
        headings beginning with the word
        Laser
    x Light amplification by stimulated
        emission of radiation
        Masers, Optical
        Optical masers
    xx Astronautics—Optical
        communication systems
        Light
        Light amplifiers
        Nonlinear optics
        Optical pumping
        Photoelectronic devices
        Photons
 —Cooling
 —Experiments
 —Juvenile literature
 —Patents
 —Physiological effect
 —Safety measures
Lasers, Effect of radiation on
    xx Radiation
Lasers, Helium-neon
    See Helium-neon lasers
Lasers in art   *(N6494.L3)*
    xx Art
Lasers in biology
    xx Biological apparatus and supplies
Lasers in chemistry
    sa Laser spectroscopy
    xx Chemical apparatus
        Photochemistry
Lasers in medicine
    sa Lasers in surgery
    xx Medical instruments and apparatus
Lasers in surgery   *(RD73.L3)*
    sa Laser coagulation
    xx Laser coagulation
        Lasers in medicine
        Surgical instruments and apparatus
Lasers in surveying
    xx Surveying—Instruments

SYMBOLS	
sa (see also)	indicates a reference to a related or subordinate topic
x (see from)	indicates a reference from an expression not itself used as a heading
xx (see also from)	indicates a related heading from which a *sa* reference is made

As you begin looking in the public (card) catalog for sources of information, first check to see if the alphabetizing is letter by letter or word by word. Most dictionaries alphabetize letter by letter, but encyclopedias and indexes may use either alphabetical order or some other order such as chronological, tabular, regional. Knowing this information is essential; otherwise you might incorrectly assume the library has no materials on a subject. The following example illustrates these two methods of alphabetizing:

Letter by Letter	*Word by Word*
art ballad	art ballad
art epic	art epic
article	art lyric
art lyric	art theatre
art theatre	Arthurian legend
Arthurian legend	article
artificial comedy	artificial comedy
artificiality	artificiality

Indexes

Indexes are to periodicals (magazines, newspapers) what the public (card) catalog is to books. By consulting indexes to periodicals, specific sources of information on a subject can be found without looking through hundreds of thousands of magazines.

Much of any needed information on a technical or business subject is likely to come from magazines. For one thing, there is a great deal of information in magazines that is never published in book form. Furthermore, because the writing and publishing of a book usually takes at least a year, the information in magazines is likely to be much more current.

At the beginning of any index, there are directions for use, a key to abbreviations, and a list of periodicals indexed.

Magazine Index   *Magazine Index* is on microfilm. Because of its coverage, organization, and ease of use, *Magazine Index* makes magazine research simple. It is a "continuous" five-year index of all significant items in some 400 of the most popular magazines in America. It includes all articles indexed in the *Readers' Guide to Periodical Literature* (discussed later in this chapter) and more. *Magazine Index* indexes articles, short stories, poems, biographical pieces, recipes, reviews (books, movies, records, restaurants, concerts, etc.), product evaluations, editorials, and the like. Coverage began in 1976.

Magazine Index provides a five-year "rolling" cumulation; that is, as a new month is added, the corresponding month five years previous is deleted from the microfilm. Cumulative microfiche of deletions are provided periodically, so the subscriber will have a complete listing.

Given below are printed excerpts from the *Magazine Index* for the entry WORD PROCESSING for the period 1 January 1979 – 1 May 1984.° The some 350 entries in the full listing were categorized under 72 headings.

WORD PROCESSING

—ACHIEVEMENTS AND AWARDS
1982—WP executive: pioneering on an international scale. (Mary Jo Greil) il Modern Office Procedures v27
June'82-p62(2)
A showcase of technology from around the globe. (West Germany) il Modern Office Procedures v26   June'81-p122(2)

. . .

—AIMS AND OBJECTIVES
Can you adjust to new secretarial structures? by Bette Primrose   Modern Office Procedures v24   Sept'79-p92(3)

—ANALYSIS
Typeset-perfect prose: writers with word processors are now telecommunicating with typesetters, but there are still a significant number of obstacles to overcome before the process is letter-perfect. by Jeff Frane il   PC v3
April 3'84-p269(3)

. . .

—APPRECIATION
The right wording. (word processors) (column) by Ken Uston il   Penthouse v15
Sept'83-p48(1)

—ASIA, EASTERN
Softward lets typists key in ideographs. il   Electronics v54   Nov 3'81-p40(2)

—AUTOMATION
IBM lowers prices on Displaywriter and several other office products.   Office Administration and Automation v44
Aug'83-p17(1)   1980713
Clustered systems: configured for productivity. il   Office Administration and Automation v44   June'83-p53(9)
18D2363

. . .

—CASES
Convergent, Savin reach accord.   Office Administration and Automation v44
March'83-p13(1)   16M5834

—COMPUTER PROGRAMS
The whimsical world of Samna. (evaluation) by Jared Taylor   PC v3
May 1'84-p263(5)

The Leading Edge Word Processor. (evaluation) il   Computers & Electronics v22   May'84-p44(3)

. . .

—COSTS
Monitoring and controlling information— WP costs. by Bette Primrose   Modern Office Procedures v26   March'81-p24(2)

—DO-IT-YOURSELF
Word processing: 7 commandments. Writer's Digest v64   Feb'84-p53(2)

—ECONOMIC ASPECTS
Commit or hold off? The short- vs. the long-term tug of war. (office automation) il   Administrative Management v43
Sept'82-p24(4)

. . .

—EXHIBITIONS
IWP Syntopican IX word processing show featured many new "writer" systems, as well as sophisticated standalone text-editing machines. (International Information-Word Processing Association) (column) il   Administrative Management v42   Aug'81-p74(1)
World's biggest office show. il Administrative Management v41
July'80-p34(4)   03F1480

—FINANCE
Pitney Bowes moves into word processing. Business Week   Jan 21'80-p31(2)

—FORECASTS
Is word processing dead? (editorial) Modern Office Procedures v28
May'83-p12(1)   17K1336

. . .

—SCIENTIFIC APPLICATIONS
Changing the way people write.   Modern Office Procedures v25   April'80-p162(2)
0203394

—SECURITY MEASURES
Theft of computer time (or, is your operator secretly writing romances?) il Office Administration and Automation v44   Nov'83-p41(3)
Office security. by Belden Menkus Administrative Management v43
Feb'82-p84B(1)

—SERVICES

A way with word processing: ventures, profile. (Colorado word processing company) il   Colorado Business v9
Jan'82-p13(1)

—SOCIAL ASPECTS

A new home for the mind. (storing libraries in computer and allowing creative revisions) by Ted Nelson il   Datamation v28   March'82-p168(6)

—SOCIETIES AND CLUBS

IWP will change name later this year. (International Information-Word Processing Assoc.)   Office Administration and Automation
v44Feb'83-p11(1)
. . .

—TROUBLESHOOTING

The case for proofreading.   Modern Office Procedures v24   Feb'79-p106(2)

—USAGE

Exit the Dim Ages. (creative word processing) (column) by William Brohaugh   Writer's Digest v63
Nov'83-p18(2)

WP speeds judicial process. il   Office Administration and Automation v44
Aug'83-p95(2)   19B0789

Read any good texts lately? (Reading and Writing) (column) by Le Anne Schreiber il   New York Times Book Review v88
April 10'83-p47(1)

Yet another word about word processors. by Herman Holtz   Sales and Marketing Management v130   April 4'83-p50(1)
17F1232
. . .

The last entry in the *Magazine Index* excerpts shows that "Yet Another Word about Word Processors" is by Herman Holtz. The article appears in *Sales and Marketing Management,* volume 130, the April 4, 1983, issue on page 50. The article, for copying, is one page and in the "Magazine Collection" (see following paragraph) is number 17F1232.

Magazine Index, for all practical purposes, is one of the first resources a student researcher should turn to.

- The headings, subheadings, and cross references can be quite valuable in suggesting subject areas and topics for a library research report. In particular, the subheadings with subsequent entries indicate restricted, usable possibilities for report topics and titles.
- Headings in *Magazine Index* conform to the *Library of Congress: Subject Headings.* Magazine search can easily be coordinated with search for material in the public (card) catalog.
- The chronological listing of entries reflects the order of most recent information.
- "Hot Topics" gives ready reference to popular issues. A spin-off of *Magazine Index,* "Hot Topics" is a monthly printout (in a loose-leaf binder) of current magazine articles on such topics as abortion, child abuse, computer crime, and health care costs.
- The "Magazine Collection" gives ready reference to selected articles. The "Magazine Collection" consists of sets of 16 mm microfilm cartridges containing the complete texts of articles from many periodicals indexed in the *Magazine Index.* The "Magazine Collection" dates back to 1980 and is updated twice a month.

Readers' Guide to Periodical Literature   The *Readers' Guide* is a general index of over 180 leading popular magazines published from 1900 to the present. There are two issues a month except for January, February, May, July, and August, when there is only one issue a month. The second issue of each month includes the material from the first issue of that month. There are cumulative issues every three months, and a bound cumulation each year. This cumulation saves the researcher from having to look in so many different issues and keeps the index up to date.

The main body of the *Readers' Guide* is a listing, by subject and by author, of periodical articles. Each entry gives the title of the article, the author (if known), the name of the magazine, the volume, the page numbers, and additional notations for such items as bibliography, illustration, or portrait. Following the main body of the index is an author listing of citations to book reviews.

The excerpt below from the May 1984 issue of the *Readers' Guide to Periodical Literature* is the complete listing for the subject "Word processors and processing."*

Word processors and processing
  Hand-held word processor [Microwriter] W. J. Hawkins. il *Pop Sci* 224:116–17 F '84
  The word-processing maze. A. Lewis. *Byte* 9:235–6+ F '84

Programming
Bank Street Writer. M. Pagnoni. *Byte* 9:282–4 Mr '84
Behavior modification [WordStar] J. M. Fallows. il *Atlantic* 253:90–2+ Ja '84
Beyond the word processor. P. Lemmons. il *Byte* 9:53–4+ Ja '84
Electric Pencil PC. E. B. Staples. il *Creat Comput* 10:126+ Mr '84
Electronic editor helps you write. J. P. Lucas. il *Sci Dig* 92:84–5 F '84

Evaluating word-processing programs. A. Naiman. il *Byte* 9:243–6 F '84
Good words: four new word processors for the Apple. S. Arrants. il *Creat Comput* 10:106+ Ja '84
What's new in word processors. N. L. Shapiro il *Sci Dig* 91:93+ D '83
The word-processing software. il *Consum Rep* 49:90–4 F '84
A word processor with power [Word Juggler IIe] C. Rubin. il *Pers Comput* 8:213–14+ Ja '84
Word processors, il *Consum Rep* 48:101–17 D '83

Testing
Home computers for word-processing [special section] il *Consum Rep* 49:82–97 F '84

The first entry gives this information: title of article—"Hand-Held Word Processor [Microwriter] (annotation inserted in brackets by the editors of *Readers' Guide* to identify the particular word processor); author—W. J. Hawkins; illustration(s); magazine—*Popular Science;* volume 224; pages 116–117; date—February 1984.

With cumulative quarterly and yearly issues, the *Readers' Guide* is an easy-to-use, up-to-date source of articles in general interest magazines such as *Nation's Business, Popular Mechanics, Reader's Digest, Newsweek, Time, Health, Today's Education, Architectural Record, Flying,* and *Car and Driver.*

Applied Science & Technology Index The *Applied Science & Technology Index* indexes about 400 English language periodicals in the fields of aeronautics and space service, atmospheric sciences, chemistry, computer technology and applications, construction industry, energy resources and research engineering, engineering, fire and fire prevention, food and food industry, geology, machinery, mathematics, metallurgy, mineralogy, oceanography, petroleum and gas, physics, plastics, textile industry and fabrics, transportation, and other industrial and mechanical arts. The main body of the *Index* lists subject entries to periodical articles. Additionally, there is an author listing of citations to book reviews.

First published in 1958 (until 1957 it was part of the *Industrial Arts Index*), the *Applied Science & Technology Index* is issued monthly except July, and has quarterly and annual cumulations.

The arrangement of entries in the *Applied Science & Technology Index* is similar to that in the *Readers' Guide to Periodical Literature.*

Below are excerpts of entries under "Text editors" from the June 1984 issue of the *Applied Science & Technology Index.*° (The entry "Word processors" was followed by "*See* Text editors [Computer programs].")

Text editors (Computer programs)
Andra: the document preparation system of the personal workstation Lilith. J. Gutknecht and W. Winiger. bibl diags *Softw Pract Exper* 14:73–100 Ja '84
Bank Street Writer; word processor. M. Pagnoni. *Byte* 9:282–4 Mr '84
Beyond the word processor. P. Lemmons. *Byte* 9:53–4+ Ja '84
Choosing an IP system. P. Dunford. il *Data Process* 25:19–20 D '83

· · ·

Generation of syntax-directed editors with text-oriented features. B. A. Bottos and C. M. R. Kintala. bibl diags *Bell Syst Tech J* 62 pt2:3205–24 D '83
Juggling words with a word processor. L. Holz. il *Am City Cty* 99:22 Ja '84

Kaypro: all keyed up [Config program] R. Gaissert. *Microcomputing* 8:56–8 Ap '84
Managing multi-version programs with an editor. V. Kruskal. bibl *IBM J Res Dev* 28:74–81 Ja '84

· · ·

Select-86 word processor for the Rainbow. *Byte* 9:176 Ap '84
This word processor does it all. T. Bonoma. *Microcomputing* 8:16+ Mr '84
Trends in word processing. *Data Process* 25:2 D '83
Word processing holds the line [Structural Design Northeast, Inc.] il *Eng News-Rec* 212:62 F 9 '84
The word-processing maze. A. Lewis. *Byte* 9:235–6+ F '84

· · ·

The last entry in the excerpt indicates that the article "The Word-Processing Maze," by A. Lewis, appears in *Byte,* volume 9, pages 235–236 and is continued on other pages, in the February 1984 issue.

Business Periodicals Index This is an index to over 300 English language periodicals in the fields of accounting, advertising and public relations, banking, building and buildings, chemicals, communications, computer technology and applications, drugs and cosmetics, economics, electronics and electricity, finance and investments, industrial relations, insurance, international business, management and personnel administration, marketing, occupational health and safety, paper and pulp, petroleum and gas, printing and publishing, real estate, transportation, and other specific businesses, industries, and trades.

The main body of the *Index* lists subject entries to business periodical articles. Additionally, there is an author listing of citations to book reviews.

The *Business Periodicals Index* is published monthly except August and has quarterly and annual cumulations. It is very similar in format and arrangement to the *Readers' Guide* and the *Applied Science and Technology Index.*

The general subject headings are divided into subclassifications; thus, locating articles on a particular topic is easy. These subclassifications of a general subject may be useful to the student in another way: they may serve as a guide to a suitable subject for a library research report.

Below are excerpts from the May 1984 issue of the *Business Periodicals Index.*†

° *Applied Science & Technology Index.* Copyright © 1984 by The H. W. Wilson Company. Material reproduced by permission of the publisher.

† *Business Periodicals Index.* Copyright © 1984 by The H. W. Wilson Company. Material reproduced by permission of the publisher.

Word processing
  See also
Dictation

Management

Office applications for word-processing management. E. H. Jackson. il *Office* 99:77–8 F '84

Supplies

  See also
Word processing equipment

Word processing equipment
  See also
Automatic typewriters
Dictating machines
Work stations (Office automation)
Disaster to success in difficult & costly lessons. J. V. Simms. *J Syst Manage* 35:38–40 Ja '84
The word processor: a tool and a temptation [editorial] D. Wightman. *Tech Commun* 31 no1:3 '84

Add-ons

  See Word processing equipment—Plug compatible equipment

Energy usage

Power-line disturbances can play havoc with WP [AC line-monitoring equipment] il *Office* 99:109 F '84

Plug compatible equipment

Computerized paper pushing. *Eng News-Rec* 212:61 F 9 '84
Words, data work together. il *Eng News-Rec* 212:61–2 F 9 '84

Power supply

  See Word processing equipment—Energy usage

Printers

  See Printers (Data processing systems)

Programs

Evaluating word-processing programs. A. Naiman. *Byte* 9:243–6 F '84

. . .

Rating

And the race goes on [survey] tab *Comput Decis* 15:94+ D '83, 16:68+ Ja '84
Sony heads up WP honor roll. tab *Comput Decis* 16:26+ Ja '84

Selection

The word-processing maze. A. Lewis. *Byte* 9:235–6+ F '84

Word processing equipment industry
  See also
Data General Corp.
NCR Corp.
Wang Laboratories Inc.

Marketing

Changes in automation: some old friends will go. D. W. Murphy. *Office* 99:152 Ja '84

Word processors
  See Word processing equipment

Other Indexes to Professional Journals

In addition to the *Magazine Index*, *Readers' Guide to Periodical Literature*, *Applied Science & Technology Index*, and *Business Periodicals Index*, the following indexes to periodicals may be useful:

> *Applied Arts Index* (since 1913; formerly *Industrial Arts Index*)
> *Biological and Agricultural Index* (since 1916; formerly *Agricultural Index*)
> *Business Periodicals Index* (since 1958)
> *Cumulative Index to Nursing and Allied Health Literature* (since 1956; formerly *Cumulative Index to Nursing Literature*)
> *Engineering Index* (since 1884)
> *Hospital Literature Index* (since 1945)
> *Public Affairs Information Service Bulletin* (PAIS) (since 1915)
> *Social Sciences Index* (since 1974; formerly part of *Social Sciences and Humanities Index*, 1965–1974, and of *International Index*, 1907–1965)
> On microfilm: *Business Index* (since 1979). Has a "Business Collection" similar to the "Magazine Collection" for use with the *Magazine Index* (see page 381)

Indexes to Newspapers

Newspaper indexes include:

> *Christian Science Monitor Index* (since 1960, monthly)
> *Newspaper Index* (since 1972, monthly)

The London Times Index (1906–1977, bimonthly and quarterly; since 1977, monthly)

The New York Times Index (since 1851, semimonthly, annual cumulation). Also on-line

Wall Street Journal Index (since 1950, monthly, annual volume). Also on-line

On microfilm: *The National Newspaper Index,* covering *The New York Times, Christian Science Monitor, Wall Street Journal, Los Angeles Times,* and *Washington Post* (since 1 January 1979, monthly; updated daily). Also on-line

The New York Times Index is especially useful. The *Times* covers all major news events, both national and international. Because of its wide scope and relative completeness, the *Times Index* provides a wealth of information. It is frequently used even without reference to the individual paper of the date cited. A brief abstract of the news story is included with each entry. Thus, someone seeking a single fact, such as the date of an event or the name of a person, may often find all that is needed in the Index. In addition, since all material is dated, the *Times Index* serves as an entry into other, unindexed newspapers and magazines. *The New York Times Index* is arranged in dictionary form with cross-references to names and related topics.

Indexes to Government Publications The U.S. Government prints all kinds of books, reports, pamphlets, and periodicals for audiences from the least to the most knowledgeable. The best-known index to government documents is the *Monthly Catalog of United States Government Publications,* published by the U.S. Superintendent of Documents. Each monthly issue lists the documents published that month.

U.S. Government Books is a selective list of government publications of interest to the general public.

Also available from the U.S. government are some 250 subject bibliographies of government publications. These are listed in the *Subject Bibliographies Index;* subjects of bibliographies are as varied as "Accidents and Accident Prevention," "United States Army in World War II," and "Zoology."

A guide to reports from research is *Government Reports Announcements* (GRA) and its accompanying index *Government Reports Index,* both published twice a month.

Government Reference Books is an annotated guide that provides access to important reference works issued by agencies of the United States government. The guide is published every two years; the entries are arranged by subject.

Essay Index It is often difficult to locate essays and miscellaneous articles in books. The *Essay and General Literature Index* is an index by author, subject, and some titles of essays and articles published in books since 1900. The index is kept up to date by supplements.

Other "Helps" in Library Research

In addition to the public (card) catalog and the indexes, other tools or sources of information may be valuable in research.

Computer-Aided Search In a computer search, various databases (databases are electronic file cabinets) produced by the government, by nonprofit organizations, or by private companies are accessed through a computer terminal.

Some indexes are available in printed form and in a database, in which case the information is the same but the format (or appearance) is different. Also, the database may contain additional access points because more subject approaches may be used and key words in the titles may be searched.

Using the computer terminal to access the database is a two- or three-step procedure. First, contact is established with the computer containing the database via telephone lines. Some computers contain only one database; some contain many. The database needed must be accessed. Then, using carefully formulated search logic, the computer searches the database for the desired materials.

Search strategies should be formed, using one or more key words before going "on-line" (on-line is the time actually spent interacting with the computer). A thesaurus or a subject heading list, if available for the index, should be used. These have "see" and "see also" terms to help in selecting the proper subject headings to use.

During the computer search, the search strategy may be modified if the results are not satisfactory. Thus, if no items are located, another term may be used. If too many citations are found, the search may be limited. Limitations may include time, place, or more specific descriptors.

A computer search is fast (particularly for searches covering several years), current (some information is available on-line weeks or months before the printed version), accurate, thorough (more in-depth coverage since there is more access to the information), and convenient. Printouts of citations can also save time and energy.

Computer searches require the assistance of a librarian and during busy times may need to be scheduled in advance. In addition, computer searches may be expensive, although the cost of using databases varies greatly. The user is charged for on-line time (cost per minute of time the user is "connected" to the database) and for each citation printed. Some users have the citations printed off-line and mailed to cut costs, but it may take two days to a week to receive them.

Most thorough searches for information require several indexes. Computer searches may be considered to complement manual searches when many issues of a printed index must be consulted, when numerous sources are needed, and when currency is important.

Traditionally, database searches have been used for locating citations for journal and newspaper articles on a subject. Now with entire works — periodical articles, books, and even encyclopedias on-line — databases may be used for locating detailed financial data and directory listings on companies, statistics, biographical information, newswire stories, information on colleges and universities, and quotations. The information itself is becoming on-line, not just the citations to it.

NewsBank NewsBank is a microfiche newspaper reference service in the field of urban and public affairs. Articles are collected from more than 100 leading newspapers all over the United States and indexed by subject. The printed indexes are published monthly and are cumulated quarterly in March, June, and September, with an annual cumulation in December. The articles, reproduced on microfiche, are provided monthly with the index. NewsBank is a particularly useful help because of the on-the-spot availability of all indexed articles.

Given below is an excerpt from the April 1984 Index with an explanation of how to use the Index.°

Computer Industries
      See also Computers, Social Aspects;
      Electronic Equipment and Supplies;
      Electronic Information Handling;
      Manufacturing Industries – robots
      Japan – INT – 28:F7 – 8
competition
      AT&T vs. IBM – BUS – 47:A6 – 7
      IBM
         suppliers – BUS – 47:A8 – 9
bankruptcies and failures
      Magnuson Computer Systems – BUS – 47:A10, 47:A11
      CAD/CAM (computer-aided design and manufacturing) – BUS – 47:A12 – 13, 47:A14
disc drives
    expansion
      Jotech Inc. – BUS – 47:B1
    financial problems
      Shugart Corp. – BUS – 47:B2 – 3
discs
    laser optical system
      Colorado: Control Data Corp. – BUS –

47:B4
    earnings and profits
      Eagle Computer – BUS – 47:B5

mini computers
    marketing
      Wisconsin: General Robotics – BUS – 47:C3
    modems
      reviews – BUS – 47:C4
    peripherals

      Texas: STB Systems – BUS – 47:C5 – 6
    earnings and profits
      California: Microtek – BUS – 47:C7
personal computers
    See also Computers, Social Aspects – personal computers
    competition
      IBM vs. Apple Computer – BUS – 47:C8

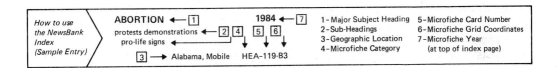

Social Issues Resources Series A valuable help in library research is the Social Issues Resources Series (SIRS). SIRS is a selection of articles reprinted from newspapers, magazines, journals, and government publications. The articles are organized into volumes with each volume, in a loose-leaf notebook format, dealing with a different social issue. Among the issues addressed (and thus titles for the volumes) are Aging, Alcohol, Communication, Consumerism, Corrections, Defense, Energy, Family, Food, Health, Human Rights, Mental Health, Pollution, Privacy, Sports, Technology, and Women. Each volume contains a minimum of 20 articles and is updated with an annual supplement of another 20 articles. (Each volume eventually contains 100 articles.) The articles are selected to represent various reading levels, differing points of view, and many aspects of the issue.

Audiovisual Materials Most colleges have an audiovisual department, a media or learning resources center, or a library department that supervises audiovisual

° *NewsBank Index.* Copyright 1984 by NewsBank, Inc. Material reproduced by permission of the publisher.

materials. Check with the librarian or person in charge concerning the cataloging of such materials as audio tapes, video tapes, phonograph recordings, films, filmstrips, and slides. These items may be alphabetized in the public (card) catalog or in a separate catalog. They may contain valuable information on a research topic.

Periodicals Holdings List The periodicals holdings list is a catalog of all the periodicals in a library. The alphabetical list gives the name of each magazine and the dates of the available issues. The list may also indicate whether the issues are bound or unbound and where in the library the magazines are located.

The periodicals holdings list may be in various forms, such as a drawer of 3- by 5-inch cards, a visible index file, a typed sheet, a microform, or automated printouts. Some libraries combine the periodicals holdings list with the public (card) catalog.

It is essential to know where the periodicals holdings list in a library is located. When in the various periodical indexes you find titles of articles that seem usable, you need to know if the library has the specified magazines. The periodicals holdings list will give this information; you can save time by checking the list yourself.

Reference Works Libraries are filled with all kinds of reference books. Common among these are encyclopedias, dictionaries, books of statistics, almanacs, bibliographies, handbooks, and yearbooks.

ENCYCLOPEDIAS Encyclopedias may be general encyclopedias or specialized encyclopedias. General encyclopedias may be a good starting point for locating information about a subject and for gaining an overall view of it. *Americana, Britannica, Colliers,* and *World Book* are well-known general encyclopedias that provide articles written for the general reader.

A valuable specialized encyclopedia is the *McGraw-Hill Encyclopedia of Science and Technology,* an international reference work in 15 volumes including an index. The articles, arranged in alphabetical order (word by word), cover pertinent information for every area of modern science and technology. Each article includes the basic concepts of a subject, a definition, background material, and multiple cross-references.

Specialized encyclopedias are numerous. Included are the *Encyclopedia of Athletics, Encyclopedia of Chess, Encyclopedia of U.S. Coins, Encyclopedia of Sea Warfare, Encyclopedia of Superstitions, Encyclopedia of the Horse, Encyclopedia of Athletic Medicine, Encyclopedia of Angling, Encyclopedia of Textiles, Encyclopedia of Advertising, Glen G. Munn's Encyclopedia of Banking and Finance,* and *Encyclopedia of Business Information Sources.*

DICTIONARIES General-use dictionaries include *The American College Dictionary, The American Heritage Dictionary of the English Language, The Random House Dictionary of the English Language,* and *Webster's New Collegiate Dictionary.* Specialized dictionaries include those of computer languages, architecture, welding, decorative arts, technical terms, the occult, U.S. military terms, Christian ethics, and economics.

BOOKS OF STATISTICS Statistics are often an important part of a report because they support conclusions, show trends, and lend validity to statements. Since statistics change frequently, currency is usually essential.

Up-to-date statistics on a subject may be located in such sources as almanacs, yearbooks, and encyclopedias as well as recent newspaper and magazine articles on the topic. Statistical information on the past, such as wages in the 1930s, may be located in *Historical Statistics of the United States, Colonial Times to 1970.*

Statistics for the United States and other countries in such areas as industry, business, society, and education are found in *Statistics Sources.*

For annual updates of statistical data, see the *Statistical Abstract of the United States* (since 1878) and the *Statistical Yearbook* (since 1949), which covers yearly events for about 150 countries.

Two monthly indexes which provide access to a large area of statistical information are *American Statistical Index* (ASI) and *Statistical Reference Index* (SRI). ASI (since 1973) indexes most statistical sources published by the federal government and SRI (since 1980) indexes statistical information in U.S. sources other than those published by the federal government. Both of these complementing indexes have annual cumulations.

For statistical works held by the library on your topic, look in the public catalog under the subject headings "Statistics" and "United States — Statistics." Also look under your topic for the subheading "Statistics," for example "Agriculture — Statistics."

ALMANACS Perhaps the best-known general almanac is *The World Almanac and Book of Facts.* It includes such diverse facts as winners of Academy Awards, accidents and deaths on railroads, civilian consumption of major food commodities per person, fuel economy in 1985 cars, National Football League champions, notable tall buildings in North American cities, and major new U.S. weapons systems.

Other almanacs include *Information Please Almanac*, the *Readers' Digest Almanac and Yearbook*, and the *Hammond Almanac.*

BIBLIOGRAPHIES Bibliographies are guides to sources of information on specific subjects. They do not generally provide answers but rather list sources, such as periodicals, books, pamphlets, and audiovisuals, which contain the needed information.

Most bibliographies contain specific citations to information on a subject; however, others, such as the *Encyclopedia of Business Information Sources*, give types of sources available on a subject. The *Encyclopedia of Business Information Sources* lists by subject such types of sources as encyclopedias and dictionaries, handbooks and manuals, periodicals, statistical sources, and almanacs and yearbooks. This type of work is particularly useful when researching a topic about which little is known or few sources seem to be available.

For bibliographies available in the library on a specific subject, consult the public catalog. Look under the subject for the subheading "Bibliography," for example, "Business — Bibliography," "Marketing — Bibliography," or "Nursing — Bibliography."

HANDBOOKS Handbooks contain specialized information for specific fields. The variety of handbooks is illustrated by the following examples. There are handbooks for word processor users, secretaries, electronics engineers, prospectors, and construction superintendents, as well as handbooks for the study of suicide, transistors, air conditioning systems design, food additives, simplified television service, and law of sales, to list a few.

Persons interested in information about job opportunities will find the *Occupational Outlook Handbook* quite useful. Published biennially by the U.S. Bureau of Labor Statistics, it tells the jobs available and where, the possible salary, educational requirements, possibility for advancement, and so on.

YEARBOOKS   Yearbooks, as the name suggests, cover events in a given year. Encyclopedia yearbooks update material covered in a basic set — this is an example of a general yearbook.

Specialized yearbooks include the *Yearbook of Adult and Continuing Education, Yearbook of Agriculture, Yearbook of American and Canadian Churches, Yearbook of Anesthesia, Yearbook of Drug Therapy, Yearbook of World Affairs, Yearbook of Industrial Statistics, Yearbook of Labour Statistics,* and *Yearbook of Landscape Architecture.*

Note that the above examples of encyclopedias, dictionaries, books of statistics, almanacs, bibliographies, handbooks, and yearbooks illustrate the number and variety of these types of reference works. A quick glance at *Books in Print,* under these categories, further emphasizes the number and variety.

Guides to Reference Works   For a quick review of what reference materials exist, the following guides are useful. If you find in these guides materials not available in your library, ask your librarian about an interlibrary loan. But remember that interlibrary loans take time.

PERIODICALS   *Ulrich's International Periodicals Directory* includes an alphabetical listing (by subject and title) of in-print periodicals, both American and foreign, and lists some of the works which index the periodicals.

BOOKS   Sheehy's *Guide to Reference Books* lists approximately 10,000 reference titles of both general reference works and those in the humanities, social sciences, history, and the pure and applied sciences. This guide also includes valuable information on how to use reference works.

The information in Sheehy's *Guide* may be updated by using *American Reference Books Annual* (ARBA), which lists by subject the reference books published each year in the United States.

The *Cumulative Book Index* lists books printed in the English language each year. *Books in Print* is a listing of books in print in America.

Vertical File   Much printed information exists in other than book and magazine forms. Pamphlets, booklets, bulletins, clippings, and other miscellaneous unbound materials are usually in a collection called the vertical file. These materials are filed or cataloged by subject. The vertical file and the *Vertical File Index,* which lists current pamphlets, may be valuable sources of information.

PLANNING AND WRITING A RESEARCH REPORT

Now that you are familiar with the four general sources of information — personal observation or experience, personal interviews, free or inexpensive materials from various agencies, and library materials and their use — you are ready to begin planning and writing a research report.

A research report is the written result of an organized investigation of a specific topic. It requires systematic searching out and bringing together information from various sources. It requires that the gathered information be presented in a conventional, easy-to-follow form.

Writing a research report can be profitable and rewarding. Knowing how and where to search for information and then how to present that information in a practical, understandable, and logical manner is a real accomplishment.

The procedure for writing a research report centers around four major steps:

1. Selecting a subject and defining the problem
2. Finding the facts
3. Recording and organizing the facts
4. Reporting the facts

Selecting a Subject and Defining the Problem

Selecting a Subject The success of the research project depends on a wise choice of subject. If a specific subject is assigned, of course the selection problem is solved. However, if you choose the subject, consider the following guidelines.

1. *Choose a subject that fulfills a need.* Doing research should not be a chore or just another assignment — it should be a pleasant adventure that fulfills a need to know. Investigating some aspect of a future vocation, following up a question or a statement in a class, finding out more about an invention or a discovery, wanting to know the functions and uses of a particular mechanism — whatever the subject, let it be something that appeals to you because you want and need to know the information.

2. *Choose a subject that can be treated satisfactorily in the allotted time.* No one expects a college student to make an earthshaking contribution to human knowledge by presenting the result of months and years of research and study. Library research gives the student experience in finding, organizing, and reporting information on a specific subject. Therefore, the topic chosen should be sufficiently limited for adequate treatment in the few weeks allotted for the paper. The subject "Dogs," for instance, is much too broad to try to cover in a few weeks. Even "Hunting Dogs" would require far more time than is available. But "The Care and Training of Bird Dogs" is a specific topic that could reasonably be investigated in the usual time designated for a research report.

3. *Choose a subject on which there is sufficient available material.* Before deciding definitely on a subject, check with instructors and the library to be sure that the topic has sufficient accessible material. Generally, it is wise to choose another topic if the principal library you use has little or no information on the proposed topic. If the topic is highly specialized or has information in only very select journals, locate several references before deciding definitely to use the topic. Sometimes a news broadcast or a current event may suggest a subject. Again, be sure that enough material can be secured to write an effective report.

Defining the General Problem   After the selection of the subject for the research report, the central problem or idea being investigated should be specifically stated. The formulation of this central problem, or basic question, is important because it determines the kind of information to look for. In writing a report, the idea is not simply to gather information that happens to fall under a general heading; the idea is to gather information that relates directly to the subject and that can give it form and meaning. For the subject "The Effects of Alcohol on People," for example, the central problem might be defined as the following: "How does alcohol affect people: how does it affect their bodies, behavior, relationships with other people?" This question gives direction to the researcher's reading and to the investigation as a whole.

Defining the Specific Problems   As a guide in searching for information, divide the central problem into specific problems, or questions. These questions serve as a preliminary outline for more selective reading. Again, take the subject "The Effects of Alcohol on People" with the central problem, "How does alcohol affect people: how does it affect their bodies, behavior, relationship with other people?" Divide this general question into smaller ones. such as these:

1. Does alcohol kill brain cells?
2. Why do people drink?
3. Why do some people become silly and giggle a lot and others become morose and withdrawn when they drink?
4. What organs of the body does alcohol affect?
5. How does excessive drinking affect family relationships?
6. How much alcohol does it take to have an effect on the body?
7. Why can some people take or leave alcohol while others become addicted to it?

Other questions, of course, might be added to these.

As the investigation proceeds and the body of collected data increases, change or drop or add to the questions in the preliminary outline.

Finding the Facts

Finding the facts for a research report requires a search of all available resource materials on the subject of the report. As discussed earlier in this chapter the possible sources of information can be classified as: (1) personal observation, (2) personal interviews, (3) free or inexpensive materials from various agencies, and (4) library materials.

Make a thorough, systematic search of all available materials. A good place to start is a general encyclopedia. From there move to the card catalog, remembering to check every possible topic you can think of that is related to the subject of the report. Then check indexes to periodicals; if the subject requires current information, check only the issues of current date. If, however, time is not a factor, check in all available issues. Remember to check in more than one index, too. You might start with the *Magazine Index* or the *Reader's Guide* and then the *Applied Science & Technology Index* or the *Biological and Agricultural Index* or one of the specialized indexes.

A check of these basic resources gives you a good start in finding the facts. Then you can go to any other available materials.

Sample Card for an Essay in a Book

Portias, John E. "Computer Graphics."
Computer Delineations. Ed. Roberto L.
Guille, Jr., and Maria C. Dumais. 3rd
ed. New York: McGraw-Hill, 1984.
92 - 104.

BIBLIOGRAPHY CARD FOR AN ARTICLE IN A JOURNAL   On each bibliography card for an article from a journal, record:

1. Author's name (last name first)
2. Title of the article (in quotation marks)
3. Title of the journal (underlined)
4. Volume number
5. Date of publication (in parentheses)
6. Page numbers

Sample Card for an Article in a Journal

Greytak, David, Richard McHugh, and others.
"Inflation and the Individual Income
Tax." *Southern Economic
Journal* 50 (1983): 168 - 180.

BIBLIOGRAPHY CARD FOR AN ARTICLE IN A POPULAR MAGAZINE On each bibliography card for an article from a popular magazine, record:

1. Author's name (last name first), if given
2. Title of the article (in quotation marks)
3. Title of the magazine (underlined)
4. Date of publication
5. Page numbers

Sample Card for an Article in a Popular Magazine

DeLaughton, Lynn C. "New Rules in Soccer." <u>Time</u> 4 January 1985: 61.

BIBLIOGRAPHY CARD FOR AN ITEM IN A NEWSPAPER On each bibliography card for an item from a newspaper, record:

1. Author's name (last name first), if given
2. Title of the item (in quotation marks)
3. Name of the newspaper and, if applicable, the edition. (If needed for publication clarification, insert in brackets the name of the city or state, or both.)
4. Date
5. Section and page

Sample Card for an Item in a Newspaper

> Subokof, Alle. "Which Way for Defense."
> Courier [Columbus, Ohio]
> 24 Feb. 1984, late ed.: B11.

BIBLIOGRAPHY CARD FOR AN ITEM FROM NEWSBANK   For a newspaper item appearing in NewsBank (on microfiche) it is necessary to give two sets of bibliographical data: citation of the newspaper in which the item originally appeared and citation of the NewsBank location. On each bibliography card for an item from NewsBank, record:

1. Author's name (last name first), if given
2. Title of the item (in quotation marks)
3. Name of the newspaper. (If needed for publication clarification, insert in brackets the name of the city or state, or both.)
4. Date
5. NewsBank identification, subject heading, year, fiche number and grid location

Sample Card for an Item from NewsBank

> Berman, Laura. "Utilities Battle Natural
> Gas Hike." Detroit [Mich.] Free Press,
> 11 Aug. 1982. NewsBank,
> Business and Economic
> Development, 1982, 77:C13.

BIBLIOGRAPHY CARD FOR AN ITEM REPRINTED FROM ANOTHER SOURCE   For an item reprinted (rpt.) from another source, it is necessary to give two sets of bibliographical data: citation of the original source of the item, and citation of the immediate source of the item. (This bibliography card is somewhat similar to a bibliography card for an item from NewsBank.) For the citation of the original source, follow the standard format for citing the particular item: essay from a book, a magazine article, newspaper item, or whatever. Then identify the immediate source of the item.

For example, for a bibliography card of a magazine article reprinted in the Social Issues Resources Series, record:

1. Author's name (last name first), if given
2. Title of the article (in quotation marks)
3. Title of the magazine (underlined)
4. Date of publication
5. Page numbers
6. Social Issues Resources Series identification, volume title, volume number, article number

Sample Card for an Item Reprinted from Another Source

Stephens, Gene. "Crime in the Year 2000." _Futurist_ April 1981: 49 – 52. Rpt. in Social Issues Resources Series, Crime 2: art. 73.

BIBLIOGRAPHY CARD FOR AN ENCYCLOPEDIA ARTICLE   For a bibliography card for an article in a well-known encyclopedia, record:

1. Author's name (last name first), if given. (Encyclopedia articles are often signed with initials; it may be necessary to look in a separate listing for identification of the initials.)
2. Title of the article (in quotation marks)
3. Name of the encyclopedia (underlined)
4. Edition year. (Note that volume and page numbers are given if the reference is to material on a single page of an article covering several pages.)

Note: For other than well-known encyclopedias, give full publication information as for any other book.

Sample Card for an Encyclopedia Article

"Computer." <u>McGraw-Hill Encyclopedia of Science and Technology.</u> 1982 ed.

BIBLIOGRAPHY CARD FOR A PAMPHLET   For a bibliography card for a pamphlet or any individual printed work of less than book length, give the following:

1. Author's or editor's name, if given (last name first), or name of sponsoring organization
2. Title of pamphlet (underlined)
3. Other identifying information, such as series name and number
4. City of publication
5. Publishing company
6. Date of publication. (It might be helpful to remember that a pamphlet reference is very similar to a book reference.)

Sample Card for a Pamphlet

United States. Dept. of Justice. National Criminal Justice Information and Statistics Service. <u>The Characteristics of Burglary Incidents.</u> Washington: GPO, 1985.

BIBLIOGRAPHY CARD FOR A PERSONAL INTERVIEW   On each bibliography card for a personal interview (for a telephone interview, substitute the word "telephone"), record:

1. Interviewee's name (last name first)
2. Kind of interview and, if applicable, subject of the interview
3. Date of the interview

Sample Card for a Personal Interview

> *Strong, Alicia M. Personal
> interview on employment
> opportunities. 2 Feb. 1984.*

Taking Notes   While investigating each source in the working bibliography, save time by first consulting the table of contents and the index for the exact pages that may contain helpful information. After locating the information, scan it to get the general idea. Then, if the information is of value, read it carefully. If certain material may be specifically used in the paper, write it down on note cards.

GENERAL DIRECTIONS FOR TAKING NOTES   Regardless of the shortcuts you may think you have devised for taking notes, following these directions will be the shortest shortcut:

1. Take notes in ink on either 3- by 5- or 4- by 6-inch cards. Ink is more legible than pencil, and cards are easier to handle than pieces of paper.
2. If it is difficult to decide when to take notes and when not to, stop *trying* to take notes. Read a half dozen or so of the sources, taking no notes. Study the preliminary outline. (Do not hesitate to revise the outline — it is purely for your use.) Then return to the sources with a clearer idea of what facts are needed.
3. Write one item of information on a note card. Write on one side of the card. Cards can then be rearranged easily.
4. Always write notes from different sources on different cards.
5. Take brief notes — passages that may possibly be quoted in the paper,

statistics, and other such specific data, proper names, dates, and only enough other information to jog the memory. Writing naturally or well cannot be done if the paper is based solely on notes rather than on overall knowledge and understanding. One caution: write enough so that you can use the information after it is "cold."

6. Write a key word or phrase indicating the content of each note in the upper left corner for quick reference. This key word or phrase will be especially helpful in arranging cards according to topic; often these key words or phrases become headings in the final outline.

7. In the upper right corner, identify the source (author's name and, if necessary, title of the work) and give the specific page number from which the material comes. This information in the right corner keys the note card to the bibliography card, needed for writing notes and bibliography.

8. Remember that proper credit must be given in the paper for all borrowed material—quotations, exact figures, or information and ideas that are not widely known among educated people. Remember, too, that an idea stated in one's own words is just as much borrowed as an idea quoted in the author's exact words. Therefore, take notes carefully so that you know which notes are direct quotes, or paraphrase, or summary.

TYPES OF NOTE CARDS   Notes may be direct quotations, paraphrases, or summaries.

Direct Quotation   Some notes will be direct quotations, that is, the author's exact words.

There may be passages in which the author has used particularly concise and skillful wording, and you may want to quote them; in this case, the author's exact words are written on the note card. Generally, however, take down few direct quotations—they create a tendency to rely on someone else's phrasing and organization for the paper. If it is desirable to leave out part of a quotation, use ellipsis points, that is, three spaced dots (. . .) or four spaced dots if the omission includes an end period (. . . .). Be sure to put quotation marks around all quoted material.

Sample Note Card Containing a Direct Quotation

> *Potential of miracle chip*   *"The Computer Society,"*
> *p. 467*
>
>
>   *"Far from rendering the big computer*
>   *obsolete, the miracle chip has opened*
>   *the way for the design of custom-made*
>   *supercomputers more powerful than anything*
>   *dreamed possible a few years ago."*

Paraphrase and Summary   Most of the notes for a library report will be paraphrases and summaries rather than direct quotations. A paraphrase is a restatement in different words of someone else's statement. A summary is the gist — it includes the main points — of a passage or article. In reading, get main ideas and record them in your own words. Jot down key phrases and sentences that summarize ideas clearly. Do not bother taking down isolated details and useless illustrative material. It is not necessary to write notes in complete sentences, but each note should be sensible, factual, and legible — and meaningful after two weeks.

Following are examples of the paraphrase and the summary note cards.

Sample Note Card Containing a Paraphrase

> *Effect of miracle chip*   *"The Computer Society,"*
> *on computer industry*   *p. 467*
>
>   *The miracle chip makes possible*
>   *more powerful computers. It will*
>   *lower the cost of minicomputers and*
>   *enable the small computers to perform*
>   *more and more functions previously*
>   *requiring large computers. Such*
>   *use will result in future cost*
>   *reduction.*

Sample Note Card Containing a Summary

Potential use   *"The Computer Society,"*
                                                  pp. 468-469

Key areas for potential use of miracle chips:

1. *Automobiles*
2. *Communications*
3. *Office equipment*

Stating the Central Idea and Constructing a Formal Outline At the very beginning of the research project a basic question or problem was formulated; then this general question was divided into specific questions, or aspects, as a preliminary outline. As investigation has progressed, you probably have added to, changed, and perhaps even omitted some of the original questions. Thus, the present list of questions looks quite different from the beginning list. (The preliminary outline should be revised and brought up to date after all notes are taken.)

By this stage in the research you should have clearly in mind the central idea of the report. Write this central idea (thesis statement or controlling idea) as a one-sentence summary at the top of what will be the working outline page.

From the central idea, the list of questions or divisions in the revised preliminary outline, and the key words in the upper left corner of the note cards, structure a formal outline to serve as the working outline for the first draft of the paper. Every major division in the outline should reflect a major aspect of the central idea. Taken as a whole, all of the major divisions should cover the central idea and adequately explain it.

The formal outline may be either a sentence outline or a topic outline. Remember, in a sentence outline all the headings are complete statements (no heading should be a question), and in a topic outline all the headings are phrases or single words. The sentence outline is more complete and helps to clarify the writer's thinking on each point as he or she goes along; it brings him or her one step nearer the writing of the paper. The topic outline is briefer and shows at a glance the divisions and subdivisions of the subject. Whichever type of outline is chosen, be consistent; do not mix topics and sentences. (For further treatment of outlining, see pages 114–115, 135, 145, 414, and 444.)

The working outline will serve as a work plan in writing the first draft of the report; it will let you know where you are and will provide a systematic organization of the information.

Arranging the Note Cards to Fit the Outline When the working outline is completed, mark each note card with a roman numeral, letter of the alphabet, or Arabic numeral to show to what section and subsection of the outline the note card corresponds. Then rearrange the note cards accordingly. If the note cards are insufficient, look up additional material; if there are irrelevant note cards, discard them. When you have enough material to cover each point in the outline adequately, you are ready to begin writing the report. Each main heading in the outline should correspond to a major section of the report; each subheading to a supporting section.

REPORTING THE FACTS

Writing the First Draft

With the working outline for a guide and the note cards for content, write the first draft of the report rapidly and freely. Concentrate on getting thoughts down on paper in logical order; take care of grammar, punctuation, and mechanical points later. In writing the first draft, it will be necessary to write short transitional passages to connect the material on the note cards. Also, it will be necessary to rephrase notes (except for direct quotations) to suit the exact thought and style of writing. Add any headings that would help to make the material clearer. (See pages 4–5 and 313 for a discussion of headings.) Think through the layout and design of the report (see pages 1–4, 23–25).

Introduction and Conclusion In the first paragraph or in a section headed "Introduction," state the thesis, or central idea, of the report. Let the reader know what to expect, to what extent the subject will be explored, as indicated in the major headings of the outline. The introduction, designed to attract the reader's attention, serves as a contract between writer and reader. It may be a sentence, a single paragraph, several paragraphs, or even several pages. In it, the writer commits the report to a subject, a purpose, and an organization of material. (See also Chapter 8, Reports, page 311, for further discussion of the introduction.)

In the introduction, make clear the subject to be covered and the extent of the coverage. Stating the thesis or the central idea usually is sufficient to identify the subject; a sentence listing the major headings of the outline will show the extent of coverage.

Supply any information needed to help the reader understand the material to follow; this information might include a definition of the subject itself or of terms related to the subject. Explain the significance of your investigation and reporting.

After completing the body of the paper, close with a paragraph that is a summary, a climax, conclusions, or recommendations drawn from the material that has been presented.

Quotations and Paraphrases If the exact words of another writer are used, put them in quotation marks. If the quotation is four lines or more in length, however, instead of using quotation marks, single space the quotation and indent each line ten spaces from both the left and right margins.

Incorporate paraphrased matter and indirect quotations into the body of the paper, and do not use quotation marks. However, document *all* borrowed information, whether quoted directly or paraphrased. (Documentation is discussed in detail later in this chapter.)

A NOTE ABOUT PLAGIARISM Plagiarism is implying that another person's ideas or words are your own ideas or words. Sometimes plagiarism is unintentional; sometimes intentional. To avoid the problem of plagiarism, keep the following suggestions in mind.

1. Place quotation marks around any material that you yourself did not write and credit the source with a footnote. Indicate material copied on note cards by using quotation marks. In the report you may wish to introduce the material by using the name of the person who wrote it or the title of the work in which it appeared.
2. Write paraphrased material in your own style and language. Simply rearranging the words in a sentence or changing a few words does not paraphrase.

There is no excuse for plagiarism. A careful handling of information should help you avoid any problem.

Documentation Documenting information means supplying references to support assertions and to acknowledge ideas and material that you borrow. Documentation is usually done by inserting in the text a shortened parenthetical identification or a number that corresponds to a work identified fully in a footnote at the bottom of the page, in a note at the end of the report, or, most often, in a list of "References Cited" at the end of the report. Sometimes included is a bibliography listing all the sources used in writing the report, whether specifically referred to or not. (Documentation practices are discussed in detail on pages 406–411.)

Revising the Outline and First Draft After writing the first draft of the report, study it carefully for accuracy of content, mechanical correctness, logical organization, clarity, proportion, and general effectiveness. Check to see if the intended reader has been kept in mind. The writer may understand perfectly well what is written, but the real test of writing skill is whether or not the reader will understand the report.

Make needed revisions in the outline and the first draft. Make sure that the headings in the report correspond exactly to the headings in the outline. (For a further discussion of headings, see pages 4–5 and 313.) Plan and prepare visuals. Think through the kinds of visuals that will be the most effective and decide where to place the visuals. (For a detailed discussion, see Chapter 11, Visuals.)

The revising process may involve making several drafts of the outline and the report. But after the hours, days, and weeks already invested in this project, a few more hours spent polishing the report is worth the effort. Careful revision may mean the difference between an excellent and a mediocre report. (See also the checklist for revising on the inside back cover.)

Writing the Final Draft

When the outline, the text of the paper, and the documentation are completed, carefully recopy the pages. Prepare a letter of transmittal, a title page, and an abstract (see pages 310–311). For the entire report, follow the general format directions for writing, on the inside front cover. Double space a typewritten report. In a handwritten report, space as if it were typewritten.

Proofread the report thoroughly. Clip the pages together in this order: letter of transmittal, title page, outline, abstract, body of the report, and as applicable: notes, list of works cited, bibliography. The research report is finished at last and ready to be handed in! (For a detailed discussion of reports, see Chapter 8, Reports, pages 309–312.)

Documentation

Documentation provides a systematic method for identifying sources or references used in a research report.

The format or style used for documentation varies from discipline to discipline and even within disciplines. Societies or organizations of persons in a specific discipline may offer style manuals to be used in documenting papers in that discipline. Examples include the American Mathematical Society's *Manual for Authors of Mathematical Papers,* the Council of Biology Editors' *CBE Style Manual: A Guide for Authors, Editors, and Publishers in the Biological Sciences,* the American Chemical Society's *Handbook for Authors of Papers in American Chemical Society Publications,* the American Institute of Physics' *Style Manual for Guidance in the Preparation of Papers,* and the International Steering Committee of Medical Editors' "Uniform Requirements for Manuscripts Submitted to Biomedical Journals."

Then there are basic manuals that are used by various disciplines, such as the *MLA Handbook for Writers of Research Papers* (2nd ed.; New York: MLA, 1984); *The Chicago Manual of Style* (13th ed.; Chicago: U of Chicago P, 1982); *Publication Manual of the American Psychological Association* (3rd ed.; Washington: American Psychological Assn., 1983); Turabian's *Manual for the Writers of Term Papers, Theses, and Dissertations* (4th ed.; Chicago: U of Chicago P, 1973; Campbell, Ballou, and Slade's *Form and Style: Theses, Reports, Term Papers* (6th ed.; Boston: Houghton Mifflin, 1982); or the United States Government Printing Office *Style Manual* (rev. ed.; Washington: GPO, 1973).

Although documentation practices in literature, history, and the arts are somewhat uniform, documentation in other areas follows various practices. Among the science disciplines, for instance, there is little uniformity of procedure.

While the *reason* for documentation is the same in all areas—citation of sources for statements presented or to acknowledge borrowed matter—the *procedures* for citing sources are somewhat different.

The following discussion is presented with these reservations and with this advice: regarding documentation practices, consult with the instructor assigning the report, consult with instructors in the subject area of the report, and study the practices in pertinent professional journals.

Remember: whatever format you choose, be consistent.

Four Styles of Documentation   In documenting information, the important thing is to cite the source of the information. The source can be given in the text:

> Many of us would agree, as is pointed out on page 33 in David Marc's article "Understanding Television" in the August 1984 issue of *The Atlantic*, pages 33–44, that a well-pronounced distaste for TV has become a prerequisite for claims of intellectual and even of ethical legitimacy.

Such a citation within the text, however, detracts from the emphasis in the sentence; and several such citations within the text are likely to annoy the reader and hinder readability.

Various styles or systems of documentation are used, but four styles seem to dominate. They will be referred to as Style A, Style B, Style C, and Style D.

Style A, recommended by the Modern Language Association, is distinguished by a textual parenthetical listing of the reference (author's last name and page number) and at the end of the report, a full citation of the reference.

EXAMPLE:

> Many of us would agree that a well-pronounced distaste for TV has become a prerequisite for claims of intellectual and even of ethical legitimacy (Marc 33).

The full citation in the list of references:

> Marc, David. "Understanding Television." *The Atlantic* Aug. 1984: 33–44.

Style A is favored by writers in literature, history, and the arts.

Style B, recommended by *The Chicago Manual of Style* (Chicago) and the *Publication Manual of the American Psychological Association* (APA), is distinguished by a textual parenthetical listing (author's last name and year of publication) and at the end of the report, a full citation of the reference.

EXAMPLE:

> Many of us would agree that a well-pronounced distaste for TV has become a prerequisite for claims of intellectual and even of ethical legitimacy (Marc 1984). [APA inserts a comma between author and year.]

The full citation in the list of references:

Chicago: Marc, David. 1984. Understanding television. *The Atlantic*, Aug., 33–44.
APA: Marc, D. (1984, August). Understanding television. *The Atlantic*, pp. 33–44.

ANOTHER EXAMPLE OF STYLE B:

TEXT OF PAPER:

Field (1971) cited 11 references to indicate that the estimated retail yield favored rams over wethers. Shelton and Carpenter (1972) found that not only is the amount of fat less in rams than in wethers or ewes, but the rate of fat deposition is also much lower at heavy weights (64 kg live weight) in rams. Kemp et al. (1972) observed that fat measurements were greater for wethers than for rams in light weight groups and that these differences between sexes became greater as weight increased. Crouse et al. (1981) found ram lamb carcasses to be significantly leaner than ewe or wether lamb carcasses.

ENTRIES FROM "LITERATURE CITED" AT THE END OF THE PAPER:

Crouse, J. D., J. R. Busboom, R. A. Field and C. L. Ferrell, 1981. The effects of breed, diet, sex, location and slaughter weight on lamb growth, carcass composition and meat flavor. J. Anim. Sci. 53:376.

Crouse, J. D., R. A. Field, J. L. Chant, Jr., C. L. Ferrell, G. M. Smith and V. L. Harrison, 1978. Effect of dietary energy intake on carcass composition and palatability of different weight carcasses from ewe and ram lambs. J. Anim. Sci. 47:1207.

Deweese, W. P., H. A. Glimp, J. D. Kemp and D. G. Ely, 1969. Performance and carcass characteristics of rams and wethers slaughtered at different weights. Kentucky Agr. Exp. Sta. Prog. Rep. 181.

Dolezal, H. G., G. C. Smith, J. W. Savell and Z. L. Carpenter, 1982. Comparison of subcutaneous fat thickness, marbling and quality grade for predicting palatability of beef. J. Food Sci. 47:942.

Style B is favored by writers in the natural sciences and social sciences.

Style C is a number system. A number is usually placed in parentheses or in brackets (sometimes the number is written as a superscript—slightly above the regular line of type) in the text. This number refers to an entry in the numbered list of references at the end of the paper.

EXAMPLE:

TEXT OF PAPER:

Of the anatomic indices that have been developed, the most widely used is the Injury Severity Score (ISS) *(1,2)*. This index is a modification of an earlier index, the Abbreviated Injury Scale (AIS) which was originally developed for motor vehicle injuries. The AIS-ISS system of grading severity has undergone considerable evolution as experience in its use has accumulated, and an updated version appeared in 1984 *(3)*.

ENTRIES FROM "REFERENCES" AT THE END OF THE PAPER:

1. Baker, S. P., O'Neill, B., Haddon, W., and Long, W.: The injury severity score: a method for describing patients with multiple injuries and evaluating emergency care. J Trauma 14: 187–193 (1974).

2. Baker, S. P., and O'Neill, B.: The injury severity score: an update. J Trauma 16: 882–885 (1976).

3. The abbreviated injury scale—1984 revision. American Association for Automotive Medicine, Morton Grove, Ill., 1984.

The list of references at the end of the paper may be given in (a) alphabetical order or in (b) the order in which the sources are mentioned in the text of the paper (as in the above example).

References in science papers may be written in a number of ways; there is no one uniform format. Given below is a sampling of notes using various formats. (Remember, whatever format you choose for your paper, be consistent.)

EXAMPLES (each example from a different paper):

(4) Guthrie, Robert D.; Nutter, Dale E. *Amer. Chem. Soc.,* 106:7478 (1984).

17. Lombard CW, Tilly LP, Yoshioka MM: Pacemaker implantation in the dog. *J Am Anim Hosp Assoc* 17:746–750, 1981.

9. Walters, S., "The Age of Fusion: On the Brink," *Mechanical Engineering*, July 1982, pp. 22–23.

6. McKelvey, J., and Grotch, H., *Physics for Science and Engineering*, text ed. (New York: Harper & Row, 1982), chap. 1, p. 25.

Style C is favored by writers in the sciences and in engineering.

Style D is the traditional, humanities system of documenting through footnotes or endnotes and with or without a list of works cited or a bibliography. A superscript number in the text is keyed to a full citation at the bottom of the page or, more commonly, at the end of the report.

EXAMPLE

Juveniles under the age of 18 constitute only one-fifth of our country's population but they account for nearly one-half of those arrested for serious crimes.[1]

The full citation as a footnote or endnote:

[1] George M. Anderson, "Juvenile Justice: A Long Way to Go," *America*, 8 Mar. 1984, p. 190.

If there is a list of references, the citation is as follows:

Anderson, George M. "Juvenile Justice: A Long Way to Go." *America*, 8 Mar. 1984, p. 190.

In Style D the first reference to a source is a complete citation, as illustrated in the example above. Frequently, reference is made to a source a second, third, or more times. Any source reference after the first usually gives the author's last name and the page number(s). The reference may also include an intelligible short title if necessary to make clear which work is cited.

First reference: [2] Annie Dillard, *Pilgrim at Tinker Creek* (New York: Harper's Magazine Press, 1974), p. 204.

[3] . . . .

[4] . . . .

Second reference: [5] Dillard, p. 19.

Notice that footnotes/endnotes are indented as if they were paragraphs and that the items of information are separated by commas, not periods.

Citations List and Bibliography   A citations list or bibliography typically concludes a library research report. A citations list gives author, title, and publishing information about all source materials referred to in the text. The citations list is headed "Works Cited," "Works Consulted," "References," or a similar title.

The citations list is usually in alphabetical order. If Style C documentation (a number system) is used, however, the numbered list of citations may be either alphabetical or in the order in which the sources are mentioned in the text.

A bibliography is an alphabetical listing of all source materials — whether specifically referred to or not — used in preparing and writing a research report.

An annotated bibliography includes descriptive or evaluative comments about each entry. (See Chapter 7, The Summary, especially pages 191–192.)

The citations list and bibliography observe hanging indentation, that is, in every entry each line after the first is indented.

Examples of Citations Given below are examples of citations to various kinds of references: books, periodicals, and nonprint materials. These examples follow Style A documentation (author-page parenthetical insertion in the text and an end-of-report citations list). The sample library research paper that concludes this chapter follows Style A documentation.

Remember that although documentation styles differ, they differ only in details — details of punctuation and abbreviation and of order in the placement of information.

CITATIONS FOR BOOKS

One author	Custer, Cleve. *Raising Dandelions.* New York: Viking, 1984.
Two authors	Tompkins, Jayne V., and Russell Atkins. *Microprocessor Applications.* Boston: High Tech, 1984.
Three or more authors	Baell, A. Walter, Paul Edson Johnson, and Jone Goldman. *Retailing Ideas.* San Francisco: Hindemann, 1983.
	Adams, Robert K., and others. *Hanging Wallpaper.* New York: Crowell, 1984.
Corporate author	American National Red Cross. *Standard First Aid and Personal Safety.* Garden City, NY: Doubleday, 1981.
	United States. The President's Commission on Higher Technology. *The Role of Higher Technology in the 1990s.* Washington: GPO, 1985.
Editor	Battista, O. A., ed. *Synthetic Fibers in Papermaking.* New York: Wiley, 1981.
Essay	Levinson, Harry. "Alcoholism in Industry." *Health and the Community.* Ed. Alfred H. Katz and Jean Spencer Felton. New York: Free Press, 1975. 187–191.
	Williams, Kathleen. "Venus and Diana: Some Uses of Myth in *The Faerie Queene.*" *English Literary History* 28 (1961): 50–61. Rpt. in *Spenser: A Collection of Critical Essays.* Ed. Harry Berger, Jr. Twentieth Century Views. Englewood Cliffs: Prentice-Hall, 1968. 101–112.
Republished book	Finck, Henry. *Romantic Love and Personal Beauty.* 1891. Havertown, Pa.: R. West, 1973.
Encyclopedia article	"Field Effect Transistor." *McGraw-Hill Encyclopedia of Science and Technology.* 1982 ed.
	"Photochemical Reactions." *Encyclopaedia Britannica: Macropaedia.* 1982 ed.

CITATIONS FOR ARTICLES IN PERIODICALS

Article in a journal	Graves, J. T., and Helene O. Pornov. "Inheritance Tax Reforms." *Journal of Economics* 50 (1983): 168–180.
Article in a popular magazine	Woods, Anna. "Robots on the Loose." *U.S. News and World Report* 21 Aug. 1984: 48–49, 52.
	"A Maverick in the Cockpit." *Flying* June 1980: 14.

Article reprinted in another source	Holstik, G. G. "Robotics Engineering." *Electronics Tomorrow* Nov. 1984: 8–11, 42–45. Rpt. in Social Issues Resources Series, Technology 3: art. 37.
Item in a newspaper	Hillary, Dale F. "Millions in CETA Spending Undocumented." *Jackson* [Miss.] *Daily News* 5 Jan. 1983: A1.
	"Time for Judicial Reform." Editorial. *Washington Post* 20 July 1983: A20.

CITATIONS FOR NONPRINT MATERIALS

NewsBank (microfiche)	Bertolli, Mario. "Gasoline Mileage Comparisons." *Portland* [Ore.] *Times* 10 May 1983. NewsBank, Consumer Affairs, 1983, 41:E12.
Filmstrip (or film or video tape)	"Parenteral Fluid Therapy—Venipuncture." Filmstrip and cassette tape. Nutrition and Fluid Balance. Train-Aide Corp., 1984. 76 frames, 19 min.
Computer software	*The Write Stuff: Word Processing Program.* Computer software. Harper & Row, 1984. Version 1.0, Apple IIPlus or IIe, 64K, DOS 3.3, disk.
Personal interview (or telephone interview or lecture)	James, Clyde D. Personal interview. 4 March 1983.

A SAMPLE RESEARCH REPORT

Following is a sample research report prepared by a student concerned about the worldwide loss of forestland. Included are the letter of transmittal, the title page, the outline, an abstract, the paper, and list of works cited. Note the use of headings throughout the paper.

6801 Paxton Road
Vicksburg, MS 39180
April 30, 1984

Dr. Nell Ann Pickett
Department of English
Raymond Campus
Hinds Junior College District
Raymond, MS 39154

Dear Dr. Pickett:

   Enclosed is the report entitled "The Future of the World's
Forests: A Look at Mother Nature on the Run" as required in
English 1123-Technical Approach. It discusses the current
problem the world is facing because of rapid loss of forest
resources, some reasons it is that way, and some possible
solutions.

   All research for this paper was done at the McLendon
Library. Since I am a Forestry major, this subject is of great
interest to me. This subject is not as widely publicized as the
current energy shortage is; yet the magnitude and importance of
these two problems are similar and I feel all of us need to
better understand this problem in order to solve it for future
generations.

                              Sincerely,

                              William E. Bratcher, Jr.
                              William E. Bratcher, Jr.

THE FUTURE OF THE WORLD'S FORESTS:
A LOOK AT MOTHER NATURE ON THE RUN

by
William E. Bratcher, Jr.

English 1123-40
Raymond Campus
Hinds Junior College District
Raymond, Mississippi
May 1, 1984

THE FUTURE OF THE WORLD'S FORESTS:
A LOOK AT MOTHER NATURE ON THE RUN

Purpose Statement: The purpose of this paper is to present the current worldwide forest situation, some reasons for its being that way, the effects of a worldwide timber shortage, and some possible answers to the problem we face.

    I. Geographical analysis
   II. Forest deprivants
       A. Agriculture
       B. Forest harvesting
          1. Lumber
          2. Pulpwood
          3. Fuel
       C. Urbanization
  III. Effects of deforestation
       A. Ecological effects
          1. Water supply
          2. Erosion
          3. The greenhouse effect
          4. Oxygen
          5. Wildlife
       B. Economic effects
          1. Underdeveloped countries
          2. Developed countries
   IV. Possible solutions
       A. Research
          1. Agroforestry
          2. American forestry
       B. Reforestation
       C. Land management

ABSTRACT

A pressing international problem is the ever increasing worldwide loss of forestland due to overuse and indirect involvement of man, both intended and unintended. Third World countries at the present time face dire situations in respect to forestland and forest resources. The human race is depriving itself of forest resources with its own consumption and so-called "progress." Solutions to this very serious world problem are possible through research, refor- estation, and land management.

THE FUTURE OF THE WORLD'S FORESTS:
A LOOK AT MOTHER NATURE ON THE RUN

In the time it takes for you to read this sentence, eight acres of forest will disappear (Reiss 117).

This alarming statement is a good representation of the speed by which the world's forests are being lost. The tropical forests of South America alone are being cleared at the rate of 250,000 square kilometers a year and are believed to make up a mere half of their original area (Raven 633). In a world so dependent on forests and their products, these facts cannot be overlooked, and, as years pass, the figures become more and more ominous. What does the future hold for the world's forests? That is the question that is the basis of this report.

GEOGRAPHICAL ANALYSIS

The world's forests are rapidly disappearing all over the globe, on all the continents, and in nearly every country in the world. The problems involved in deforestation, however, are far more noticeable in the world's underdeveloped countries, which are located primarily around the equator. (See Figure 1.) This fact is due not only to the population and poor economic conditions of these countries but also to the lack of technological advancements in these countries. These countries include such states as Brazil, Peru, Colombia, Mexico, and Venezuela in South America; Niger, Mali, Gabon, Congo, and Zaire in Africa; and India, Burma, Bangladesh, and Thailand in Asia.

The developed countries of this world, on the other hand, are not as vulnerable to the rapid deforestation of the earth because of their low population density and because of the relative economic stability they possess. Therefore, the de-, veloped countries, which occur primarily north of the equator, have established the northern hemisphere as the last great stronghold of the earth's forests.

FOREST DEPRIVANTS

The reason behind the rapid deforestation of the earth is our need to exploit our natural resources toward our own good. Due to the skyrocketing rate of population growth, consumption of forest materials is the major threat to our forests.

Agriculture

One of the major deprivants of our forests is another of our exploitations of the earth, agriculture. In the rush to

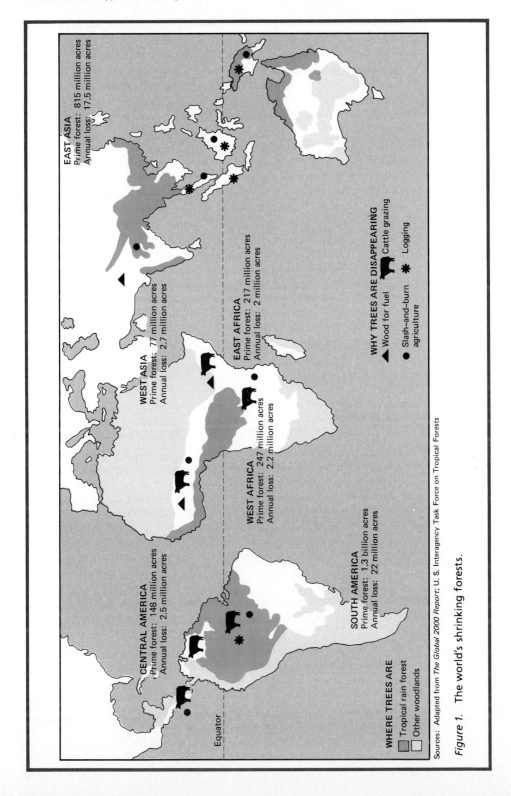

EAST ASIA
Prime forest: 815 million acres
Annual loss: 17.5 million acres

WEST ASIA
Prime forest: 77 million acres
Annual loss: 2.7 million acres

EAST AFRICA
Prime forest: 217 million acres
Annual loss: 2 million acres

WEST AFRICA
Prime forest: 247 million acres
Annual loss: 2.2 million acres

CENTRAL AMERICA
Prime forest: 148 million acres
Annual loss: 2.5 million acres

SOUTH AMERICA
Prime forest: 1.3 billion acres
Annual loss: 22 million acres

Equator

WHY TREES ARE DISAPPEARING
Cattle grazing
Wood for fuel   ✳ Logging
● Slash-and-burn
   agriculture

WHERE TREES ARE
Tropical rain forest
Other woodlands

Sources: Adapted from *The Global 2000 Report*; U. S. Interagency Task Force on Tropical Forests

Figure 1.   The world's shrinking forests.

feed our starving world, agriculture is becoming more and more
important. Unfortunately, land needed for crops is often
cleared from existing forestland. As Carl Eckholm states in his
report on deforestation, "When soil fertility is lost, cultiva-
tion is abandoned and the land is often grazed. The bare soil
will frequently return to the forest, unless, as is often the
case, it is first destroyed by erosion" (14). Often, this
replacement of forest lands with crops is attempted at
high altitudes where forests thrive and crops do poorly,
leaving bare, eroded patches of earth when the crops die.

Forest Harvesting
        Another form in which our forests are being destroyed is
the actual harvesting of trees for consumption. Lumber is still
the major use of forest products, the major consumers of which
are the United States and other developed countries.
        Pulpwood is another use of timber that is growing in need
of resources daily. Besides being used for paper and press-
board, the cellulose from pulpwood can be used in the production of cellophane, rayon and plastic. Each Sunday edition of
The New York Times requires 153 acres of southern pines;
similarly, the paper used by McDonald's alone for paper bags
and napkins requires 315 square miles of trees each year
(The Renewable Tree). Also, paper is the driving force
behind the current "information boom," as the feedstock
of government, education, and most interpersonal
communications (Eckholm 13).
        Another major use of timber and forest products is fuel. In
a world that is rapidly losing its natural sources of energy,
more and more people are turning to wood for fuel, an uneasy
answer to a very complex problem. Wood is the principal source
of fuel for cooking and warmth in the underdeveloped countries
of Africa, Asia, and Latin America (Maersch). Vast areas
around the towns and cities of these countries are totally
denuded due to the clearing of these forests to supply the
energy-hungry masses, and, in these poorer countries, the
money is not available for reforestation and the land is
destroyed by erosion or overrun by useless deserts.
        The recent energy crunch has also shown its effects on
American forests with the increased interest shown in heating
homes with woodburning stoves. The Department of Energy estimates that there are over 5 million woodburning stoves in the
United States and that wood provides the United States with
two-thirds as much energy as does nuclear power. A comparison
of the cost of energy obtained from the four major fuels
(Starnes 12) shows that the economics of wood burning is sound.

```
                    COST PER MILLION Btu's
            Oil.......... $7.81   Coal.......... $2.38
            Natural Gas... $4.64   Wood.......... $2.30
```

In an ever tightening economy, these figures are increasing the
consumption of cordwood in the United States astronomically.

Another use of wood as an energy source, which was first
developed by the Germans in World War II as an alternative fuel
source to oil, is ethanol. Ethanol is a combustible fuel
produced by breaking down the cellulose in woody material into
sugars that are fermented into ethanol. Although ethanol is not
projected to replace oil, it is a good way to stretch our
currently depleted oil supplies to last longer than expected.

Due to new technology, it is now possible to convert fiber
into wood pellets by pressure. These pellets can be used in
much the same way as coal while eliminating the bad points of
coal such as mining and shoveling, not to mention the mess involved in household heating by coal. Trucks carrying wood
pellets make deliveries to homes and simply dump the
pellets down a chute, where they are automatically fed
into a furnace (Harris 42).

Urbanization

There is yet another threat to our forests that seems un-
controllable; that is the rapid urbanization of the earth as
the population explosion continues. Urbanization destroys many
millions of acres of forests yearly, through clearing land for
industry as well as for homes. Along with this urbanization
come the usual human tendencies to pollute and exploit our
natural resources.

EFFECTS OF DEFORESTATION

The effects of deforestation are twofold: ecological and
economic.

Ecological Effects

First and most noticeable of these effects are the effects
on the ecology. Clearcuts, areas of forests where the land
has been totally denuded, are seen all over the world and have
much the same aesthetic values as strip mines. However, there
are more ways than just the actual loss of trees in which
the loss of our forests is affecting the earth's ecology.

The earth's water supply is one of the victims of deforestation (Brett 10). Tree roots collect and hold water
during rains, keeping the balance of water even over large
tracts of land. Also the roots of trees hold the soil
together, preventing the formation of silt in our
waterways as water travels through its cycle.

The soil of the earth is also endangered by deforestation. Trees are one of, if not the most, effective preventives of erosion. The leaves of the trees stop rainfall from hitting the ground full force and loosening the soil for erosion. That, along with the spongy soil of the forest, which absorbs excess water, is a very good, natural way of preventing erosion.

Another of the ill effects of deforestation is what scientists call the greenhouse effect. This situation is currently happening on the earth, and is growing in proportion every day. The greenhouse effect is a global warming trend due to the overabundance of carbon dioxide in the air, which is compounded by the extensive clearing and burning of tropical and temperate forests. If left unchecked, this phenomenon could melt the polar ice caps and raise the sea level by over 20 feet in 70 years (Reiss 120). The clearing and burning of the world's forests account for a full third of the carbon dioxide in the atmosphere, while removing carbon deposits from the earth (Delcourt 35). Along with the increase of carbon dioxide due to deforestation, the oxygen supply of the earth is shrinking due to the destruction of trees, which are a major source of the earth's oxygen.

Yet another victim of our greed for timber is wildlife. This statement is best shown in the deforestation of the tropics, which is expected to be complete within a few decades. The consequences of this are expected to include the extinction of upwards of one-third of the estimated three million species of plants, animals, and microorganisms in the tropics (Raven 633). In a world where extinction of species occurs repeatedly, this trend can only produce ominous circumstances that no act of ours can reverse. Once a species becomes extinct, there is no bringing it back.

These ecological disasters that appear imminent cannot be simply overlooked. They will not go away by themselves; and, like all of the problems brought up in viewing our world's deforestation, they have no simple answers.

Economic Effects

Deforestation by humans has also brought about some problems that bear direct importance on the nations of the earth, economic shortages being the most obvious and important. Economics is defined as the allocation of scarce goods and resources, which becomes more and more difficult as this scarcity increases. As Peter Raven states it: "The loss of resources worldwide is a leading factor in inflation and unemployment, but it is not often stressed by economists (633). This callousness shown by our social leaders is only one of the many reasons the rapidly growing population of the earth

is starved for natural resources, and will be even more so
in the future unless the proper actions are taken.

The underdeveloped countries of the world, with their un-
stable political leadership and overabundance of people, are
now, and have been for quite some time, feeling the hunger
pains of a starving world. The question to these people is not
whether or not to conserve; rather they must ask where the next
day's meal or fuel for cooking and heat will come from. As is
obvious, a cold and starving man is not going to consider the
consequences of cutting a tree for fuel or of clearing a few
acres of forest to grow his crops. As one Malaysian forestry
official put it, "Our hardwoods take 90 years to grow. What
bank will lend us 90-year money?" (Reiss 122). Consequently,
the Third World countries of the tropics are moving
rapidly toward mass starvation, social disorder, and a
profound disruption of international economics (Watson and
Bickers).

The developed countries of the earth are not much better
off because the entire world must feel the pains eventually.
The developed countries are losing the Third World as a market
for their goods, as well as a source of raw materials. Along
with that, there will be a mass migration out of the Third
World countries into the developed countries (Polsgrove 43).

Yet, on the more optimistic side, the developed countries
of the world still have the technology necessary to create more
of these natural resources as well as conserving them more efficiently and using them to our best advantage. Let us hope
that our technology can stay one step ahead of our growing
population.

POSSIBLE SOLUTIONS

What kind of technology exists to relieve the world of this
timber crunch? It all depends on the advancement of our
research technology, proper land management, and reforestation.

Research

Research in the field of forestry is currently being conducted all over the world, from the highly energy intensive
tree farms of the United States to the infant forestry program
in India.

Despite the lack of research funds spent in underdeveloped
countries, only 5 percent of the world total, many important
advancements are being made in forestry in the Third World.
First among these advancements is the advancement of a relatively new science called agroforestry.

Agroforestry is the scientific rotation of food crops and
timber, thereby eliminating the destruction of millions of
acres of forests, while at the same time producing much needed

food. Crops are rotated with timber, using the timber growth period as rest for the soil. Agroforestry is a partial answer to the Third World countries' fuel and food problems, producing food, fuel, and forests simultaneously (Polsgrove 43).

Another form of research currently being done in the Third World countries is being done with legumes. These are small, fast growing trees that are extremely weather resistant and can be used for food as well as for fuel and paper (Reiss 122). Two of the most successful legumes are Gmelina and Leucaena, two fast growing tropical trees that could provide part of the answer to the Third World countries' severe timber shortage.

The American forestry situation is only marginally better. The U.S. Forest Service predicts that the volume of wood produced in the United States must double over the next 50 years to meet domestic needs (Starnes 12). This fact, along with the current inflation rate and the increasing thirst for energy (which has direct effects on our timber resources), presents us with a grim outlook for the future of our forest resources.

What can the United States do to curb the tide of our growing timber shortage? The key lies, Weigner contends, in the advancement of our forest technology. Currently, our forest technology leads the world, resulting in a greater yield per acre in the United States than anywhere else in the world. Also, the U.S. Forest Service predicts that, with proper management, the country could double, perhaps triple, the productivity of its forests within 50 years (41).

Reforestation

Another key to staying one step ahead of global deforestation is reforestation. Reforestation is necessary to stem the tide of deforestation, yet it lacks economic support in most cases; the exceptions are large industry and government, which can afford such a long-time investment. Once a seedling is planted, the economic return will not show up for at least 25 years.

Despite the ever increasing cost of reforestation, American landowners, industry, and government are seeing the need of reforestation in a growing world. In 1979, over 600 million seedlings were planted commercially in the South alone (The Renewable Tree).

Land Management

To support reforestation and advancing technology, proper land management must be practiced in order to receive the full effect of a necessary concerted effort. The responsibility for land management in the South lies primarily with the private landowner, who owns approximately 73 percent of the timberland in the South. Government land management is foremost in the West, however, where government lands make up approximately 71 percent of the forested land area.

Although the United States is leading the way in technology and development, we must share our valuable knowledge with the other countries of the world in order to help them meet the increasing shortage of timber with resources of their own. For just as all people are the cause of deforestation, so should all people be the cause of reforestation.

WORKS CITED

Brett, R. M. "A Different View of the Forest." American
    Forests Dec. 1982: 10, 43-44.
Delcourt, Hazel R. "The Virtue of Forests, Virgin and
    Otherwise." Natural History June 1981: 33-39.
Eckholm, Erik. "The Shrinking Forests." Focus Sept.-Oct.
    1982: 12-16.
Harris, Michael. "Farewell Forests." The Progressive Feb.
    1983: 42-43.
Maersch, Stephen. "Fuel That Grows on Trees." Milwaukee
    Journal 17 Jan. 1982. NewsBank, Consumer Affairs, 1982, 2:C6.
Polsgrove, Carol. "The Vanishing Forests of the Third World."
    The Progressive Aug. 1982: 42-43.
Raven, Peter H. "Raven Warns of Rapid Tropical Deforestation."
    Bioscience Oct. 1982: 633.
Reiss, Spencer, "Vanishing Forests." Newsweek 24 Nov. 1982:
    117-122.
The Renewable Tree. Videotape. Educational Resources, 1983. 60 min.
Starnes, Richard. "The Tree Eaters Are Coming." Outdoor Life
    Oct. 1981: 12-13.
Watson, Steve, and Chris Bickers. "Timber!" Southern World
    Mar./Apr. 1981: 36-38. Rpt. in Social Issues Resources
    Series, 3:art. 25.
Wiegner, Kathleen K. "America's Green Gold." Forbes 24 (Dec.
    1982): 40-46.

APPLICATION 1 WRITING A RESEARCH REPORT

Answer the following concerning your college library.

1. What are the library hours?
2. Which system of classifying books (Library of Congress or Dewey Decimal System) does the library use?
3. What is the procedure for checking out a book?
4. For how long a period of time may books be checked out?
5. Where are reserve books shelved?
6. What is the procedure for requesting a magazine?
7. Where are current magazines located?
8. If the library has audiovisual materials, where are they located?
9. Where are microfilm and microfiche materials and readers located?

APPLICATION 2 WRITING A RESEARCH REPORT

Draw a floor plan of your college library. Indicate the location of the following: public (card) catalog; periodical indexes; periodicals holdings list; general encyclopedias; technical encyclopedias, dictionaries, and guides; biographical reference works; and works in your major field.

APPLICATION 3 WRITING A RESEARCH REPORT

In a periodical index (such as the *Magazine Index, Readers' Guide to Periodical Literature, Applied Science & Technology Index,* or *Business Periodicals Index*) look up a general subject, such as hydraulics, nutrition, computers, office machines, metals, recreation, stock market, space research, antipollution laws, soils, retailing, fibers, eye, electronic circuits, personnel management, internal-combustion engines, and so on. For the general subject, list at least ten subclassifications that would be sufficiently limited for a research report.

APPLICATION 4 WRITING A RESEARCH REPORT

Choose one of the following topics (or pick a topic of your own). Formulate a possible basic question, or basic problem, to be investigated in a research report. Then divide the basic question into a list of specific questions (preliminary outline).

1. Problems in developing an electric automobile
2. Early results of the discovery of penicillin
3. Effects of nicotine on the body
4. Benjamin Franklin's minor inventions
5. Architectural problems in restoring the Statue of Liberty
6. The shooting down of Korean Airliner Flight 007
7. July 20, 1969
8. Cooking food electronically
9. The next ten years in space exploration
10. The American office—100 years ago and today

APPLICATION 5   WRITING A RESEARCH REPORT

Explain each of the items on the following card from a public (card) catalog.

```
657
M47a3    Meigs, Walter B
              Accounting: the basis for business de-
         cisions [by] Walter B. Meigs, A.N. Mosich
         [and] Charles E. Johnson. 4th ed.    New
         York, McGraw-Hill [1982]
              xxiv, 936p. 24cm.

              1. Accounting.  I. Mosich, A.N., joint
         author.  II. Johnson, Charles E., joint author
```

APPLICATION 6   WRITING A RESEARCH REPORT

Turn to page 383. Look at the last three entries from the *Applied Science & Technology Index*. Explain the items in each of the entries.

APPLICATION 7   WRITING A RESEARCH REPORT

Select a topic that is sufficiently restricted for a research report. Find and list at least two magazine articles, two books, and one encyclopedia article that contain information on the topic. Use conventional bibliographical forms. (See pages 410–411 for examples.)

APPLICATION 8   WRITING A RESEARCH REPORT

Using the article on pages 186–188, "Controversy Over the Clean Air Act" (appearing on page 132 of the January 1982 *Congressional Digest*) do the following:

1. Make a bibliography card for the article.
2. Make a direct-quotation note card for the first sentence in paragraph 2.
3. Make a paraphrased note card of the information in paragraph 5.
4. Make a direct-quotation note card for the second sentence in paragraph 3, omitting the phrase "a weather condition known as."
5. Make a summary note of paragraph 7.
6. Of the information on the preceding note cards, which would require documentation in a paper? Why?
7. Write a sentence that includes information requiring documentation. Give the parenthetical reference.

8. Write a sentence about pollution in which you quote these words: "economics touches most aspects of the controversy."

APPLICATION 9   WRITING A RESEARCH REPORT

Arrange the following information as if it were the final bibliography for a report. Include only needed words and information.

Computer Science in Social and Behavioral Science Education, edited by Daniel E. Bailey, published in 1985 by Educational Technology Publications, Inc., in Englewood Cliffs, New Jersey.

Computer Security and Protection Structures, by G. J. Walker and Ian F. Blake, published in 1984 by Academic Press, Inc., in New York.

Computer Security, by John M. Carroll, published in 1984 by Security World Publishing Company, Inc., Los Angeles, California.

"Multiprocessing Boosts Micro Computer Power," by K. Rozsa, in *Electronic Design,* the 15 March 1985 issue, vol. 31, pp. 72–75.

"Stimulation Studies of Energy Saving with Chopper Control on the Jubilee Line," by B. Mellitt and others, in *Proceedings of the Institute of Electrical Engineers,* the April 1984 issue, vol. 129, pp. 304–310.

"Microprocessor Design Problems" by Susan B. Elleby, in *The New York Times,* Section 3, page 2, columns 1–2, on 18 April 1984.

APPLICATION 10   WRITING A RESEARCH REPORT

Write a research report as directed by your instructor. Use the schedule below as a checklist of steps in writing the paper. Make and fill in the appropriate Plan Sheet (like the Plan Sheets on pages 429–435) before beginning each major step.

Schedule for Writing a Research Report

ASSIGNMENT	DATE DUE
Choice of general subject	_____
Choice of specific topic	_____
Statement of basic problem (basic question)	_____
Statement of specific questions (preliminary outline)	_____
Working bibliography	_____
Note cards	_____
Working outline	_____
Purpose statement or central idea	_____
First draft With correct documentation	

Final report, including outline and documentation   _____
    (Your instructor may also require that bibliography
    cards, note cards, outlines, preliminary drafts, etc.,
    be turned in with the final report.)

APPLICATION 11 WRITING A RESEARCH REPORT

As directed by your instructor, adapt your research report for oral presentation. Ask your classmates to evaluate your speech by making an Evaluation of Oral Presentations sheet like the one on page 459 and filling it in.

PLAN SHEET 1
FOR WRITING A RESEARCH REPORT: SELECTING
A SUBJECT

Major Field

My major is:

Allotted Time

Today's date is:

The completed report is due on:

That means I have _____ weeks to work on this report.

Possible Subjects

Five to ten possible subjects for my research report are the following:

1.   6.

2.   7.

3.   8.

4.   9.

5.   10.

Specific Topics

From the preceding list of possible subjects, the one that interests me the most is:

I can narrow this subject to at least three topics that I could treat satisfactorily in the allotted time:

1.

2.

3.

Chosen Topic

After checking in the library and with my instructors to be sure there is sufficient available material, I have chosen the following as the topic for my research report:

Questions

I need to ask my instructor these questions:

Subject

The topic for my research report is:

General Problem

I can state the general problem or idea that I am investigating as this question:

Specific Problems

I can divide the general problem into these specific problems or questions:

Questions

I need to ask my instructor these questions:

PLAN SHEET 3
FOR WRITING A RESEARCH REPORT: FINDING THE FACTS

Subject

The subject for my research report is:

Sources to Be Researched

Personal Observation or Experience   In gathering information for writing, I will need to visit the following places to observe conditions:

Personal Interviews   In gathering information for writing, I may want to interview the following people:

Library Materials   The library (or libraries) I will use are:

A tentative bibliography of available materials includes:

432

Free and Inexpensive Materials In gathering information for writing, I may write or call the following companies or agencies:

Questions

I need to ask my instructor these questions:

PLAN SHEET 4
FOR WRITING A RESEARCH REPORT: RECORDING AND ORGANIZING THE FACTS

Subject

The subject for my research report is:

Central Idea or Thesis

I can sum up the main idea of my report in the following sentence:

Formal Outline

The formal outline is a _____ (sentence or topic) outline. The outline is as follows:

Introduction

The introductory material for the report is as follows:

Closing

The closing material for the report is as follows:

Visuals

Kinds of visuals and what they will show are as follows:

Questions

I need to ask my instructor these questions:

CHAPTER 10

Oral Communication: Saying It Clearly

OBJECTIVES   438
INTRODUCTION   438
SPEAKING DIFFERS FROM WRITING   438
CLASSIFICATION AS INFORMAL AND FORMAL   439
    Modes of Delivery for Formal Presentations   439
CLASSIFICATION ACCORDING TO GENERAL PURPOSE   439
    To Entertain   440
    To Persuade   440
      Basic Considerations in Persuasion   440
        Needs, Wants, and Desires of People   440
        Appeals—Emotional and Rational, Direct and Indirect   441
      The Persuasive Presentation   441
        Opening   441
        Need and Desire Intensified   441
        Supporting Proof   441
        Close   441
    To Inform (Emphasis of Remainder of Chapter)   442
PREPARATION OF AN ORAL PRESENTATION   442
    Determine the Specific Purpose   442
    Analyze the Type of Audience   442
    Gather the Material   443
    Organize the Material   443
    Determine the Mode of Delivery   443
    Outline the Speech, Writing It Out If Necessary   444
    Prepare Visual Materials   444
    Rehearse   444
DELIVERY   445
    Walk to the Podium with Poise and Self-Confidence   445
    Capture the Audience's Attention and Interest   445
    Look at the Audience   445
    Stick to an Appropriate Mode of Delivery   445
    Put Some Zest in Your Expression   445
    Get Your Words Out Clearly and Distinctly   445
    Adjust the Volume and Pitch of Your Voice   446
    Vary Your Rate of Speaking to Enhance Meaning   446
    Stand Naturally   446

Avoid Mannerisms   446
Show Visuals with Natural Ease   446
Close — Don't Just Stop Speaking   446
VISUAL MATERIALS   446
General Types of Visuals in Oral Presentations   447
Flat Materials   447
Exhibits   447
Projected Materials   447
Preparing and Showing Visuals   448
Preparation of Visuals   448
Showing of Visuals   448
EVALUATING AN ORAL PRESENTATION   449
JOB INTERVIEWS   449
Preparing for an Interview   449
Acquaintance with the Job Field   451
Company Analysis   451
Job Analysis   451
Interviewer Analysis   452
Personal Analysis   452
Preparation of a Resumé   452
Rehearsing an Interview   452
Holding an Interview   453
Observance of Business Etiquette   453
Establishing the Purpose of the Interview   453
Questions and Answers   453
Closing the Interview   453
Following Up an Interview   454
INFORMATIONAL INTERVIEWS   454
Preparing for an Interview   455
The Interview   455
Courtesy Follow-Up   455
GENERAL PRINCIPLES IN ORAL COMMUNICATION   455
APPLICATIONS   456

OBJECTIVES

Upon completing this chapter, the student should be able to:

- List ways in which an oral presentation differs from a written presentation
- List and identify the modes of delivery for a formal speech
- Classify oral presentations according to general purpose
- Prepare and use visuals in oral presentations
- Prepare and deliver to a specific audience an oral presentation that meets a clearly stated purpose
- Evaluate an oral presentation
- Demonstrate a knowledge and an understanding of how to hold a job interview
- Demonstrate a knowledge and an understanding of how to hold an informational interview

INTRODUCTION

Oral expression is the most important communication skill that you need to master. In school or on the job, you probably speak thousands of times as often as you communicate in any other way. Even a moment's consideration of how people make a living will point to the importance of being able to express ideas orally.

Every time you speak, you convey something of who you are and what you think. Your vocabulary, pronunciation, grammatical usage, phrasing, and expressed ideas are aspects of speech that make an impression on your listeners and by which they then form opinions about you. Unfortunately, sometimes the impression you make can be a negative or poor one simply because you cannot orally express what you want to say. Such a situation shows a lack of self-confidence and knowledge in handling oral communication.

This chapter will acquaint you with various group and individual communication situations and will give suggestions to help you develop the self-confidence and knowledge needed for effective oral expression.

SPEAKING DIFFERS FROM WRITING

Speaking and writing have much in common because they are both forms of communication based on language. Speaking differs, however, in several important ways:

1. *Level of diction.* In speaking, a simpler vocabulary and shorter sentences of less involved structure are typically used.
2. *Amount of repetition.* More repetition is needed in speaking to emphasize and to summarize important points.
3. *Kind of transitions.* Transitions from one point to another must be more obvious in speaking. Such transitions as *first, second,* and *next* signal movement often conveyed on the printed page through paragraphing and headings.

4. *Kind and size of visuals.* Speaking lends itself to the use of exhibits and projected materials; some kinds of flat materials such as charts, drawings, and maps must be constructed on a large scale.

CLASSIFICATION AS INFORMAL AND FORMAL

Oral communication might be broadly classified as informal and formal. The term *informal* describes nonprepared speech and *formal* describes well-planned, rehearsed speech. Most of us spend a large percentage of each day in informal communication: we talk with friends, parents, fellow workers, neighbors, other family members. Often, individuals may be asked to share views or knowledge about events, people, places, or things with a group, such as a service club, a professional organization, or a class. They may have been asked at the meeting to respond impromptu; or they may have been asked ahead of time but made little or no preparation. In both cases, their information will be shared through informal oral communication.

On the other hand, formal oral communication involves a great deal of preparation and attention to delivery. Professional and learned people are often asked to share their views and knowledge regarding their field. The deliberate, planned, carefully organized and rehearsed presentation of ideas and information for a specific purpose constitutes formal communication.

Modes of Delivery for Formal Presentations

Formal presentations may be categorized according to the speaker's mode of delivery as:

- Extemporaneous
- Memorized
- Read from a manuscript

In the extemporaneous mode—the most often used of the three—the speaker refers to brief notes or an outline, or simply recalls from memory the points to be made. In this way, the speaker is able to interact with the audience and convey sincerity and self-assurance. In the memorized mode, the speaker has written out the speech and committed it to memory, word for word. The memorized speech is typically lacking in spontaneity and an at-ease tone; too, the speaker has the very real possibility of forgetting what comes next. In the third mode of delivery, the speaker reads from a manuscript. While this type of delivery may be needed when exact wording is required in a structured situation, the manuscript speech has serious limitations. It is difficult for the speaker to show enthusiasm and to interact with the audience, delivery is usually stilted, and the audience may soon become inattentive.

The effective speaker considers the occasion, the audience, and the purpose of the speech in determining the mode of delivery to be used.

CLASSIFICATION ACCORDING TO GENERAL PURPOSE

In addition to informal and formal, another way to classify oral communication is according to its general purpose: to entertain, to persuade, or to inform. Any one of these types of communication could be presented formally or informally.

To Entertain

Oral communication that is meant to entertain is intended to provide enjoyment for those who listen. Probably neither an employee nor a student would have many occasions to communicate solely for the purpose of entertaining except on an informal basis with friends and relatives.

To Persuade

The goal of communication that is meant to persuade is to affect the listeners' beliefs or actions. As an employee you may well find yourself responsible for persuading supervisory personnel or customers or employees to change a method or a procedure, to hire additional personnel, to buy a certain piece of machinery or equipment, and so forth. Whether presenting an idea, explaining a plan, or selling a product, the same basic principles of persuasion are involved.

The art of persuasion can be summed up in two sentences: Present a need, want, or desire of the customer (buyer). Show the customer how your idea, service, or product can satisfy that need, want, or desire.

Basic Considerations in Persuasion If you are to be able to prepare and present a persuasive speech effectively, you must be aware of several factors: needs, wants, and desires of people; and kinds of appeals.

NEEDS, WANTS, AND DESIRES OF PEOPLE The actual needs of people in order to exist are few: food, clothing, and shelter. In addition to these physical needs, people have numerous wants and desires. Among these are:

- *Economic security.* This includes a means of livelihood and ownership of property and material things.
- *Recognition.* People want social and professional approval. They want to be successful.
- *Protection of self and loved ones.* Safety and physical well-being of self and of family and friends are important.
- *Aesthetic satisfaction.* Pleasant surroundings and pleasing the senses can be very satisfying.

Consideration of people's needs, wants, and desires is essential in order to effectively present an idea, plan, or product. For example, if you were to try to persuade your employer to purchase micro-computers, you probably would appeal to the employer's economic and aesthetic desires; that is, you probably would emphasize the time that could be saved with computers and the improved appearance of word-processed material. Or if you were a supervisor trying to impress upon a worker the importance of following dress regulations, you would stress protection (safety) of self and the possible loss of economic security for the worker and his family should injury or accident occur. Or if you were to try to persuade a co-worker to take college courses in the evening, you would point out the recognition and economic security aspects—gaining recognition and approval for furthering education and skills and the possible subsequent financial rewards.

APPEALS — EMOTIONAL AND RATIONAL, DIRECT AND INDIRECT   Persuasion is the process of using combined emotional and rational appeals and principles. Emotional appeals are directed toward feelings, inclinations, and senses; rational appeals are directed toward reasoning, logic, or intellect. Undoubtedly, many times emotional appeals carry more weight than do rational appeals.

The most satisfying persuasion occurs when people make up their own minds or direct their own feelings toward a positive reception of the idea, plan, or product — but without being told to do so. Thus, indirect appeals, suggestions, and questions are usually much more effective than a direct statement followed by proof.

The Persuasive Presentation   The persuasive presentation involves four steps or stages: opening, need and desire intensified, supporting proof, and close. For timing in moving from one step to another, you must use your judgment by constantly analyzing conditions and audience mood.

In approaching a single listener or a small group of listeners, be sincere and cordial. A firm handshake should set a tone of friendliness. It is natural also to exchange a few brief pleasantries (How are you? — How is business? — Beautiful weather we are having — etc.) before getting down to business. With a large group of listeners, such a personal approach is impossible. You can, however, be sincere and cordial.

OPENING   In the opening, the listener's attention is aroused. Thus the opening should immediately strike the listener's interest and should present the best selling points. This may be done directly or indirectly.

> DIRECT: Our new Top Quality razor blades get a closer, cleaner shave than any others on the market.
> INDIRECT: Do your customers ask for razor blades that get a closer, cleaner shave?

NEED AND DESIRE INTENSIFIED   When the audience's attention is aroused, each main selling point is then developed with explanatory details.

Both emotional and logical appeals are used to show how the proposal will help satisfy one or more of these basic desires: economic security, recognition, protection of self and loved ones, and aesthetic satisfaction.

At this stage and throughout the proposal presentation, the listener may raise objections. The best way to handle these is to be a step ahead of the listener; that is, to be aware of all possible objections, prepare effective responses, and incorporate them into your main presentation.

SUPPORTING PROOF   Description and explanation must be supported by evidence or proof. Visual exhibits, demonstrations, testimony of users, examples of experience with and uses of the product, and statistics showing specifications and increased productivity are methods to prove the worth of your proposal.

CLOSE   In closing a presentation, you usually are wise to assume the positive attitude that the audience will accept the idea or plan or will buy the product. The following suggestions reflect such an attitude: *When may we begin using this procedure? Which model do you prefer?* Reaffirmation of how the proposal will enhance the listener's business often helps to conclude the deal and to reinforce his or her satisfaction. If you detect a negative attitude, avoid a definite "no" by suggesting further consideration of the proposal or a trial use of the product and another meeting at a later date.

To Inform (Emphasis of Remainder of Chapter)

Of the three general purposes of oral communication—to entertain, to persuade, and to inform—the informative purpose is most frequently employed by the person on the job. In communicating instructions and processes, descriptions of mechanisms, definitions, analyses through classification and partition, analyses through effect and cause and through comparison and contrast, summaries, and reports (Chapters 1 – 6, and 8), the speaker will have as a major goal *informing* the listeners.

Giving oral informative presentations is a very significant aspect of the employee's communication responsibilities. The next three sections of this chapter—Preparation of an Oral Presentation, Delivery, and Visual Materials—are geared to the informative speech. The basic principles discussed in these sections are, of course, applicable to any speech situation. For instance, the steps in preparing a speech are essentially the same, whether the purpose of the speech is to entertain, to persuade, or to inform.

PREPARATION OF AN ORAL PRESENTATION

Preparing an oral presentation includes these steps:

- Determine the specific purpose
- Analyze the type of audience
- Gather the material
- Organize the material
- Determine the mode of delivery
- Outline the speech, writing it out if necessary
- Prepare visual materials
- Rehearse

Determine the Specific Purpose

The general purpose of an employee's speech typically is to inform; sometimes the general purpose is to persuade, or, occasionally, to entertain. The *specific* purpose, however, must be determined if the speech is to be effective. The reason for the speech and who will use the information must be established. Data that completely, accurately, and clearly present the subject must be given, analyzed, and interpreted thoroughly and honestly. Recommendations can then be made accordingly.

Analyze the Type of Audience

A speech, if it is to be effective, must be designed especially for the knowledge and interest level of the intended audience or listeners. Vocabulary and style must be adapted to the particular audience. For instance, if you were to report on recent applications of the laser, your report to a group of nurses, to a group of engineers, to a college freshman class of physics students, or to a junior high science club would differ considerably. Each group represents a different level of knowledge and a different partisan interest.

Gather the Material

The material is gathered primarily from three sources: interviews and reading, field investigation, and laboratory research.

The extent to which one or more of these sources will be used depends on the nature of the speech. A student reading report in history, for instance, may simply call for the reading of certain material in a book. An investigation of parking facilities in a particular location may call for personal interviews plus on-site visits. Or an analysis of the hardiness of certain shrubs when exposed to sudden temperature changes may involve both field investigation and experimental observation.

Organize the Material

To organize the material, select the main ideas; do not exceed three or four. (Remember that your audience is listening, not reading.) Arrange supporting data under each main idea. Use only the supporting data necessary to develop each main idea clearly and completely.

After the main body of material is organized, plan the introduction. Let the audience know the reason for the speech, the purpose, the sources of data, and the method or procedure for gathering the data. Then state the main ideas to be presented. The function of the introduction is to set an objective framework in which the audience will accept the information as accurate and as significant.

Plan the conclusion. It should contain a summary of the data, a summary of the significance or of the interpretation of the data, and conclusions and recommendations for action or further study.

A suggested outline for the introduction, body, and conclusion are given below, under the heading Outline the Speech, Writing It Out if Necessary.

(The organization of a persuasive speech is treated earlier in the chapter.)

Determine the Mode of Delivery

Once you have analyzed the speaking situation and gathered the material and organized it, you are in position to determine the appropriate mode of delivery. Is it more appropriate to speak extemporaneously, to recite a memorized speech, or to read from a manuscript? (Of course, you may have been told which mode to use; thus the decision has already been made for you.) The memorized speech is most appropriate in such situations as competing in an oratorical contest or welcoming an important visiting dignitary. Reading from a script is most appropriate if presenting a highly technical scientific report, giving a policy speech, or the like. For most other situations, extemporaneous speaking is the most appropriate.

Outline the Speech, Writing It Out If Necessary

Outline your speech. A suggested outline form is as follows:

> *Introduction*
>
> I. Reason for the speech
>   A. Who asked for it?
>   B. Why?
> II. Purpose of the speech
> III. Sources of data
> IV. Method or procedure for gathering the data
> V. Statement of main ideas to be presented
>
> *Body*
>
> I. First main idea
>   A. Sub-idea
>   1., 2., etc. Data
>   B., etc. Sub-ideas
>   1., 2., etc. Data
> II., III., etc. Second, third, etc., main ideas
>   A., B., etc. Sub-ideas
>
> *Conclusion*
>
> I. Summary of the data
> II. Summary of the significance or of the interpretation of the data
> III. Conclusions and recommendations for action or further study

If you plan to present a memorized speech or read from a script, write out the speech. Special care should be given to manuscript form and to the construction of visuals if you are to distribute copies of the speech (copies should be distributed *after* the oral presentation, not before or during it).

Prepare Visual Materials

Carefully select and prepare visuals to help clarify information and to crystallize ideas. See the section below entitled Visual Materials.

Rehearse

For an extemporaneous speech: From your outline, make a note card (3- by 5-inch, narrow sides up and down) of the main points that you want to make. Indicate on the card where you plan to use visuals. Rehearse the entire speech several times, using only the note card (not the full outline). Get fixed in your mind the ideas and supporting data and the order in which you want to present them. For a memorized speech: Commit to memory the exact wording of the script. As you practice the speech, put some feeling into the words; avoid a canned, artificial sound. For a speech read from a manuscript: Just because you are to read a speech doesn't mean you shouldn't practice it. Go over the speech until you know it so thoroughly that you can look at your audience almost as much as you look at the script. Number the pages so that they can be kept in order easily. Leave the pages loose (do not clip or staple them together); you can then unobtrusively slide a finished page to the back of the stack.

Some speakers find it helpful to tape record their speech once or twice while rehearsing; then they play back the recording for an objective analysis of their strengths and weaknesses.

Rehearsing your presentation several times is very important; it gives you self-confidence and it prepares you to stay within the time allotted for the speech.

DELIVERY

A major factor in oral communication is effective delivery, or *how* you say what you say. When giving a speech, observe the following suggestions.

Walk to the Podium with Poise and Self-Confidence

From the moment the audience first sees you, give a positive impression. Even if you are nervous, the appearance of self-confidence impresses the audience and helps you to relax.

Capture the Audience's Attention and Interest

Begin your speech forcefully. Opening techniques include asking a question, stating a little-known fact, and making a startling assertion (all, of course, should pertain directly to the subject at hand).

Look at the Audience

Interact with the audience through eye-to-eye contact, but without special attention to particular individuals. You should not overdo looking at your notes, the floor, the ceiling, over the heads of your audience, or out the window.

Stick to an Appropriate Mode of Delivery

If, for instance, your speech should be extemporaneous, don't read a script to the audience.

Put Some Zest in Your Expression

Relax; be alive; show enthusiasm for your subject. Avoid a monotonous or "memorized" tone and robot image. Have a pleasant look on your face.

Get Your Words Out Clearly and Distinctly

Make sure that each person in the audience can hear you. Follow the natural pitches and stresses of the spoken language. Speak firmly, dynamically, and sincerely. Enunciate distinctly, pronounce words correctly, use acceptable grammar, and speak on a language level appropriate for the audience and the subject matter.

Adjust the Volume and Pitch of Your Voice

This adjusting may be necessary for emphasis of main points and because of distance between speaker and audience, size of audience, size of room, and outside noises. Be certain everyone can hear you.

Vary Your Rate of Speaking to Enhance Meaning

Don't be afraid to pause; pauses may allow time for an idea to become clear to the audience or may give emphasis to an important point.

Stand Naturally

Stand in an easy, natural position, with your weight distributed evenly on both feet. Bodily movements and gestures should be natural; well-timed, they contribute immeasurably to a successful presentation.

Avoid Mannerisms

Mannerisms detract. Avoid such mannerisms as toying with a necklace or pin, jangling change, or repeatedly using an expression such as "You know" or "Uh."

Show Visuals with Natural Ease

For specific suggestions, see Showing of Visuals on pages 448–449.

Close — Don't Just Stop Speaking

Your speech should be a rounded whole, and the close may be indicated through voice modulation and a simple "Thank you" or "Are there any questions?"

VISUAL MATERIALS

Visual materials can significantly enhance your oral presentation. Impressions are likely to be more vivid when visuals are used. In general, they are more accurate than the spoken word. Showing rather than telling an audience something is often clearer and more efficient. And showing *and* telling may be more successful than either method by itself. For instance, a graph, a diagram, or a demonstration may present ideas and information more quickly and simply than can words alone.

In brief, visual materials are helpful in several ways. They can convey information, supplement verbal information, minimize verbal explanation, and add interest.

See Chapter 11, Visuals, for a discussion of all types of visual materials for both oral and written communication.

General Types of Visuals in Oral Presentations

Visuals for use with oral presentations can be grouped into three types: flat materials, exhibits, and projected materials. A brief survey of these can help you determine which visuals are most appropriate for your needs.

Flat Materials   Included in flat materials are two-dimensional materials such as the chalkboard, bulletin board, flannel board, magnetic boards, handout sheets, pictures, posters, cartoons, charts, maps, scale drawings, and the like.

Although these are usually prepared in advance and revealed at the appropriate time (as in the poster used in the oral presentation "Description of Acco 20/30 Staplers," page 69), sometimes they are created spontaneously during the presentation (as in the outlining of steps on the chalkboard in the oral presentation "How Plywood Is Made," pages 42–43). A chalkboard or easel and paper (a pad of newsprint is excellent) serves beautifully. Actually, the visuals should be created in advance and reproduced from memory or notes during the presentation.

In using printed handout material, careful attention should be given to its time and manner of distribution. The main thing that the speaker should guard against is competing with his or her own handout material—the audience reading when it should be listening.

An easel is almost essential in displaying pictures, posters, cartoons, charts, maps, scale drawings, and other flat materials. Various lettering sets, tracing and template outfits, and graphic supplies can be purchased in hobby or art supply stores and facilitate a neat visual.

For a more detailed discussion of flat materials, see pages 465–479 in Chapter 11, Visuals.

Exhibits   Visual materials such as demonstrations, displays, dramatizations, models, mock-ups, dioramas, laboratory equipment, and real objects comprise exhibits. These are usually shown on a table or stand.

Undoubtedly the demonstration is one of the best aids in an oral presentation. (Several models of staplers are demonstrated in the oral description on page 69.) In fact, at times the entire presentation can be in the form of a demonstration. When performing a demonstration, be sure that all equipment is flawlessly operable and that everyone in the audience can see; if practical, allow the audience to participate actively.

For a more detailed discussion of exhibits, see pages 477–479 in Chapter 11, Visuals.

Projected Materials   Projected materials are those shown on a screen by use of a projector: pictures, slides, films, filmstrips, and transparencies. When using projected materials, a long pointer is essential, and an assistant often is needed to operate the machine.

For a more detailed discussion of projected materials, see pages 479–480 in Chapter 11, Visuals.

Preparing and Showing Visuals

The most effective use of visual materials occurs when the most appropriate kind of visual is selected and when the visual is prepared and shown well.

Preparation of Visuals   Once you have chosen specific kinds of visuals from the general types of flat materials, exhibits, and projected materials, careful attention should be given to their preparation. The following should assist you.

1. *Determine the purpose of the visual.* Select visuals that will help the audience understand the subject. Adapt them to your overall objective and to your audience.
2. *Organize the visual.* Information and its arrangement should be geared to quick visual comprehension.
3. *Consider the visibility of the aid: its size, colors used, and typography.* The size of the visual aid is determined largely by the size of the presentation room and the size of the audience. Visuals should be large enough to be seen by the entire audience.
4. *Keep the visual simple.* Do not include too much information.
5. *In general, portray only one concept or idea in each visual.*
6. *Make the visual neat and pleasing to the eye.* Clean, bold lines and an uncrowded appearance contribute to the visual's attractiveness.
7. *Select and test needed equipment.* If you need equipment to show your visuals—an overhead projector, a filmstrip projector, a movie projector—select the equipment and test it to be sure it is operable. Check the room if possible for locations and types of electrical outlets; these may affect the placement of the visual equipment. Perhaps a long extension cord will be needed. Determining needs and setting up equipment ahead of time allow you to make your presentation in a calm, controlled manner.

Showing of Visuals   Visual materials should be shown with natural ease, avoiding awkwardness. This is the basic principle in showing visuals in any kind of oral communication. The following suggestions are simply aspects of that basic principle.

1. Place the visual so that everyone in the audience can see it.
2. Present the visual at precisely the correct time. If an assistant is needed, rehearse with the assistant. The showing of a visual near the beginning of a presentation often helps the speaker to relax and to establish contact with the audience.
3. Face the audience, not the visual, when talking. In using a chalkboard, for instance, be sure to talk to the audience, not the chalkboard.
4. Keep the visual covered or out of sight until needed. After use, cover or remove the visual, if possible. Exposed drawings, charts, and the like, are distracting to the audience.
5. Correlate the visual with the verbal explanation. Make the relationship of visual and spoken words explicit.
6. When pointing, use the arm and hand next to the visual, rather than reaching across the body. Point with the index finger, with the other

fingers loosely curled under the thumb; keep the palm of the hand toward the audience.

7. Use a pointer as needed, but don't make it a plaything.

Visuals should not be a substitute for the speaker, or a prop, or a camouflage for the speaker's inadequacies. Further, the use of visuals should not constitute a show, obviating the talk.

Appropriately used, visuals can decidedly enhance an oral presentation.

EVALUATING AN ORAL PRESENTATION

On the following page is a class evaluation form for oral presentations. The vertical spaces across the top are for students' names. The evaluative criteria are listed under two headings, *Delivery* and *Content & Organization;* to these is added *Overall Effectiveness.* The members of the class are to evaluate one another on each criterion, using this scale:

4 = Outstanding
3 = Good
2 = Fair
1 = Needs improvement

Then the total number of points for each speaker is tabulated. Total scores can range from a high of 64 to a low of 16.

The evaluation procedure can be simplified, if desired, by using only the Overall Effectiveness criterion. The highest number of points for a speaker would then be 4; and the lowest, 1.

JOB INTERVIEWS

Whether or not an applicant gets the job is usually a direct result of the interview. Certainly, the information in the application letter and resumé are important, but the *person* behind that information is the real focus (see pages 253–269 in Chapter 7, Memorandums and Letters for a discussion of the application letter and resumé). The personal circumstance of the job interview allows the applicant to be more than written data. The impression that the applicant makes is often the deciding factor in whether he/she gets the job.

Following the suggestions below will help ensure your making the right impression. The suggestions are grouped according to the three steps in the job interview process: preparing for an interview, holding an interview, and following up an interview.

Preparing for an Interview

Careful attention should be given to preparing for an interview. This involves acquaintance with the job field, company analysis, job analysis, interviewer analysis, personal analysis, and preparation of a resumé. A procedure for rehearsing an interview is suggested at the end of this section.

EVALUATION OF ORAL PRESENTATIONS
(See page 449 for directions.)

Course and Section _____ Date _____ Evaluated by (Name) _____

Students' Names

DELIVERY

Forceful introduction																					
Poise																					
Eye contact																					
Sticking to mode of delivery																					
Zest (enthusiasm)																					
Voice control																					
Acceptable pronunciation and grammar																					
Avoidance of mannerisms																					
Ease in showing visuals																					
Clear-cut closing																					
Sticking to specified length																					

CONTENT & ORGANIZATION

Stating of main points at outset																					
Development of main points																					
Needed repetition and transitions																					
Effective kinds and sizes of visuals																					

OVERALL EFFECTIVENESS

TOTAL POINTS

COMMENTS:

4 = Outstanding   2 = Fair
3 = Good   1 = Needs improvement

Acquaintance with the Job Field Part of preparing for a job interview involves learning as much as you can about the field in which you seek a job. Become familiar with the possible career choices, job opportunities, advancement possibilities, salaries, and the like. An excellent way of learning about your field is talking with persons who are currently employed in that field, especially in the kind of job you are interested in.

Another excellent way of becoming acquainted with your job field is by reading in occupational guides, such as *The Occupational Outlook Handbook*, or by consulting brochures published by various professional societies. (All these reading materials usually are available in a college or public library or in a counselor's office.)

Company Analysis Find out as much as you can about the company by which you are to be interviewed. Your investigation may lead you to conclude that you really don't want to work for that particular company. More likely, however, your investigation will provide you with information useful for your letter of application, for the interview, and for later if you get the job.

Your analysis of the company should take into account such items as the following:

> *Background.* How old is the company? Who established it? What are the main factors or steps in its development?
> *Organization and management.* Who are the chief executives? What are the main divisions?
> *Product (or service).* What product does it manufacture or handle? What are its manufacturing processes? What raw materials are used and where do they come from? Who uses the product? Is there keen competition? How does the quality of the product compare with that of other companies?
> *Personnel.* How many persons does the company employ? What is the rate of turnover? What is the range of skills required for the total work force? What are company policies concerning hiring, sick leave, vacation, overtime, retirement? What kinds of in-service training are provided? What is the salary range? Are there opportunities for advancement?

To obtain answers to these and other pertinent questions may require consulting various sources. Remember that the enterprising applicant who really wants the job will overcome whatever difficulties or expend whatever energy is required to find needed information.

This information can be obtained from the Chamber of Commerce, trade and industrial organizations, local newspapers, interviews with company personnel, inspection tours through the company, company publications, and correspondence with the company.

Job Analysis Just as you analyze the various aspects of the company with which you will interview, you also should analyze the particular job for which you will interview. That is, you should be as knowledgeable as possible about such job factors as the following:

Educational requirements
Necessary skills

Significance of experience
On-the-job responsibilities
Desirable personal qualities
Promotion possibilities
Salary range
Special requirements

This analysis can help you to see yourself and your qualifications more objectively and thereby contribute to self-confidence.

Sources of information concerning a particular job are likely to be the same as those for the company analysis.

Interviewer Analysis Learn something about the person who will interview you as it usually is well worth the effort. Of course, the communication that gained you an interview provided some information about the interviewer; but more information would relieve undue anxiety and help to smooth the way and establish rapport.

Just as the salesperson analyzes a prospective customer — his or her wants, needs, and interests — before making a big sales effort, so you should analyze the person who will interview you.

Personal Analysis In preparing for the job interview, analyze yourself. Think through your attitudes, your qualifications, and your career goals. Be prepared to answer such questions as the following:

Why did I apply for this job?
Do I really want this job?
Have I applied for jobs with other companies?
What do I consider my primary qualifications for this job?
Why should I be hired over someone else with similar qualifications?
What do I consider my greatest accomplishment?
Can I take criticism?
(If you have held other positions) Why did I leave other jobs?
Do I prefer to work with people or with objects?
How do I spend my leisure time?
What are my ambitions in life?
What are my salary needs?

Preparation of a Resumé If your letter of application did not include a resumé, or data sheet, prepare one to take with you to the interview. This orderly listing of information about yourself will help you organize your qualifications. Further, having the resumé with you at the interview will help you to present all significant information and will provide the interviewer, at a glance, with an outline of pertinent information about your ability.

See pages 254 – 255 and 266 – 269 in Chapter 7, Memorandums and Letters for specific directions in preparing a resumé.

Rehearsing an Interview With the help of friends, practice an interview. Set up an office situation with desk and chairs. Ask a friend to assume the role of the interviewer and to ask you questions about yourself (see the questions listed in the section on Personal Analysis) and questions about the information on your resumé. Ask your friends to comment honestly on the rehearsal. Then swap roles; you be the interviewer and a friend, the applicant. If possible, tape the interview and play it back for critical analysis.

Another way to rehearse is by yourself, in front of a full-length mirror. Dress in the attire you will wear for the interview. Study yourself impartially; go over aloud the points you plan to discuss in the interview. Keep your gestures and facial expressions appropriate.

Rehearsals can help you gain self-confidence and organize your thoughts.

Holding an Interview

Ordinarily, you cannot know exactly how an interview will be conducted. Thus it is impossible to be prepared for every situation that can arise. It is possible, however, to become acquainted with the usual procedure so that you can more easily adapt to the particular situation.

The usual procedure for an interview includes observance of business etiquette, establishing the purpose of the interview, questions and answers, and closing the interview.

Observance of Business Etiquette Dressing appropriately is extremely important. Good business manners, if not common sense, demand that you arrive on time, be pleasant and friendly but businesslike, avoid annoying actions (such as chewing gum or tapping your feet), let the interviewer take the lead, and listen attentively.

Establishing the Purpose of the Interview At the outset of the interview, establish why you are there. If you seek a specific position, say so. If you seek a job within a general area of a company, let that be known. Be flexible, but give the interviewer a clear idea of your job preferences.

Questions and Answers During most of the interview, the interviewer will ask questions to which you respond. Your responses should be frank, brief, and to the point—yet complete.

Be honest in discussing your qualifications, neither exaggerating nor minimizing them. The interviewer's questions and comments can help you determine the type of employee sought; then you can emphasize your suitable qualifications. For instance, if you apply for a business position and the interviewer mentions that the job requires some customer contact, present your qualifications that show you have dealt with many people. That is, emphasize any work, experience, or courses that pertain to direct contact work.

In the course of the interview, you will likely be asked if you have any questions. Don't be afraid to ask what you need to know concerning the company or the job and its duties (such as employee insurance programs, vacation policy, overtime work, travel).

Closing the Interview Watch the interviewer for clues that it is time to end the interview. Express appreciation for the time and courtesies given you, say goodbye, and leave. Lingering or prolonging the interview usually is an annoyance to the interviewer.

At the close of the interview, you may be told whether or not you have the job; or the interviewer may tell you that a decision will be made within a few days. If the interviewer does not definitely offer you a job or indicate when you will be informed about the job, ask when you may telephone to learn the decision.

Following Up an Interview

Following up an interview reflects good manners and good business. Whether the follow-up is in the form of a telephone call, a letter, or another interview usually depends on whether you got the job, did not get the job, or no decision has been made.

If you got the job, a telephone call or a letter can serve as confirmation of the job, its responsibilities, and the time for reporting to work. Too, the communication can express appreciation for the opportunity to become connected with the company.

If you did not get the job, thank the interviewer by telephone or by letter for his or her time and courtesy. This kind of goodwill is essential to business success.

Perhaps a final decision has not yet been reached concerning your employment. A favorable decision may well hinge on a wisely executed follow-up. If the interview ended with "Keep in touch with us" or "Check with us in a few days," you have the go-ahead. Have another interview. A telephone call or a letter would be less effective, for they would not be as forceful in maintaining the good impression that has been made. If the interview ended with "We'll keep your application on file" or "We may need a person with your qualifications a little later," follow up the lead. After a few days, write a letter. Mention the interview, express appreciation for it, include any additional credentials or emphasize credentials that since the interview seem to be particularly significant, and state your continued interest in the position.

INFORMATIONAL INTERVIEWS

A student writing a report about careers in sociology visits a sociologist, a social worker, and an occupational counselor. An employee who has been promoted to a higher position talks with his associates concerning his new job responsibilities. A member of a service organization polls the membership for suggested projects to undertake. The prospective buyer of a used car questions the owner about its condition. All these situations call for informational interviews—that is, conversing with another person to gain needed information. In addition, the preparer of a field report (see pages 341–353 in Chapter 8, Reports) and of a research report (see Chapter 9, The Research Report) frequently derives information from knowledgeable people. In seeking such information, especially from those not obliged to give it, you must prepare carefully for the interview.

Preparing for an Interview

Knowledgeable people usually are willing to share their knowledge, provided the time required to do so seems worthwhile to them. Follow these steps to ensure that time is well spent for both interviewee and interviewer:

1. Ask for an interview. A frank, informal request usually is sufficient. Identify yourself, and explain briefly why the interview is important. State the kind of information being sought.
2. Set a convenient time and place for the interview. Accommodation of the person who must grant the interview is especially important.
3. Carefully plan the questions to be asked. Think through the reason for the interview and the kind of information desired.
4. The parties to the interview should be aware of each other's knowledge and resources so that a valuable exchange of information results.

The Interview

After making the arrangements for the interview and planning specifically your contribution, you are prepared for the interview itself.

Follow this guide for a more satisfactory interview.

1. Be persuasive in explaining the significance of the interview and the value of the information sought. Make the other person feel that the time and knowledge shared can be of value to both parties.
2. Explain how you will use the information. Assure the interviewee that the information will be treated honestly and that confidential information will remain confidential.
3. Ask well-planned questions. Refer to your notes if necessary.
4. Take notes on what is said. One technique is to bring to the interview written questions. Space can be left to write in the interviewee's responses. Instead, if the interviewee does not object, you may want to tape the interview.
5. Review the information, clarifying where necessary. Especially if you intend to quote, read the quotation back to the interviewee as a check for accuracy.
6. Close the interview by sincerely thanking the person giving the information.

Courtesy Follow-Up

After the interview, a brief letter of appreciation should be written to the person who granted the interview. This courteous gesture is both good manners and good business. See "Application Follow-Up Letters," pages 273–277.

GENERAL PRINCIPLES IN ORAL COMMUNICATION

1. *An oral presentation differs from a written presentation.* Differences occur in level of diction, amount of repetition, kind of transitions, and kind and size of visuals.

2. *Modes of delivery include extemporaneous, memorized, and read from a manuscript.* The speaker selects a mode appropriate for a given situation.
3. *The general purpose of a presentation may be to entertain, to persuade, or to inform.*
4. *An effective presentation requires preparation.* The steps in preparation for a presentation include determining the specific purpose; analyzing the type of audience; gathering the material; organizing the material; determining the mode of delivery; outlining the speech, writing it out if necessary; preparing visual materials; and rehearsing.
5. *The delivery of the presentation is very important.* Effective delivery includes walking to the podium with poise and self-confidence; capturing the audience's attention and interest; looking at the audience; sticking to an appropriate mode of delivery; putting some zest in expression; getting words out clearly and distinctly; adjusting the volume and pitch of voice; varying the rate of speaking to enhance meaning; standing naturally; avoiding mannerisms; showing visuals with natural ease; and closing appropriately.
6. *Visuals for oral presentations include flat materials, exhibits, and projected materials.*
7. *Evaluating a presentation requires considering the purpose and audience, the delivery, and the content and organization of the presentation.*

APPLICATION 1 ORAL COMMUNICATION

Select five advertisements and bring them to class. To what needs, wants, and desires do the ads appeal? Decide for each one whether the major appeal is emotional or rational.

APPLICATION 2 ORAL COMMUNICATION

Assume that you are in *one* of the situations below. What would you say?

a. Gather your supporting material.
b. Organize the material.
c. Outline the presentation.
d. Prepare appropriate visuals.
e. Rehearse.
f. Give the presentation.

Assume:

1. You have been employed in a firm for six months. You are asking your employer for a raise.
2. You have a plan for facilitating the flow of traffic for campus events. Present your plan to the local police chief (or other appropriate official).
3. You have an automobile (or some other piece of personal property) for sale. A prospective buyer is coming to talk with you.
4. You are a football coach getting ready to talk to your team at halftime. Your team is losing 17–0.

5. You want your parents to buy an automobile (or some other expensive item) for you.
6. Select any other situation in which you present an idea, plan, or product.

Ask your classmates to evaluate your speech by making an Evaluation of Oral Presentations sheet like the one on page 459 and filling it in.

APPLICATION 3　ORAL COMMUNICATION

As directed by your instructor, prepare one of the topics below for an oral presentation.

a. Analyze the type of audience.
b. Gather the material.
c. Organize the material. Prepare an appropriate Plan Sheet.
d. Determine the mode of delivery.
e. Outline the presentation.
f. Prepare appropriate visuals.
g. Rehearse.
h. Give the presentation.

Prepare:
1. A set of instructions or description of a process. (Review Chapter 1.)
2. A description of a mechanism. (Review Chapter 2.)
3. An extended definition. (Review Chapter 3.)
4. An analysis through classification or partition. (Review Chapter 4.)
5. An analysis through effect and cause or comparison and contrast. (Review Chapter 5.)
6. A report. (Review Chapter 8.)

Ask your classmates to evaluate your speech by making an Evaluation of Oral Presentations sheet like the one on page 459 and filling it in.

APPLICATION 4　ORAL COMMUNICATION

Team up with a classmate for practice job interviews. Alternate roles of interviewer and interviewee. Be constructively critical of each other. If you have access to a tape recorder, record your practice sessions and play them back for study.

APPLICATION 5　ORAL COMMUNICATION

Assume that your instructor is the personnel manager of a company you would like to work for. (*a*) Prepare for the interview by making a written job field analysis, company analysis, job analysis, interviewer analysis, personal analysis, and resumé. (*b*) Write a letter of application, including a resumé, to the personnel manager. See pages 253–269. If the letter is successful, you will be granted an interview. (*c*) Attend the interview at the scheduled time in the office of the personnel manager. (*d*) Use an appropriate follow-up.

APPLICATION 6   ORAL COMMUNICATION

Arrange for an interview (conference) with an instructor in whose class you would like to be making better grades. Then write a one-page report on the interview.

APPLICATION 7   ORAL COMMUNICATION

Arrange for an interview with your program adviser, a school counselor, an employment counselor, or some other person knowledgeable in your major field of study. Try to determine the availability of jobs, pay scale, job requirements, promotion opportunities, and other such pertinent information for the type of work you are preparing for. Present your findings in an oral report.

a. Gather the material.
b. Organize the material.
c. Outline the presentation.
d. Prepare appropriate visuals.
e. Rehearse.
f. Give the presentation.

Ask your classmates to evaluate your speech by making an Evaluation of Oral Presentations sheet like the one on page 459 and filling it in.

EVALUATION OF ORAL PRESENTATIONS
(See page 449 for directions.)

Course and Section _____ Date _____ Evaluated by (Name) _____

Students' Names

DELIVERY

Forceful introduction

Poise

Eye contact

Sticking to mode of delivery

Zest (enthusiasm)

Voice control

Acceptable pronunciation and grammar

Avoidance of mannerisms

Ease in showing visuals

Clear-cut closing

Sticking to specified length

CONTENT & ORGANIZATION

Stating of main points at outset

Development of main points

Needed repetition and transitions

Effective kinds and sizes of visuals

OVERALL EFFECTIVENESS

TOTAL POINTS

4 = Outstanding   2 = Fair

3 = Good   1 = Needs improvement

COMMENTS:

CHAPTER 11

Visuals: Seeing Is Convincing

OBJECTIVES 461
INTRODUCTION 461
ADVANTAGES OF VISUALS 461
USING VISUALS EFFECTIVELY 462
COMPUTER GRAPHICS 464
    Basic Visuals — Charting 464
    More Complex Visuals 465
    Effect on Manually Produced Visuals 465
TABLES 465
    General Directions for Constructing Tables 466
CHARTS 467
    General Directions for Constructing Charts 467
    Pie Chart 467
    Bar Chart 468
    Organization Chart 469
    Flow Chart 471
GRAPHS 472
    General Directions for Constructing Graphs 472
PHOTOGRAPHS 475
DRAWINGS AND DIAGRAMS 476
    Drawings 476
    Diagrams 476
    Schematic Diagram 477
EXHIBITS 477
    Demonstration 478
    Display 478
    Real Object 478
    Model 478
    Diorama 478
    Poster 479
    Chalkboard 479
PROJECTED MATERIALS 479
    Film 479
    Filmstrip 479
    Slide 480
    Transparency 480
GENERAL PRINCIPLES IN USING VISUALS 480
APPLICATIONS 481

OBJECTIVES

Upon completing this chapter, the student should be able to:

- List ways in which visuals can be helpful
- Explain how to use visuals effectively
- Explain how computers are influencing the use and the production of visuals
- Explain the special characteristics of tables, charts, graphs, photographs, drawings, diagrams, exhibits, and projected materials
- Use visuals in written and in oral presentations

INTRODUCTION

Visuals can help immeasurably in your communication needs. Both in written and in oral presentations, visuals can clarify the information and impress it upon the minds of your audience.

The various kinds of visuals have unique qualities that make each type the "right" one to use in certain circumstances. All kinds require careful planning and preparation. Some are usable only in written or only in oral presentations, although most types are adaptable to either; some require a great deal of technical knowledge to prepare — others can be rather easily constructed by an amateur. In order to select and show the visuals that best serve your purpose, you should consider both the reasons for using visuals and the best way to use them effectively. Further, you should become familiar with the most frequently used types (tables, charts, graphs, photographs, drawings, diagrams, exhibits, and projected materials), their specific contributions, and their special characteristics. (See also pages 446–449 in Chapter 10, Oral Communication.)

ADVANTAGES OF VISUALS

Visuals can be helpful in several ways:

1. Visuals can capitalize on *seeing*. For most people, the sense of sight — more so than hearing, smell, touch, or taste — is the most highly developed of the senses.
2. Visuals can convey some kinds of messages better than words can. Ideas or information difficult or impossible to express in words may be communicated more easily through visuals.
3. Visuals can simplify or considerably reduce textual explanation. Accompanying visuals often clarify words.
4. Visuals can add interest and focus attention.

Of course, visuals can work against you as well as for you. So guard against an overreliance on visuals, against poorly planned visuals, and, most of all, against snafus in timing or presentation.

Remember, however, that appropriately used, visuals can richly enhance your presentation.

USING VISUALS EFFECTIVELY

Visuals can be a simple, effective way of presenting information that will make a lasting, positive impression on your audience. Following are suggestions that will help ensure your using visuals to the best advantage.

1. *Study the use of visuals by others.* Analyze their use in books and periodicals and by speakers and lecturers, especially in your field of study. Note such things as intended audience, the kinds of information presented or supplemented, the kind of visual selected for a particular purpose, the design and layout of the visual, the amount of accompanying textual explanation, and the overall effectiveness of the visual.

2. *Select the kinds of visuals that are most suitable.* Consider the purpose of your presentation, the needs of your audience, and the specific information or idea to be presented.

3. *Prepare the visual carefully.* Organize information logically, accurately, completely, and consistently. Include all needed labels, symbols, titles, and headings.

   a. *Do not include too much in a visual.* Plan one overall focus. Information should be easy to grasp visually and intellectually.

   b. *Make the visual pleasing to the eye.* It should be neat, uncrowded, attractive, and should have sufficient margins on all sides.

   c. *Use lettering to good advantage.* Avoid carelessly mixing styles of lettering or typefaces and mixing uppercase (capital) letters with lowercase ones. Space consistently between letters and between words. Suggestion: Using a pencil, lightly rule guidelines and block out the words. Then do the actual lettering. Erase the pencil lines with art gum after the lettering has dried. Examples of lettering:

Poor	Good
EX pensez for the Y EAR	Expenses for the year
	Expenses for the Year
	EXPENSES FOR THE YEAR

   d. *Give each visual a caption.* State clearly and concisely what the viewer is looking at. For tables, place the caption above the visual; in all other instances, place the caption below the visual.

4. *Decide whether to make the visual "run on" in the text or to separate it from the text.* The run-on visual is a part of the natural sequence of information within a paragraph. It is not set apart with a title, a number, or lines (rules). Usually the run-on visual is short and the information contained is uncomplicated. The separate visual is "dressed up" with a number (unless the communication contains only one visual), a caption, and rule lines. Such a visual usually is more complicated and requires more space than the run-on visual. In addition, the separate visual is movable; that is, it can be located other than at the place where it is mentioned in the text (see number 5 below).

5. *Determine where to place the visual.* Ideally a visual is placed within the text at the point where it is discussed. The visual may be more practically placed, however, other than at the point of reference (such as on a

following page, on a separate page, or at the end of the communication) if (1) a visual too large for the remaining space on a page unavoidably causes a noticeable blank space; (2) a visual that merely supplements verbal explanation interferes with reader comprehension; or (3) a number of visuals are used and seem to break the content flow of a presentation. (When visuals form a significant part of a report, they are *listed*, together with page numbers, under a heading such as "List of Illustrations." This list appears on a separate page immediately following the table of contents.)

6. *Refer to the visual in the textual explanation.* The audience should never be left to wonder "Why is this visual included?" It is essential that you establish a proper relationship between the visual and the text. The extent of textual explanation is determined largely by the complexity of the subject matter, the purpose of the visual, and the completeness of labels on the visual. In referring to the visual, use such pointers as *see Figure 1, as illustrated in the following diagram,* or *Table 3 indicates the pertinent factors.*

7. *Use correct terminology in referring to visuals.* Tables are referred to as tables; all other visuals are usually referred to as figures. Examples: *Study the amounts of salary increases shown in Table 2. Note the position of the automobile in Figure 6. As the graph in Figure 4 indicates* . . .

8. *Give credit for borrowed material.* The credit line, usually in parentheses, typically is placed immediately following the title of the visual or just below the visual. For bibliographical forms other than those illustrated below, see pages 409 – 411 in Chapter 9, The Research Report.

   a. *If you have borrowed or copied an entire visual, give the source.* Although there is no one standard format for giving the source, the following examples use acceptable formats.

EXAMPLE 1

TABLE 4
CAUSES OF INDUSTRIAL ACCIDENTS

[The table goes here.]

Source: John R. Barnes, Industry on Trial (New
York: Harper & Row, 1983), p. 221.

EXAMPLE 2

Figure 6. Automobile troubleshooting using
the charging system (Source: Ford Division—
Ford Motor Co.)

EXAMPLE 3

Table 2. Projected College Enrollments for
1985 (Education Almanac [New York: Educational
Associates, Inc., 1983], p. 76.)

(Note the brackets where parentheses ordinarily are used; another pair of parentheses would be confusing.) For other examples, see in this Chapter, Table 3 (page 466), Figure 4 (page 469), Figure 6 (page 471), Figure 7 (page 472), Figure 10 (page 474), Figure 11 (page 475), Figure 13 (page 477), and Table 4 (page 484).

b. *If you have devised the visual yourself but gotten the information from another source, give the source.* The following examples use acceptable formats.

EXAMPLE 1

```
Figure 5. Per Capita Income in Selected
States. (Source of Information: U.S. Dept. of
Urban Affairs)
```

EXAMPLE 2

```
Figure 1. Average size of American families.
(Data from U.S. Bureau of the Census)
```

For other examples, see page 74 and Figure 7 in this chapter (page 472).

9. *If necessary, mount the visual.* Photographs, maps, and other visuals smaller than the regular page should be mounted. Attach the visual with dry mounting tissue, spray adhesive, or rubber cement (glue tends to wrinkle the paper).

COMPUTER GRAPHICS

The computer is revolutionizing both the role and the production of visuals in communication. This computer revolution can be largely attributed to three conditions: (1) the increasing availability of terminals for mainframe systems, (2) the widespread availability and downward pricing of microcomputers, and (3) the continuous additions to a growing array of graphic software, that is, commercially produced programs for easily and swiftly transforming data into various kinds of graphics. For the novice or intermediate level computer user, the software aspect is of most interest.

Graphics software provides programs for creating basic kinds of visuals and programs for creating more complex visuals.

Basic Visuals — Charting

Persons in business and industry — regardless of the size of the company — are using computer graphics to enlarge upon the time-proved positive difference that visuals make. The general term for producing basic visuals on the computer is charting.

The computer user can create line graphs, pie graphs (pie charts), bar graphs (bar charts), consumer marketing maps, forecasting charts, and a host of other basic visuals. These can be produced in black-and-white hard copies, that is, on a sheet of paper; or with a color plotter (a device that acts as a mechanical arm and that "draws" with a pen), the visuals can be produced in multiple colors and on clear polyester film for overhead projection.

What this means in terms of preparing a business report is that the data in the computer can be programmed to produce such visuals as a pie chart of percentages of sales for particular products, a graph displaying a sales matrix, a line graph depicting total sales and fixed expenses, or bar charts reflecting sales, gross profits, and overhead expenses. The visuals are generated as an integral aspect of the report.

More Complex Visuals

In addition to charting, other software programs provide for more complex, more sophisticated kinds of visuals.

One kind of such graphics is the slide-show program. This program permits the user to select computerized charts for demonstration; the user sets up the charts in sequence, times the needed intervals, and programs the charts for projection on a screen. Some slide-show programs offer graphic editing and such design features as borders and multiple typefaces.

Other slide-show programs include those that splice such media as videotape, film, off-air broadcasts, and interactive computer programs and those that produce 3-D computerized graphics.

Effect on Manually Produced Visuals

Computer graphics are rapidly replacing manually produced graphs and charts. Manually produced visuals — whether by hand, with a rapidograph or other such aids, or through a company's graphic arts department — are increasingly being replaced by electronically produced visuals.

The computer generated visuals can be produced quickly, accurately, and economically. Futhermore, they can be easily updated.

TABLES

Tables are an excellent form for presenting large amounts of data concisely. (See the tables on pages 123, 131, 179, and 339.) Although tables lack the eye appeal and interest-arousing dramatization of such visuals as charts or graphs, they are unexcelled as a method of organizing and depicting statistical information compiled through research. In fact, information in most other visuals showing numerical amounts and figures derives from data originally calculated in tables.

Study Table 3 below, noting the quantity of information given and its arrangement.

Tables may be classified as informal (such as those on pages 176–177 and 331–332) or as formal (such as Table 3 below). Informal tables are incorporated as an integral part of a paragraph and thus are not given an identifying number or title. Formal tables are set up as a separate entity (with identifying number and title) but are referred to and explained as needed in the pertinent paragraphs.

Table 3 American Family Characteristics: 1980

Characteristic	Families	Per-cent	Characteristic	Families	Per-cent
All families	58,426,000	100.0	Nonmetropoli-		
White	51,389,000	88.0	tan	19,377,000	33.2
Black and Other	7,037,000	12.0	Headed by		
Family Size:			Women	8,540,000	14.6
2 persons. . . .	22,913,000	39.2	Age of Family		
3 persons. . . .	13,332,000	22.8	Head:		
4 persons. . . .	12,180,000	20.8	Under 25 years	3,725,000	6.4
5 persons. . . .	5,871,000	10.0	25–34 years . .	13,743,000	23.5
6 persons. . . .	2,439,000	4.2	35–44 years . .	12,159,000	20.8
7 persons or			45–54 years . .	10,709,000	18.3
more	1,691,000	2.9	55–64 years . .	9,298,000	15.9
Own Children			65 years or		
under 18 Years			older	8,792,000	15.0
Old:			Marital Status of		
No children. . .	27,909,000	47.8	Household Heads:		
1 child	12,231,000	20.9	All Households	79,108,000	100.0
2 children. . . .	11,280,000	19.3	Married.	51,867,000	65.6
3 children. . . .	4,616,000	7.9	Separated . .	2,944,000	3.7
4 children or			Widowed. . . .	10,462,000	13.2
more.	2,390,000	4.1	Divorced	7,421,000	9.4
Residence:			Single	9,359,000	11.8
Metropolitan. .	39,049,000	66.8			

SOURCE: U.S. Bureau of Census

General Directions for Constructing Tables

As you prepare tables, observe the following basic practices:

1. Number each table (the number may be omitted if only one table is included) and give it a descriptive title (number and title are omitted in informal tables). Center the number and the title *above* the table. Often the word *table* is written in all capitals, the number written in Arabic numerals, and this label centered above the title (caption) written in all capitals. Example:

TABLE 2

LEADING CAUSES OF DEATH AMONG AMERICANS

Just as acceptable:

Table 2. Leading Causes of Death among Americans

Table 2. Leading causes of death among Americans

Other acceptable practices include giving the table number in Roman numerals or as a decimal sequence.

2. Label each column accurately and concisely. If a column shows

amounts, indicate the unit in which the amounts are expressed; example: Wheat (in metric tons).

3. To save space, use standard symbols and abbreviations. If items need clarification, use footnotes, placed immediately below the table. (Table footnotes are separate from ordinary footnotes placed at the bottom of the page.)
4. Generally use decimals instead of fractions, unless it is customary to use fractions (as in the size of drill bits or hats).
5. Include all factors or information that affect the data. For instance, omission of wheat production in a table "Production of Chief United States Crops" would make the table misleading.
6. Use ample spacing and rule lines (straight lines) to enhance the clarity and readability of the table. Caution: Generally, use as few rule lines as necessary.
7. If a table is divided for continuation, as in Table 3 on page 466, repeat the column headings.
8. If a table is more than a page long and must be continued to another page, use the word *continued* at the bottom of each page to be continued and at the top of each continuation page. If column totals are given at the end of the table, give subtotals at the end of each page; and at the top of each continuation page, repeat the subtotals from the preceding page.

CHARTS

Although the term *chart* is often used as a synonym for *graph*, a chart is distinguished by the various shapes it can take, by its use of pictures and diagrams, and by its capacity to show nonstatistical as well as statistical relationships. More importantly, a chart can show relationships better than other types of visuals can. Frequently used types of charts are the pie chart, the bar chart, the organization chart, and the flow chart.

General Directions for Constructing Charts

Manually constructing charts, as well as other visuals, requires careful attention to details, a bit of arithmetic, and a few basic materials: ruler, pen or pencil, and paper.

In the construction process:

1. Number each chart as Figure 1 or Fig. 1, Figure 2, and so on (this may be omitted if only one visual is included), and give the chart a descriptive title. Center the number and title (both on the same line) *below* the chart.
2. Label each segment concisely and clearly.
3. Use lines or arrows if necessary to link labels to segments.
4. Place all labels and other information horizontally for ease in reading.

Pie Chart

The pie chart, also called circle chart or circle graph, is a circle representing 100 percent. It is divided into segments, or slices, that represent amounts or proportions. The pie chart is especially popular for showing monetary proportions and is often used to show proportions of expenditures, income, or taxes. Although not the most accurate form for presenting information, it has strong pictorial impact. More than any other kind of visual, the pie chart permits simultaneous comparison of the parts to one another and comparison of one part to the whole.

Constructing a pie chart is relatively simple if you will follow the general directions given above and these additional suggestions:

1. Begin the largest segment in the "twelve o'clock" position; then, going clockwise, give the next largest segment, and so on.
2. Lump together, if practical, items that individually would occupy very small segments. Label the segment "Other," "Miscellaneous," or a similar title, and place this segment last.
3. Put the label and the percentage or amount on or near each segment.

Pie Chart

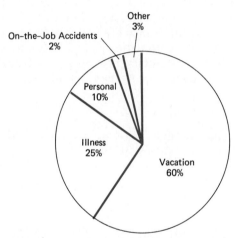

Figure 2. Work loss for all employees.

Bar Chart

The bar chart, also called column chart or bar graph, is one of the simplest and most useful of the visual aids, for it allows the immediate comparison of amounts. (Bar charts are shown on pages 122 and 469.)

The bar chart consists of one or more vertical or horizontal bars of equal width, scaled in length to represent amounts. (When the bar is vertical, the visual is called a column chart; when the bar is horizontal, the visual is called a bar chart.) The bars are often separated to improve appearance and readability.

To give multiple data, a bar may be subdivided, or multiple bars may be used, with crosshatching, colors, or shading to indicate different divisions.

Note the difference in the two accompanying examples of bar charts, Figure 3 and Figure 4.

Vertical Bar Chart with Shading and Crosshatching

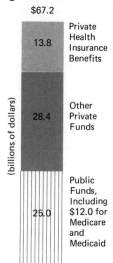

Figure 3. How health care is paid for.

Horizontal Bar Chart with Multiple Bars

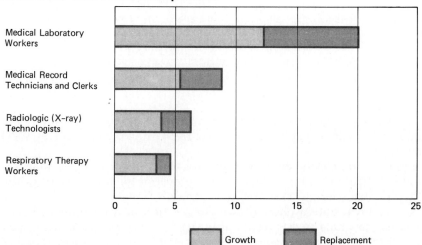

Figure 4. Average annual openings, 1978–1987 (in thousands), selected medical technologist, technician, and assistant occupations. (*Source:* Bureau of Labor Statistics)

Organization Chart

The organization chart is effective in showing the structure of such organizations as businesses, institutions, and governmental agencies. (An organization chart appears in Figure 5 and in a sample report in Chapter 4, page 140.) Unlike most

Organization Chart

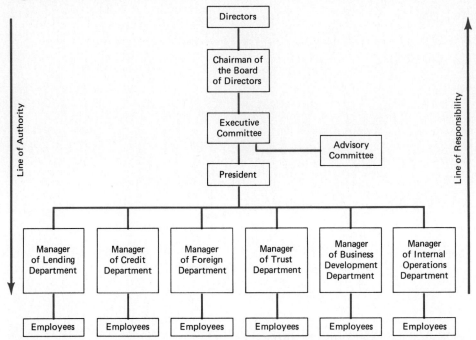

Figure 5. A line organization plan of a medium-sized bank. In this plan, the department head must perform highly specialized functions and at the same time direct or supervise subordinates.

other charts, the organization chart does not present statistical information. Rather, it reflects lines of authority, levels of responsibility, and kinds of working relationships.

Organization charts depict the interrelationships of (1) staff, that is, the personnel; (2) administrative units, such as offices or departments; or (3) functions, such as sales, production, and purchasing.

A staff organization chart shows the position of each individual in the organization, to whom each is responsible, over whom each has control, and the relationship to others in the same or different divisions of the organization. The administrative unit organization chart shows the various divisions and subdivisions. The administrative units of a large supermarket, for instance, include the produce department, the meat department, the grocery department, and the dairy department, among others. The functions organization chart shows the interrelationships of different activities, operations, and responsibilities. A college organization chart, for instance, might show its structure by functions: teaching, community service, research, and the like.

An organization chart must be internally consistent; that is, it should not jump randomly from, say, depicting personnel to depicting functions.

Blocks or circles containing labels are connected by lines to indicate the organizational arrangement. Heavier lines are often used to show chain of authority, while broken lines may show coordination, liaison, or consultation. Blocks on the same level generally suggest the same level of authority.

Flow Chart

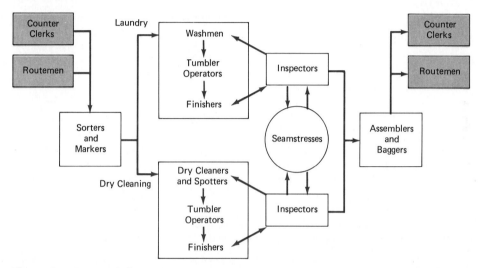

Figure 6. How work flows through a laundry and dry cleaning plant. (*Source:* Bureau of Labor Statistics)

Flow Chart

The flow chart, or flow sheet, shows the flow or sequence of related actions. The flow chart pictorially presents events, procedures, activities, or factors and shows how they are related. (Sample presentations, pages 39, 42–43, and 74, contain a flow chart.)

The flow chart is an effective visual for showing the flow of a product from its beginning as raw material to its completed form, or the movement of persons in a process, or the steps in the execution of a computer operation. Labeled blocks, triangles, circles, and the like (or simply labels) represent the steps, although sometimes simplified drawings that suggest the actual appearance of machines and equipment indicate the various steps. Usually, arrowhead lines show the direction in which the activity or product moves.

The flow chart in Figure 6 uses labeled blocks and a circle, arrowhead lines, and screened and unscreened lettering to explain the work process in a laundry and dry cleaning plant. The flow chart below depicts a natural process: nerve supply from the brain to the teeth.

Flow Chart

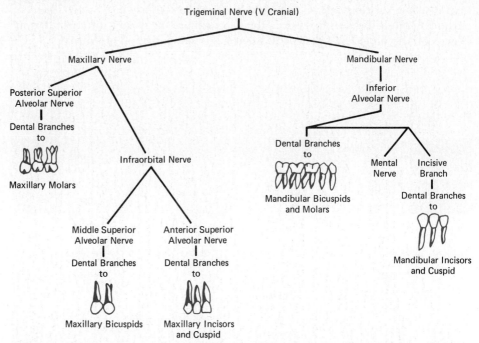

Figure 7. Nerve supply to the teeth. (Redrawn by permission from Russell C. Wheeler, *Dental Anatomy and Physiology* [Philadelphia: W. B. Saunders, 1965], p. 94)

GRAPHS

Graphs present numerical data in easy-to-read form. They are often essential in communicating statistical information, as a glance through a business periodical, a report, or an industrial publication will attest.

Graphs are especially helpful in identifying trends, movements, relationships, and cycles. Production or sales graphs, temperature and rainfall curves, and fever charts are common examples. Graphs simplify data and make their interpretation easier. But whatever purpose a specific graph may serve, all graphs emphasize *change* rather than actual amounts.

Consider, for instance, the graph on page 473, showing the changes over a ten-year period in the cost of stock in a company.

At a glance you can see the change in cost over the years. Presented verbally or in another visual form, such as in a table, the information would be less dramatic and would require more time for study and analysis. But presented in a graph, the information is immediately impressed upon the eyes and the mind.

General Directions for Constructing Graphs

Consider the following as you prepare graphs:

1. A graph is labeled as Figure 1 or Fig. 1, Figure 2, etc. (this may be omitted if only one visual is included), and is given a descriptive caption, or title. The label and caption (same line) are placed below the graph.

2. A graph has a horizontal and a vertical scale. The vertical scale usually appears on the left side (the same scale may also appear on the right side if the graph is large), and the horizontal scale appears underneath the graph.

Graph

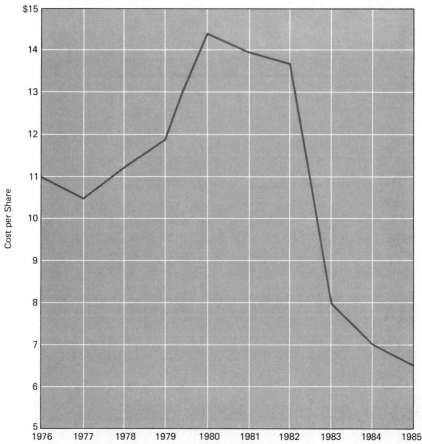

Figure 8.   Average cost per share in Threadrite, Inc., 1976–1985.

3. Generally, the independent variable (time, distance, etc.) is shown on the horizontal scale; the dependent variable (money, temperature, number of people, etc.) is shown on the vertical scale.

4. The horizontal scale increases from left to right. If this scale indicates a value other than time, labeling is necessary. The vertical scale increases from bottom to top; it should always be labeled. Often this scale starts at zero, but it may start at any amount appropriate to the data being presented.

5. The scales on a graph should be planned so that the line or curve creates an accurate impression, an impression justified by facts. To the viewer, sharp rises and falls in the line mean significant changes. Yet the angle at which the line goes up or down is controlled by the scales. If a change is important, the line indicating that change should climb or drop sharply;

if a change is unimportant, the line should climb or drop less sharply. See the graph in Figure 9 below.

Graph

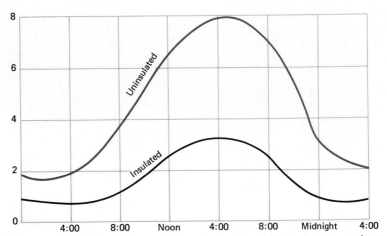

Figure 9. Heat flow into air-conditioned house (BTU per square foot per hour).

6. A graph may have more than one line. The lines should be amply separated to be easily recognized and distinguished, yet close enough for clear comparison. Each line should be clearly identified either above or to the side of the line or in a legend. Often, variations of the solid unbroken line are used, such as a dotted line or a dot/dash line. Note the kinds of lines and their identification in Figure 9 above and Figure 10 below.
7. The line connecting two plotted points may be either straight, as in Figure 8, or smoothed out (faired, curved), as in Figure 9. A straight line

Multiple-Line Graph

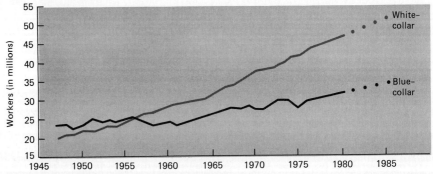

Figure 10. The shift toward white-collar occupations will continue through 1985. (*Source:* Bureau of Labor Statistics)

is usually desired if the graph shows changes that occur at stated intervals; a faired line, if the graph shows changes that occur continuously.

PHOTOGRAPHS

Photographs provide a more exact impression of actual appearance than other visual aids. Photographs on page 353 are used to validate a report. They supply far more concreteness and realism than drawings. Though helpful in supplementing verbal description and for giving information, photographs are of the greatest value as evidence in proving or showing what something is.

Photographs have certain limitations, however. Since they present only appearance (except, of course, for such specialties as X-ray photography or holography), internal or below-the-surface exposure is impossible, and drawings or diagrams might be necessary. Further, unless retouched (or cropped) or taken with proper layout for a given purpose, photographs may unavoidably present both significant and insignificant elements of appearance with equal emphasis; or they may even miss or misrepresent important details.

The photograph in Figure 11 was used in filing an insurance claim.

Photograph

Figure 11. Damage to police car. (Photograph courtesy of Jack Coppenbarger)

DRAWINGS AND DIAGRAMS

Drawings

Drawings are especially helpful in all kinds of technical communication. (Among the many drawings in the text are those on pages 18–20, 21, 31–32, 61, 63–64, 71, 86, 94, 134, 135, and 158–159.)

A drawing, though sometimes suggestive or interpretive, ordinarily portrays the actual appearance of an object. Like a photograph, it can picture what something looks like; but unlike a photograph — and herein lies one of its chief values — it can picture the interior as well as the exterior. A drawing makes it possible to place the emphasis where needed and thus omit the insignificant. Furthermore, a drawing can show details and relationships that might be obscured in a photograph. And a drawing can be tailored to fit the need of the user: it can show, for example, a cutaway view (see pages 63, 71, and 74) or an enlarged view of a particular part (see Figure 12).

Drawing

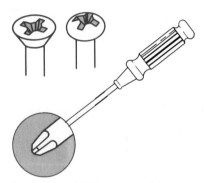

Figure 12. Phillips screwdriver.

Making a simple drawing is relatively uncomplicated and usually is much easier and less expensive than preparing a photograph. If the object being drawn has more than one part, the parts should be proportionate in size (unless enlargement is indicated). The name of each part that is significant in the drawing should be clearly given, either on the part or near it, connected to it by a line or arrow. If the drawing is complex and shows a number of parts, symbols (either letters or numbers) may be used with an accompanying key.

Diagrams

A diagram is a plan, sketch, or outline, consisting primarily of lines and symbols. A diagram is designed to demonstrate or explain a process, object, or area, or to clarify the relationship existing among the parts of a whole. Diagrams are especially valuable for showing the shape and relative location of items and the manner in which equipment functions or operates (see the diagrams on pages 74 and 145). Too, diagrams are helpful in showing the principles involved in an operation or concept (as in defining horsepower, page 99).

Diagrams are indispensable in modern construction, engineering, and manufacturing. A typical example is the design for a fireplace in Figure 13.

Diagram

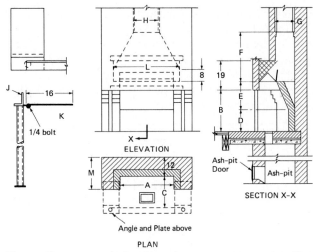

Figure 13. Proven design for a three-way, conventionally built fireplace. (Courtesy of Donley Brothers Co.)

Schematic Diagram

The schematic diagram, a specialized diagram, is an invaluable aid in various mechanical fields, particularly in electronics. As with all visuals, the schematic diagram, like that below and on page 338 of an electronic device, has standard symbols, terminology, and procedures that should be followed in its preparation.

Schematic Diagram

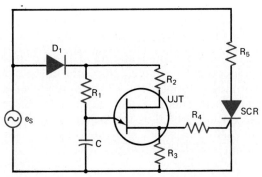

Figure 14. Basic circuit of an SCR controller.

EXHIBITS

Exhibits, particularly valuable in oral presentations, are designed as learning experiences that involve people, objects, or representations presented in orderly sequence. Among the most frequently used kinds of exhibits are demonstrations, displays, real objects, models, dioramas, posters, and the chalkboard. (See Chapter 10, Oral Communication, especially page 447.)

Demonstration

A demonstration describes, explains, or illustrates a procedure or idea. A demonstration provides realism, for it is an enactment of actual steps or aspects using real objects. For instance, an explanation of how to apply a tourniquet, a description of what happens when acid is applied to copper, or a discussion of Newton's law of gravity is more realistic to an audience if it is demonstrated. In the oral description of several models of staplers on page 69, the speaker uses demonstration to good advantage.

Display

A display is an arrangement of materials, such as photographs, news clippings, mobiles, or three-dimensional objects, designed to dramatize significant information or ideas. Often displays are presented on a bulletin board, flannel board, table, or similar area.

For an effective showing of displays, observe the following suggestions:

1. Plan the display around a specific theme.
2. Arrange the material so that it tells a story.
3. Use neat, clear lettering.
4. Show the material in an attractive setting with pleasing backgrounds and accessories.

Real Object

Real objects are especially effective in a presentation. More so than pictures, models, or other representations, real objects give immediacy. Both animate and inanimate, real objects provide an opportunity to show actual size, weight, sound, movement, and texture.

Model

A model is a three-dimensional representation of a real object. A model can be used when the real object is not available, is too large or too small, or is otherwise unsuitable for use with the presentation. Although models are of various types, generally they permit easy handling and convenient observation; they can provide interior views of objects; they can be stripped of some details so that other details can be easily observed; and they can be disassembled and put together to show the interrelationship of parts.

Diorama

A diorama is a three-dimensional scene of proportionately scaled objects and figures in a natural setting. A diorama is framed by a box, pieces of cardboard fastened together at right angles, or other such delineating devices. The diorama gives an in-depth, realistic view.

Dioramas are commonly used in museums, advertising displays, and instructional materials.

Poster

A poster is a very versatile visual aid, for it can contain a wide range of information and include a number of other visuals such as charts, photographs, pictures, drawings, and diagrams. In addition, anyone can design a good poster. (A poster is used in the oral presentation describing several models of staplers, page 69.)

In preparing a poster, review Using Visuals Effectively, pages 462–464, especially number 3, on preparing a visual. Remember that everything on a poster must be large enough for *all* viewers to see.

Chalkboard

The chalkboard, though not really an exhibit in itself, is one of the most convenient means for visually communicating information. The chalkboard can be erased quickly, and new material can be added as the learning sequence progresses. (The chalkboard is used in the outlining of steps in the oral presentation of how plywood is made, pages 42–43.)

When using a chalkboard, be sure to write large enough for all material to be visible from the rear of the room; develop one point at a time; remove or cover distracting material; and stand to one side when pointing out material.

PROJECTED MATERIALS

Projected materials are uniquely effective in oral presentations. (See Chapter 10, Oral Communication, especially page 447.) Among the most common projected materials are films, filmstrips, slides, and overhead-projected transparencies. These materials require a certain room illumination, a screen, and specialized projectors.

Film

Films, or more accurately motion pictures, are excellent, of course, for portraying the action and movement inherent in a subject. They present a sense of continuity and logical progression. And sound can be added easily. However, since the preparation of films requires specialized knowledge and is expensive in terms of time, equipment, and materials, commercially prepared 8-millimeter or 16-millimeter films are often borrowed, rented, or purchased.

Filmstrip

A filmstrip is a series of still pictures photographed in sequence on 35-millimeter film. They may be supplemented by captions on the frames (pictures), recorded narration, or script reading. Filmstrips are compact, easily handled, and, unlike slides, always in proper sequence. Although rather difficult to prepare locally, filmstrips from commercial producers are inexpensive and cover a wide array of topics.

Slide

Slides, usually 2 inches by 2 inches, are taken with a simple 35-millimeter camera; they provide colorful, realistic reproductions of original subjects. Exposed film is sent to a processing laboratory, which then returns the slides mounted and ready for projection. Also, sets of slides on particular topics can be purchased; these often are accompanied by taped narrations.

Slides are quite flexible: they are easily rearranged, revised, handled, and stored; and automatic and remotely controlled projectors are available for greater efficiency and effectiveness. If handled individually, however, slides can get out of order, be misplaced, or even be projected incorrectly.

Transparency

Transparencies have become quite popular in conveying information to groups of people. They are easy and inexpensive to prepare and to use, and the projector is simple to operate.

The overhead projector permits a speaker to stand facing an audience and project transparencies (sheets of acetate usually 8½ inches by 10 inches) onto a screen behind the speaker. The projection may be enlarged to fit the screen, so the speaker may more easily point to features or mark on the projected image. Room light is at a moderate level.

In preparing a transparency, you may write on the film with a grease pencil, India ink, or special acetate ink; or you may use a special copying machine.

GENERAL PRINCIPLES IN USING VISUALS

1. *Visuals can be extremely helpful.* They can capitalize on seeing, convey information, reduce textual explanation, and add interest.
2. *Effective use of visuals requires careful planning.* Appropriate selection, placement, and reference to visuals are crucial to their effective use. The visual should not include too much, should be pleasing to the eye, and should use lettering to good advantage.
3. *Credit should be given for borrowed material.* Whether an entire visual or simply the information is borrowed, credit should be given for the source.
4. *Layout of text on the page can visually aid the reader.* Such layout devices as headings, paragraphing, indentation, list formats, double columns, and ample white space can enhance a report.
5. *Computers have both simplified and expanded the production of graphic illustrations.*
6. *Tables present large amounts of data concisely.* Although tables lack eye appeal and interest-arousing dramatization, they are unexcelled as a method of organizing and depicting research data.
7. *Charts show relationships.* Common types of charts are the pie chart, the bar chart, the organization chart, and the flow chart.
8. *Graphs show change.* Graphs portray numerical data helpful in identifying trends, movements, and cycles.
9. *Photographs show actual appearance.* Photographs are of particular value as evidence in proving or showing what something is.

10. *Drawings and diagrams show isolated or interior views, exact details, and relationships.* Drawings and diagrams can be easily tailored to fit the needs of the user.
11. *Exhibits dramatize a concept or objects before an audience.* Frequently used kinds of exhibits are demonstrations, displays, real objects, models, dioramas, posters, and the chalkboard.
12. *Projected materials show pictures and other forms of information on a screen before an audience.* Common projected materials include films, filmstrips, slides, and overhead-projected transparencies.

APPLICATION 1 USING VISUALS

From periodicals, reports, brochures, government publications, etc., make a collection of ten visuals pertaining to your major field of study. If necessary, copy the visual from the source. Mount the visuals on sheets of paper, give the sources, and write a two- to three-sentence comment concerning each visual.

APPLICATION 2 USING VISUALS

Make a survey of 20 persons near your age concerning their preferences in automobiles: make, color, accessories. Present your findings in a table.

APPLICATION 3 USING VISUALS

From a bank or home finance agency, obtain the following information concerning a $30,000 house loan, a $40,000 house loan, and a $50,000 house loan:

Interest rate
Total monthly payment for a 20-year loan
Total interest for 20 years
Total cost of the house after 20 years
Cost of insurance for 20 years
Estimated taxes for 20 years

Present this information in a table.

APPLICATION 4 USING VISUALS

Present the following information in the form of a pie chart.

From Steer to Steak

Choice steer on hoof	1000 lbs
Dresses out 61.5%	615 lbs
Less fat, bone, and loss	183 lbs
Salable beef	432 lbs

APPLICATION 5 USING VISUALS

Prepare a pie chart depicting your expenses at college for a term. Indicate the total amount in dollars. Show the categories of expenses in percentages.

APPLICATION 6   USING VISUALS

> Roy McGowan is transportation maintenance supervisor for Denis County Public Schools. His salary is $20,000 per year. McGowan participates in a retirement plan into which annually he pays 5 percent of his salary, Denis County pays 4 percent of his salary, and the state pays 2 percent of his salary.

Prepare a bar chart showing the total amount in dollars paid annually in Mc-Gowan's retirement plan and the individual amounts paid by McGowan, by Denis County, and by the state.

APPLICATION 7   USING VISUALS

Make a bar chart showing the sources of income and areas of expenditure for a household, your college or some other institution, or a firm.

APPLICATION 8   USING VISUALS

Make an organization chart of the administrative personnel of your college or of some other institution or of the personnel in a firm.

APPLICATION 9   USING VISUALS

Make an organization chart of a club or organization with which you are familiar.

APPLICATION 10   USING VISUALS

Make a flow chart of the registration procedures or some other procedure in your college or of a procedure in your place of employment.

APPLICATION 11   USING VISUALS

Make a flow chart depicting from beginning to completion the flow of a process or product in your field of study.

APPLICATION 12   USING VISUALS

Construct a line graph depicting your growth in height *or* weight, or someone else's growth, for a ten-year period. (Make estimates if actual amounts are unknown.)

APPLICATION 13   USING VISUALS

Prepare a multiple-line graph showing the enrollment in your college and in another college in your area for the past ten years. If you are unable to obtain the exact enrollment figures, use your own estimates.

APPLICATION 14   USING VISUALS

Find two photographs (from your own collection; in newspapers, periodicals, etc.) that present evidence as only a photograph can. Write a brief comment about each photograph.

APPLICATION 15   USING VISUALS

Visualize a situation pertinent to your major field of study in which a photograph would be essential. Then find or make a suitable photograph. Finally, write a paragraph that describes the situation and include the photograph.

APPLICATION 16   USING VISUALS

Make a drawing of a piece of equipment used in your major field of study and indicate the major parts. Then write a paragraph identifying the piece of equipment and include the drawing.

APPLICATION 17   USING VISUALS

> The ancient Greek philosopher Aristotle thought that the heavier something is, the faster it falls to the ground. The Renaissance physicist Galileo discovered that this is not true. Rather, everything falls to the ground at the same rate; for example, a baseball and a lead cannon ball dropped from a tower would both hit the ground at the same time.

Make a drawing or diagram that illustrates this concept.

APPLICATION 18   USING VISUALS

Make a floor plan (diagram) of your living quarters, including the location of all pieces of furniture.

APPLICATION 19   USING VISUALS

Prepare an oral presentation in which you use exhibits and/or projected materials.

APPLICATION 20   USING VISUALS

Present the following information in an appropriate visual or visuals: Government service, one of the nation's largest fields of employment, provided jobs for 15 million civilian workers in 1984, about one out of six persons employed in the United States. Nearly four-fifths of these workers were employed by state or local governments, and more than one-fifth worked for the federal government.

APPLICATION 21   USING VISUALS

Select information from Table 3, page 466. Present the selected information in a nontable visual.

Table 4 Marital Status of Adults (Persons 14 years old and over)

Marital Status and Sex	1955*	1960	1970	1980
Total (millions)	107	114	147	168
Single (millions)	16	17	37	43
Married (millions)	79	84	94	104
Widowed (millions)	10	11	11	12
Divorced (millions)	2	3	5	10
Male, total (millions)	51	55	70	80
Percent distribution	100.0	100.0	100.0	100
Single	17.4	17.8	28.2	29.3
Married	76.1	76.0	66.6	63.4
Wife separated	1.5	1.7	1.3	1.3

Marital Status and Sex	1955*	1960	1970	1980
Male, total (cont.)				
Widowed	4.6	4.1	3.0	2.5
Divorced	1.9	2.1	2.2	4.8
Female, total (millions)	56	59	77	88
Percent distribution	100.0	100.0	100.0	100.0
Single	12.0	11.8	22.1	22.4
Married	71.9	71.3	62.0	59.0
Husband separated	2.5	2.2	2.2	2.8
Widowed	13.6	14.0	12.5	11.9
Divorced	2.4	2.9	3.5	6.6

* Excludes Alaska and Hawaii.
Source: U.S. Bureau of Census

APPLICATION 22   USING VISUALS

Select information from the table on page 484. Present the selected information in a nontable visual.

APPLICATION 23   USING VISUALS

Select any 15 consecutive pages in this book. Analyze the visuals (including layout and design).

   a. List the selected page numbers.
   b. List the various techniques used in layout and design.
   c. List the kinds of visuals included.
   d. Write a paragraph evaluating the effectiveness of the layout and design and the visuals.

APPLICATION 24   USING VISUALS

Look up your major field of study in the latest edition of *Occupational Outlook Handbook* (published biennially by the U.S. Department of Labor's Bureau of Labor Statistics). From the information given, prepare a report, using visuals where appropriate. Create your own visuals; do not merely copy the ones in the *Handbook.*

HANDBOOK

CHAPTER 1
   Grammatical Usage   489

CHAPTER 2
   Mechanics   521

The handbook consists of two chapters to be used as a guide to accepted practices in grammatical usage and mechanics. These practices, developed through the centuries, are conventions through which communication of meaning is made easier.

CHAPTER 1

Grammatical Usage

OBJECTIVES   490
INTRODUCTION   490
PARTS OF SPEECH: DEFINITION AND USAGE   490
 Adjectives   490
 Adverbs   491
 Conjunctions   492
 Interjections   493
 Nouns   493
 Prepositions   494
 Pronouns   495
 Verbs   497
 Verbals   499
PROBLEMS OF USAGE   500
 Sentence Fragments   500
 Parallelism in Sentences   501
 Run-on or Fused Sentence   502
 Comma Splice   503
 Shift in Focus   503
 Agreement of Pronoun and Antecedent   504
 Shifts in Person, Number, and Gender   505
 Agreement of Subject and Verb   505
 Modifiers   507
  Dangling Modifiers   507
  Dangling Elliptical Clauses   507
  Misplaced Modifiers   508
  Squinting Modifiers   508
EMPHASIS IN SENTENCES   509
WORDS OFTEN CONFUSED AND MISUSED   510
APPLICATIONS   518

OBJECTIVES

Upon completing this chapter, the student should be able to:

- Recognize and revise nonstandard English for communication in business, industry, and government
- Solve typical usage problems: sentence fragments; parallelism in sentences; run-on or fused sentence; comma splice; shift in focus; agreement of nouns; shifts in person, number, and gender; agreement of subject and verb; and use of modifiers
- Write sentences to emphasize certain material within the sentence.
- Select an appropriate word for a specific communication need

INTRODUCTION

English language usage varies and constantly changes. Attempts made to classify language according to its usage in different dialects (the form of language spoken in different geographical areas), social statuses, educational levels or styles (formal and informal) are all incomplete and overlapping. However, amid these differences in grammatical usage, there are generally accepted standard practices in business and industry.

Usage does make a difference. Select the usage most likely to get the desired results, recognizing that usages, like people, have different characteristics. For example, you say or write *I have known him a week* rather than *I have knowed him a week* because *I have known him a week* is more acceptable to most people. You base this decision, consciously or unconsciously, on the grammatical expressions of people you respect or of people with whom you want to "fit in," and on the reactions of people to these expressions.

Because judgments are based on knowledge, the following guides are designed to improve your judgment by increasing your knowledge of acceptable grammatical usages and word choice in standard English.

PARTS OF SPEECH: DEFINITION AND USAGE

A customary way of examining the English language is to divide the vocabulary into eight major divisions called parts of speech: adjectives, adverbs, conjunctions, interjections, nouns, prepositions, pronouns, and verbs. Added to these divisions in the following discussion is another group, called verbals.

Adjectives

Adjectives describe, limit, or qualify a noun or pronoun by telling "Which one?" "What kind?" or "How many?" An adjective may be a word, a phrase, or a clause.

DESCRIBING ADJECTIVE	the *gray* paint *with a yellow tint* (Tells "What kind?")
LIMITING ADJECTIVE	*three* pencils (Tells "How many?")
QUALIFYING ADJECTIVE	*younger* sister *who lives in Denver* (Tells "Which one?")

● Adjectives show degrees of comparison in quality, quantity, and manner by affixing *-er* and *-est* to the positive form or by adding *more* and *most* or *less* and *least* to the positive form.

Degrees of Comparison

POSITIVE	tall	beautiful	wise
COMPARATIVE	taller	more beautiful	less wise
SUPERLATIVE	tallest	most beautiful	least wise

The comparative degree is used when speaking of two things, and the superlative when speaking of three or more. One-syllable words generally add *-er* and *-est* while words of two or more syllables generally require *more* and *most*. To show degrees of inferiority, *less* and *least* are added.

● Do not use a double comparison such as *most beautifulest;* either *-est* or *most* makes the superlative degree, not both.

● Adjectives that indicate absolute qualities or conditions (such as *dead, round,* or *perfect*) cannot be compared. Thus: *dead, more nearly dead, most nearly dead* (not *deader, deadest*).

● Adjective clauses are punctuated according to the purpose they serve. If they are essential to the meaning of the sentence, they are not set off by commas. If they simply give additional information, they are set off from the rest of the sentence. (See comma usage, pages 533–534.) Adjective clauses beginning with *that* are essential and are not set off (with one exception: when *that* is used as a substitute for *which* to avoid repetition).

Edward Jenner is the man *who experimented with smallpox vaccination.* (Essential to meaning)
Bathrooms are often decorated in colors *that suggest water.* (Essential to meaning)
My ideas about exploration of space, *which are different from most of my friends' ideas,* were formulated mainly through reading. (Gives additional information)

Adverbs

Adverbs modify verbs, adjectives, or other adverbs by telling "When?" (time), "Where?" (place), "Why?" (reason), "How?" (manner), "How much?" (degree), or "How often?" (frequency). An adverb may be a word, a phrase, or a clause.

The class began *after everyone arrived.* (Tells "When?")
The recording session will take place *in Booth A.* (Tells "Where?")
Medical technicians often go to developing nations *to help the people.* (Tells "Why?")
Experienced salespeople can recognize a quality product *by inspection.* (Tells "How?")
In our laboratories we have containers of *very* clear plastic. (Tells "How much?")
The agricultural experts have a meeting *once a year* to exchange new knowledge. (Tells "How often?")

● Do not use an adjective when an adverb is needed.

> INCORRECT   The new employee did *good* on her first report. (Adverb needed)
> CORRECT   The new employee did *well* on her first report.
>
> INCORRECT   For a department to operate *smooth* and *efficient*, all employees must
>   cooperate. (Adverbs needed)
> CORRECT   For a department to operate *smoothly* and *efficiently*, all employees
>   must cooperate.

● Introductory adverb clauses are generally followed by a comma. Adverb
clauses at the end of a sentence are not set off. (See comma usage, page 534.)

> *Although most people agree clothes do not make the person,* they spend considerable
>   time and money dressing themselves in the latest fashions.
> *When the investigation is completed,* the company will make its decision.
> The company will make its decision *when the investigation is completed.*

Conjunctions

A conjunction connects words, phrases, or clauses. Conjunctions may be divided
into two general classes: coordinating conjunctions and subordinating conjunctions.

**1. COORDINATING CONJUNCTIONS—SUCH AS *AND, BUT, OR*—CONNECT
WORDS, PHRASES, OR CLAUSES OF EQUAL RANK.**

> I bought nails, brads, staples, *and* screws. (Connects nouns in a series)
> Nancy *or* Elaine will serve on the committee. (Connects nouns)

● Conjunctive adverbs—such as *however, moreover, therefore, consequently,
nevertheless*—are a kind of coordinating conjunction. They link the independent clause in which they occur to the preceding independent clause. The clause
they introduce is grammatically independent, but it depends on the preceding
clause for complete meaning. Note that a semicolon separates the independent
clauses (see semicolon usage, pages 536–537) and that the conjunctive adverb is
usually set off with commas (see comma usage, page 534).

> The film was produced and directed by students; other students, *therefore,* should
>   be interested in viewing the film.
> Jane had a severe cold; *consequently,* she was unable to participate in the computer
>   tournament.

● Correlative conjunctions—*either . . . or, neither . . . nor, both . . . and,
not only . . . but also*—are a kind of coordinating conjunction. Correlative
conjunctions are used in pairs to connect words, phrases, and clauses of equal
rank.

> The movie was *not only* well produced *but also* beautifully filmed.

● Be sure that the units joined by coordinate conjunctions are the same *grammatically.* (See also Coordination, page 112, and Parallelism in Sentences, pages
501–502.)

CONFUSING | Our store handles two kinds of drills—manual *and* electricity. (Adjective and noun)

REVISED | Our store handles two kinds of drills—manual *and* electric. (Adjective and adjective)

CONFUSING | I *either* will go today *or* tomorrow. (Verb and adverb)

REVISED | I will go *either* today *or* tomorrow. (Adverb and adverb)

● Be sure that the units joined by coordinate conjunctions are the same *logically*. (See also Coordination, page 112, and Parallelism in Sentences, pages 501–502.)

CONFUSING | I can't decide whether I want to be a lab technician, a nurse, *or* respiratory therapy. (Two people and a field of study)

REVISED | I can't decide whether I want to be a lab technician, a nurse, *or* a respiratory therapist. (Three people)

REVISED | I can't decide whether I want to study lab technology, nursing, *or* respiratory therapy. (Three fields of study)

2. SUBORDINATE CONJUNCTIONS—SUCH AS *WHEN, SINCE, BECAUSE, ALTHOUGH, AS, AS IF*—INTRODUCE SUBORDINATE CLAUSES.

Because the voltmeter was broken, we could not test the circuit.

The instructor gave credit for class participation *since the primary purpose of the course was to stimulate thought.*

Interjections

An interjection indicates sudden or strong feeling. It has no grammatical relationship to the sentence following, if there is one.

Ouch!

Darn!

Good grief, I dropped the thermometer.

Oh, you wouldn't believe what happened.

Nouns

Nouns name persons *(Ms. Jones)*, places *(Portland, Oregon)*, things *(motorcycle)*, actions *(sterilization)*, and qualities *(mercy)*. A noun may be a word, a phrase, or a clause.

The *record* sold one million *copies.*

Making my first record was a satisfying *experience.*

The *group* believed *that the record would be a hit.*

Note: The second and third sentences above may be analyzed in two ways. Generally, the italicized sections may be identified simply as nouns. More specifically, they may also be analyzed on the basis of elements within them. For example, *Making my first record* includes *making,* a gerund used as subject; *my,* a pronoun functioning as an adjective; *first,* adjective; *record,* a noun used as the object of *making.*

● Nouns can also be characterized by their ability to have an affix added to show possession or plurality.

> The *man's* overcoat protected him from the cold. (*man* + *'s* forms a possessive)
> *Experiences* teach vivid *lessons*. (*experience* and *lesson* add *s* to form plurals)

● Nouns have many uses in sentences:

SUBJECT   A noun identifying *who* or *what* the sentence is about.

Da Vinci invented the bicycle in 1493.

DIRECT OBJECT   A noun identifying *what* or *who* receives the action expressed by the verb.

Da Vinci's bicycle did not have *pedals*.

PREDICATE NOUN (also called PREDICATE NOMINATIVE and SUBJECTIVE COMPLEMENT)   A noun following a linking verb and referring to the subject of the sentence.

The inventor of the turbojet engine was *Sir Frank Whittle*.

INDIRECT OBJECT   The noun identifying *to whom (what, which)* or *for whom (what, which)* the action expressed by the verb is done. If the *to* or *for* appears in the sentence, the indirect object becomes a prepositional phrase.

INDIRECT OBJECT   The children gave *Spot* a bath.
                       He gave the *plan* a second chance.
                       They bought *him* a new leash.
PREPOSITIONAL PHRASE   They bought a new leash *for him*.

OBJECT OF PREPOSITION   The noun answering the question "What?" following a preposition.

The first step in the *procedure* is sanding the wood surface.

APPOSITIVE   The noun following another noun or pronoun and renaming that noun or pronoun.

My gift to John, my oldest *brother*, was a calculator.

OBJECTIVE COMPLEMENT   The noun (or adjective) following a direct object, referring to the direct object and completing its meaning.

The employees selected Sarah Smith *spokesperson*.

Prepositions

Traditionally a preposition (such as *in, by, to, with, at, into, over*) is a word that precedes a noun or a pronoun and shows its relationship to some other word in the sentence, generally a noun, adjective, or verb. A preposition is also a function word whose form does not change; the importance of the preposition lies in its grammatical function, not in its meaning. A prepositional phrase is composed of the preposition, its object, and any modifiers with them. It functions as an adjective, adverb, or noun.

> The tools *on the shelves* need dusting. (Adjective)
> Most commuting students live *at home*. (Adverb)
> *Under the mattress* is our hiding place. (Noun)

● A preposition may end a sentence when any other placement of the preposition would result in a clumsy, unnatural sentence.

UNNATURAL   Sex is a topic *about* which many people think.
NATURAL   Sex is a topic which many people think *about*.

Pronouns

A pronoun takes the place of or refers to a noun.

> *They* worked overtime.
> *Who* is *that?*
> *She* gave the tube to *him*.
> *These* belong to *someone*.

● The personal pronouns and *who* have different forms, or cases, for different uses in the sentence. These pronoun forms divide into three groups—nominative case, objective case, and possessive case.

  1. Nominative case forms

	Singular	*Plural*
FIRST PERSON	I	we
SECOND PERSON	you	you
THIRD PERSON	he, she, it	they
	who, whoever	who, whoever

Nominative case forms may be used in the following ways:

Subject of Dependent or Independent Clauses

We know about bacteria because of the microscope.
A student hands in an assignment when *it* is completed.
Ferdinand Cohn, *who* was a German botanist, worked out the first scheme for classifying bacteria as plants rather than as animals.

Subjective Complement (Predicate Pronoun) Following a Linking Verb

(Linking verbs include forms of "to be" and such verbs as *appear, seem, remain, become*.)

The delegates to the convention are *he* and *she*.
The most qualified applicant seemed to be *I*.

Appositive Following a Subject or a Subjective Complement

Two students, *Joan* and *I*, received awards for achievement.
The representatives to the DECA convention are club members *Dale* and *I*.

2. Objective case forms

	Singular	*Plural*
FIRST PERSON	me	us
SECOND PERSON	you	you
THIRD PERSON	her, him, it	them
	whom, whomever	whom, whomever

Objective case forms may be used in the following ways:

Direct Object of a Verb or of a Verbal (Infinitive, Participle, Gerund)

The flying chips hit *me* in the face. (Object of verb *hit*)
The artist carefully handled the clay, shaping *it* so that it did not crack. (Object of verbal *shaping*)

Indirect Object

The flight attendant told *them* the reason for the change in plans.

Object of Preposition

Persons like Marie and *him* will make excellent workers.
Give the plans only to Jack or *me*.

Subject of Infinitive

I believe *her* to be the best choice.
Let *me* help Tom.

Appositive Following a Direct Object, Indirect Object, Object of a Preposition, or Subject of an Infinitive

We gave the article to the editors, James and *him*.

3. Possessive case forms

	Singular	*Plural*
FIRST PERSON	my, mine	our, ours
SECOND PERSON	your, yours	your, yours
THIRD PERSON	his, her, hers, its	their, theirs
	whose, whosever	whose, whosever

Possessive pronoun forms are used in the following way:

Show Ownership or Possession

Pasteur was also experimenting while Koch and *his* disciples were busy perfecting new techniques.
Whose guitar is this?

● Compound personal pronouns are formed by combining personal pronoun forms with *-self* or *-selves: myself, yourself, herself, himself, itself, ourselves, yourselves,* and *themselves.*

● Avoid using *myself* in the place of *I* or *me*.

INCORRECT	Mother or *myself* will be present.
CORRECT	Mother or *I* will be present.

INCORRECT   Reserve the conference room for the supervisor and *myself*.
CORRECT   Reserve the conference room for the supervisor and *me*.

- Never use *themself, theirselves,* and *hisself;* they are not acceptable forms.

CORRECT   The members of the team *themselves* voted not to go.
CORRECT   Henry cut *himself*.

Verbs

Verbs indicate state of being or express action.

That machine *is* a very expensive piece of equipment. (State of being)
The engineer *studied* the local water problem carefully. (Action)

- Verb tense indicates the time of the state of being or action. There are six tenses.

1. Present tense verbs indicate action taking place now or continuing action. There are three kinds of present tense: simple present, emphatic present, and progressive present.

I *work* eight hours a day. (Simple present tense)
I *do work* eight hours a day. (Emphatic present tense)
I *am working* eight hours a day. (Progressive present tense)

2. Past tense verbs indicate action completed before the present time. There are three kinds of past tense: simple past, emphatic past, and progressive past.

I *worked* eight hours a day. (Simple past tense)
I *did work* eight hours a day. (Emphatic past tense)
I *was working* eight hours a day. (Progressive past tense)

3. Future tense verbs indicate action that will occur sometime in the future, that is, sometime after the present. There are two kinds of future tense: simple future and progressive future.

I *will work* eight hours a day. (Simple future tense)
I *will be working* eight hours a day. (Progressive future tense)

4. Present perfect tense verbs indicate action completed prior to the present but connected in some way with the present or action begun in the past and continuing in the present. There are two kinds of present perfect tense: simple present perfect and progressive present perfect.

I *have worked* eight hours a day. (Simple present perfect tense)
I *will have been working* eight hours a day. (Progressive present perfect tense)

5. Past perfect tense verbs indicate action completed prior to some stated past time. There are two kinds of past perfect tense: simple past perfect and progressive past perfect.

I *had worked* eight hours a day. (Simple past perfect tense)
I *had been working* eight hours a day. (Progressive past perfect tense)

6. Future perfect tense verbs indicate action to be completed prior to some stated future time. There are two kinds of future perfect tense: simple future perfect and progressive future perfect.

I *will have worked* eight hours a day. (Simple future perfect tense)
I *will have been working* eight hours a day. (Progressive future perfect tense)

● Do not needlessly shift from one tense to another. Since verb tenses tell the reader when the action is happening, inconsistent verb tenses confuse the reader.

SHIFTED VERBS (CONFUSING)   As time *passed*, technology *becomes* more complex.

passed—past tense verb
becomes—present tense verb

Since the two indicated actions occur at the same time, the verbs should be in the same tense.

CONSISTENT VERBS   As time *passed*, technology *became* more complex.
CONSISTENT VERBS   As time *passes*, technology *becomes* more complex.

passed
became—past tense verbs

passes
becomes—present tense verbs

SHIFTED VERBS (CONFUSING)   While I *was installing* appliances last summer, I *had learned* that customers appreciate promptness.

was installing—past tense verb
had learned—past perfect tense verb

The verb phrase *was installing* indicates a past action in progress while the verb phrase *had learned* indicates an action completed prior to some stated past time. To indicate that both actions were in the past, the sentence might be written as follows:

CONSISTENT VERBS   While I *was installing* appliances last summer, I *learned* that customers appreciate promptness.

was installing
learned—past tense verbs

● Verbs have two voices, active and passive.

1. The active voice indicates action done by the subject. The active voice is forceful and emphatic.

Roentgen *won* the Nobel Prize for his discovery of X rays.
Meat slightly marbled with fat *tastes* better.
The scientist *thinks*.

2. The passive voice indicates action done to the subject. The recipient of the action receives more emphasis than the doer of the action. A passive voice verb is always at least two words, a form of the verb *to be* and the past participle (third principal part) of the main verb.

My husband's surgery *was performed* by Dr. Petro Vanetti.
Logarithm tables *are found* on page 210.

See also pages 9–10, 510.

● Choose the voice of the verb that permits the desired emphasis.

ACTIVE VOICE   The ballistics experts *examined* the results of the tests. (Emphasis on *ballistics experts*)
PASSIVE VOICE   The results of the tests *were examined* by the ballistics experts. (Emphasis on *results of the tests*)
ACTIVE VOICE   Juan *gave* the report. (Emphasis on *Juan*)
PASSIVE VOICE   The report *was given* by Juan. (Emphasis on *report*)

● Avoid needlessly shifting from the active to the passive voice.

NEEDLESS SHIFT IN VOICE (CONFUSING)   Management and labor representatives *discussed* the pay raise, but no decision *was reached*.

discussed—active voice
was reached—passive voice

CONSISTENT VOICE   Management and labor representatives *discussed* the pay raise, but they *reached* no decision.

$\dfrac{discussed}{reached}$ —active voice

Verbals

Verbals are formed from verbs and are used as modifiers or naming words.

The trees *planted on the slope* have prevented further erosion. (Modifier)
The persons who wanted *to scale the mountain* have done so. (Naming word)
Delegating authority is a simple and natural process. (Naming word)

Verbals are divided into three groups—participles, gerunds, and infinitives.

● Participles are verb forms that function as adjectives, and they have three forms: present participle (ends in *-ing*), past participle (ends in *-d, -ed, -n, -en*, or *-t*), and present perfect participle (*having* plus the past participle).

Designing his own home, the architect used an ultramodern decor.
Pictures *produced by colored light* may replace painted pictures in future homes.
Having completed the experiment, I was convinced that silver was a better conductor than copper.

Participles that are not necessary to identify the word modified are set off by commas. (See comma usage, pages 533–534.) Participles that identify the noun modified are *not* set off by commas.

Mr. Owens, *presiding at the council meeting*, called for the committee's report.
A picture *improperly mounted and insecurely fastened* may come loose from the mounting and fall to the floor.

Participles introducing a sentence are set off by a comma. (See comma usage, page 534.)

> *Representing the company*, the salesmen can sign contracts.

● Gerunds are verb forms that end in *-ing, -d, -ed, -n, -en,* or *-t* and that function as nouns.

> *Measuring the pattern* is necessary for proper fit.
> The *unrecognized* are often the backbone of a company.

● Infinitives are verb forms that function as nouns, adjectives, or adverbs, depending on their use in a sentence. There are two forms of the infinitive: present (*to* plus first principal part of main verb) and present perfect (*to* plus *have* plus the third principal part of the main verb).

> My purpose is *to become involved in ecological discussion.* (Noun)
> By the first of the year I hope *to have completed the tests.* (Noun)
> This is the equipment *to be returned.* (Adjective)
> *To prevent injury to the worker or damage to materials*, safe practice must be
>   observed at all times. (Adverb)

The *to* sign of an infinitive is sometimes omitted for the sake of conventional sentence sense.

> We saw him *perform.*
> Let them *go* when they have finished.

Introductory infinitive phrases used as adjectives or adverbs are usually followed by a comma. (See comma usage, page 534.)

> *To secure the most satisfactory results*, buy a good quality material.
> *To choose the best job*, Lin first talked with an employment counselor.

PROBLEMS OF USAGE

The following section is designed to help you solve typical usage problems: sentence fragments; parallelism in sentences; run-on or fused sentences; comma splice; shift in focus; agreement of pronoun and antecedent; shifts in person, number, and gender; agreement of subject and verb; and modifiers.

Sentence Fragments

A group of words containing a subject and a verb and standing alone as an independent group of words is a sentence. If a group of words lacks a subject or a verb or cannot stand alone as an independent group of words, it is called a sentence fragment. Sentence fragments generally occur because:

● A noun (subject) followed by a dependent clause or phrase is written as a sentence. The omitted unit is the verb.

> FRAGMENT   The engineer's scale, which is graduated in the decimal system.
> FRAGMENT   Colors that are opposite.

To make the sentence fragment into an acceptable sentence, add the verb and any modifiers needed to complete the meaning.

SENTENCE   The engineer's scale, which is graduated in the decimal system, is often called the decimal scale.
SENTENCE   Colors that are opposite on the color circle are used in a complementary color scheme.

● Dependent clauses or phrases are written as complete sentences. These are introductory clauses and phrases that require an independent clause.

FRAGMENT   While some pencil tracings are made from a drawing placed underneath the tracing paper.
FRAGMENT   Another development that has promoted the recognition of management.

To make the fragments into sentences, add the independent clause.

SENTENCE   While some pencil tracings are made from a drawing placed underneath the tracing paper, most drawings today are made directly on pencil tracing paper, cloth, vellum, or bond paper.
SENTENCE   Another development that has promoted the recognition of management is the separation of ownership and management.

Acceptable Fragments   There are occasions when types of fragments are acceptable.

Emphasis

Open the window. Right now.

Transition between ideas in a paragraph or composition

Now to the next point to be discussed.

Dialogue

"How many different meals have been planned for next month?"
"About ten."

Parallelism in Sentences

Parallel structure involves getting like ideas into like constructions. A coordinate conjunction, for example, joins ideas that must be stated in the same grammatical form. Other examples: an adjective should be parallel with an adjective, a verb with a verb, an adverb clause with an adverb clause, and an infinitive phrase with an infinitive phrase. Parallel structure in grammar helps to make parallel meaning clear.

A *typewriter,* a *table,* and a *filing cabinet* were delivered today. (Nouns in parallel structure)
Whether you accept the outcome of the experiment or *whether I accept it* depends on our individual interpretation of the facts. (Dependent clauses in parallel structure)

Failure to express each of the ideas in the same grammatical form results in faulty parallelism.

FAULTY   This study should help the new spouse *in budgeting* and *to learn* homemaking skills. (Prepositional phrase and infinitive phrase)

REVISED   This study should help the new spouse *in budgeting* and *in learning homemaking skills.* (Prepositional phrases in parallel structure)

FAULTY   Three qualities of tungsten steel alloys are *strength, ductility,* and *they have to be tough.* (Noun, noun, and independent clause)

REVISED   Three qualities of tungsten steel alloys are *strength, ductility,* and *toughness.* (Nouns in parallel structure)

FAULTY   The best lighting in a study room can be obtained *if windows are placed in the north side, if tables are placed so that the light comes over the student's left shoulder,* and *by painting the ceiling a very light color.* (Dependent clause, dependent clause, phrase)

REVISED   The best lighting in a study room can be obtained *if windows are placed in the north side, if tables are placed so that the light comes over the student's left shoulder,* and *if the ceiling is painted a very light color.* (Dependent clauses in parallel structure)

See also Chapter 4, Analysis Through Classification and Partition, especially Coordination, page 112; and Coordinating Conjunctions, pages 492–493.

Run-on or Fused Sentence

The run-on or fused sentence occurs when two sentences are written with no punctuation to separate them. (See also Comma Splice below.)

The evaluation of the Automated Drafting System is encouraging we expect to operate the automated system in an efficient and profitable manner.

Obviously the sentence above needs some punctuation to make it understandable. Several methods could be used to make it into an acceptable form:

(a) Period between "encouraging" and "we"

The evaluation of the Automated Drafting System is encouraging. We expect to operate the automated system in an efficient and profitable manner.

(b) Semicolon between "encouraging" and "we"

The evaluation of the Automated Drafting System is encouraging; we expect to operate the automated system in an efficient and profitable manner.

(c) Comma plus "and" between "encouraging" and "we"

The evaluation of the Automated Drafting System is encouraging, and we expect to operate the automated system in an efficient and profitable manner.

(d) Recasting the sentence

Since the evaluation of the Automated Drafting System is encouraging, we expect to operate the automated system in an efficient and profitable manner.

See also Punctuation, especially usage of the period, the comma, and the semicolon, pages 531, 532, 533, 534, 536–537.

Comma Splice

The comma splice occurs when a comma is used to connect, or splice together, two sentences. The comma splice, a common error in sentence punctuation, is also called the comma fault. (See also Run-on or Fused Sentence above.)

> Mahogany is a tropical American timber tree, its wood turns reddish brown at maturity.

The comma splice in the above sentence may be corrected by several methods:

(a) Replacing the comma with a period

> Mahogany is a tropical American timber tree. Its wood turns reddish brown at maturity.

(b) Replacing the comma with a semicolon

> Mahogany is a tropical American timber tree; its wood turns reddish brown at maturity.

(c) Adding a coordinate conjunction, such as "and"

> Mahogany is a tropical American timber tree, and its wood turns reddish brown at maturity.

(d) Recasting the sentence

> Mahogany is a tropical American timber tree whose wood turns reddish brown at maturity.

Shift in Focus

The writer may begin a sentence that expresses one thought but, somehow, by the end of the sentence has unintentionally shifted the focus. Consider this sentence:

> There are several preparatory steps in spray painting a house, which is easy to mess up if you are not careful.

The focus in the first half of the sentence is on preparatory steps in spray painting a house; the focus in the second half is on how easy it is to mess up when spray painting a house. Somehow, in the middle of the sentence, the writer shifted the focus of the sentence. The result is a sentence that is confusing to the reader.

To correct such a sentence, the writer should think through the intended purpose and emphasis of the sentence and should review preceding and subsequent sentences. The poorly written sentence above might be divided into two sentences:

> There are several preparatory steps in spray painting a house. Failure to follow these steps may result in a messed-up paint job.

or might be recast as one sentence:

> Following several preparatory steps in spray painting a house will help to keep you from messing up.

or

> To help assure satisfactory results when spray painting a house, follow these preparatory steps.

Agreement of Pronoun and Antecedent

Pronouns take the place of or refer to nouns. They provide a good way to economize in writing. For example, writing a paper on Anthony van Leeuwenhoek's pioneer work in developing microscopes, you could use the pronoun forms *he*, *his*, and *him* to refer to Leeuwenhoek rather than repeat his name numerous times. Since pronouns take the place of or refer to nouns, there must be number (singular or plural) agreement between the pronoun and its antecedent (the word the pronoun stands for or refers to).

● A singular antecedent requires a singular pronoun; a plural antecedent requires a plural pronoun.

> NONAGREEMENT   Gritty ink *erasers* should be avoided because *it* invariably damages the working surface of the paper.
>
> AGREEMENT   Gritty ink *erasers* should be avoided because *they* invariably damage the working surface of the paper.

● Two or more subjects joined by *and* must be referred to by a plural pronoun.

> The *business manager* and the *accountant* will plan *their* budget.

● Two or more singular subjects joined by *or* or *nor* must be referred to by singular pronouns.

> *Ms. Pullen* or *Ms. Merton* has left *her* purse.
> Neither *Mr. Conway* nor *Mr. Freeman* will appear to give *his* report.

● Nouns such as *part, rest,* and *remainder* may be singular or plural. The number is determined by a phrase following the noun.

> The *remainder* of the *students* asked that *their* grades be mailed.
> The *rest* of the coffee was stored in *its* own container.

● The indefinite pronouns *each, every, everyone* and *everybody, nobody, either, neither, one, anyone* and *anybody,* and *someone* and *somebody* are singular and thus have singular pronouns referring to them.

> *Each* of the sorority members has indicated *she* wishes *her* own room.
> *Neither* of the machines has *its* motor repaired.

● The indefinite pronouns *both, many, several,* and *few* are plural; these forms require plural pronouns.

> *Several* realized *their* failure was the result of not studying.
> *Both* felt that nothing could save *them.*

● Still other indefinite pronouns—*most, some, all, none, any,* and *more*—may be either singular or plural. Usually a phrase following the indefinite pronoun will reveal whether the pronoun is singular or plural in meaning.

> *Most* of the *patients* were complimentary of *their* nurses.
> *Most* of the *money* was returned to *its* owner.

Shifts in Person, Number, and Gender

Avoid shifting from one person to another, from one number to another, or from one gender to another—such shifting creates confusing, awkward constructions.

SHIFT IN PERSON When *I* was just an apprentice welder, the boss expected *you* to know all the welding processes. (*I* is first person; *you* is second person)

REVISION When *I* was just an apprentice welder, the boss expected *me* to know all the welding processes.

SHIFT IN NUMBER *Each* person in the space center control room watched *his* dial anxiously. *They* thought the countdown to "0" would never come. (*Each* and *his* are singular pronouns; *they* is plural)

REVISION *Each* person in the space center control room watched *his* dial anxiously and thought the countdown to "0" would never come.

SHIFT IN GENDER The mewing of my cat told me *it* was hungry, so I gave *her* some food. (*It* is neuter; *her* is feminine)

REVISION The mewing of my cat told me *she* was hungry, so I gave *her* some food.

Agreement of Subject and Verb

A subject and verb agree in person and number. Person denotes person speaking (first person), person spoken to (second person), and person spoken of (third person). The person used determines the verb form that follows.

Present Tense

FIRST PERSON	I go	we go	I am	we are
SECOND PERSON	you go	you go	you are	you are
THIRD PERSON	he goes	they go	he is	they are
IMPERSONAL	one goes		one is	

● A subject and verb agree in number; that is, a plural subject requires a plural verb and a singular subject requires a singular verb.

The *symbol* for Hydrogen *is* H. (Singular subject; singular verb)
Comic *strips are* often vignettes of real-life situations. (Plural subject; plural verb)

● A compound subject requires a plural verb.

Employees and *employers work* together to formulate policies.

● The pronoun *you* as subject, whether singular or plural in meaning, takes a plural verb.

You were assigned the duties of staff nurse on fourth floor.
Since *you are* new technicians, *you are* to be paid weekly.

● In a sentence containing both a positive and a negative subject, the verb agrees with the positive.

The *employees,* not the *manager, were asked* to give their opinions regarding working conditions. (Positive subject plural; verb plural)

- If two subjects are joined by *or* or *nor,* the verb agrees with the nearer subject.

  > *Graphs* or a *diagram aids* the interpretation of statistical reports. (Subject nearer verb singular; verb singular)
  > A *graph* or *diagrams aid* the interpretation of this statistical report. (Subject nearer verb plural; verb plural)

- A word that is plural in form but names a single object or idea requires a singular verb.

  > The *United States has changed* from an agricultural to a technical economy.
  > Twenty-five *dollars was offered* for any usable suggestion.
  > Six *inches is* the length of the narrow rule.

- The term *the number* generally takes a singular verb; *a number* takes a plural verb.

  > *The number* of movies attended each year by the average American *has decreased.*
  > *A number* of modern inventions *are* the product of the accumulation of vast storehouses of smaller, minor discoveries.

- When followed by an *of* phrase, *all, more, most, some,* and *part;* fractions; and percentages take a singular verb if the object of the *of* is singular and a plural verb if the object of the *of* is plural.

  > *Two-thirds* of his *discussion was* irrelevant. (Object of *of* phrase, *discussion,* is singular; verb is singular)
  > *Some* of the *problems* in a college environment *require* careful analysis by both faculty and students. (Object of *of* phrase, *problems,* is plural; verb is plural)

- Elements that come between the subject and the verb ordinarily do not affect subject-verb agreement.

  > *One* of the numbers *is* difficult to represent because of the great number of zeros necessary.
  > Such *factors* as temperature, available food, age of organism, or nature of the suspending medium *influence* the swimming speed of a given organism.

- Occasionally the subject may follow the verb, especially in sentences beginning with the expletives *there* or *here;* however, such word order does not change the subject-verb agreement. (The expletives *there* and *here,* in their usual meaning, are never subjects.)

  > There *are* two common temperature *scales:* Fahrenheit and Celsius.
  > There *is* a great *deal* of difference in the counseling techniques used by contemporary ministers.
  > Here *are* several *types* of film.

- The introductory phrase *It is* or *It was* is always singular, regardless of what follows.

  > *It is* these problems that overwhelm me.
  > *It was* the officers who met.

● Relative pronouns *(who, whom, whose, which, that)* may require a singular or a plural verb, depending on the antecedent of the relative pronoun.

> She is one of those people *who keep* calm in an emergency. (Antecedent of *who* is *people*, a plural form; verb plural)
> The earliest lab *that is* offered is at 11:00. (Antecedent of *that* is *lab*, a singular form; verb singular)

Modifiers

Modifiers are words, phrases, or clauses, either adjective or adverb, that limit or restrict other words in the sentence. Careless construction and placement of these modifiers may cause problems such as dangling modifiers, dangling elliptical clauses, misplaced modifiers, and squinting modifiers.

Dangling Modifiers Dangling modifiers or dangling phrases occur when the word the phrase should modify is hidden within the sentence or is missing.

WORD HIDDEN IN SENTENCE	Holding the bat tightly, the ball was hit by the boy. (Implies that the ball was holding the bat tightly)
REVISION	Holding the bat tightly, the boy hit the ball.
WORD MISSING	By placing a thermometer under the tongue for approximately three minutes, a fever can be detected. (Implies that a fever places a thermometer under the tongue)
REVISION	By placing a thermometer under the tongue for approximately three minutes, anyone can tell if a person has a fever.

● To correct dangling modifiers, either rewrite the sentence so that the word modified by the phrase immediately follows the phrase (this word is usually the subject of the sentence) or rewrite the sentence by changing the phrase to a dependent clause.

DANGLING MODIFIER	*Driving down Main Street,* the city auditorium came into view.
SENTENCE REWRITTEN TO CLARIFY WORD MODIFIED	Driving down Main Street, I saw the city auditorium.
SENTENCE REWRITTEN WITH A DEPENDENT CLAUSE	As I was driving down Main Street, the city auditorium came into view.

Dangling Elliptical Clauses In elliptical clauses some words are understood rather than stated. For example, the dependent clause in the following sentence is elliptical: *When measuring the temperature of a conductor, you must use the Celsius scale;* the subject and part of the verb have been omitted. The understood subject of an elliptical clause is the same as the subject of the sentence. This is true in the example: *When (you are) measuring the temperature of a conductor, you must use the Celsius scale.* If the understood subject of the elliptical clause is not the same as the subject of the sentence, the clause is a dangling clause.

DANGLING CLAUSE	*When using an electric saw,* safety glasses should be worn.
REVISION	When using an electric saw, wear safety glasses.

• Dangling elliptical clauses may be corrected by either including within the clause the missing words or rewriting the main sentence so that the stated subject of the sentence and the understood subject of the clause will be the same.

DANGLING CLAUSE	*After changing the starter switch,* the car still would not start.
SENTENCE REVISED; MISSING WORDS INCLUDED	After *the mechanic* changed the starter switch, the car still would not start.
SENTENCE REVISED; UNDERSTOOD SUBJECT AND STATED SUBJECT THE SAME	After changing the starter switch, the *mechanic* still could not start the car.

Misplaced Modifiers   Place modifiers near the word or words modified. If the modifier is correctly placed, there should be no confusion. If the modifier is incorrectly placed, the intended meaning of the sentence may not be clear.

MISPLACED MODIFIER	The machinist placed the work to be machined in the drill press vise *called the workpiece.*
CORRECTLY PLACED MODIFIER	The machinist placed the work to be machined, *called the workpiece,* in the drill press vise.
MISPLACED MODIFIER	Where are the shirts for children *with snaps?*
CORRECTLY PLACED MODIFIER	Where are the children's shirts *with snaps?*

Squinting Modifiers   A modifier should clearly limit or restrict *one* sentence element. If a modifier is so placed within a sentence that it can be taken to limit or restrict either of two elements, the modifier is squinting; that is, the reader cannot tell which way the modifier is looking.

SQUINTING MODIFIER	When the student began summer work *for the first time* he was expected to follow orders promptly and exactly. (The modifying phrase could belong to the clause that precedes it or to the clause that follows it.)

Punctuation may solve the problem. The sentence might be written in either of the following ways, depending on the intended meaning.

REVISION	When the student began summer work *for the first time,* he was expected to follow orders promptly and exactly.
REVISION	When the student began summer work, *for the first time* he was expected to follow orders promptly and exactly.

• Squinting modifiers often are corrected by shifting their position in the sentence. Sentence meaning determines placement of the modifier.

SQUINTING MODIFIER	The students were advised *when it was midmorning* the new class schedule would go into effect.
REVISION	*When it was midmorning,* the students were advised that the new class schedule would go into effect.
REVISION	The students were advised that the new class schedule would go into effect *when it was midmorning.*

• Particularly difficult for some writers is the correct placement of *only, almost,* and *nearly.* These words generally should be placed immediately before the word they modify, since changing position of these words within a sentence changes the meaning of the sentence.

> In the reorganization of the district the congressman *nearly* lost a hundred voters. (Didn't lose any voters)
> In the reorganization of the district the congressman lost *nearly* a hundred voters. (Lost almost one hundred voters)
> The customer *only* wanted to buy soldering wire. (Emphasizes *wanted*)
> The customer wanted to buy *only* soldering wire. (Emphasizes *soldering wire*)

EMPHASIS IN SENTENCES

In sentence construction, important parts of the sentence should stand out and less important parts should be subordinate. In the English sentence, word order controls emphasis.

1. Put material to be emphasized either at the beginning or at the end of the sentence.

   EXAMPLES

   The *tape rule* is a common measuring device in the machine shop.
   A common measuring device in the machine shop is the *tape rule.*
   In the machine shop a common measuring device is the *tape rule.*

2. Emphasize important details by putting them in independent clauses and subordinate the less important details in dependent clauses and phrases.

   EXAMPLES

   The dimensions on a blueprint, which are given in terms of a fraction, *are called scale dimensions.* (Dependent clause)

   Note: A dependent clause or phrase that gives additional information not essential to the basic sentence meaning is set off by commas. (See Nonrestrictive Modifiers, pages 533–534.)

   The generator acts like an electron pump, causing electrons to flow through the circuit provided by the wire in the direction indicated by the arrow. (Participial phrase)

   One method for treating posts, called double diffusion, *is fairly inexpensive and can be done on the farm.* (Participial phrase)

   The roping type of saddletree, as the name implies, *is used by professional ropers.* (Dependent clause)

   The vernier caliper, one of the machinist's most versatile precision instruments, *is used to take either inside or outside measurements accurate to .001 of an inch.* (Phrase used as appositive)

3. Invert the normal order of the sentence to gain emphasis.

   EXAMPLES

   Unexpected was the reaction to the new plant rules.
   Fragile and brittle is the tap tool.

4. Add emphasis by placing the adjective after the noun modified instead of before it.

EXAMPLES

Helium is a gas, *light, inert,* and *colorless.*
The drill press, *dangerous when not properly operated,* is commonly employed for drilling holes.
The personnel manager, *tired and hungry,* interviewed the final applicant.
The tap tool, *fragile and brittle,* is easily broken.

5. Add emphasis by using verbs in the active voice.

EXAMPLES

The Greeks first *noticed* that lodestones had a peculiar and invisible quality they named magnetism.
The candidate *realized* her campaign was a risk.
The column *supports* the head and the table of the drill press.
Use of an iron centerpiece or core greatly *increases* the magnetizing effect of a wire loop.
The resistance of most conductors *increases* if the temperature of the conductor increases.
To convert from Fahrenheit to Centigrade, *subtract* 32 from the Fahrenheit value and *multiply* the remainder by 5/9.

Active voice verbs are usually stronger than passive voice verbs because the emphasis is on action; the writer mentions who or what is being talked about first. However, passive voice verbs sometimes may be used more emphatically. (The passive verb includes a form of *be* plus the past participle of the main verb.)

a. When the who or what is not as significant as the action or the result, use passive voice.

EXAMPLE

The shop *has been* burglarized again. (More emphatic than "Someone has burglarized the shop again.")

b. When the who or what is unknown, preferably unnamed, or relatively insignificant, use passive voice.

EXAMPLES

The strike *was begun* yesterday.
The artificial heart *was implanted* by a world renowned surgeon.
Comfortable working conditions *are provided* in the contract.

WORDS OFTEN CONFUSED AND MISUSED

Here is a list of often confused and misused words, with suggestions for their proper use.

a, an *A* is used before words beginning with a consonant sound; *an* is used before words with a vowel sound. (Remember: Consider sound, not spelling.)

> EXAMPLES   This is *a* banana.
> This is *an* orange.

accept, except *Accept* means "to take an object or idea offered" or "to agree to something"; *except* means "to leave out" or "excluding."

> EXAMPLES   Please *accept* this gift.
> Everyone *except* Joe may leave.

access, excess *Access* is a noun meaning "way of approach" or "admittance"; *excess* means "greater amount than required or expected."

> EXAMPLES   The children were not allowed *access* to the laboratory.
> His income is in *excess* of $50,000.

ad *Ad* is a shortcut to writing *advertisement.* In formal writing, however, write out the full word. In informal writing and speech, such abbreviated forms as *ad, auto, phone, photo,* and *TV* may be acceptable.

advice, advise *Advice* is a noun meaning "opinion given," "suggestions"; *advise* is a verb meaning "to suggest," "to recommend."

> EXAMPLES   We accepted the lawyer's *advice.*
> The lawyer *advised* us to drop the charges.

affect, effect *Affect* as a verb means "to influence" or "to pretend"; as a noun, it is a psychological term meaning "feeling" or "emotion." *Effect* as a verb means "to make something happen"; as a noun, it means "result" or "consequence."

> EXAMPLES   The colors used in a home may *affect* the prospective buyer's decision to buy.
> The new technique will *effect* change in the entire procedure.

aggravate, irritate *Aggravate* means "to make worse or more severe." Avoid using *aggravate* to mean "to irritate" or "to vex," except perhaps in informal writing or speech.

ain't A contraction for *am not, are not, has not, have not.* This form is still regarded as substandard; careful speakers and writers do not use it.

all ready, already *All ready* means that everyone is prepared or that something is completely prepared; *already* means "completed" or "happened earlier."

> EXAMPLES   We are *all ready* to go.
> It is *already* dark.

all right, alright Use *all right.* In time, *alright* may become accepted, but for now *all right* is generally preferred.

> EXAMPLE   Your choice is *all right* with me.

all together, altogether *All together* means "united"; *altogether* means "entirely."

EXAMPLES We will meet *all together* at the clubhouse.
There is *altogether* too much noise in the hospital area.

almost, most *Almost* is an adverb meaning "nearly"; *most* is an adverb meaning "the greater part of a whole."

EXAMPLES The emergency shift *almost* froze.
The emergency shift worked *most* of the night.

a lot, alot, allot *A lot* is written as two separate words and is a colloquial term meaning "a large amount"; *alot* is a common miswriting for *a lot; allot* is a verb meaning "to give a certain amount."

among, between Use *among* when talking about more than two. Use *between* to express the relation between two things or the relation of a thing to many surrounding things.

amount, number *Amount* refers to mass or quantity; *number* refers to items, objects, or ideas that can be counted individually.

EXAMPLES The *amount* of money for clothing is limited.
A large *number* of people are enrolled in the class.

and/or This pairing of coordinate conjunctions indicates appropriate alternatives. Avoid using *and/or* if it misleads or confuses the reader, or if it indicates imprecise thinking. In the sentence, "Jones requests vacation leave for Monday–Wednesday and/or Wednesday–Friday," the request is not clear because the reader does not know whether three days' leave or five days' leave is requested. Use *and* and *or* to mean exactly what you want to say.

EXAMPLES She is a qualified lecturer *and* consultant.
For our vacation we will go to London *or* Madrid *or* both.

See also Virgule, page 539.

angel, angle *Angel* means "a supernatural being"; *angle* means "corner" or "point of view." Be careful not to overuse *angle* meaning "point of view." Use *point of view, aspect,* and the like.

anywheres, somewheres, nowheres Use *anywhere, somewhere,* or *nowhere.*

as if, like *As if* is a subordinate conjunction; it should be followed by a subject-verb relationship to form a dependent clause. *Like* is a preposition; in formal writing *like* should be followed by a noun or a pronoun as its object.

EXAMPLES He reacted to the suggestion *as if* he never heard of it.
Pines, *like* cedars, do not have leaves.

as regards, in regard to Avoid these phrases. Use *about* or *concerning.*

average, mean, median *Average* is the quotient obtained by dividing the sum of the quantities by the number of quantities. For example, for scores of 70, 75, 80, 82, 100, the *average* is 81⅖. *Mean* may be the simple average or it may be the value midway between the lowest and the highest quantity (in the scores above, 85). *Median* is the middle number (in the scores above, 80).

balance, remainder *Balance* as used in banking, accounting, and weighing means "equality between the totals of two sides." *Remainder* means "what is left over."

> EXAMPLES The company's bank *balance* continues to grow.
> Our shift will work overtime the *remainder* of the week.

being that, being as how Avoid using either of these awkward phrases. Use *since* or *because*.

> EXAMPLE *Because* the bridge is closed, we will have to ride the ferry.

beside, besides *Beside* means "alongside," "by the side of," or "not part of"; *besides* means "furthermore" or "in addition."

> EXAMPLES The tree stands *beside* the walk.
> *Besides* the cost there is a handling charge.

bi-, semi- *Bi-* is a prefix meaning "two," and *semi-* is a prefix meaning "half," or "occurring twice within a period of time."

> EXAMPLES Production quotas are reviewed *biweekly*. (Every two weeks)
> The board of directors meets *semiannually*. (Every half year, or twice a year)

brake, break *Brake* is a noun meaning "an instrument to stop something"; *break* is a verb meaning "to smash," "to cause to fall apart."

> EXAMPLES The mechanic relined the *brakes* in the truck.
> If the vase is dropped, it will *break*.

can't hardly This is a double negative; use *can hardly*.

capital, capitol *Capital* means "major city of a state or nation," "wealth," or, as an adjective, "chief" or "main." *Capitol* means "building that houses the legislature"; when written with a capital "C," it usually means the legislative building in Washington.

> EXAMPLES Jefferson City is the *capital* of Missouri.
> Our company has a large *capital* investment in preferred stocks.
> The *capitol* is located on Third Avenue.

cite, sight, site *Cite* is a verb meaning "to refer to"; *sight* is a noun meaning "view" or "spectacle"; *site* is a noun meaning "location."

> EXAMPLES *Cite* a reference in the text to support your theory.
> Because of poor *sight*, he has to wear glasses.
> This is the building *site* for our new home.

coarse, course *Coarse* is an adjective meaning "rough," "harsh," or "vulgar"; *course* is a noun meaning "a way," "a direction."

> EXAMPLES The sandpaper is too *coarse* for this wood.
> The creek followed a winding *course* to the river.

consensus *Consensus* means "a general agreement of opinion." Therefore, do not write *consensus of opinion*; it is repetitious.

contact *Contact* is overused as a verb, especially in business and industry. Consider using in its place such exact forms as *write to, telephone, talk with, inform, advise,* or *ask.*

continual, continuous *Continual* means "often repeated"; *continuous* means "uninterrupted" or "unbroken."

EXAMPLES The conference has had *continual* interruptions.
The rain fell in a *continuous* downpour for an hour.

could of The correct form is *could have.* This error occurs because of the sound heard in pronouncing such statements as: We *could have* (could've) completed the work on time.

council, counsel, consul *Council* is a noun meaning "a group of people appointed or elected to serve in an advisory or legislative capacity." *Counsel* as a noun means "advice" or "attorney"; as a verb, it means "to advise." *Consul* is a noun naming the official representing a country in a foreign nation.

EXAMPLES The club has four members on its *council.*
The *counsel* for the defense advised him to testify.
The *consul* from Switzerland was invited to our international tea.

criteria, criterion *Criteria* is the plural of *criterion,* meaning "a standard on which a judgment is made." Although *criteria* is the preferred plural, *criterions* is also acceptable.

EXAMPLES This is the *criterion* that the trainee did not understand.
On these *criteria,* the proposals will be evaluated.

device, devise *Device* is a noun meaning "a contrivance," "an appliance," "a scheme"; *devise* is a verb meaning "to invent."

EXAMPLES This *device* will help prevent pollution of our waterways.
We need to *devise* a safer method for drilling offshore oil wells.

different from, different than Although *different from* is perhaps more common, *different than* is also an acceptable form.

discreet, discrete *Discreet* means "showing good judgment in conduct and especially in speech." *Discrete* means "consisting of distinct, separate, or unconnected elements."

EXAMPLES The administrative assistant was *discreet* in her remarks.
Discrete electronic circuitry was the standard until the advent of integrated circuits.

dual, duel *Dual* means "double." *Duel* as a noun means a fight or contest between two people; as a verb, it means "to fight."

EXAMPLES The car has a *dual* exhaust.
He was shot in a *duel.*

due to Some authorities object to *due to* in adverbial phrases. Acceptable substitutes are *owing to* and *because of.*

each and every Use one or the other. *Each and every* is a wordy way to say *each* or *every*.

> EXAMPLE *Each* person should make a contribution.

except for the fact that Avoid using this wordy and awkward phrase.

fact, the fact that Use *that*.

field Used too often to refer to an area of knowledge or a subject.

had ought, hadn't ought Avoid using these phrases. Use *ought* or *should*.

> EXAMPLE He *should not* speak so loudly.

hisself Use *himself*.

imply, infer *Imply* means to "express indirectly." *Infer* means to "arrive at a conclusion by reasoning from evidence."

> EXAMPLES The supervisor *implied* that additional workers would be laid off.
> I *inferred* from her comments that I would not be one of them.

in case, in case of, in case that Avoid using this overworked phrase. Use *if*.

in many instances Wordy. Use *frequently* or *often*.

in my estimation, in my opinion Wordy. Use *I believe* or *I think*.

irregardless Though you hear this double negative and see it in print, it should be avoided. Use *regardless*.

its, it's *Its* is the possessive form; *it's* is the contraction for *it is*. The simplest way to avoid confusing these two forms is to think *it is* when writing *it's*.

> EXAMPLES The tennis team won *its* match.
> *It's* time for lunch.

lay, lie *Lay* means "to put down" or "place." Forms are *lay, laid*, and *laying*. It is a transitive verb; thus it denotes action going to an object or to the subject.

> EXAMPLES *Lay* the books on the table.
> We *laid* the floor tile yesterday.

> *Lie* means "to recline" or "rest." Forms are *lie, lay, lain*, and *lying*. It is an intransitive verb; thus it is never followed by a direct object.

> EXAMPLES The pearls *lay* in the velvet-lined case.
> *Lying* in the velvet-lined case were the pearls.

lend, loan *Lend* is a verb. *Loan* is used as a noun or a verb; however, many careful writers use it only as a noun.

loose, lose *Loose* means "to release," "to set free," "unattached," or "not securely fastened"; *lose* means "to suffer a loss."

> EXAMPLE We turned the horses *loose* in the pasture, but we locked the gate so that we wouldn't *lose* them.

lots of, a lot of In writing, use *many, much, a large amount*.

might of, ought to of, must of, would of   *Of* should be *have*. See *could of*.

off of   Omit *of*. Use *off*.

on account of   Use *because*.

one and the same   Wordy. Use *the same*.

outside of   Use *besides, except for,* or *other than*.

passed, past   *Passed* identifies an action and is used as a verb; *past* means "earlier" and is used as a modifier.

> EXAMPLES   He *passed* us going 80 miles an hour.
> In the *past,* bills were sent out each month.

personal, personnel   *Personal* is an adjective meaning "private," "pertaining to the person"; *personnel* is a noun meaning "body of persons employed."

> EXAMPLES   Please do not open my *personal* mail.
> He is in charge of hiring new *personnel*.

plain, plane   *Plain* is an adjective meaning "simple," "without decoration"; *plane* is a noun meaning "airplane," "tool," or "type of surface."

> EXAMPLES   The *plain* decor of the room created a pleasing effect.
> We worked all day checking the engine in the *plane*.

principal, principle   *Principal* means "highest," "main," or "head"; *principle* means "belief," "rule of conduct," or "fundamental truth."

> EXAMPLES   The school has a new *principal*.
> His refusal to take a bride was a matter of *principle*.

proved, proven   Use either form.

put across   Use more exact terms, such as *demonstrate, explain, prove, establish*.

quiet, quite   *Quiet* is an adjective meaning "silence" or "free from noise"; *quite* is an adverb meaning "completely" or "wholly."

> EXAMPLES   Please be *quiet* in the library.
> It's been *quite* a while since I've seen him.

raise, rise   *Raise* means "to push up." Forms are *raise, raised, raising*. It is a transitive verb; thus it denotes action going to an object or to the subject.

> EXAMPLES   *Raise* the window.
> The technician *raised* the impedance of the circuit 300 ohms.

Rise means "to go up" or "ascend." Forms are *rise, rose, risen*. It is an intransitive verb and thus it is never followed by a direct object.

> EXAMPLES   Prices *rise* for several reasons.
> The sun *rose* at 6:09 this morning.

rarely ever, seldom ever   Avoid using these phrases. Use *rarely* or *seldom*.

read where   Use *read that*.

reason is because, reason why   Omit *because* and *why*.

respectfully, respectively *Respectfully* means "in a respectful manner"; *respectively* means "in the specified order."

> EXAMPLES I *respectfully* explained my objection.
> The capitals of Libya, Iceland, and Tasmania are Tripoli, Reykjavik, and Hobart, *respectively.*

sense, since *Sense* means "ability to understand"; *since* is a preposition meaning "until now," an adverb meaning "from then until now," and a conjunction meaning "because."

> EXAMPLES At least he has a *sense* of humor.
> I have been on duty *since* yesterday.

set, sit *Set* means "to put down" or "place." Its basic form does not change: *set, set, setting.* It is a transitive verb; thus it denotes action going to an object or to the subject.

> EXAMPLES Please *set* the test tubes on the table.
> The electrician *set* the breaker yesterday.

Sit means "to rest in an upright position." Forms are *sit, sat, sitting.* It is an intransitive verb and thus it is never followed by a direct object.

> EXAMPLES Please *sit* here.
> The electrician *sat* down when the job was finished.

state Use exact terms such as *say, remark, declare, observe. To state* means "to declare in a formal statement."

stationary, stationery *Stationary* is an adjective meaning "fixed"; *stationery* is a noun meaning "paper used in letter writing."

> EXAMPLES The workbench is *stationary.*
> The school's *stationery* is purchased through our firm.

their, there, they're *Their* is a possessive pronoun; *there* is an adverb of place; *they're* is a contraction for *they are.*

> EXAMPLES *Their* band is in the parade.
> *There* goes the parade.
> *They're* in the parade.

this here, that there Avoid this phrasing. Use *this* or *that.*

> EXAMPLE *This* machine is not working properly.

thusly Use *thus.*

till, until Either word may be used.

to, too, two *To* is a preposition; *too* is an adverb telling "How much?"; *two* is a numeral.

try and *Try to* is generally preferred.

type, type of In writing, use *type of.*

used to could Use *formerly was able* or *used to be able.*

where . . . at Omit the *at*. Write *"Where* is the library?" (not "Where is the library at?")

who's, whose *Who's* is the contraction for *who is; whose* is the possessive form of *who*.

> EXAMPLES *Who's* on the telephone?
> *Whose* coat is this?

-wise Currently used and overused as an informal suffix in such words as *timewise, safetywise, healthwise*. Better to avoid such usage.

would of The correct form is *would have*. This error occurs because of the sound heard in pronouncing such a statement as this: He *would have* (would've) come if he had not been ill.

APPLICATION 1 GRAMMATICAL USAGE AND WORD CHOICE

Think for a few minutes about your choice of career and the study necessary to prepare for that career. Then write five sentences about your thoughts. Analyze the sentences by answering the following questions.

1. Do your sentences contain any *adjectives, adverbs, conjunctions, interjections, nouns, prepositions, pronouns, verbs,* or *verbals*? Divide a page into nine columns; head Column I "Adjectives," Column II "Adverbs," and so on. Then, list the words from your sentences in the appropriate column.
2. Identify the subject(s) and verb(s) in each of the five sentences. Explain the agreement in number of each subject and verb.
3. For every pronoun listed in Question 1 above, identify an antecedent. Explain how each pronoun agrees with its antecedent.

APPLICATION 2 GRAMMATICAL USAGE

Make a list of usage problems you have had in writing assignments. (Study this chapter and other available sources that explain how to solve your usage problems. Then, as you write, try to correct these problems.)

APPLICATION 3 GRAMMATICAL USAGE

Rewrite the following sentences to correct errors in usage.

1. The team only managed to practice two days.
2. The glass face of the meter.
3. The workers were injured by the blast security officers were on the scene immediately to help.
4. The children's ward located in the hospital's east wing which houses patients from age 2 through age 10 was completed last year.
5. According to a report I read in last night's newspaper.
6. The project was quite complex, nevertheless I managed to complete it.

7. The instructors taught the new employees to serve customers efficiently, and while teaching them they seemed alert and knowledgeable.
8. If one understands a set of instructions, they will have little difficulty in following them.
9. We washed the windows to make the room clean and for more light.
10. Though tired, the suggestion that we go out to dinner was appealing to us.
11. Molly wanted to go to school and continuing with her work.
12. Because of the shortage of trained personnel.
13. While working for IBM, Walt received many honors one of them was being selected as the outstanding speaker at the annual convention.
14. After observing the assembly workers for a period of time, the supervisor made suggestions for improving production, then the suggestions were analyzed and implemented.
15. One of the workers have left their tools here.
16. The committee chairperson or myself will prepare the annual report.
17. My department manager insists on.
18. Tables or a graph aid the clear presentation of these statistics.
19. The number of calories are easily reduced.
20. The diesel engine is an increasingly popular engine in automobiles it does however have some disadvantages.

APPLICATION 4 GRAMMATICAL USAGE

On pages 510–518 is a list of words often confused and misused. Study this list. Choose ten of the words that you confuse and/or misuse and write sentences using the words in an acceptable way.

APPLICATION 5 GRAMMATICAL USAGE

Keep a list of words that you often confuse and/or misuse. Study definitions of these words; practice using the words in writing and in speaking.

APPLICATION 6 GRAMMATICAL USAGE

Students should separate into two groups. From each group select a leader who will write on the board words from the list of words often confused and misused. The students in the first group will take turns using the words acceptably in sentences. If a student in that group cannot use a word acceptably, the opportunity passes to the other group. Count five points for each acceptable usage.

APPLICATION 7 GRAMMATICAL USAGE

The following paragraph contains many misused and confused terms; for each unacceptable usage substitute an acceptable one.

Joe Schmoe was a good worker in regard to his actual performance on the job. But in many instances he complained about the access amount of responsibilities. He all ready had sought the council of alot of his fellow workers, trying to find an angel to use in devicing a duel plan to present to his superiors. He hisself wanted to try and establish a consensus of opinion, establish some principal, and then offer his advise to his superiors. Joe felt that altogether the workers between them could device a coarse of action that would be exceptable to management personal sense they had proved quiet agreeable to passed suggestions, irregardless of the fact that their had been too few personal added. The workers could of let there emotions guide them, but they didn't. Led by Joe, they sited plane facts, showing how in many instances workers were assigned to many responsibilities. Thusly they avoided a brake between management and workers. Its better generally to site facts!

CHAPTER 2

Mechanics

OBJECTIVES   522
INTRODUCTION   522
ABBREVIATIONS   522
CAPITALIZATION   524
NUMBERS   526
    Numerals (figures)   527
    Words   527
PLURALS OF NOUNS   528
PUNCTUATION   531
    Punctuation Marks Used Primarily at the End of a Sentence   531
      Period   531
      Question Mark   532
      Exclamation Point   532
    Internal Marks That Set Off and Separate   533
      Comma   533
      Semicolon   536
      Colon   537
      Dash   538
      Virgule (sometimes called "slash")   539
    Enclosing Marks Always Used in Pairs   539
      Quotation Marks   539
      Parentheses   541
      Brackets   542
    Punctuation of Individual Words and Terms   542
      Apostrophe   542
      Ellipsis Points   543
      Hyphen   544
      Italics (underlining)   544
SPELLING   545
    Suggestions for Improving Spelling   545
    Using ie and ei   546
    Spelling Changes When Affixes Are Added   546
      Prefixes   547
      Suffixes   548
      Final Letters   549
      Ceed, Sede, Cede Words   550
SYMBOLS   551
APPLICATIONS   552

OBJECTIVES

Upon completing this chapter, the student should be able to:

- Use accepted forms of abbreviations, capitalization, numbers, plurals of nouns, punctuation, and spelling
- Explain the difficulty in using symbols
- Give examples to show how conventional use of mechanics (abbreviations, capitalization, etc.) helps make meaning clearer
- Identify the different punctuation marks and illustrate the various uses of each

INTRODUCTION

Threw the yrs. certin, conventions in the mechanics of written communication; have developed? These convention: Or generally accepted practicen; eze the communication process for when. These conventional usages or followed! the (readers attention) can be-rightly focused on the c. of the wtg.

Through the years certain conventions in the mechanics of written communication have developed. These conventions, or generally accepted practices, ease the communication process, for when these conventional usages are followed, the reader's attention can be rightly focused on the content of the writing.

Which is easier to follow — the first or the second paragraph? Undoubtedly the second, because it follows generally accepted practices in the mechanics of written English. The second paragraph permits you to concentrate on what is being said; further, it is thoughtful of you, the reader, in not requiring you to spend a great deal of time in simply figuring out the words and the sentence units before beginning to understand the subject material. The matter of mechanics, in short, is a matter of convention and of courtesy to the reader.

The following are accepted practices concerning abbreviations, capitalization, numbers, plurals of nouns, punctuation, spelling, and symbols. Applying these practices to your writing will help your reader understand what you are trying to communicate.

ABBREVIATIONS

Always consult a recent dictionary for forms you are not sure about. Some dictionaries list abbreviations together in a special section; other dictionaries list abbreviated forms as regular entries in the body of the dictionary.

Always acceptable 1. Abbreviations generally indicate informality. Nevertheless,
abbreviations there are a few abbreviations always acceptable when used to specify a time or a person, such as a.m. (ante meridiem, before noon), BC (before Christ), AD (anno Domini, in the year of our Lord), Ms. or Ms (combined form of Miss and Mrs.), Mrs. (mistress), Mr. (mister), Dr. (doctor).

Dr. Ann Meyer and Mrs. James Brown will arrive at 7:30 p.m.

*Titles following
names*

2. Certain titles following a person's name may be abbreviated, such as Jr. (Junior), Sr. (Senior), MD (Doctor of Medicine), SJ (Society of Jesus).

> Martin Luther King, Jr., was assassinated on April 4, 1968. (The commas before and after "Jr." are optional.)
> George B. Schimmet, MD, signed the report.

*Titles preceding
names*

3. Most titles may be abbreviated when they precede a person's full name, but not when they precede only the last name.

> Lt. James W. Smith or Lieutenant Smith but *not* Lt. Smith
> The Rev. Arthur Bowman or the Reverend Bowman but *not* Rev. Bowman or the Rev. Bowman

*Terms with
numerals*

4. Abbreviate certain terms only when they are used with a numeral.

a.m., p.m., BC, AD, No. (number), $ (dollars)

(Careful writers place "BC" after the numeral and "AD" before the numeral: 325 BC, AD 597)

> ACCEPTABLE   He arrives at 2:30 p.m.
> Julius Caesar was killed in 44 BC.
> The book costs $12.40.
> UNACCEPTABLE   He arrives this p.m.
> Julius Caesar was killed a few years BC.
> The book costs several $.

*Repeated term or
title*

5. To avoid repetition of a term or a title appearing many times in a piece of writing, abbreviate the term or shorten the title. Write out in full the term or title the first time it appears, followed by the abbreviated or shortened form in parentheses.

> Many high school students take the American College Test (ACT) in the eleventh grade; however, a number of students prefer to take the ACT in the twelfth grade.
> *A Portrait of the Artist as a Young Man (Portrait)* is an autobiographical novel by James Joyce. *Portrait* shows the struggle of a young man in answering the call of art.

*Periods with
abbreviations*

6. Generally, place a period after each abbreviation. However, there are many exceptions:

• The abbreviations of organizations, of governmental divisions, and of educational degrees usually do not require periods (or spacing between the letters of the abbreviation).

> IBM (International Business Machines), DECA (Distributive Education Clubs of America), IRS (Internal Revenue Service), AAS (Associate of Applied Science) degree

• The U.S. Postal Service abbreviations for states are written without periods (and in all uppercase — capital — letters).

For a complete list of these abbreviations, see pages 221–222 in Chapter 7, Memorandums and Letters.

- Roman numerals in sentences and contractions are written without periods.

  Henry VIII didn't let enemies stand in his way.

- Units of measure, with the exceptions of in. (inch) and at. wt. (atomic weight), are written without periods. See 9 below.

  He weighs 186 lbs and stands 6 ft tall.

Plural terms

7. Abbreviations of plural terms are written in various ways. Add *s* to some abbreviations to indicate more than one; others do not require the *s*. See 9 below.

  ABBREVIATIONS ADDING "s"   Figs. (or Figures) 1 and 2
  20 vols. (volumes)
  ABBREVIATIONS WITHOUT "s"   pp. (pages)
  ff. (and following)

Lowercase letters

8. Generally use lowercase (noncapital) letters for abbreviations except for abbreviations of proper nouns.

  mpg (miles per gallon)   Btu (British thermal unit)
  c.d. (cash discount)   UN (United Nations)

Units of measure as symbols

9. Increasingly, the designations for units of measure are being regarded as symbols rather than as abbreviations. As symbols, the designations have only one form — regardless of whether the meaning is singular or plural — and are written without a period.

  100 kph (kilometers per hour)   200 rpm (revolutions per minute)
  50 m (meters)   1 T (tablespoon)

CAPITALIZATION

There are very few absolute rules concerning capitalization. Many reputable businesses and publishers, for instance, have their own established practices of capitalization. However, the following are basic conventions in capitalization and are followed by most writers.

Sentences

1. Capitalize the first word of a sentence or of a group of words understood as a sentence (except a short parenthetical sentence within another).

  After the party no one offered to help clean up. Not one person.

Quotations

2. Capitalize the first word of a direct quotation.

  Melissa replied, "Tomorrow I begin."

Proper nouns

3. Capitalize proper nouns:

People
- Names of people, and titles referring to specific persons

    Frank Lloyd Wright   Mr. Secretary
    Aunt Marian   the Governor

Places
- Places (geographic locations, streets), but not directions

    Canada   Golden Gate Bridge
    Canal Street the Smoky Mountains
    the South   the Red River

    Go three blocks south; then turn west.

Groups
- Nationalities, organizations, institutions, and members of each

    Indian   Bear Creek High School
    British   League of Women Voters
    a Rotarian International Imports, Inc.

Calendar divisions
- Days of the week, months of the year, and special days, but not seasons of the year

    Monday   Halloween New Year's Day
    January spring   summer

Historic occurrences
- Historic events, periods, and documents

    World War II   the Industrial Revolution
    the Magna Carta   Battle of San Juan Hill

Religions
- Religions and religious groups

    Judaism   the United Methodist Church

Deity
- Names of the Deity and personal pronouns referring to the Deity

    God   Son of God
    Creator His, Him, Thee, Thy, Thine

Bible
- Bible, Scripture, and names of the books of the Bible These words are not italicized (underlined in handwriting).

    My favorite book in the Bible is Psalms.

Proper noun derivatives
4. Capitalize derivatives of proper nouns when used in their original sense.

    Chinese citizen *but* china pattern
    Salk vaccine   *but* pasteurized milk

Pronoun I
5. Capitalize the pronoun *I*.

    In that moment of fear, I could not say a word.

Titles of publications
6. Capitalize titles of books, chapters, magazines, newspapers, articles, poems, plays, stories, musical compositions, paint-

ings, motion pictures, and the like. Ordinarily, do not capitalize articles *(a, an, the)*, coordinate conjunctions *(and, or, but)*, and prepositions *(or, by, in, with)*, unless they are the first word of the title. It is acceptable to capitalize prepositions of five or more letters *(against, between)*.

Newsweek (magazine)
"The Purloined Letter" (short story)
"Tips on Cutting Firewood" (article)
Godspell (musical composition)
Man Against Himself (book)
Madonna and Child (painting)

Titles with names   7. Capitalize titles immediately preceding or following proper names.

Juan Perez, Professor of Computer Science
Dr. Alicia Strumm
Dale Jaggers, Member of Congress

Substitute names   8. Capitalize words or titles used in place of the names of particular persons. However, names denoting kinship are not capitalized when immediately preceded by an article or a possessive.

Last week Mother and my grandmother gave a party for Sis.
Jill's dad and her uncle went hunting with Father and Uncle Bob.

Trade names   9. Capitalize trade names.

Dodge trucks   Hershey bars

Certain words with numerals   10. Capitalize the words *Figure, Number, Table* and the like (whether written out or abbreviated) when used with a numeral.

See Figure 1. See the accompanying figure.
This is Invoice No. 6143. Check the number on the invoice.

School subjects   11. Capitalize school subjects only if derived from proper nouns (such as those naming a language or a nationality) or if followed by a numeral.

English   Spanish
history   History 1113
algebra   Algebra II

NUMBERS

The problem with numbers is knowing when to use numerals (figures) and when to use words.

Numerals (figures)

Dates, houses, telephones, ZIPs, specific amounts, math, etc.

1. Use numerals for dates, house numbers, telephone numbers, ZIP codes, specific amounts, mathematical expressions, and the like.

> July 30, 1984 *or* 30 July 1984   857–5969
> 600 Race Street   10:30 p.m.
> 61 percent   Chapter 12, p. 14

Decimals

2. Use numerals for numbers expressed in decimals. Include a zero before the decimal point in writing fractions with no whole number (integer).

> 12.0006
> 0.01
> 0.500 (The zeros following "5" show that accuracy exists to the third decimal place.)

10 and above; three or more words

3. Use numerals for number 10 and above or numbers that require three or more written words.

> She sold 12 new cars in 2½ hours.

Several numbers close together

4. Use numerals for several numbers (including fractions) that occur within a sentence or within related sentences.

> The recipe calls for 3 cups of sugar, ½ teaspoon of salt, 2 sticks of butter, and ¼ cup of cocoa.
> The report for this week shows that our office received 127 telephone calls, 200 letters, 30 personal visits, and 3 telegrams.

Adjacent numbers

5. Use numerals for one of two numbers occurring next to each other.

> 12 fifty-gallon containers
> two hundred 24 × 36 mats

Words

Approximate or indefinite numbers

1. Use words for numbers that are approximate or indefinite.

> If I had a million dollars, I'd buy a castle in Ireland.
> About five hundred machines were returned because of faulty assembling.

Fractions

2. Use words for fractions.

> The veneer is one-eighth of an inch thick.
> Our club receives three-fourths of the general appropriation.

Below 10

3. Use words for numbers below 10.

> There are four quarts in a gallon.

Beginning of sentence

4. Use words for a number or related numbers that begin a sentence.

Fifty cents is a fair entrance fee.

Sixty percent of the freshmen and seventy percent of the sopho-mores come from this area.

Note: If using words for a number at the beginning of a sentence is awkward, recast the sentence.

UNACCEPTABLE 2175 freshmen are enrolled this semester.

AWKWARD Two thousand one hundred and seventy-five fresh-men are enrolled this semester.

ACCEPTABLE This semester 2175 freshmen are enrolled.

Adjacent numbers 5. Use words for one of two numbers occurring next to each other.

50 six-cylinder cars   four 3600-pound loads

Repeating a number 6. Except in special instances (such as in order letters or legal documents), it is not necessary to repeat a written-out num-ber by giving the numerals in parentheses.

ACCEPTABLE: The drumpet was invented five years ago.

UNNECESSARY: The drumpet was invented five (5) years ago.

PLURALS OF NOUNS

The English language has been greatly influenced not only by the original English but also by a number of other languages, such as Latin, Greek, and French. Some nouns in the English language, especially those frequently used, continue to retain plural forms from the original language.

Most nouns: s or es 1. Most nouns in the English language form their plural by adding -*s* or -*es*. Add -*s* unless the plural adds a syllable when the singular noun ends in *s*, *ch* (soft), *sh*, *x*, and *z*.

pencil	pencils	mass	masses
desk	desks	church	churches
flower	flowers	leash	leashes
boy	boys	fox	foxes
post	posts	buzz	buzzes

Nouns ending in y 2. If a noun ends in *y* preceded by a consonant sound, change the *y* to *i* and add -*es*.

history   histories
penny   pennies

For other nouns ending in *y*, add -*s*.

monkey   monkeys
valley   valleys

Nouns ending in f or fe 3. A few nouns ending in *f* or *fe* change the *f* to *v* and add -*es* to form the plural. These nouns are:

calf	calves	life	lives	shelf	shelves
elf	elves	loaf	loaves	thief	thieves
half	halves	leaf	leaves	wife	wives
knife	knives	sheaf	sheaves	wolf	wolves

In addition, several nouns may either add *-s* or change the *f* to *v* and add *-es*. These nouns are:

beef	beefs (slang for "complaints"), beeves
scarf	scarfs, scarves
staff	staffs (groups of officers), staffs or staves (poles or rods)
wharf	wharfs, wharves

Nouns ending in o   4. Most nouns ending in *o* add *-s* to form the plural. Among the exceptions, which add *-es*, are the following:

echo	echoes	potato	potatoes
hero	heroes	tomato	tomatoes
mosquito	mosquitoes	veto	vetoes

Compound nouns   5. Most compound nouns form the plural with a final *-s* or *es*. A few compounds pluralize by changing the operational part of the compound noun.

handful	handfuls	son-in-law	sons-in-law
go-between	go-betweens	(and other in-law compounds)	
good-by	good-bys	passer-by	passers-by
court-martial	courts-martial	editor in chief	editors in chief

Internal vowel change   6. A few nouns form the plural by an internal vowel change. These nouns are:

foot	feet	mouse	mice
goose	geese	tooth	teeth
louse	lice	woman	women
man	men		

-en plurals   7. A few nouns form the plural by adding *-en* or *-ren*. These nouns are:

ox	oxen
child	children
brother	brothers, brethren

Foreign plurals   8. Several hundred English nouns, originally foreign, have two acceptable plural forms: the original form and the conventional American English *-s* or *-es* form.

memorandum	memoranda	memorandums
curriculum	curricula	curriculums
index	indices	indexes
criterion	criteria	criterions

Some foreign nouns always keep their original forms in the plural.

crisis	crises	die	dice
analysis	analyses	alumna	alumnae (feminine)
bacterium	bacteria	alumnus	alumni (masculine)
basis	bases	thesis	theses
ovum	ova		

Terms being discussed

9. Letters of the alphabet, signs, symbols, and words used as a topic of discussion form the plural by adding the apostrophe and -*s*.

The *i*'s and *e*'s are not clear.
The sentence has too many *and*'s and *but*'s.

Note: Abbreviations and numbers form the plural regularly, that is, by adding *s* or *es*.

The three *PhDs* were born in the *1950s*.
The number has two *sixes*.

Same singular and plural forms

10. Some nouns have the same form in both the singular and the plural. In general, names of fish and of game birds are included in this group.

cod	swine	sheep
trout	cattle	Chinese
deer	species	Japanese
quail	corps	Portuguese

Two forms

11. Some nouns have two forms, the singular indicating oneness or a mass, and the plural indicating different individuals or varieties within a group.

a string of fish	four little fishes
a pocketful of money	moneys (or monies) appropriated by Congress
fresh fruit	fruits from Central America

Only plural forms

12. Some nouns have only plural forms. A noun is considered singular, however, if the meaning is singular.

measles	dynamics
(Measles is a contagious	mumps
disease.)	news
economics	physics
mathematics	molasses

A noun is considered plural if the meaning is plural.

scissors   (The scissors are sharp.)
pants

PUNCTUATION

Punctuation is a necessary part of the written language. Readers and writers depend on marks of punctuation to help prevent vagueness by indicating pauses and stops, separating and setting off various sentence elements, indicating questions and exclamations, and emphasizing main points while subordinating less important sentence content.

Punctuation usage is presented here according to marks used primarily at the end of a sentence (period, question mark, and exclamation point), internal marks that set off and separate (comma, semicolon, colon, dash, and virgule), enclosing marks always used in pairs (quotation marks, parentheses, and brackets), and punctuation of individual words and of terms (apostrophe, ellipsis points, hyphen, and italics).

Punctuation Marks Used Primarily at the End of a Sentence

Period (.)

Statement, command, or request

1. Use a period at the end of a sentence (and of words understood as a sentence) that makes a statement, gives a command, or makes a request (except a short parenthetical sentence within another).

    James Naismith invented the game of basketball. (Statement)
    Choose a book for me. (Command)
    No. (Understood as a sentence)
    Naismith (he was a physical education instructor) wanted to provide indoor exercise and competition for students. (Parenthetical sentence with no capital and no period)

    See also Sentence Fragments, pages 500–501.

    Note: The polite request phrased as a question is usually followed by a period rather than a question mark.

    Will you please send me a copy of your latest sale catalog.

Initials and abbreviations

2. Use a period after initials and most abbreviations.

    Dr. H. H. Wright   p. 31
    437 mi.   no. 7

    The abbreviations of organizations, of governmental divisions, and of educational degrees usually omit periods.

    BA (Bachelor of Arts) degree
    NFL (National Football League)
    FBI (Federal Bureau of Investigation)

    The U.S. Postal Service abbreviations for states (see page 221–222 in Chapter 7, Memorandums and Letters for a list of the abbreviations), contractions, parts of names used as a whole, roman numerals in sentences and units of measure with the exception of in. (inch) and at. wt. (atomic weight) are written without periods. (Designations for units of measure are increasingly being regarded as symbols rather than as abbreviations. See item 9, page 524.)

Hal C. Johnson IV, who lives 50 mi. away in Sacramento, CA, won't be present.

See also Abbreviations, item 6, pages 551–552.

Outline   3. Use a period after each number and letter symbol in an outline.

I.
  A.
  B.

For other examples see page 115.

Decimals   4. Use a period to mark decimals.

$10.52
A reading of 1.260 indicates a full charge in a battery; 1.190, a half charge.

Question Mark (?)

Questions   1. Use a question mark at the end of every direct question, including a short parenthetical question within another sentence.

Have the blood tests been completed?
When you return (when will that be?), please bring the reports.

An indirect question is followed by a period.

He asked if John were present.

A polite request is usually followed by a period.

Will you please close the door.

Uncertainty   2. Use a question mark in parentheses to indicate there is some question as to certainty or accuracy.

Chaucer, 1343(?)–1400
The spindle should revolve at a slow (?) speed.

Exclamation Point (!)

Sudden or strong emotion or surprise   1. Use an exclamation point after words, phrases, or sentences (including parenthetical expressions) to show sudden or strong emotion or force, or to mark the writer's surprise.

What a day!
The computer (!) made a mistake.

Note: The exclamation point can be easily overused, thus causing it to lose its force. Avoid using the exclamation point in place of vivid, specific description.

Internal Marks That Set Off and Separate

Comma (,)

Items in series

1. Use a comma to separate items in a series. The items may be words, phrases, or clauses.

   How much do you spend each month for food, housing, clothing, and transportation?

Compound sentence

2. Use a comma to separate independent clauses joined by a coordinate conjunction (*and, but, or, either, neither, nor,* and sometimes *for, so, yet*). (An independent clause is a group of related words that have a subject and verb and that could stand alone as a sentence.)

   There was a time when the homemaker had few interests outside the home, but today she is a leader in local and national affairs.

   Note: Omission of the coordinate conjunction results in a comma splice (comma fault), that is, a comma incorrectly splicing together independent clauses. See page 503.

   If the clauses are short, the comma may be omitted.

   I aimed and I fired.

   See also Semicolon, pages 536–537.

Equal adjectives

3. Use a comma to separate two adjectives of equal emphasis and with the same relationship to the noun modified.

   The philanthropist made a generous, unexpected gift to our college.

   Note: If *and* can be substituted for the comma or if the order of the adjectives can be reversed without violating the meaning, the adjectives are of equal rank and a comma is needed.

Misreading

4. Use a comma to prevent misreading.

   Besides Sharon, Ann is the only available organist.
   Ever since, he has gotten to work on time.

Number units

5. Use a comma to separate units in a number of four or more digits (except telephone numbers, **ZIP** numbers, house numbers, and the like).

   2,560,781   7,868 *or* 7868

   Note: The comma may be omitted from four-digit numbers.

Nonrestrictive modifiers

6. Use commas to set off nonrestrictive modifiers, that is, modifiers which do not limit or change the basic meaning of the sentence.

   The Guggenheim Museum, *designed by Frank Lloyd Wright*, is in New York City. (Nonrestrictive modifier; commas needed)

A museum *designed by Frank Lloyd Wright* is in New York City. (Restrictive modifier; no comma needed)

Leontyne Price, *who is a world-renowned soprano,* was awarded the Presidential Medal of Freedom. (Nonrestrictive modifier; commas needed)

A world-renowned soprano *who was awarded the Presidential Medal of Freedom* is Leontyne Price. (Restrictive modifier; no commas needed)

Introductory adverb clause

7. Use a comma to set off an adverb clause at the beginning of a sentence. An adverb clause at the end of a sentence is not set off.

When you complete these requirements, you will be eligible for the award.

If given the proper care and training, a dog can be an affectionate and obedient pet.

A dog can be an affectionate and obedient pet *if given the proper care and training.*

Introductory verbal modifier

8. Use a comma to set off a verbal modifier (participle or infinitive) at the beginning of a sentence.

Experimenting in the laboratory, Sir Alexander Fleming discovered penicillin. (Participle)

To understand the continents better, researchers must investigate the oceans. (Infinitive)

Appositives

9. Use commas to set off an appositive. (An appositive is a noun or pronoun that follows another noun or pronoun and renames or explains it.)

Joseph Priestley, *a theologian and scientist,* discovered oxygen.

Opium pain-killers, *such as heroin and morphine,* are narcotics.

Note: The commas are usually omitted if the appositive is a proper noun or is closely connected with the word it explains.

My friend Mary lives in Phoenix.

The word *occurred* is often misspelled.

Parenthetical expressions, conjunctive adverbs

10. Use commas to set off a parenthetical expression or a conjunctive adverb.

A doughnut, *for example,* has more calories than an apple.

I was late; *however,* I did not miss the plane.

See also Semicolon, items 2 and 5, page 537.

Address, dates

11. Use commas to set off each item after the first in an address or a date.

My address will be 1045 Carpenter Street, Columbia, Missouri 65201, after today. (House number and street are considered one item; state and ZIP code are considered one item.)

Thomas Jefferson died on July 4, 1826, at Monticello. (Month and day are considered one item.)

Note: If the day precedes the month or if the day is not given, omit the commas.

Abraham Lincoln was assassinated on 14 April 1865.
In July 1969 man first landed on the moon.

Quotations 12. Use commas to set off the *he said* (or similar matter) in a direct quotation.

"I am going," Mary responded.
"If you need help," he said, "a student assistant will be in the library."

Person or thing addressed 13. Use commas to set off the name of the person or thing addressed.

If you can, Ms. Yater, I would prefer that you attend the meeting.
My dear car, we are going to have a good time this weekend.

Mild interjections 14. Use commas to set off mild interjections, such as *well, yes, no, oh.*

Oh, this is satisfactory.
Yes, I agree that farming is still the nation's single largest industry.

Inverted name 15. Use commas to set off, in an inverted name, a person's given name when the surname appears first.

Adams, Lucius C., is the first name on the list.

Title after a name 16. Use commas to set off a title following a name. (Setting off *Junior* or *Senior,* or their abbreviations, following a name is optional.)

Patton A. Houlihan, President of Irish Imports, is here.
Gregory McPhail, DDS, and Harvey D. Lott, DVM, were classmates.

Contrasting elements 17. Use commas to set off contrasting elements.

The harder we work, the sooner we will finish.
Leif Ericson, not Columbus, discovered the North American continent.

Elliptical clause 18. Use a comma to indicate understood words in an elliptical clause.

Tom was elected president; Jill, vice-president.

Inc., Ltd. 19. Use commas to set off the abbreviation for *incorporated* or *limited* from a company name.

Drake Enterprises, Inc., is our major competitor.
I believe that Harrells, Ltd., will answer our request.

Note: Some companies omit the comma.

Introductory elements 20. Use a comma to introduce a word, phrase, or clause.

His destination was clearly indicated, New York City.
I told myself, you can do this if you really want to.

See also Colon, item 1, page 537.

Before conjunction "for"

21. Use a comma to precede *for* when used as a conjunction.

The plant is closed, for the employees are on strike.
The plant has been closed for a week. (No comma; *for* is a preposition, not a conjunction.)

Correspondence

22. Use a comma to follow the salutation and complimentary close in a social letter and usually the complimentary close in a business letter.

Dear Mother,   Sincerely,
Dear Lynne,   Yours truly,

Note: The salutation in a business letter is usually followed by a colon; a comma may be used if the writer and the recipient know each other well. Some newer business letter formats omit all punctuation following the salutation and the complimentary close. For a full discussion, see pages 222–223, Chapter 7, Memorandums and Letters.

Tag question

23. Use commas to set off a tag question (such as *will you, won't you, can you*) from the remainder of the sentence.

You will write me, won't you?

Absolute phrase

24. Use commas to set off an absolute phrase. An absolute phrase (also called a nominative absolute) consists usually of a participle phrase plus a subject of the participle and has no grammatical connection with the clause to which it is attached.

I fear the worst, *his health being what it is.*

Semicolon (;)

Independent clauses, no coordinate conjunction

1. Use a semicolon to separate independent clauses not joined by a coordinate conjunction *(and, but, or)*.

Germany has a number of well-known universities; several of them have been in existence since the Middle Ages.
There are four principal blood types; the most common are O and A.

Note 1: If a comma is used instead of the needed semicolon, the mispunctuation is called a comma splice, or comma fault (see page 503).
Note 2: If the semicolon is omitted, the result is a run-on, or fused, sentence (see page 502).

Short, emphatic clauses may be separated by commas.

I came, I saw, I conquered.

Independent clauses, transitional connective

2. Use a semicolon to separate independent clauses joined by a transitional connective. Transitional connectives include conjunctive adverbs such as *also, however, moreover, nevertheless, then, thus,* and explanatory expressions such as *for example, in fact, on the other hand.*

> We have considered the historical background of the period; thus we can consider its cultural achievements more intelligently.
> During the Renaissance the most famous Humanists were from Italy; for example, Petrarch, Boccaccio, Ficino, and Pico della Mirandola were all of Italian birth.

See also Comma, item 10, page 534.

Certain independent clauses, coordinate conjunction

3. Use a semicolon to separate two independent clauses joined by a coordinate conjunction when the clauses contain internal punctuation or when the clauses are long.

> The room needs a rug, new curtains, and a lamp; but my budget permits only the purchase of a lamp.
> Students in an occupational program of study usually have little time for electives; but these students very often want to take courses in the humanities.

Items in series

4. Use a semicolon to separate items in a series containing internal punctuation.

> The three major cities in our itinerary are London, Ontario, Canada; Washington, DC, USA; and Tegucigalpa, Honduras, Central America.
> The new officers are Brady Harrison, president; Corkren Samuels, vice-president; and Tony McBride, secretary.

Examples

5. Use a semicolon to separate an independent clause containing a list of examples from the preceding independent clause when the list is introduced by *that is, for example, for instance,* or a similar expression.

> Many great writers have had to overcome severe physical handicaps; for instance, John Milton, Alexander Pope, and James Joyce were all handicapped.

Colon (:)

List or series

1. Use a colon to introduce a list or series of items. An expression such as *the following, as follows,* or *these* often precedes the list.

> A child learns responsibility in three ways: by example, by instruction, and by experience.
> The principal natural fibers used in the production of textile fabrics include the following: cotton, wool, silk, and linen.

See also Comma, item 20, page 535.

Explanatory   2. Use a colon to introduce a clause that explains, reinforces, or
clause   gives an example of a preceding clause or expression.

> Until recently, American industry used the English system of linear
>   measure as standard: the common unit of length was the inch.
> "Keep cool: it will be all one a hundred years hence." (Emerson)

Emphatic   3. Use a colon to direct attention to an emphatic appositive.
appositive

> We have overlooked the most obvious motive: love.
> That leaves me with one question: When do we start?

Quotation   4. Use a colon to introduce a long or formal quotation.

> My argument is based on George Meredith's words: "The attitudes,
>   gestures, and movements of the human body are laughable in
>   exact proportion as that body reminds us of a machine."

Formal greeting 5. Use a colon to follow a formal greeting (usually in a business
                   letter).

> Dear Ms. Boxeman: Dear Sir or Madam: Greenway, Inc.:

> (See also comma, item 22, page 536.)

Relationships 6. Use a colon to indicate relationships such as volume and page,
                   ratio, and time.

> 42:81–90 (volume 42, pages 81–90)   x:y
> Genesis 4:8   3:1
> 2:50 a.m.

Dash (—)

The dash generally indicates emphasis or a sudden break in thought. Often the
dash is interchangeable with a less strong punctuation mark: if emphasis is
desired, use a dash; if not, use an alternate punctuation mark (usually a comma,
colon, or parentheses). The dash is made with two hyphens when writing by
hand or typing; there is no spacing before or after the dash within a sentence.

> I want one thing out of this agreement—my money.
> My mother—she is president of the company—will call this to the
>   attention of the board of directors.
> If we should succeed—God help us!—all mankind will profit.

> *Note:* In some sentences the writer may have a choice among
> dashes, parentheses, or commas. Dashes emphasize the
> words set off; parentheses subordinate them; and commas
> simply show that the words are not essential to the basic
> meaning of the sentence.

Sudden change 1. Use a dash to mark a sudden break or shift in thought.

> The murderer is—but perhaps I shouldn't spoil the book for you.
> And now to the next point, the causes of—did someone have a
>   question?

Appositive series   2. Use a dash to set off a series of appositives.

Four major factors—cost, color, fabric, and fit—influence the purchase of a suit of clothes.

Because of these qualities—beauty, durability, portability, divisibility, and uniformity of value—gold and silver have gradually displaced all other substances as material for money.

Summarizing clause   3. Use a dash to separate a summarizing clause from a series.

Tests, a term paper, and class participation—these factors determined the student's grade.

Note: The summarizing clause usually begins with *this, that, these, those,* or *such.*

Emphasis   4. Use a dash to set off material for emphasis.

Flowery phrases—regardless of the intent—have no place in reports.

Sign of omission   5. Use a dash to indicate the omission of letters or words.

The only letters we have in the mystery word are —*a* —*lm.*

Virgule (sometimes called "slash") (/)

Alternative   1. Use a virgule to indicate appropriate alternatives.

Identify/define these persons, occurrences, and terms.

Poetry   2. Use a virgule to separate run-in lines of poetry. For readability, space before and after the virgule.

"Friends, Romans, countrymen, lend me your ears. / I come to bury Caesar, not to praise him." (Shakespeare, *Julius Caesar*)

Per   3. Use a virgule to represent *per* in abbreviations.

12 ft/sec   260 mi/hr

Time   4. Use a virgule to separate divisions of a period of time.

the fiscal year 1985/86

Enclosing Marks Always Used in Pairs

Quotation Marks (" ")

Direct quotations   1. Use quotation marks to enclose every direct quotation.

The *American Heritage Dictionary* defines dulcimer as "a musical instrument with wire strings of graduated lengths stretched over a sound box, played with two padded hammers or by plucking."

"Marriage is popular," said George Bernard Shaw, "because it combines the maximum of temptation with the maximum of opportunity."

Note: Quotations of more than one paragraph have quotation marks at the beginning of each paragraph and at the end of the last paragraph. Long quotations, however, are usually set off by indentation, eliminating the need for quotation marks.

Titles

2. Use quotation marks to enclose titles of magazine articles, short poems, songs, television and radio shows, and speeches.

Included in this volume of Poe's works are the poem "Annabel Lee," the essay "The Philosophy of Literary Criticism," and the short story "The Black Cat."

Note: Titles of magazines, books, newspapers, long poems, plays, operas and musicals, motion pictures, ships, trains, and aircraft are italicized (underlined in handwriting).

Different usage level

3. Use quotation marks to distinguish words on a different level of usage.

The ambassador and his delegation enjoyed the "good country eating."

Note: Be sparing in placing quotation marks around words used in a special sense, for this practice is annoying to many readers. Rather than apologizing for a word with quotation marks, either choose another word or omit the quotation marks. Avoid using quotation marks for mere emphasis.

Nicknames

4. Use quotation marks to enclose nicknames.

William J. "Happy" Kiska is our club adviser.

Note: Quotation marks are usually omitted from a nickname that is well known (Babe Ruth, Teddy Roosevelt) or after the first use in a piece of writing.

Single quotation marks

5. Use single quotation marks (' ') for a quotation within a quotation.

"I was puzzled," confided Mary, "when Jim said that he agreed with the writer's words, 'The world wants to be deceived.'"
This writer states, "Of all the Sherlock Holmes stories, 'The Red-Headed League' is the best plotted."

Own title not quoted

6. At the beginning of a piece of writing, do not put your own title in quotation marks (unless the title is a quotation).

How to Sharpen a Drill Bit
The Enduring Popularity of the Song "White Christmas"

With other punctuation marks

7. Use quotation marks properly with other marks of punctuation.

Period or comma

• The closing quotation mark *always* follows the period or comma.

"File all applications before May," the director of personnel cautioned, "if you wish to be considered for summer work."

Colon or
semicolon
- The closing quotation mark *always* precedes the colon or semicolon.

I have just finished reading Shirley Ann Grau's "The Black Prince"; the main character is a complex person.

Question mark,
exclamation
point, or dash
- The closing quotation mark precedes the question mark, exclamation point, or dash when these punctuation marks refer to the entire sentence. The closing quotation mark follows the question mark, exclamation point, or dash when these punctuation marks refer only to the quoted material.

Who said, "I cannot be here tomorrow"?
Was it you who yelled, "Fire!"?
Bill asked, "Did you receive the telegram?"

Parentheses ( )

Additional
material
1. Use parentheses to enclose additional material remotely connected with the remainder of the sentence.

If I can find a job (I hope I won't need a driver's license), I will pay part of my college expenses.
Ernest Hemingway (1899–1961) won the Nobel Prize in literature.

Note: In some sentences the writer may have a choice among using parentheses, dashes, or commas. Dashes emphasize the words set off; parentheses subordinate them; and commas simply show that the words are not essential to the basic meaning of the sentence.

Itemizing
2. Use parentheses to enclose numbers or letters that mark items in a list.

Government surveys indicate that students drop out of school because they (1) dislike school, (2) think it would be more fun to work, and (3) need money for themselves and their families.

"See" references
3. Use parentheses to enclose material within a sentence directing the reader to see other pages, charts, figures, etc.

The average life expectancy in the United States is 70 years (see Figure 3).

Capitalization
and punctuation
with
parentheses
4. Use capitalization and punctuation properly within parentheses.

Capitalization
- Do not capitalize the first word of a sentence enclosed in parentheses within a sentence.

The table shows the allowable loads on each beam in kips (a kip is 1000 pounds).

Period

- Omit the period end punctuation in a sentence enclosed in parentheses within a sentence.

  The Old North Church (the name is now Christ Church) is the oldest church building in Boston.

Question mark, exclamation point

- Use a needed question mark or exclamation point with matter enclosed in parentheses.

  Pour the footings below the frost line (what is the frost line?) for a stable foundation.

Separate sentence

- If the matter enclosed in parentheses is a separate sentence, place the end punctuation inside the closing parentheses.

  The regular heating system will be sufficient. (Infrared heaters are available for spotheating.)

Brackets ([ ])

Insertion in quotation

1. Use brackets for parentheses within parentheses.

   Susan M. Jones (a graduate of Teachers' College [now the University of Southern Mississippi]) was recognized as Alumna of the Year.

2. Use brackets to insert comments or explanations in quotations.

   "Good design [of automobiles] involves efficient operation, sound construction, and pleasing form."
   "It is this decision [*Miller* v. *Adams*] that parents of juvenile offenders will long remember," said the judge.

Sic in quotation

3. Use brackets to enclose the Latin word *sic* ("so," "thus") to indicate strange usage or an error such as misspelling or incorrect grammar in a quotation.

   According to the report, "Sixty drivers had there [sic] licenses revoked."

4. Use brackets to indicate missing or unverified information in documentation.

   James D. Amo. *How to Hang Wallpaper.* [Boston: McGuire Institute of Technology.] 1985.

Punctuation of Individual Words and of Terms

Apostrophe (')

Contractions

1. Use an apostrophe to take the place of a letter or letters in a contraction.

   I'm (I am)
   we've (we have)
   Don't come until one o'clock (Do not, of the clock)

Singular possessive

2. Use an apostrophe to show the possessive form of singular nouns and indefinite pronouns.

citizen's responsibility   Rom's car
someone's book   everybody's concern

Note: To form the possessive of a singular noun, add the apostrophe + *s*.

doctor + ' + s = doctor's, as in "doctor's advice"
Keats + ' + s = Keats's, as in Keats's poems

Note: The *s* may be omitted in a name ending in *s*, especially if the name has two or more syllables.

James's (or James') book
Ms. Tompkins's (or Ms. Tompkins') cat

Note: Personal pronouns (*his, hers, its, theirs, ours*) do not need the apostrophe because they are already possessive in form.

Plural possessive

3. Use an apostrophe to show the possessive form of plural nouns.

boys' coats   children's coats

Note: To show plural possessive, first form the plural; if the plural noun ends in *s*, add only an apostrophe. If the plural noun does not end in *s*, add an apostrophe + *s*.

Certain plurals

4. Use an apostrophe to form the plurals of letters and words used as words.

Don't use too many *and's,* and eliminate *I's* from your report.

Note: The apostrophe is usually omitted in the plurals of abbreviations and numbers.

Ellipsis Points (. . . or. . . .)

Omission sign in quotations

1. Use ellipsis points (plural form: ellipses) to indicate that words have been left out of quoted material. Three dots show that words have been omitted at the beginning of a quoted sentence or within a quoted sentence. Four dots show that words have been omitted at the end of a quoted sentence (the fourth dot being the period at the end of the sentence.)

"The average American family spent about $4000 on food . . . in 1984."
"The adoption of standard time in North America stems from the railroads' search for a solution to their chaotic schedules. . . . In November, 1883, rail companies agreed to set up zones for each 15 degrees of longitude, with uniform time throughout each zone."

Hesitation in dialogue	2. Use ellipsis points to indicate hesitation, halting speech, or an unfinished sentence in dialogue.

"If . . . if it's all right . . . I mean . . . I don't want to cause any trouble," the bewildered child stammered.

Hyphen (-)

Word division	1. Use a hyphen to separate parts of a word divided at the end of a line. (Divide words only between syllables.) Careful writers try to avoid dividing a word because divided words may impede readability.

On April 15, 1912, the *Titanic* sank after colliding with an iceberg.

Compound numbers; fractions	2. Use a hyphen to separate parts of compound numbers and fractions when they are written out.

seventy-four people   twenty-two cars
one-eighth of an inch   one-sixteenth-inch thickness

Compound adjectives	3. Use a hyphen to separate parts of compound adjectives when they precede the word modified.

an eighteenth-century novelist   40-hour week

Compound nouns	4. Use a hyphen to separate parts of compound nouns.

brother-in-law   U-turn
kilowatt-hour   vice-president

Note: Many compound nouns are written as a single word, such as *notebook* and *blueprint*. Others are written as two words without the hyphen, such as *card table* and *steam iron*. If you do not know how to write a word, look it up in a dictionary.

Compound verbs	5. Use a hyphen to separate parts of a compound verb.

brake-test   oven-temper

Numbers or dates	6. Use a hyphen to separate parts of inclusive numbers or dates.

pages 72-76   the years 1984-87

Prefixes	7. Use a hyphen to separate parts of some words whose prefix is separated from the main stem of the word.

ex-president   self-respect
semi-invalid   pre-Renaissance

Note: A good dictionary is the best guide for determining which words are hyphenated.

Italics (underlining)

Italics *(such as these words)* are used in print; the equivalent in handwriting is underlining.

Titles 1. Italicize (underline) titles of books, magazines, newspapers, long poems, plays, operas and musicals, motion pictures, ships, trains, and aircraft.

> At the library yesterday I checked out the book *Roots*, read this month's *Reader's Digest*, looked at the sports section in the *Daily Register*, and listened to parts of *Jesus Christ Superstar*.

> *Note:* Use quotation marks to enclose titles of magazine articles, book chapters, short poems, songs, television and radio shows, and speeches.

> Do not italicize or put in quotation marks titles of sacred writings, editions, series, and the like: Bible, Psalms, Anniversary Edition of the Works of Mark Twain.

Terms as such 2. Italicize words, letters, or figures when they are referred to as such.

> People often confuse *to* and *too.*
> I cannot distinguish between your *a*'s and *o*'s.

Foreign terms 3. Italicize words and phrases that are considered foreign.

> His novel is concerned with the *nouveau riche.*
> This item is included gratis. (The last word in this sentence is no longer considered foreign.)

Emphasis 4. Italicize a word or phrase for special emphasis. If the emphasis is to be effective, however, italics must be used sparingly.

> My final word is *no.*

SPELLING

Because of the strong influence of other languages, spelling in the English language is fairly irregular.

Suggestions for Improving Spelling

If you are currently having difficulty with spelling, here are several helpful suggestions:

1. *Keep a study list of words misspelled.* Review the list often, dropping words that you have learned to spell and adding any new spelling difficulties.
2. *Attempt to master the spelling of these words from the study list.* Use any method that is successful for you. Some students find that writing one or several words on a card and studying them while riding to school or waiting between classes is an effective technique. Some relate the word in some way, such as "There is 'a rat' in sep*arat*e."
3. *Use a dictionary.* It is the poor speller's best friend. If you have some idea of the correct spelling of a word but are not sure, consult a dictionary. If

you have no idea about the correct spelling, get someone to help you find the word in a dictionary. Or look in a dictionary designed for poor spellers, which lists words by their common misspellings and then gives the correct spelling.

4. *Proofread everything you write.* Look carefully at every word within a piece of writing. If a word does not "look right," check its spelling in a dictionary.

5. *Take care in pronouncing words.* Words sometimes are misspelled because of problems in pronouncing or hearing the words. Examples: *prompness* (misspelled) for *promptness, accidently* (misspelled) for *accidentally, sophmore* (misspelled) for *sophomore.* Pronunciation, of course, is not a guide for a small portion of the words in our language (typically words not of English origin). Examples: *pneumonia, potpourri, tsunami, xylophone.*

Although spelling may be difficult, it can be mastered—primarily because many spelling errors are a violation of conventional practices for use of "ie" and "ei" and of spelling changes when affixes are added.

Using *ie* and *ei*

The following jingle sums up most of the guides for correct *ie* and *ei* usage:

Use *i* before *e*,
Except after *c*,
Or when sounded like *a*,
As in *neighbor* and *weigh*.

● Generally use *ie* when the sound is a long *e* after any letter except *c*.

believe	chief
grief	niece
piece	relieve

● Generally use *ei* after *c*.

deceive	receive	receipt

Note: An exception occurs when the combination of letters *cie* is sounded *sh*; in such instances *c* is followed by *ie*.

sufficient	efficient	conscience

● Generally use *ei* when the sound is *a*.

neighbor	freight	sleigh
weigh	reign	vein

Spelling Changes When Affixes Are Added

An affix is a letter or syllable added either at the beginning or at the end of a word to change its meaning. The addition of affixes, whether prefix or suffix, often involves spelling changes.

Prefixes A prefix is a syllable added to the beginning of a word. One prefix may be spelled in several different ways, usually depending on the beginning letter of the base word. For example, *com, con, cor,* and *co* are all spellings of a prefix meaning *together, with.* They are used to form such words as *commit, collect,* and *correspond.*

Following are some common prefixes and illustrations showing how they are added to base words. The meaning of the prefix is in parentheses.

ad (to, toward) In adding the prefix *ad* to a base, the *d* often is changed to the same letter as the beginning letter of the base.

ad + breviate = abbreviate
ad + commodate = accommodate

com (together, with) The spelling is "com" unless the base word begins with *l* or *r*; then the spelling is *col* and *cor,* respectively.

com + mit = commit
com + lect = collect
com + respond = correspond

de (down, off, away) This prefix is often incorrectly written *di.* Note the correct spellings of words using this prefix.

describe   desire
despair   destroyed

dis (apart, from, not) The prefix *dis* is usually added unchanged to the base word.

dis + trust = distrust
dis + satisfied = dissatisfied

in (not) The consonant *n* often changes to agree with the beginning letter of the base word.

in + reverent = irreverent
in + legible = illegible

The *n* may change to *m.*

in + partial = impartial
in + mortal = immortal

sub (under) The consonant *b* sometimes changes to agree with the beginning letter of the base word.

sub + marine = submarine
sub + let = sublet
sub + fix = suffix
sub + realistic = surrealistic

un (not) This is added unchanged.

un + able = unable
un + fair = unfair

Suffixes A suffix is a syllable added to the end of a word. One suffix may be spelled in several different ways, such as *ance* and *ence*. Also, the base word may require a change in form when a suffix is added. Because of these possibilities, adding suffixes often causes spelling difficulties. Learning the following suffixes and the spelling of the exemplary words will improve your vocabulary and spelling immeasurably. The meaning of the suffix is in parentheses.

able, ible (capable of being)   Adding this suffix to a base word, usually a verb or a noun, forms an adjective.

rely — reliable	sense — sensible
consider — considerable	horror — horrible
separate — separable	terror — terrible
read — readable	destruction — destructible
laugh — laughable	reduce — reducible
advise — advisable	digestion — digestible
commend — commendable	comprehension — comprehensible

ance, ence (act, quality, state of)   Adding this suffix to a base word, usually a verb, forms a noun.

appear — appearance	exist — existence
resist — resistance	prefer — preference
assist — assistance	insist — insistence
attend — attendance	correspond — correspondence

Other nouns using *ance, ence* include:

ignorance	experience
brilliance	intelligence
significance	audience
importance	convenience
abundance	independence
performance	competence
guidance	conscience

ary, ery (related to, connected with)   Adding this suffix to base words forms nouns and adjectives.

boundary	gallery
vocabulary	cemetery
dictionary	millinery
library	
customary	

efy, ify (to make, to become)   Adding this suffix forms verbs.

liquefy	ratify
stupefy	testify
rarefy	falsify
putrefy	justify
	classify

ize, ise, yze (to cause to be, to become, to make conform with)   These suffixes are verb endings all pronounced the same way.

recognize revise   analyze
familiarize advertise paralyze
generalize exercise
emphasize supervise
realize
criticize
modernize

Also, some nouns end in *ise*.

exercise   enterprise
merchandise franchise

ly (in a specified manner, like, characteristic of) Adding this suffix to a base noun forms an adjective; adding *ly* to a base adjective forms an adverb. Generally *ly* is added to the base word with no change in spelling.

monthly   surely
heavenly softly
earthly   annually
randomly clearly

If the base word ends in *ic*, usually you add *ally*.

critically   drastically
basically   automatically

An exception is *public — publicly*.

ous (full of) Adding this suffix to a base noun forms an adjective.

courageous outrageous grievous
dangerous   humorous   mischievous
hazardous   advantageous beauteous
marvelous   adventurous bounteous

Other suffixes include:

ant (ent, er, or, ian) meaning "one who" or "pertaining to."

ion (tion, ation, ment) meaning "action," "state of," "result."

ish meaning "like a."

less meaning "without."

ship meaning "skill," "state," "quality," "office."

Final Letters Final letters of words often require change before certain suffixes can be added.

● **Final *e*.** A final silent *e* usually is kept before a suffix beginning with a consonant but dropped before a suffix beginning with a vowel.

use — useful write — writing
love — lovely hire — hiring

Exceptions: true — truly due — duly argue — argument

Note: In adding *ing* to some words ending in *e*, retain the *e* to avoid confusion with another word.

dye — dyeing	die — dying
singe — singeing	sing — singing

● Final *ce* and *ge*. Retain the *e* when adding *able* to keep the *c* or *g* soft. If the *e* were dropped, the *c* would have a *k* sound in pronunciation and the *g* a hard *g* sound. For example, the word *change* retains the *e* when *able* is added: *change-able.*

● Final *ie*. Before adding *ing*, drop the *e* and change the *i* to *y* to avoid doubling the *i*.

tie — tying	lie — lying

● Final *y*. To add suffixes to words ending in a final *y* preceded by a consonant, change the *y* to *i* before adding the suffix. In words ending in *y* preceded by a vowel, the *y* remains unchanged before the suffix.

survey — surveying	try — tries

● Final consonants. Double the final consonant before adding a suffix beginning with a vowel if the word is one syllable or if the word is stressed on the last syllable.

hop — hopping — hopped	occur — occurred — occurring
plan — planning — planned	refer — referred — referring
stop — stopping — stopped	forget — forgotten — forgetting

● In adding suffixes to some words, the stress shifts from the last syllable of the base word to the first syllable. When the stress is on the first syllable, do *not* double the final consonant.

prefer — preference	confer — conference
refer — reference	defer — deference

Ceed, Sede, Cede Words   The base words *ceed, sede,* and *cede* sound the same when they are pronounced. However, they cannot correctly be interchanged in spelling.

● *ceed:* Three words, all verbs, end in *ceed.*

proceed	succeed	exceed

● *sede:* The only word ending in *sede* is *supersede.*

● *cede:* All other words, excluding the four named above, ending in this sound are spelled *cede.*

recede	secede	accede
concede	intercede	precede

SYMBOLS

Symbols are used mostly in tables, charts, figures, drawings, diagrams, and the like; they are not used generally within the text of pieces of writing for most audiences (intended readers).

Symbols cannot be discussed as definitely as abbreviations, capitalization, and numbers because no one group of symbols is common to all areas. Most organizations and subject groups—medicine and pharmacy, mathematics, commerce and finance, engineering technologies—have their own symbols and practices for the use of these symbols. A person who is a part of any such group is obligated to learn these symbols and the accepted usage practices. The following are examples of symbols common to these groups:

- Medicine and Pharmacy

  ℞ take (Latin, *recipe*): used at the beginning of a prescription
  ℥ ounce
  ʒ dram
  s write (Latin, *signā*): on prescription indicates directions to be printed on medicine label)

- Mathematics

+	plus	>	is greater than
−	minus	=	equals
×	times	∫	integral
÷	divide	∠	angle

- Commerce and Finance

  # number, as in #7, or pounds, as in 50#
  £ pound sterling, as in British currency
  @ *at*: 10 @ 1¢ each

- Engineering Technologies

More specialized fields, such as electronics, hydraulics, welding, and technical drawing use standard symbols for different areas. These symbols are usually determined by the American Standards Association.

For example, one electricity text has nine pages of symbols used by electricians. There are resistor and capacitor symbols, contact and push-button symbols, motor and generator symbols, architectural plans symbols, transformer symbols, and switch and circuit breaker symbols. Some examples are illustrated below.

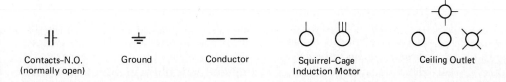

Contacts-N.O. (normally open)   Ground   Conductor   Squirrel-Cage Induction Motor   Ceiling Outlet

A technical drawing text has eight pages of symbols including topographic symbols; railway engineering symbols; American Standard piping symbols; heating, ventilating, and ductwork symbols; and plumbing symbols. Some examples are:

⊙	County seat	⧺	Flanged joint
----	National or state line	⊙	Hot water tank
▨	Wood—with the grain	⊗	Exit outlet

● Nonspecialized Areas

Common among symbols that the average person would recognize and use are:

%	percent	' and "	feet and inches
°	degree	$ and ¢	dollars and cents
&	and		

See also units of measure as symbols, page 524, and flowchart symbols, pages 124–125.

Most dictionaries have a section on common signs and symbols.

APPLICATION 1   USING MECHANICS

Rewrite the following sentences making corrections in the use of abbreviations, capitalization, and numbers.

1. Atmospheric pressure decreases with increase in Altitude, about 1 in of mercury for every 1,000 ft of altitude.
2. 9 out of 10 pounds of all the metal used today is steel.
3. In may 1927 Charles a lindberg flew the atlantic ocean nonstop from new york to paris.
4. The scientific monthly reported findings about the microbiology of the atmosphere.
5. The cashier counted two hundred one dollar bills in the register.
6. Hardness of tool materials is further explained in chapter 23, "heat treatment Of metals."
7. The correct point for a ruling pen is shown in fig. 40.
8. The phenomenon of radioactivity was discovered by a french scientist Henri becquerel.
9. Steel exists from eight hundredths percent carbon to two percent carbon.
10. On the drawing board were two twelve inch rulers.
11. Mister Curtis Berry owns Berry Appliance company.
12. Milling machines are provided with a large range of speeds, from fifteen to one thousand six hundred revolutions per minute.
13. In a desirable classroom for teaching drafting, window areas on the north side should be as large as practical and not less than twenty percent of the floor area.
14. The mechanic put a set of champion spark plugs in mister bronson's mustang.

15. Arthur Winchester manager of tri-d ranch in Cody Wyoming purchased a john deere tractor.
16. The measurement was within an in. of an acceptable length.
17. That small wheel may turn 100 RPM.
18. Many engineers belong to ASTME.
19. Our company uses gmc trucks for delivering building supplies.
20. If I pass the state exams, I will become an rn.
21. Magnax Corporation was located at 501 south street, Chicago, Illinois, from may 15, 1965, to september 1, 1968.
22. Mr. Williams, instructor in refrigeration, said, "turn to page one hundred twenty-six and consult figure 14."
23. The lab team completed 1/2 the assigned experiments.
24. A survey revealed that a lab technician can see about 9 patients an hour.
25. We received your order for 5 50 h.p. boat motors.

APPLICATION 2   USING MECHANICS

List at least ten terms (noun forms) used in your major field. Write the plural of each term.

APPLICATION 3   USING MECHANICS

Using material in your major field, write sentences using the following punctuation marks.

Possessive Forms

1. A sentence containing a singular possessive noun
2. A sentence containing a plural possessive pronoun
3. A sentence containing the possessive form of an indefinite pronoun

Colon

4. A sentence containing a colon to signal that a list or series of items is to follow an independent clause

Comma

5. A sentence containing commas to separate items in a series
6. A sentence containing a comma before "and" joining two independent clauses
7. A sentence containing commas to set off a city from a state
8. A sentence containing commas to set off a month and a day from a year
9. A sentence containing commas to separate units in a number longer than four digits

Dash

> 10. A sentence containing a dash used to introduce a list of items following an independent clause
> 11. A sentence containing a dash (or dashes) to mark a sudden break in thought

Ellipsis Points

> 12. A sentence (quoted from a source) containing ellipsis points to show that words have been left out of the quoted material

Hyphen

> 13. A sentence containing a compound adjective preceding the word modified
> 14. A sentence containing a fraction expressed in words, not numerals

Parentheses

> 15. A sentence containing parentheses to enclose material not grammatically connected to the remainder of the sentence

Period

> 16. A sentence containing a period to mark decimals

Quotation Marks

> 17. A sentence containing quotation marks to enclose material quoted exactly from a printed source

Semicolon

> 18. A sentence containing a semicolon to separate two independent clauses not joined by a coordinate conjunction
> 19. A sentence containing a semicolon as a strong comma to separate items in a series that contains commas
> 20. A sentence containing a semicolon between two independent clauses containing commas that are joined by a coordinate conjunction

APPLICATION 4 USING MECHANICS

Punctuate the following sentences.

> 1. When a large volume of liquid is to be lifted a short distance or pumped against relatively low pressure the centrifugal pump is generally used

2. The combustion chamber and general design of the jet are somewhat similar to the gas turbine but the thrust is delivered in a different manner
3. Modern Miss Shoe Company produces womens shoes to sell in a low price range
4. Since all assumptions cannot be verified there will always remain incomplete data errors in perception of facts and distortion in communication
5. Does the fact that annual reports show a high correlation of sales volume and advertising expense mean that more advertising will increase sales
6. American designers particularly the modern ones have learned to employ artificial light with excellent results
7. Persons engaged in industries dealing with paints batteries gasoline glazes for pottery and insecticides are exposed to unhealthy concentrations of lead unless suitable precautions are observed
8. The term sewage is applied to the pipes mains tanks etc that constitute a disposal system
9. Some decorators believe that the exposure of a room should influence its color scheme for example a north room should employ yellow to produce a feeling of sunshine
10. Finances are often referred to in terms of gain or loss time is referred to as future or past and temperature is denoted as above or below some preassigned zero
11. How many skilled men are now employed
12. The English system of linear measure measuring in a straight line is the standard adopted by American industry
13. A combination set measuring tool used in a machine shop consists of the following principal parts a steel rule a square stock incorporating a level a scriber and a 45 degree angle a protractor head and a center head
14. A taper or starting tap a plug tap and a bottoming tap are used in the order indicated when tapping a blind hole a hole that does not go entirely through the workpiece
15. Like charges repel unlike charges attract
16. Included in the broad classification of tool steels used for both cutting and noncutting purposes are water hardened air hardened shock resisting air hardened and hot worked types
17. Many of our chemical metallurgical and physical laws were discovered by the ancient Egyptians Greeks East Indians Chinese and Tibetans
18. In a drafting classroom an illumination of 50 footcandles at the drawing board level is generally specified as the minimum
19. Early electrical experimenters not fully understanding the nature of the flow of electricity believed that the electricity flowed from the positive terminal of the generator into the conducting wire this was given the name current flow
20. To thumbtack the paper in place on the drawing board the designer presses the T-square head firmly against the working edge of the drawing board

APPLICATION 5   USING MECHANICS

Review the papers that you have written this term. Make a list of the words that you misspelled, indicating words misspelled more than once. Try to determine why you misspelled each word.

APPLICATION 6   USING MECHANICS

Find at least ten symbols used in your major field. Reproduce them as accurately as you can and explain the meaning of each.

Index

Abbreviations, 221–222, 522–524
 in addresses, 221–222
 always acceptable, 522
 in *Library of Congress Subject Headings*, 378–379
 lowercase letters, 524
 in periodical indexes, 379–385
 periods with, 523–524
 plural terms, 524
 repeated term or title, 523
 for states, 221–222
 terms with numerals, 523
 titles following names, 523
 units of measure, 524
Abridgment, 189
Abstract, 191–193, 311, 415. *See also* Summary
Abstract words, 6
Active voice, 9–10, 498–499
Adjectives, 490–491
Adjustment letter, 243–247
Adverbs, 491–492
Agreement
 in gender, 505
 in number, 505
 in person, 505
 of pronoun and antecedent, 504
 of subject and verb, 505–507
Almanacs, 389
Alphabetizing, 379
 letter by letter, 379
 word by word, 379
Analysis
 through classification, 107–133
 through comparison and contrast, 171–183
 through effect and cause, 151–170
 through partition, 134–150
Annotation, 192
Antecedent, pronoun and, 504
Apostrophe, 542–543
 certain plurals, 543
 contractions, 542
 plural possessive, 543
 singular possessive, 543
Appendix, 312
Application follow-up letters, 273–277

Application for a job, 253–277
 forms, 270–272
 interviews, 253, 449–454
 resumé, 254, 255, 268–269
Application letter, 253–262
Applied Science and Technology Index, 382–383
Appositive, 494, 495, 496
 punctuation of, 534
Attention line, in business letters, 225–226, 228
Audience, 13, 20–22, 27, 37–48, 58, 85–87, 96–98, 155, 185–186, 442–443
Audiovisual materials, 387–388
Author card, or author entry, 374, 375

Bar chart, 468
 examples of, 122, 469
Bibliographies, books of, 389
Bibliography
 cards for, 393–400
 citations, 409, 410–411
 compiling a working, 393–400
 definition of, 200, 409
 evaluating sources for, 393
 examples of, 394, 395, 396, 397, 398, 399, 400
  for an article in a journal, 395
  for an article in a popular magazine, 396
  for a book, 393–394
  for an encyclopedia article, 398–399
  for an essay in a book, 394–395
  for a NewsBank item, 397
  for a newspaper item, 396–397
  for a pamphlet, 399
  for a personal interview, 400
  for a reprinted item, 398
 final, 409, 410–411
 forms for, 410–411
 preliminary, 393
 in a report, 312
 in a summary, 200
Block form, for business letters, 220

Book report. *See* Book review; Reading report

Book review, 198–199

Books
  bibliography card for, 393–394
  bibliography forms for, 410
  systems for classifying, 372–374

Books in Print, 390

Brackets, 542
  insertion in quotation, 542
  sic, 542

Bullet, 2, 24–25, 26

Business letters, 218–302
  abbreviations for states, 221–222
  adjustment letter, 243–247
    example of, 247
    sample plan sheet for, 244–245
  application follow-up letters, 273–277
    example of, 277
    sample plan sheet for, 275–276
  application form, 270–272
  application letter, 253–262
    background information in, 253
    examples of, 255–262
    no resumé in, 253
    purpose of, 253
    request for an interview in, 253
    resumé, data sheet, or vita in, 254–255
    sample plan sheets for, 256–257, 260–261
  applications for writing, 278–302
  claim letter, 243–247
    example of, 246
    sample plan sheet for, 244–245
  collection letters, 248–252
    examples of, 249, 252
    sample plan sheet for, 250–251
  content of, 218–219
  envelope sizes, 227
  format for, 220–221
    appearance of, 220
    block, 220
    full block, 220–221
    handwriting or typewriting, 220
    letterhead stationery, 222
    modified block, 220
    paper, 220
    simplified block, 220–221
  inquiry or request letter, 229–232
    example of, 222
    sample plan sheet for, 230–231
  layout forms, 220–221
  order form, 237–238
  order letter, 232–238
    examples of, 236, 237
    printed form for, 237–238
    sample plan sheet for, 234–235
  parts of, 221–227
    attention line, 225–226, 228
    body, 223
    complimentary close, 223
    copy line, 226–227
    enclosure line, 226
    example of, 225
    heading, 221–222
    identification line, 226
    inside address, 222
    mailing, 227
    personal line, 227, 228
    regular parts of, 221–225
    salutation, 222–223
    signature, 223–224
    special parts, 225–227
    subject or reference line, 226
  parts of the envelope, 227–229
    illustration of, 229
    outside address, 227
    return address, 227
    special parts, 228
  positive approach, 219
  principles in writing, 278
  report letter, 309
  resumé, data sheet, or vita, 254, 255, 263–269
    example of, 264, 265, 268–269
    sample plan sheet for, 266–267
  sales, 239–242
    example of, 242
    sample plan sheet for, 240–241
  second page of, 223
  transmittal letter, 310, 347, 412
  types of, 229
  "you" emphasis in, 218–219
  wording in, 219

Business Periodicals Index, 383–384

Capitalization, 524–526
  certain words with numerals, 526
  pronoun *I,* 525
  proper noun derivatives, 525
  proper nouns, 524–525
  quotations, 524
  school subjects, 526
  sentences, 524
  substitute names, 526
  titles with names, 526
  titles of publications, 525–526
  trade names, 526

Card catalog. *See* Public catalog

Cause and effect. *See also* Effect and cause

actual cause, 159–160
cause-to-effect analysis, 162
effect-to-effect reasoning, 154–155
probable cause, 159–160
Central idea, 392
Chalkboard, 479
Charting, 464–465
Charts, 467–472
  bar, 468–469
  flow, 471–472
  organization, 469–471
  pie, 467–468
Checklist for revising, inside back cover
Citations, in research report, 409,
    410–411
Claim letter, 243–247
Classification, analysis through, 107–
    133
  applications for, 126–133
  bases for, 113
    purpose, 113
    usefulness, 113
  categories in,
  characteristics of a system
      112–113
    completeness, 113
    coordination, 112
    mutual exclusiveness, 112
    nonoverlapping, 112–113
  combination of presentation forms in,
      123–125
  definition of, 109
  examples of, 109–111, 115, 119–
      121, 122, 123–125
  forms of data presentation for, 114, 125
  graphic illustration of, 121–125
  items that can be classified, 111–112
  order of presentation for, 113–114
  outlines for, 114–115
  plural items, 111–112
  principles in, 125
  procedure for, 125–126
  sample plan sheet for, 117–118
  verbal explanation of, 115–121
  visuals in, 121–123
Closing, in business letters, 223
Colon, 537–538
  emphatic appositive, 538
  explanatory clause, 538
  formal greeting, 538
  list, 537
  quotation, 538
  relationships, 538
  series, 537
Combining sentence elements, 9
COM catalog, 374

Comma, 533–536
  absolute phrase, 536
  address, 534
  appositive, 534
  compound sentence, 533
  conjunctive adverb, 534
  contrasting elements, 535
  correspondence, 536
  dates, 534–535
  elliptical clause, 535
  equal adjectives, 533
  "for" as conjunction, 536
  "Inc.," 535
  interjections, 535
  introductory adverb clause, 534
  introductory elements, 535–536
  introductory verbal modifier, 534
  inverted name, 535
  items in series, 533
  "Ltd.," 535
  misreading, 533
  nonrestrictive modifiers, 533–534
  number units, 533

  person or thing
  quotations, 535
  tag question, 635
  title after a name, 535
Comma fault, 503
Comma splice, 503
Comparison-contrast, 171–183
  applications for, 180–183
  examples of, 176–178
  organizational patterns of, 171–173
    point by point, 171–172, 173
    similarities/differences, 172, 173
    subject by subject, 172, 173
  principles in, 178–179
  procedure for, 179–180
  relation to other forms of communica-
      tion, 178
  sample plan sheet for, 174–175
Comparison of general and specific
      mechanism descriptions, 70–73
Complaint letter, 243–247
Complimentary close, 223
Compound personal pronouns, 496
Computer-aided search, 386
Computer graphics, 464–465
  basic visuals—charting, 464–465
  complex visuals, 465
  effect on manually produced visuals,
      465
Computer-output-microform (COM)
      catalog, 374
Conciseness, 8–9, 25, 306–307

Conclusions and recommendations in
　　reports, 309, 311–312
Condensation. *See* Summary
Confused words, 510–518
Conjunctions, 492–493
　coordinate conjunctions, 492–493
　subordinate conjunctions, 493
Conjunctive adverbs, 492
Connotation, 5–6, 307
Contrast. *See* Comparison-contrast
Controlling idea. *See* Central idea
Coordinate conjunctions, 492–493
Coordination, 10–12, 112
Copy line in business letters, 226–227
Correlative conjunctions, 492
Correspondence. *See* Business letters;
　　Memorandum
Cumulative Book Index, 390

Dangling elliptical clauses, 507–508
Dangling modifiers, 507
Dash, 538–539
　appositive series, 539
　emphasis, 539
　omission sign, 539
　sudden change, 538
　summarizing clause, 539
Definition, 84–106
　adapted to purpose, 85–87
　applications for, 100–106
　essence in, 88–89
　examples of, 86–87, 89, 94–95,
　　96–98, 99
　extended, 91–95
　extent of, 88
　　for an abstract term, 88
　　for an object, 88
　in general reference works, 96
　how to define, 88–95
　importance of, 85
　intended audience for, 96–98
　oral, 98
　as part of longer communication, 98
　principles in, 99
　procedure for, 99–100
　purpose in, 96–98
　sample plan sheet for, 92–93
　sentence, 88–90
　　inadequate definition, 90
　　parts of, 88–89
　in specialized reference works, 96–98
　visuals in, 98–99
　when to define, 87
Demonstration, 478
Denotation, 5–6, 307

Description of a mechanism, 55–83
　accurate terminology in, 58
　applications for, 76–83
　comparing general and specific
　　descriptions, 70–73
　examples of, 61–62, 62–64, 65, 66,
　　69, 70–72, 73, 74
　frames of reference in, 57
　　function, 57
　　parts, 57
　　physical characteristics, 57
　general, 56–57
　in operation, 73
　oral, 73
　principles in, 75
　procedure for, 75–76
　　general, 75–76
　　specific, 76
　purpose and audience in, 58
　at rest, 73
　sample plan sheets for, 59–60, 67–68
　specific, 64–69
　visuals in, 74–75
Description of a process. *See* Process
　　description
Descriptive abstract, 190–192
Descriptive summary, 189–192
Design. *See* Layout and design
Dewey Decimal book classification,
　　372–373
Diagrams and drawings. *See* Drawings
　　and diagrams
Diction. *See* Word choice
Dictionary, 388. *See also* Definition
Diorama, 478
Direct object, 494, 496
Display, 478
Division. *See* Partition
Documentation, 200, 405–411,
　　463–464. *See also* Bibliography;
　　Citations; Research report
　four styles of, 407–409
　plagiarism, 405
　in summaries, 200
　of visuals, 463–464
Double comparison, 491
Drawings and diagrams, 476–477
　diagrams, examples of, 74, 99, 145,
　　477
　drawings, examples of, 18–20, 21,
　　31–32, 39, 61–64, 71, 86, 94,
　　134, 135, 158–159, 476
　schematic diagrams, 338, 477
Effect and cause, 151–170
　applications for, 166–170
　cause-to-effect analysis, 162

effect-to-effect reasoning, 154–155
establishing the cause of an effect, 159–160
examples of, 153–154, 158–159, 160
illogical and insufficient causes, 161
  following event caused by preced-ing event, 161
  hasty conclusion, 161
  oversimplification, 161
  sweeping generalization, 161
intended audience and purpose of, 155
principles in, 164
problem solving, 162–164
procedure for, 164–165
relationship of, to other communica-tion forms, 155
sample plan sheet for, 156–157
Ellipsis points, 543–544
  hesitation in dialogue, 544
  omission in quotations, 543
Emphasis in sentences, 10–13, 509–510
Emphasis markers, 2, 23–25
Enclosure line in business letters, 226
Encyclopedia, 388
  bibliography card for, 398–399
  bibliography form for, 410
  general, 388
  specialized, 388
Endnotes, 409
End punctuation, 531–532
  exclamation point, 532
  period, 531–532
  question mark, 532
Envelope, addressing the, 227–229
Envelope sizes, 227
Essay and General Literature Index, The, 385
Establishing the cause of an effect, 159–160
Evaluating oral presentation, 449
Evaluation form, oral presentations, 459
Evaluative summary, 197–199
Exclamation point, rules for, 532
Exhibits, 447, 477–479
  chalkboard, 479
  demonstration, 478
  diorama, 478
  display, 478
  model, 478
  in oral presentations, 447
  poster, 479
  real object, 478
Extemporaneous speech, 439

Faulty parallelism in sentences, 501–502
Field report, 341–353

Figures
  as numerals, 527
  with visuals, 463
  as words, 527–528
Final draft, of research report, 406
First draft, of research report, 404–405
First person, use of in business letters, 219
Flat materials, in oral presentations, 447
Flowchart, 471–472
  examples of, 39, 42–43, 74, 471, 472
Footnotes, 409
  second reference in, 409
  for visuals, 463–464
Form
  for letters, 220–229
  for reports, 310–312
Formal reports, 309–312
  examples of, 347–353, 412–424
Fragments, in sentences, 500–501
Full block form for business letters, 220–221
Fused sentences, 502

General description of a mechanism, 56–57
  examples of, 61–62, 63–64, 70–71
General words, 6
Gerunds, 500. *See also* Verbals
Gobbledygook, 7–8
Grammatical terms, 490–500
Grammatical usage, 489–518. *See also* Word choice
  agreement of pronoun and antecedent, 504
  agreement of subject and verb, 505–507
  applications for, 519–520
  modifiers, 507–509
    dangling, 507
    elliptical, 507–508
    misplaced, 508–509
    squinting, 508
  parts of speech, 490–500
    adjectives, 490–491
    adverbs, 491–492
    conjunctions, 492–493
    interjections, 493
    nouns, 493–494
    prepositions, 494–495
    pronouns, 495–497
    verbals, 499–500
    verbs, 497–499
  shifts in person, number, gender, 505
Graphics. *See* Visuals

Graphs, 472–475
  examples of, 373, 473
  suggestions for preparing, 472–475
Greeting, in business letters, 222–223

Headings
  in business letters, 221–222
  in memorandums, 215
  in outlines, 114
  in reports, 3, 4–5, 313, 405
"Hot Topics," 381
Hyphen, 544
  compound adjectives, 544
  compound nouns, 544
  compound numbers, 544
  compound verbs, 544
  dates, 544
  fractions, 544
  numbers, 544
  prefixes, 544
  word division, 544

Indefinite pronouns, 504
Indexes, 379–385
  Applied Science and Technology Index,
    382–383
  Business Periodicals Index, 383–384
  Essay and General Literature Index,
    The, 385
  government publications, 385
  Magazine Index, 379–381
  newspaper, 384–385
  New York Times Index, The, 385
  Readers' Guide to Periodical Litera-
    ture, 381–382
Indirect object, 494, 496
Infinitive, 500. *See also* Verbals
Informal reports. *See* Nonformal reports
Informational interview, 454–455
  applications for, 458
  follow-up, 455
  the interview, 455
  preparing for, 455
Informative summary, 192–197
Inquiry letter, 229–232
Inside address, 222
Instructions, 14–36
  applications for, 32–36
    nce, 20–22
    ing, 15–20
    n, 26–27
    tended audience on, 20–22
     16–17, 17–20, 21–22,
    3
  form fo

layout and design in, 23–25
length of, 27
locational, 16–17
operational, 17–20
oral presentation of, 22–23
planning and giving, 27–32
principles in, 25
procedure for giving, 26–27
sample plan sheet for, 29–30
visuals in, 23
Intended audience. *See* Audience
Interjections, 493
Interviews, 449–455
  informational, 454–455
  job, 449–454
  for research report, 371
Introduction, in a report, 311, 404
Investigative field report. *See* Field re-
    port
Italics, 544–545
  for emphasis, 545
  foreign terms, 545
  terms as such, 545
  titles, 545

Jargon, 7–8
Job application form, 270–272
  example of, 271–272
Job interview, 449–454
  applications for, 456–457
  following up, 454
  holding, 453–454
  preparing for, 449–453

Laboratory report, 333–450
Layout and design, 1–4, 23–25, 313
Letterhead stationery, 222
Lettering, in visuals, 462
Letters. *See* business letters
Library materials, 372–390
  almanacs, 389
  audiovisual materials, 387–388
  bibliographies, 389
  classifying books, systems of, 372–374
  computer-aided search, 386
  dictionaries, 388
  encyclopedias, 388
  guides to reference works, 390
  handbooks, 389–390
  indexes, 379–385
  Library of Congress Subject Headings,
    377–379
  NewsBank, 386–387
  periodicals holdings list, 388
  public (card) catalog, 374–377

reference works, 388–390
Social Issues Resources Series, 387
statistics, books of, 388–389
vertical file, 390
yearbooks, 390
Library of Congress book classification, 372, 373–374
Library of Congress Subject Headings, 377–379
Library research report. *See* Research reports
Linking verb, 494, 495

McGraw-Hill Encyclopedia of Science and Technology, 388
"Magazine Collection," 381
Magazine Index, 379–381
Magazines. *See* Periodicals
Manuscript form, front endpaper
Mechanics, 521–555
abbreviation, 522–524
applications for, 552–555
capitalization, 524–526
numbers, 526–528
plurals of nouns, 528–530
punctuation, 531–545
spelling, 545–550
symbols, 551–552
Mechanism, description of. *See* Description of a mechanism
Memorandum, 214–218, 308–309
applications for, 278–279
body in, 215
examples of, 217, 218, 226
heading in, 215
sample plan sheet for, 216
as a report, 320–321
Memorized speech, 439
Microfiche, 374, 377
Microform, 374, 377, 379–381, 384–385
Misplaced modifier, 508–509
Misused words, 510–518
Model, 478
Modified block form, for business letters, 220
Modifiers, 507–509
dangling, 507
dangling elliptical clauses, 507–508
misplaced, 508–509
squinting, 508
NewsBank, 386–387
bibliography card for, 397
Newspaper article or item
bibliography for, 411
bibliography card for, 396–397

Newspaper indexes, 384–385
New York Times Index, The, 385
Nominative case, 495
Nonformal reports, 309
examples of, 319–321, 323, 326, 328, 331–332, 336, 337–340, 344, 345–346
Note cards, 400–403, 404
arranging to fit outline, 404
direct quotation, 401–402
examples of, 402–403
general directions for writing, 400–401
paraphrase, 402
summary, 402–403
Notes. *See* Endnotes; Footnotes
Note taking for research report, 400–403
Nouns, 493–494
plurals of, 528–530
uses in sentences, 494
Numbers, rules for, 526–528
numerals, 527
words, 527–528
Numerals, 527

Objective case, 496
Objective complement, 494, 495
Objectivity, 307
Object of preposition, 494, 495, 496
Occupational Outlook Handbook, 390
Occupational writing, general principles in, 13
On-line computer systems, 386
Oral communication, 436–459
applications for, 456–459
classification of, 439, 440–442
delivery of, 445–446
difference in writing and, 438–439
evaluating, 449, 459
informational interviews, 454–455
job interviews, 449–454
modes of delivery, 439
outlining, 44
preparation for, 442–445
principles in, 455–456
purpose of, 439–442
to entertain, 440
to inform, 442
to persuade, 440–442
rehearsing for, 444–445
visuals for, 444, 446–449
Oral reports. *See* Oral communication
Order form, 237–238
Order letter, 232–238

Organizational patterns in comparison-contrast, 171–173
Organization chart, 469–471
  examples of, 140, 470
Outline
  accepted standards in, 114, 135
  decimal, 114, 115, 145
  headings in, 114
  and note cards, 403, 404
  research report, 310
  speech, 444
  traditional number-letter, 114, 115, 121, 135

Parallelism, in sentences, 501–502
Paraphrasing
  in note taking, 402
  in research report, 404–405
Parentheses, 541–542
  additional material, 541
  capitalization with, 541–542
  itemizing, 541
  punctuation with, 541–542
  "see" references, 541
Participles, 499–500. *See also* Verbals
Partition, analysis through, 134–150
  applications for, 147–150
  basis of, 144
  characteristics of, 134–136
    complete, 134
    coordinate, 134
    mutually exclusive, 134
    nonoverlapping, 134
  classification contrasted with, 145–146
  definition of, 134
  examples of, 134–135, 139–144, 145
  forms of data presentation for, 144–145
  order of presentation for, 144
  principles in, 146
  procedure for, 146–147
  sample plan sheet for, 137–138
Parts of speech, definition and usage, 490–500
Passive voice, 9–10, 498–499
Period, 531–532
  abbreviations, 531–532
  command, 531
  decimals, 532
  initials, 531–532
  outline, 532
  request, 531
  statement, 531
Periodical indexes, 379–385

Periodicals
  bibliography for, 410–411
  bibliography cards for, 395–396
Periodicals Holdings List, 388
Periodic report, 322–329
Personal line in business letters, 227, 228
Personal pronouns, 495–496
Persuasion, 440–442
Photographs, 475
  examples of, 353, 475
Pie chart, 467–468
Plagiarism, 405
Plurals of nouns, 528–530
Positive statements, 12
Possessive forms, 496
Poster, 479
Post hoc, ergo propter hoc, 161
Précis. *See* Summary
Predicate nominative. *See* Subjective complement
Predicate noun. *See* Subjective complement
Prepositional phrase, 494–495
Prepositions, 494–495
Primary and secondary sources, 393
Printed form
  application for job, 270–272
  memorandum, 215, 218
  order for merchandise, 237–238
  report, 320
Problem solving, 162–164
  choosing best solution, 163
  determination to succeed, 164
  merits of each possible solution, 163
  recognition of real problem, 163
  various possible solutions, 163
Process description, 37–54
  applications for, 50–54
  comparison with instructions, 37
  content in, 49–50
  effect of intended audience on, 37–48
    general audience, 38, 42–43
    specialized audience, 43–48
  examples of, 39, 42–43, 47–48
  form in, 49
  length of presentation of, 50
  oral presentation of, 48
  principles in, 48
  procedure for, 49–50
  sample plan sheets for, 40–41, 45–46
  visuals in, 48
Progress reports, 327–332
Projected materials, 447, 479–480
  film, 479
  filmstrip, 479
  in oral presentations, 447

slide, 480
transparency, 480
Pronouns, 495–497
  agreement with antecedent, 504
Proper nouns, 524–525
Public catalog, 374–377
Punctuation, 531–545
  applications for, 553–554
Purpose statement, 13, 311, 403, 404

Question mark, 532
  questions, 532
  uncertainty, 532
Quotation marks, 539–541
  different usage level, 540
  direct quotations, 439–440
  nicknames, 540
  with other punctuation marks,
    540–541
  own title, 540
  single quotation marks, 540
  titles, 540
Quoting
  in library research report, 404–405
  in note taking, 401–402

Readability, achieving, 1–13
  active and passive voice verbs, 9–10
  coordination and subordination,
    10–12
  design, 2–4
  headings, 4–5
  layout, 1–2
  positive statements, 12
  titles, 5
  word choice, 5–9
    conciseness, 8–9
    denotation and connotation, 5–6
    jargon, 7–8
    specific and general words, 6
  word order, 10
Reader. *See* Audience
Readers' Guide to Periodical Literature,
    381–382
Reading from a manuscript, 439
Reading report, 313–321
Real object, 478
Reasoning
  through cause to effect, 159–160
  through effect to cause, 151–153
  pitfalls to avoid in, 161
Recommendations and conclusions, in
    report writing, 311–312
Reference line, in business letters, 226
References, in job application, 253, 254

Reference works, guides to, 390
Reports, 304–367
  accuracy in, 306
  applications for, 354–367
  clarity in, 306
  conciseness in, 306–307
  conventional format for, 309–312
    formal, 309–312
    nonformal, 309
  definition of, 306–307
  examples of, 319–321, 323, 326,
    328, 331–332, 336, 337–340,
    344, 345–346, 347–353
  format of, 308–312
    letter, 309
    memorandum, 308–309
    printed form, 308
  headings, 313
  layout, 313
  letter of transmittal, 310
  objectivity in, 307
  oral, 312
  organization of, 310–312, 316, 322,
    327, 333, 341
  principles in, 354
  procedure for, 354
  qualities of report content, 306–307
  sample plan sheets for, 317–318,
    324–325, 329–330, 334–335,
    342–343
  school and professional, 307–308
  scope of, 305–306
  types, 313–353
    field, 341–353
    laboratory, 333–340
    periodic, 322–327
    progress, 327–332
    reading, 313–321
    research, 353, 368–435
    visuals, 312
Request letter, 229–232
Research paper. *See* Research report
Research report, 353, 368–435
  applications for, 425–428
  arranging note cards to fit outline for,
    404
  bibliography for
    final bibliography, 409
    working bibliography, 393–400
  citations, 409–411
  choosing the topic for, 391
  defining the problem for, 391–392
  definition of, 391
  documentation in, 405, 406–411
  evaluating resource material, 393
  example of, 411–424

Research report (*Continued*)
final draft of, 406
finding material, 392
first draft, 404–405
conclusion, 404
introduction, 404
introduction and conclusion for, 404
limiting the topic for, 391–392
locating materials for, 370
note taking for, 400–403
outlining, 403–404
paraphrasing material, 402, 404–405
plagiarism, 405
planning and writing, 390–404
quotations in, 404–405
recording and organizing the facts, 393–394
reporting the facts, 404
revising the outline and first draft of, 405
selecting the subject for, 391
sources of information for, 371–379
stating the central idea of, 403
steps in writing, 391–411
finding the facts, 392
recording and organizing the facts, 393–403
reporting the facts, 404–411
selecting the subject, 391–392
taking notes, 400–403
working outline and central idea of, 392
Resumé in letter of application, 254, 255, 263–269, 452
Revising
checklist for, inside back cover
research report, 405
Run-on sentence, 502

Salutation, in business letters, 222–223
Schematic diagram, 477
Secondary sources, 393
Second page, in business letter, 223
Selecting a subject, 391
Semicolon, 536–537
independent clauses, 536–537
introducing examples, 537
items in series, 537
Sentence combining, 8–9
Sentence definition, 88–90
Sentence fragments, 500–501
Sheehy's Guide to Reference Books, 390
Shifts
in focus, 503
in gender, 505

in number, 505
in person, 505
in tense, 498
in voice, 499
Signature
in business letters, 223–224
in memorandums, 215
in reports, 310
Slash mark. *See* Virgule
Social Issues Resources Series, 387
Solving problems. *See* Problem solving
Sources of information, research report, 371–379
free or inexpensive materials, 371–372
library materials, 372–379
personal interviews, 371
personal observation or experience, 371
Spacing between parts of business letters, 225, 229
Specific words, 6
Speech. *See* Oral communication
Spelling, 510–518, 545–550
affixes, 546–549
applications for, 556
ceed, sede, cede words, 550
final letters, 549–550
ie and *ei*, 546
prefixes, 547
suffixes, 548–549
suggestions for, 545–546
words often misused, 510–518
Squinting modifiers, 508
States, abbreviations for, 221–222
Stationery, for business letters, 220–222
Statistics, books of, 388–389
Subject
of infinitive, 496
of sentence, 494, 495
Subject card, or entry, 374, 375, 376, 377
Subjective complement, 494, 495
Subject line, in business letters, 226
Subject selection for research report, 391
Subject-verb agreement, 654–656
Subordination, 10–12
Summary, 185–211, 311, 314
abridgment, 189
accuracy of fact in, 199–200
applications for, 201–211
condensation, 189
documentation in, 200
emphasis in, 199–200
examples of, 188, 189–190, 191, 192–193, 196–197, 197–198, 198–199

forms of, 189–199
  descriptive, 189–192
  evaluative, 197–199
  informative, 192–197
in note taking, 402–403
omissions in, 186–188
placement of bibliography, 200
principles in, 200–201
procedure for, 201
purpose and intended audience in, 185–186
in a report, 311
sample plan sheet for, 194–195
understanding material for, 186–188
ways to shorten for, 188–189
Symbols, 551–552
  for flowchart, 124–125
  in *Library of Congress Subject Headings,* 378–379
Synopsis, 192
Systems of classifying books, 372–374
  Dewey Decimal, 372–373
  Library of Congress, 373–374

Table of contents, in a report, 310
Tables, 465–467
  examples of, 123, 131, 176–177, 331–332, 339, 466, 484
  formal, 465
  informal, 465
  suggestions for preparing, 466–467
Taking notes for research report, 400–403
Technical reports. *See* Reports
Tense of verbs, 497–498
  needless shift in, 498
Terminology, accuracy in, 6, 58, 306
Thesis sentence. *See* Central idea; Purpose statement
Thesis statement. *See* Central idea; Purpose statement
Title card, or entry, 374, 376
Title page, 310
Titles, 5
  punctuation of, 540, 545
Topic, deciding on, 391
Transmittal, letter or memorandum of, 310
  examples of, 347, 412

Ulrich's International Periodicals Directory, 390
Usage problems, 500–509
  agreement of pronoun-antecedent, 504

agreement of subject-verb, 505–507
comma splice, 503
emphasis in sentences, 509–510
modifiers, 507–509
parallelism in sentences, 501–509
run-on or fused sentence, 502
sentence fragments, 500–501
shifts in focus, 503
shifts in person, number, and gender, 505

Verbals, 499–500
Verbs, 497–499
Vertical file, 390
Virgule, 539
  alternative, 539
  per, 539
  poetry, 539
  time, 539
Visual aids. *See* Visuals
Visuals, 446–449, 460–485
  advantages of, 461
  applications for, 481–485
  charts, 467–472
  computer graphics, 464–465
  drawings and diagrams, 476–477
  effective use of, 462–464
  exhibits, 477–479
  graphs, 472–475
  in oral presentations, 444, 446–449
  photographs, 475
  principles in using, 480–481
  projected materials, 479–480
  tables, 465–467
  types of, 465–480
  use of, 23, 74–75, 98–99, 444
Vita. *See* Resumé
Voice of verbs, 498–499

White space providers, 2, 23–25
Word choice, 5–9
  conciseness, 8–9
  confused, 510–518
  connotation, 5–6, 307
  denotation, 5–6, 307
  gobbledygook, 7–8
  jargon, 7–8
  misused words, 510–518
  specific and general, 6
Wording in business letters, 219
Words, for numbers, 527–528
Working bibliography, 393–400

Yearbooks, 390
"You" emphasis in business letters, 218–219

CHECKLIST FOR COMMON PROBLEMS IN REVISING A REPORT

TITLE
    Clearly stated, in a phrase   5 ⎫   *See sample reports 17, 21, 31, 42, 47,*
    Precise indication of paper emphasis   5 ⎭   *61, 62, 94, 119, 139, 158, 176, etc.*
    Correctly capitalized   525 – 526
    No quotation marks around the title   540

ORGANIZATION *(See "Procedure" outline in each chapter)*
    Introductory section
        Background information, overview of topic, or identification of subject   311, 404
        Obvious thesis statement or purpose statement (key sentence, controlling statement, central idea)   13, 311, 403, 404
    Body
        Adequate development of the central idea or purpose statement   311
        Carefully chosen details, specifics, and examples   306 – 307
        Information arranged in logical sequence   113 – 114, 144, 171 – 173, 309 – 310
    Closing
        Compatible with purpose and emphasis of the paper   404

CONTENT *(See "Procedure" outline in each chapter)*
    Suitable for the intended audience and purpose   13, 20 – 22, 27, 37 – 48, 58, 85 – 87, 96 – 98, 155, 185 – 186, 442 – 443
    Accurate 48, 306, 405
    Complete
        Adequate coverage of major and minor subdivisions   25
        Length of paper appropriate   27, 50
        No significant points omitted   25
    All information directly related to the topic   306
    Concise   8 – 9, 25, 306 – 307

MECHANICS
    Careful word choice
        Accurate, precise terminology   6, 58, 306
        Level of diction suited to the intended audience   5 – 9, 20 – 22
        Correct usage of words that are often confused   510 – 518
        No careless omission of needed words   26, 306 – 307, 405, 406, 507 – 508
    Correct punctuation
        Avoidance of comma fault   503
        No careless omission of end punctuation   531 – 532
    Correct spelling
        Of common words   545 – 550
        Of words that sound alike   510 – 518, 550